Cloud Native App Google Cloud Platform

Use Serverless, Microservices and Containers to Rapidly Build and Deploy Apps on Google Cloud

Alasdair Gilchrist

www.bpbonline.com

FIRST EDITION 2022

Copyright © BPB Publications, India

ISBN: 978-93-55511-232

LIMITS OF LIABILITY AND DISCLAIMER OF WARRANTY

To View Complete
BPB Publications Catalogue
Scan the QR Code:

About the Author

Alasdair Gilchrist is an industry veteran of over 25 years spent in IT, Security, Networking, Mobile Telecoms and lately in Cloud Computing. He is the author of many technical books spanning IT, Google Cloud Platform and Industrial technologies, such as Industry 4.0 and the Industrial Internet of Things. Currently he works full-time as a Google Cloud Architect and part-time as a technical author.

About the Reviewers

❖ **Gopinath Balakrishshnan** is a Cloud advisor/Architect, Technical Advisory Board member of a startup, Advisory Council member of California State University, Chico, CA, member of Harvard Business Review Advisory Council, Judge panel for Stevie and CODiE awards, Director of Technical Steering Committee, Moja Global.

Specialized in product engineering, distributed systems/cloud platforms, built/managed high performance teams , led large transformation programs. Sales driven system engineering/solution architecting roles, worked with medium/large enterprises for their new application/infrastructure design, delivered proof-of-concept/pilots, engaged with several C level leaders at early stage startups (Series B to D) and built technology partnerships, support their digital transformation journey and help solve their business and technology challenges by helping build/migrate/modernize the application/infrastructure that can scale with better economics and resilient using Google cloud solutions with a cloud native approach.

❖ **Adnan Ahmed Khan** has 7 years of experience in Software Development, System Design and Automation. He has been a practitioner of Cloud Technologies from Google and AWS. Adnan has pursued MSc. in Computer Science from the American International University of Bangladesh. He has worked with startups like G&R, Pathao and Deligram. He is currently working as a Software Developer in Red.Digital Limited, Dhaka. His day to day life involves design, development and managing cloud-native applications.

Acknowledgement

I would first like to start with thanking BPB for giving me the opportunity to write this book. But writing the book is a team effort so I would like to thank my team mates.

A huge thank you to my editor for her patience, diligence and professionalism when editing the book. (It could never have been done without you SB).

I also need to thank Mr. Gopinath and Mr. Adnan who worked as the technical reviewers everything they so professionally contributed was a huge value add to the book.

Thank you all at BPB and I hope you the reader enjoy the book.

Preface

The purpose of this book is to demonstrate how to design develop and deploy cloud native apps on the Google Cloud Platform. The book is designed to provide theoretical lessons reinforced by step-by-step hands-on tutorials. The value of this approach is that after reading the book you will know why, where and when to use cloud native applications but most importantly you will also know how to build, test and deploy your own cloud native apps on the Google Cloud Platform.

Applications that are designed, developed and deployed by leveraging cloud-based technologies are known as Cloud-Native Applications. Cloud Native apps are built, tested and run using all the advantages of the cloud computing delivery model. However, the term, cloud native application, is not just another buzz-word as these applications have a real design purpose, which is to succeed in today's fast-paced and competitive software market. As a result, cloud native applications aim to revolutionize software delivery by simultaneously leveraging cloud platform tools, techniques, and technologies whilst also supporting cloud platform operations and DevOps capabilities.

What makes cloud native applications different from traditional web apps is that to be successful in application development today we need to speed up building new applications, optimize existing ones, and find ways to rapidly deploy them into production. Minimizing the time getting the product to market and to profit is critical in business. To this end organizations have developed operational and development strategies that involves methodologies such as DevOps and Agile development, that utilize cloud platform architectures to ensure high quality whilst also delivering continuous improvement and rapid deployment. Devops delivers the functions of continuous integration and continuous deployment pipelines (CI/CD). This is the technique used in DevOps for automated delivery of the product into production.

Cloud native apps are typically designed around microservices, which amongst their other benefits allow you to create, maintain, improve or scale one component of an application without having to refactor the whole application. Microservices are typically deployed in containers, as this provides mobility through the write once and deploy anywhere, design model as containerized apps can run on any cloud platform. For scalability, resiliency and performance the containers are typically run in Kubernetes clusters, which is a container orchestrator and cluster manager.

The cumulative effect of leveraging these techniques and methods in cloud native application development means that the apps can bring tangible value to the organization by delivering products that users need at the pace the business demands.

Over the 13 Chapters of this book you will learn the following:

Chapter 1: In this chapter we describe what a cloud native application is and lists its characteristics. You will learn about the modern concepts of Devops and the CI/CD process in particular. We discuss the Google Cloud Platform service model and you will understand the difference between each offered service. Also, through practical hands on learning you will be able to deploy a sample application to Cloud Functions, Google App Engine, and Cloud Run.

Chapter 2: Here you will learn how to download and install the Cloud SDK. Become competent in using the Shell Cloud Terminal and familiar with Cloud Code. You will also be able to build your own custom Cloud Shell Docker image and have a basic grounding in developing apps using Cloud Code. Moreover, you will have had the opportunity to deploy your first serverless app in Cloud Run.

Chapter 3: In this chapter we discuss the architecture associated with cloud native applications. You will also understand the build process and how we create cloud source repositories to store our code, containers and other artifacts. You will also have had the opportunity to create your own Docker image and push it to the artifact registry using everything you have learned so far.

Chapter 4: In this chapter we describe microservice architecture its benefits and best use cases as well as some caveats where it is best avoided. You will also be able to deploy your microservices into functions that can be run in Cloud Functions or as containers that can be deployed to Google App Engine. You will also have picked up the required practical skills to allow you to handle and deploy microservices using GCP's Cloud Function and Google App Engine.

Chapter 5: In the chapter we discuss containers and the recent trend of containerization. You will learn through a practical lesson how to create and deploy a container to Cloud Run. You will also learn how to explore and push containers to the Artifact Registry in GCP. As a practical tutorial you will also build your own application using a Google API, hosted your translation app to artifact registry and deployed it to Cloud Run.

Chapter 6: We discuss the component and services you can use to build automated pipelines in GCP. You will learn about Pub/Sub what it is how it works and how you can deploy it in practice. You will also learn how to initiate and schedule automated tasks using both Cloud Task and Cloud Scheduler. In addition, you will learn how to handle streaming data in a pipeline by using Cloud Dataflow and BigQuery.

Chapter 7: The lesson is focused on the underlying issues with managing containers at scale. You will also be introduced to the need for container orchestration and the leading solution -Kubernetes. Through practical exercises you will learn how to create a Kubernetes cluster and deploy a cloud native application to it.

Chapter 8: This chapter provides a discussion on cluster design patterns and what designs are best suited to particular scenarios. You will also learn about resource management and how you go about transforming a monolith application into microservices architecture for deployment on a Kubernetes cluster.

Chapter 9: In this chapter we take a deep-five into learning the skills required to optimize your application to run on a Kubernetes Engine. You will learn how to analyze and if necessary, refactor your applications to get the best from Kubernetes performance and scalability. You will also learn how to identify metrics and apply disruption budgets.

Chapter 10: In this chapter you will become familiar with the DevOps practice of continuous integration and continuous delivery, which is also process automation in action. You will learn how to describe each stage in the CI/CD process as well as being able to design and deploy your own pipeline in GCP.

Chapter 11: You will learn the purpose and features of Anthos and how it operates in a hybrid or multi-cloud environment. You will also become familiar with Anthos features and architecture and understand how it is deployed in real world scenarios. In addition, you will learn how to design, configure and deploy a CI/CD solution with Anthos.

Chapter 12: In this chapter you will learn about the Kubernetes technical architecture and how Kubernetes can span multi-cloud and hybrid environments. You will become familiar with Anthos as a multi-cloud, multi-cluster orchestrator and through hands on tutorials be able to connect and explore an Anthos environment.

Chapter 13: We discuss Anthos security and administering identity and access management at the GKE level and understanding the principles of least privilege and how to enforce the policy on a real cluster. You will also become familiar with some Anthos specific security modules such as the Config Controller, Config Sync and through some hands-on work the Policy Controller.

Code Bundle and Coloured Images

Please follow the link to download the
Code Bundle and the *Coloured Images* of the book:

https://rebrand.ly/sw7qdus

The code bundle for the book is also hosted on GitHub at **https://github.com/bpbpublications/Cloud-Native-Apps-on-Google-Cloud-Platform**. In case there's an update to the code, it will be updated on the existing GitHub repository.

We have code bundles from our rich catalogue of books and videos available at **https://github.com/bpbpublications**. Check them out!

Errata

We take immense pride in our work at BPB Publications and follow best practices to ensure the accuracy of our content to provide with an indulging reading experience to our subscribers. Our readers are our mirrors, and we use their inputs to reflect and improve upon human errors, if any, that may have occurred during the publishing processes involved. To let us maintain the quality and help us reach out to any readers who might be having difficulties due to any unforeseen errors, please write to us at :

errata@bpbonline.com

Your support, suggestions and feedbacks are highly appreciated by the BPB Publications' Family.

Did you know that BPB offers eBook versions of every book published, with PDF and ePub files available? You can upgrade to the eBook version at www.bpbonline.com and as a print book customer, you are entitled to a discount on the eBook copy. Get in touch with us at :

business@bpbonline.com for more details.

At **www.bpbonline.com**, you can also read a collection of free technical articles, sign up for a range of free newsletters, and receive exclusive discounts and offers on BPB books and eBooks.

Piracy

If you come across any illegal copies of our works in any form on the internet, we would be grateful if you would provide us with the location address or website name. Please contact us at **business@bpbonline.com** with a link to the material.

If you are interested in becoming an author

If there is a topic that you have expertise in, and you are interested in either writing or contributing to a book, please visit **www.bpbonline.com**. We have worked with thousands of developers and tech professionals, just like you, to help them share their insights with the global tech community. You can make a general application, apply for a specific hot topic that we are recruiting an author for, or submit your own idea.

Reviews

Please leave a review. Once you have read and used this book, why not leave a review on the site that you purchased it from? Potential readers can then see and use your unbiased opinion to make purchase decisions. We at BPB can understand what you think about our products, and our authors can see your feedback on their book. Thank you!

For more information about BPB, please visit **www.bpbonline.com**.

Table of Contents

CHAPTER 1
Introducing Cloud Native Apps

The goal of this book is to teach you how to design, build, and deploy Cloud-native apps on the Google Cloud Platform. The book describes a modern approach to building, running, and deploying software applications by leveraging the flexibility, scalability, and resilience of cloud computing. The book focuses on building Cloud Native apps based on Agile Development and DevOps/GitOps techniques using the **Google Cloud Platform (GCP's)** tools and technologies. It is designed to provide you with knowledge and information through a balance of traditional text and video reinforced by hands-on interactive labs.

In this chapter, we will learn about the modern method for rapidly developing flexible and resilient applications in the cloud. The applications are truly cloud native from pre-design through deployment and management. In this chapter, you'll begin with some crucial cloud concepts and learn about the principles, technologies, and processes that make developing cloud-native apps possible.

You will then look at three key areas of cloud thinking: automation, modernization, and continuous integration/continuous delivery. You will also learn how pipelines automate the CI/CD processes, which are the backbone of DevOps. Then, you will dive deeper into learning about the specific platforms, tools, and techniques used in GCP for developing cloud native apps. You will learn about microservices, functions, and containers and how we can build and deploy our code in GCP's serverless environment on either Cloud Functions, App Engine, or Cloud Run.

Structure

We will cover the following topics in this chapter:

- What are Cloud Native Apps?

- Cloud-native application architecture

- The dawn of modern DevOps

- The Google Cloud Platform service model

- Interactive tutorials: deploy a Nodejs app on
  - Cloud Function
  - App Engine
  - Cloud Run

Objectives

After going through this chapter, you will be able to describe what a cloud native is and list its characteristics. You will also be familiar with the modern concepts of DevOps and the CI/CD process in particular. You will have a good understanding of the Google Cloud Platform service model and understand the difference between each service offered. Through practical hands-on learning, you will also be able to deploy a sample application to Cloud Functions, Google App Engine, and Cloud Run.

About Cloud Native Apps

Traditionally, software was developed as a monolithic structure that was designed to run on a mainframe or on a single large server and developed adhering strictly to predefined features and specifications. The problems with the monolithic design were that it contained multiple tightly coupled layers, such as the user interface, the business logic layer, and the data interface layers, which made rolling-out, maintaining, upgrading, and adding features more difficult.

The solution to these drawbacks was the **service-orientated architecture (SOA)**, which split up the single all-purpose monolith into service-oriented functional blocks that were accessed via synchronous web services. Decomposing the monolith into a service orientated architecture resolved the issues of slow rollout, complex debugging, and upgrades. It also provided better scalability. However, one problem persisted: managing the complexity of interconnections between all those services, especially when run on a distributed platform such as the cloud. The solution was driven by the emergence of containers such as Docker and container orchestration solutions like Kubernetes. Now developers could fully embrace the features of the cloud and break down services into multiple microservices that ran independently. The complexity was resolved as the vast web of interconnectivity was handled by service meshes, message-brokers such as pub/sub, and asynchronous event-driven APIs.

In short, Cloud Native apps take advantage of the emerging cloud-based technologies like functions as a service, microservices, containers, Kubernetes, and declarative event-driven APIs. These are the building blocks used to design, construct, deploy, and run modern applications. These technologies are at the core of all automated pipelines for **continuous implementation and continuous delivery (CI/CD)**, which is the foundation for modern Development and Operations - DevOps. This, in turn, empowers organizations to build and deploy highly scalable applications on the Google Cloud Platform.

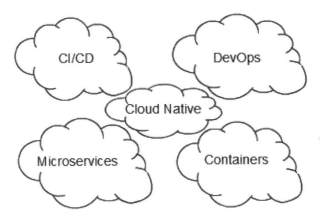

Figure 1.1: *Cloud Native apps*

In software development, an application is said to be native if it has been developed for use on a specific platform or language. Therefore, a native app is a computer program that is designed to leverage the features and functions available only on a specific computing architecture. Hence, we can say that Cloud Native applications are designed to capitalize on the inherent characteristics of a cloud computing architecture and leverage the underlying cloud's suite of technologies, tools, and software delivery model.

Cloud Native apps are, therefore, designed and built from the ground up to be deployed on the cloud. Nonetheless, a true cloud native application fully takes advantage of cloud by using technologies that are highly scalable, fully managed, distributed microservices architecture for all parts of applications with great elasticity and reliability that can only be run in the cloud. However, Cloud Native apps can still be run on-premises infrastructure, albeit without the benefits of cloud. Due to this, the boundaries of what is and what isn't cloud native have blurred.

The **Cloud Native Computing Foundation (CNCF)** defines it as:

"Cloud-native technologies empower organizations to build and run scalable applications in modern, dynamic environments such as public, private, and hybrid clouds."

The common cloud native features should provide scale, elasticity, and resilience, and serverless and microservices architecture are key technologies that help achieve those goals. The latter is where applications are broken down into functions or microservices and then packaged in lightweight containers to be deployed and orchestrated across a variety of virtual servers.

The advent and pervasiveness of the Cloud has driven the development of cloud-native applications as these components were critical in the evolution towards the integration, automation, and rapid deployment of code that businesses require today. Indeed, cloud-native apps are the foundation of the modern practice of DevOps. Indeed, the proponents of DevOps use cloud-native applications for their ability to deliver software with a shortened time to market and profit. This approach promotes business agility as cloud-native applications have shortened application lifecycle but provide faster return on investment. From the developers' point of view, a cloud native approach facilitates rapid deployment and consistent upgrades. The operational perspective is that they are highly resilient, manageable, and observable.

Cloud-native application architecture

As you just learned, cloud-native apps leverage cloud computing frameworks. They are designed and built to take advantage of the cloud platforms preference for loosely coupled cloud services. This architecture enables applications to scale out horizontally and provide redundancy, and it allows applications to dynamically scale in response to fluctuating demand and to withstand local disruptions and equipment failure.

Features of a cloud-native application

At the heart of the design Cloud-native applications are these loosely coupled services, which can be viewed as being small snippets of specialized code. They may be called functions or a microservice, depending on their characteristics. Either way, they are used to build a specific service. Typically, the ground rule is 1 microservice = 1 purpose = 1 service. This rule ensures service independence and that resources for each service are efficiently provisioned, making the application flexible and adaptable to a cloud architecture. We will go into why this is a hugely beneficial approach later in the chapter.

For now, it is sufficient to understand that previously, cloud native applications were run and deployed to serverless platforms such as Cloud Function or perhaps App Engine on the **Google Cloud Platform (GCP)**. Recently, there has been a shift towards containerization, and the functions and microservices that are part of the cloud-native application are now packaged in containers.

Key capabilities of cloud-native applications are as follows:

- **Microservices-based**

   Microservice architecture principles require an application to be decomposed into a series of independent services or modules. Each service is independent, isolated with its own data, and supports a single business purpose. In a microservices architecture the modules communicate with one another via **application program interfaces (APIs)**.

- **Container-based**

   Containers are software constructs that are similar to **virtual machines (VM)** but without the OS. Instead, a container holds the application source code and all the required dependencies and libraries it needs to run. This makes containers very easy to deploy on any platform as they can be run independent of physical resources on any operating system. Containers keep microservices from interfering with one another and stop any one from consuming all the host's shared resources, thereby solving the noisy neighbor problem. However, they also enable multiple instances of the same service, which addresses redundancy, high availability, and service resiliency.

- **API-based**

   As microservices or containers are deployed in isolation, there needs to be a way for them to communicate so that the underlying service can be invoked. This is the job of an application programming interface (API). The purpose of an API is to enable individual services, microservices, or applications to communicate, as they act as secure connectors between loosely coupled services.

- **Dynamically orchestrated**

   You might be thinking that microservices and containers are going to make life easy, but think again. As containerization becomes pervasive, managing containers becomes chaotic. As a result, there is a dire need for container orchestration tools. These tools are used to manage container lifecycles and version control, which can become challenging when there are hundreds or more containers to manage. Container orchestration tools provide the means for resource management, provisioning, and deployment using clusters of server nodes. Kubernetes is a container orchestration tool that we will work with extensively throughout this book.

- **Use declarative communication patterns**

   Cloud native apps (CNAs) follow declarative communication patterns that have trust in the network to fulfil the developer's intent of the desired state. Declarative patterns standardize a communication model, which shifts the functional tasks away from the application to a remote API or service endpoint.

- **Designed for automation in CI/CD pipelines**

  Continuous integration and deployment are fundamental to cloud native applications. This means that there must be extra logic in place to deal with the complexity of the pipelines.

- **Expose health checks**

  Understanding the status of the application is critical in automation, such as in automatic scaling, recovery, and optimization. The application needs to instruct the platform it is running on about the state it is in, and exposing health checks allows the platform to track and monitor the application state in real-time.

- **Collects telemetry data**

  CNAs often have **service level objectives** (**SLO**). Therefore, a CNA must be able to collect telemetry data to be considered a cloud native.

- **Cloud Native vs Cloud-based apps**

  The problem with defining a technology is that very rarely is something new; more often than not, it will be an evolution rather than an invention. This is clear with cloud native apps when we consider the differentiators between the terms cloud-native application, cloud-based applications, and even service-orientated architecture, as they are often confused. While they are all service orientated and superficially similar in purpose, they differ in design:

- **Service-orientated architecture (SOA)**

  This architecture is the grand-daddy of them all as it was the first architecture to be designed as a service-orientated platform. However, SOA was popular long before the cloud emerged, so services communicated across a bus connecting on-premise servers rather than across a distributed network. Hence, although the principles are similar, the technologies, protocols, and constraints are very different.

- **Cloud-based applications**

  These are applications that are designed to run on cloud platforms. As such, cloud-based applications have been redesigned to run on dynamic cloud infrastructure, but they are not typically designed to take advantage of the inherent characteristics of the cloud, such as dynamic pods, automatic scaling to infinity or zero, and zero downtime migration across nodes.

- **Cloud-native applications**

  These applications are designed specifically for the cloud. Cloud-native application development is optimized for the inherent characteristics of the cloud and is adaptable to the cloud's dynamic environment.

Benefits of Cloud-native applications

We typically build Cloud-native applications to take advantage of the speed and efficiency of the cloud. Some of the benefits we derive from them are as follows:

- **Design efficiency**

  Cloud architectures generally use a pay-for-use model, which means you no longer have to concern yourself with detailed and tiresome capacity planning for application resources.

- **Cost-effective**

  As the resources will scale as needed, which eliminates the overprovisioning of hardware. Virtual servers can be readily spun-up when needed, and cloud-native applications can be up and running in seconds. Containers are preferred over VMs to maximize the number of microservices run on a host, which saves time, resources, and money.

- **Independently scalable**

  As each microservice is logically isolated and scales independently, it is not affected by the configuration of the others.

- **Portability**

  Cloud-native applications are designed to be vendor neutral where possible to aid portability. Using containers to port functions and/or microservices between different vendors' cloud platforms provides agility and avoids vendor lock-in.

- **Reliable**

  If a failure should occur in one microservice, there's no effect on the adjacent services because these cloud-based applications are isolated in containers.

- **Easy to manage**

  Cloud-native applications use automation tools and procedures to deploy new app features and version updates. Developers can track all microservices and components as they're being deployed. Applications are decomposed into several smaller single-purpose services. By design, one team is responsible for a specific microservice.

- **Clear visibility**

  A microservice architecture isolates services, so it makes it easier for teams to monitor applications using tools such as GCP's Cloud Monitoring and Cloud Logging, which are now part of GCP's Operations Suite or Anthos.

- **The future of cloud-native applications**

  Cloud-native applications have experienced a surge in popularity recently and are predicted to be the future of software development. The Cloud Native Computing Foundation estimated that there were at the number of cloud-native developers had gone up to least 6.5 million in 2020 from 4.7 million in 2019.

  This popularity and subsequent uptake are due to Cloud-native applications being the solution to some of cloud computing's inherent problems. Nevertheless, migrating to the cloud to improve operational efficiencies has its own challenges.

- **Cloud native design considerations**

  At a high level, cloud-native applications are being designed and built to take advantage of the cloud architecture, which means they are adapting to the many new possibilities and challenges.

  When designing applications, we typically consider the following:

  - The functional requirements of a system (specifications: what it should do)

  - The non-functional requirements (requirements: how it should perform)

  - Constraints (acceptable boundaries to change)

The functional aspects don't change too much when developing Cloud Native applications, but how we go about doing things changes. Cloud architecture has very different ways to accomplish things than on-premises designs, and it imposes different constraints. If architects fail to recognize and adapt their approach to meet these constraints, the resultant systems are often sub-optimal, fragile, and hard to manage. A well-architected cloud native system, on the other hand, should be largely self-healing, cost efficient, and easily updated and maintained through **Continuous Integration/Continuous Delivery (CI/CD)**, which is the backbone of DevOps.

The Dawn of Modern DevOps

DevOps arose from the success of the Agile software development methodology at improving software development speed, flexibility, and agility. The lesson learned was that disconnects between development and operations teams — as well as between IT and the business side of the organization — significantly hinder all parties.

DevOps aims to solve the communication, competition, and priority problems between departments and IT specializations through collaboration and merger by removing the functional silos.

Development and operations teams must have a holistic understanding of the environment to build, test, deploy, and maintain viable software. This means building and testing code in realistic conditions that removes any development and operational friction.

A critical enabler for DevOps was the successful drive to virtualization in the data center for hardware, software, and networking in the early 2000s. The ability to virtualize a complete operational server as software that could be deployed on another server as a VM was revolutionary. Virtualization was, by no means, an overnight success; it took several years to dispel the sceptics and gain acceptance. One notable exception was in the development departments of enterprises who readily adopted virtualization as it dissolved many of their pain points and obstacles to software development and testing. Virtualization removed much of the developer's dependency on the operations department and set the stage for the logical merging of Development and Operations into DevOps. Nonetheless, DevOps was not the goal; streamlined, faster, reliable, and automated production was the goal!

Cloud Native DevOps

DevOps was never the goal at the organizational level, but it was a critical enabler for cloud native DevOps as it was the inspiration and landing point for combining **cloud native apps (CNAs)** and DevOps thinking:

- Cloud Native applications are specifically built for resiliency, agility, and operability with observability in mind.

- DevOps is a practice of operations and development teams working together throughout the entire lifecycle.

- Based on the above explanations, it is clear that if we merge the technologies, philosophies, and practices of both CNAs and DevOps, the result defines Cloud Native DevOps as a set of practices that involves continuous improvement, automation, cross-functional teams, and better alignment with business needs with customer expectations in mind.

Automation has always been the goal for software system development, and cloud makes it easier than ever for DevOps to automate the provisioning, building, testing, and rapid deployment of software. Applying a modern Cloud Native DevOp approach reaps benefits in terms of the resilience and performance. This is because automated processes can repair, scale, and deploy your system far faster and far more reliably than people can.

In a Cloud Native DevOps, the typical areas for automating are as follows:

- **Infrastructure**: The objective here is to automate the creation of the infrastructure using an **Infrastructure as Code (IaC)** approach. IaC is a declarative method that uses tools like Google Cloud Deployment Manager or Terraform to gain speed, consistency, and reliability.

- **Continuous Integration/Continuous Delivery**: Here, the aim is to automate the build, testing, and deployment of the software packages that constitute the application by using tools like Google Cloud Build, Jenkins, and Spinnaker. Not only should you automate the integration and deployment, but you should also automate testing processes like canary testing and rollback.

- **Scale up and scale down**: All internet facing applications face scaling issues, so you should automate the scale up of the system in response to increases in load so that the service remains available. You should also scale down in response to a sustained drop in load to reduce cost. Some applications are, by design, used sporadically; for these, you should consider scaling to zero (removing all running instances and restarting the application when it's needed next).

- **Monitoring and automated recovery**: Like security, you should bake monitoring and logging into your cloud-native systems from the very start. From a security and operations perspective, logging and monitoring the application and its environment can indicate the health of the system. For instance, cloud logging and cloud monitoring can give valuable insights into system usage and user behavior. Secondly, these disciplines can be used as a benchmark, which is the measure of overall system health. Lastly, they are an ideal point for triggering events for driving automation. For example, when a container fails, instead of just logging an error, the system can automatically restart it or spin up a replacement to allow the system to keep functioning at an optimal level.

The Cloud Service Model

Infrastructure as a service (IaaS) provides virtualized computing resources over the internet. IaaS is one of several categories of cloud computing services, alongside **software as a service (SaaS)**, **platform as a service (PaaS)**, **functions as a service (FaaS)**, and **container as a service (CaaS)**, among others; the list is growing by the day.

IaaS may well be one of the better understood benefits of the Cloud, but the Cloud is more than just infrastructure. Most cloud providers, and GCP is no different, provide a plethora of partial or fully managed services that deliver all sorts of functionalities that ease operational burden (refer to *figure 1.2*). However, many organizations are slow to take advantage of these services because they feel they know best how their applications and business logic runs. Sometimes, they are also concerned about being '*locked in*' to a given provider. These are often valid concerns, but managed services can also save time and cost and reduce operational overhead:

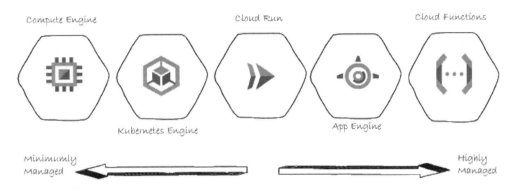

Figure 1.2: *Google Cloud Service Model*

IaaS vs PaaS vs SaaS vs FaaS

In this book, we will focus on the Google Cloud Platform. The GCP has a selection of services that provide on-demand access to cloud-hosted physical and virtual servers, storage, and networking. Which service we choose is determined mainly by our appetite for managing the underlying hardware and software. Google provides a wide range of on-demand services across the entire DIY/Google management spectrum (as shown in *figure 1.1*).

Google Compute Engine (GCE) — IaaS

GCE is Google's IaaS service, which provides the opportunity for creating virtual machines in the cloud. Building servers in this way is ideal for replication of the existing on-premises architectures. You build the virtual servers by allocating CPU, OS, and Memory, state the preferred type of local storage, for example, SSD or HDD, and the type and amount of cloud storage.

In GCE, you can select micro instances that are 0.3-Cores and 1GB of RAM to behemoth style 96-Core CPUs with over 300GB RAM.

Use cases:

- On-premises and monolithic workloads
- Raw compute to meet the existing infrastructure requirements

Examples:

- Relational databases, SAP HANA

- CRM systems

- Legacy ERP systems

The Serverless Paradigm

The Google Compute Engine is an IaaS platform, and it is extremely popular as it provides easy entry or migration points into the GCP. Operations teams like it because it delivers the speed and ease of infrastructure deployment and all the benefits of the cloud. However, it is only partially managed, so it comes without the unacceptable risk of job loss.

The alternatives to Compute Engine are what are now popularly referred to as serverless computing platforms. The term comes about because the alternative compute platforms, that is, App Engine, Google Kubernetes Engine (Autopilot), Cloud Functions, and Cloud Run, are fully managed platforms, which abstracts away the concept of there being any supporting hardware *"servers"* running the user's code.

Google Kubernetes Engine (GKE) — (CaaS)

GKE autopilot is a unique compute offering by GCP that is an abstraction over Compute Engine VM clusters. In standard form, GKE is a CaaS platform based upon the hugely popular open-source Kubernetes. Standard-edition Google Kubernetes Engine was a partially managed platform built upon a cluster of Compute engine VMs. Google retained control of the Kubernetes control plane and the master nodes and gave customer access to the cluster via the GKE API. However, the latest Autopilot mode takes GKE into the serverless domain as it is now a fully managed hands-free clustered environment.

For those who are not familiar with containers, they are handy as they help modularize services and applications. Typically, containers hold different services, for example, a container can host the front end of your web app, and another container can host the back end of your web app. Unfortunately, this ease of deployment leads to unruly container propagation and spread. Kubernetes is an open-source container orchestrator (CaaS) that comes to the rescue as it performs the automation, orchestration, management, and deployment of your containers.

Use cases:

- Microservices architecture

- Application modernization for better scale, economics

- Cloud-native Network Functions (CNF)

- Computing power for resource-hungry tasks

Google App Engine (GAE) — (PaaS)

Google App Engine is a PaaS platform that has been around as long as GCE and is best described as, *"Bring your code, we'll handle the rest"*. The original purpose of the GAE was to provide a development platform so that developers did not have to deal with the underlying hardware/middleware. GAE was designed to run apps, so it will handle the scaling up and down of the underlying infrastructure to meet the demand and ensure that your website doesn't crash because of the increased demand. This means you pay exactly for the resources that your application requires at any given point.

GAE is great for companies that are not interested in building and managing the underlying infrastructure and only care about developing their applications as efficiently as possible.

Use cases:

- Developing and hosting web applications

- Scalable mobile back-ends

- IoT, Internal IT apps

- Standard - apps

- Flexible - apps and containers

Google Cloud Functions — (FaaS)

Cloud functions was the first GCP serverless platform as it fully abstracted the hardware by allowing only specific functions as code to run. The functions or microservices are event-driven, meaning they are written to be deployed and then triggered by some event. Cloud functions are very simple and have several uses that require an event-driven mindset and no need to contemplate the hosting server. Billing is based on the number of triggered events during a billing period.

Use cases:

- Designed for event-driven workloads

- Event-driven and data processing apps

- Manipulate user-generated data and events

Examples:

- Post a comment on Slack channel following a GitHub commit
- Statistical analysis
- Image thumbnail generation

Cloud Run --- (CaaS+)

Google Cloud Run is a new serverless function based on the Knative project, so it's a fully managed service that scales container-based apps to zero. Despite Cloud Run being technically a CaaS—it does require code to be in containers that respond to web requests or event-based triggers—its serverless characteristics are considered to be better than FaaS in some cases.

Cloud Run is great for a lot of scenarios. It can do server-side streaming with gRPC, build or migrate web apps, or handle APIs that take advantage of an API Gateway. It can also coordinate apps with other serverless applications using Cloud Workflows. In addition, Cloud Run is event driven by nature, so it can respond to triggers based on events occurring anywhere within the Google Cloud.

Use cases:

- Cloud Run supports API endpoints, which makes it ideal for interfacing with container-based apps and services.

- It is flexible as it supports custom runtime environments like Rust, Kotlin, C++, and Bash and even legacy web apps using languages, such as Python 2.7, and Java 7.

- Cloud Run is also heavily adopted in use cases for native support for HTTP services and backend apps, web frameworks, and microservices.

- Developers have a wide range of supported frameworks and languages to use, such as Flask and Django for Python, the Express.js framework for JavaScript, Symfony Web framework for PHP, and Spring Boot for Java, among others.

Advantages of serverless architecture

To understand how serverless applications work in GCP, we need to realize that the architecture is divided into two parts. There is the backend, which is handled entirely by GCP. Developers have no need to concern themselves with the back end as any internal logic or integrations with hardware are fully managed.

This model allows developers to optimize the software development process and improve the performance of the front-end product. This works well as:

- **Easy deployment**: A development team doesn't have to worry about the backend functionality. Their only task is to write the code and release it. All the operational processes are handled by GCP.

- **Cost-efficiency**: Human resources, hardware, internal logic—all these aspects of software development are managed by GCP.

- **Improved scalability**: If the product you are developing suddenly exceeds forecasts, you can increase the storage space and computing power in a few seconds. Should the workload stabilize, you can scale back down again. This defeats the old enemy of over-provisioning and is a major advantage of a pay-per-use system.

- **Increased flexibility**: You can quickly release new features as most serverless architectures can be integrated with code repositories, integrated CI/CD by adding some additional functions and triggers.

- **Decreased latency**: Cloud providers such as GCP have global presence, so they can automatically provision the server that's closest to a user. Requests from users don't have to traverse the globe, so latency is reduced.

Advantages of Functions (FaaS)

Function as a Service is designed to handle the client-side functionality. GCP's Cloud Function works with code that are event-triggered functions. These are exposed to the users who can interact with them as part of the UI or the applications, which respond to their actions by running a particular component. In FaaS and Cloud Functions, the underlying hardware is completely abstracted from the code.

Advantages of a Microservices architecture

Microservices provide flexibility in development as they allow developers to work or refactor one feature at a time. Being able to decompose a large monolithic application down to key individual features or services makes an architecture scalable by design and easier to maintain.

Here are the main characteristics of microservices:

- **Made up of components**: Each system built with microservices architecture can be decomposed into many distinct services. Each of these services can be developed, tested, and deployed independently.

- **Microservices are isolated**: Developers can change one microservice without it affecting the entire application.

- **Decentralized**: A microservice has its own database. Hence, one microservice experiencing a security issue will not affect application shared data.

- **Lower risk**: Microservices mitigate risk as they provide redundancy, so a microservice can be replaced by another if it fails.

- **Scalability**: Microservices are ideal when it's time to scale an application. Additionally, microservices are aligned with the concept of modern development such as Agile and DevOps, where small teams take responsibility for a single service.

Advantages of working with APIs

Application Programmable Interfaces are the glue that connects modules within a cloud native application. APIs allow developers to save time and reduce the amount of code they need to create complex functionality within an application. APIs also help create more consistency across apps for the same platform.

For example, if you've ever seen a Google Maps object embedded on a website, that website is using the Google Maps API to embed that map. Google exposes APIs like this to web developers, who can then use the APIs to add complex objects right on their website without them needing to be experts in that field. If APIs like this didn't exist, developers might have had to create their own maps and provide their own map data just to put a little interactive map on a website.

What is the best approach?

With serverless architecture, you get access to huge computing resources that belong to large technology enterprises. Acquiring large server spaces on your own would be a risky investment, but with a serverless approach, you get access to infrastructure that is already ready to run. So, what is the best serverless system for cloud native applications?

The answer is that it depends on your application's unique requirements and specifications. To demonstrate this, we will show you each in action, with an interactive tutorial so that you can try them out for yourself.

Interactive tutorials

In this section, we will get to play with some interactive tutorials to get hands-on experience of working on the real thing. To be able to run the interactive tutorial throughout this book, you only need to have a registered Google Cloud Platform account and internet access to the Google Cloud Console (console.cloud.google.com). You can register and access your own GCP account by following these instructions:

- If you're new to Google Cloud, create an account to evaluate how our products perform in real-world scenarios. New customers also get $300 in free credits to run, test, and deploy workloads.

- Once you have access to the GCP console, you can simply click on the link provided to activate Cloud Shell and then load the interactive tutorials from the command line. The specific instructions are included in the preview for each of the interactive tutorials.

- If you cannot, for whatever reason, access the GCP console, you can follow the accompanying detailed tutorial step-through notes.

Interactive Tutorial 1.1: Deploy Node.js code in Cloud Function

Cloud Functions is a serverless execution environment for building and connecting cloud services. With Cloud Functions, you write simple, single-purpose functions that are attached to events emitted from your cloud infrastructure and services. Your function is triggered when an event being watched is fired.

Learn how to create and deploy a Node.js Cloud Function using the Cloud Console.

To run this task directly in Cloud Console, click to Activate the Cloud Shell:

Type in the Command Line:

```
$git clone https://github.com/bpbpublications/Cloud-Native-Apps-on-
Google-Cloud-Platform
cd Chapter 01
teachme tutorial-1.1
```

If you do not wish to use the Google Console for this interactive tutorial—though we strongly recommend that you do—you can watch the video and read the tutorial steps below.

The following sections take you through the same steps as the interactive tutorial.

In this tutorial, we will run a node.js function that is triggered by an HTTP request, the function writes a message to the console and a response code of **200 (OK)**.

The node.js code is shown as follows:

```
01.  **
02.   * Responds to any HTTP request.
03.   *
04.   * @param {!express:Request} req HTTP request context.
05.   * @param {!express:Response} res HTTP response context.
06.   */
07.  exports.helloWorld = (req, res) => {
08.    let message = req.query.message || req.body.message || 'Hello World!';
09.    res.status(200).send(message);
10.  };
```

Figure 1.3: API Library location

Step 1

To get started with running your first function in Google's Cloud Function, we will need to assign either an existing project or create a new one:

1. In the Google Cloud Console, on the project selector page, select or create a Google Cloud project.

   If you don't plan to keep the resources that you create in this procedure, create a project instead of selecting an existing project. After you finish these steps, you can delete the project, removing all resources associated with the project.

2. Ensure that billing is enabled for your Cloud project.

3. Enable the Cloud Functions and Cloud Build APIs.

   Go to **APIs and services** → **Library**, as shown here:

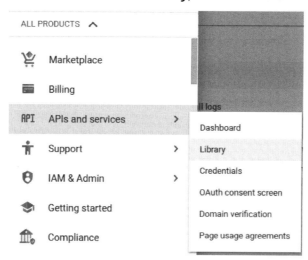

Figure 1.4: API Library location

4. Then, enter the API you want to enable in the search box:

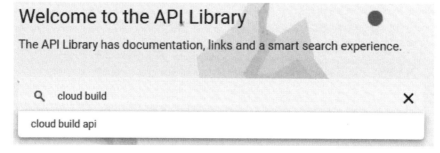

Figure 1.5: API Library Search

5. Click on Cloud Build in the **Search** Results and enable API:

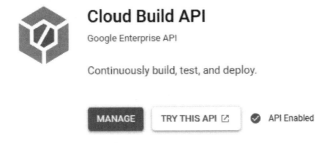

Figure 1.6: *Cloud Build Enable page*

Repeat these steps for each API you require, Cloud Functions in this case:

Figure 1.7: *Cloud Function enable page*

Note: The APIs are now enabled and will stay enabled for this Project.

Step 2. Create a function

1. Open the Functions Overview page in the Cloud Console. Ensure that the project for which you enabled Cloud Functions is selected:

Figure 1.8: *GCP Cloud Functions page*

2. Click on **CREATE FUNCTION**.

3. Name your function, as follows:

Figure 1.9: Create function – Step 1 configuration

4. In the **Trigger** field, select **HTTP**:

Trigger

⊙ HTTP

Trigger type
HTTP ▼

URL 🗗

https://us-central1-ultra-evening-331702.cloudfunctions.net/function-1

Authentication

⦿ Allow unauthenticated invocations
Check this if you are creating a public API or website.

○ Require authentication
Manage authorised users with Cloud IAM.

☐ Require HTTPS ❓

SAVE   CANCEL

NEXT   **CANCEL**

Figure 1.10: Create Function – Step 1 Configuration – Set trigger

5. In the **Authentication** field, select **Allow unauthenticated invocations**.

6. Click on **Save** to save your changes, and then click on **Next**.

7. In the **Source code** field, select **Inline editor**. In this exercise, you will use the default function provided in the editor.

8. Use the **Runtime** dropdown to select the desired Node.js runtime. (Leave as default node.js 14)

9. Ensure Entry Point field: **helloWorld**. (This is the function that will be called)

Deploy the function

1. At the bottom of the page, click on **Deploy**.

2. Cloud Console redirects you to the Cloud Functions Overview page, where you can wait as the function is being deployed.

   While the function is being deployed, which can take some time, the icon next to it is a small spinner. When it finishes deploying, the spinner turns to a green check mark:

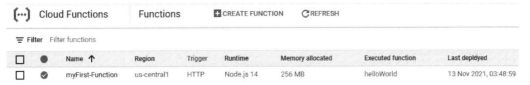

Figure 1.11: Deploy the function

Test the function

1. Clock on the 3-dot icon on the far right to display the menu for your function, and select **Test function**:

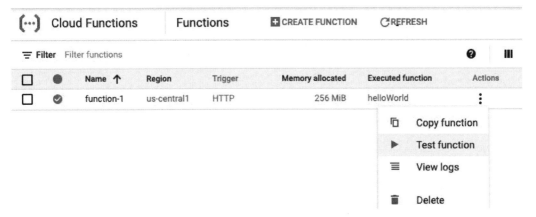

Figure 1.12: Test the function

2. On the testing page, click on **Test function**. At the bottom of the screen, the **Output** screen displays the text **Hello World!**.

Figure 1.13: *Displaying Successful Test: "Hello World"*

View logs

Check the logs to see your actions in the log history:

```
Logs    ✔Fetched (up to 100 entries). View all logs
    ⓘ  Scanned up to 30/10/2021, 22:59. Scanned 1.1 KB.
 ▶  λ  2021-11-12T20:53:43.222678640Z  myFirst-Function  1f71a29nzyhh  Function execution started
 ▶  λ  2021-11-12T20:53:43.343573585Z  myFirst-Function  1f71a29nzyhh  Function execution took 121 ms, finished with status code: 200
```

Figure 1.14: *View Cloud Function logs*

Congratulations! You've successfully deployed and tested a Node.js web service on Cloud Functions!

Tutorial 1.2: Deploy a Nodejs App in Google App Engine

Learn how to deploy and run a Nodejs app on App Engine.

To run this task directly in Cloud Console, click to Activate the Cloud Shell.

Type in the Command Line:

```
cd Chapter 01
teachme tutorial-1.2
```

The following sections take you through the same steps as the interactive tutorial.

Step 1. Project setup

GCP organizes resources into projects, which collect all the related resources for an application in one place. Begin by creating a new project or selecting an existing project for this tutorial:

Figure 1.15: *Check Project ID*

Note: Your Project number will be different from the example shown here.

Step 2. Using Cloud Shell

Cloud Shell is a built-in command-line tool for the console. We're going to use Cloud Shell to deploy our app:

1. Open Cloud Shell by clicking on the Activate Cloud Shell button in the navigation bar in the upper-right corner of the console:

Figure 1.16: *The Activate Cloud Shell icon*

2. Clone the sample code.

   In this step, we will use the Cloud Shell terminal command line (CLI) to clone the **'Hello World'** code from GitHub. Type in the following at the CLI:

   https://github.com/bpbpublications/Cloud-Native-Apps-on-Google-Cloud-Platform

   > **The sample code is cloned from GitHub to your project repository, and it is then available to the Cloud Shell terminal. If the directory already exists, remove the previous files before cloning.**

3. Switch to the tutorial directory:

   ```
   cd /Chapter 01/chapt-1
   ```

Step 3. Configuring your deployment

As you are now in the directory you just created to hold the cloned sample code, we'll take the opportunity to look at the files that configure your application.

Enter the following command to view your application code:

```
cat app.js
```

Exploring your configuration file

App Engine uses YAML files to specify a deployment's configuration. The **app.yaml** files contain information about your application, like the runtime environment, URL handlers, and a lot more.

Enter the following command to view your configuration file:

```
cat app.yaml
```

Step 4. Testing your app

Test your app on Cloud Shell. Cloud Shell lets you test your app before deploying to ensure that it's running as intended, just like debugging on your local machine.

To test your app, enter the following:

```
export PORT=8080 && npm install
```

```
alasdair_gilchrist@cloudshell:~/cloud-shell-tutorials/node.js-code/book631-tutorials
npm WARN EBADENGINE Unsupported engine {
npm WARN EBADENGINE     package: 'appengine-hello-world@0.0.2',
npm WARN EBADENGINE     required: { node: '>=14.0.0' },
npm WARN EBADENGINE     current: { node: 'v12.14.1', npm: '8.1.2' }
npm WARN EBADENGINE }

added 155 packages, and audited 156 packages in 1s

26 packages are looking for funding
  run `npm fund` for details

found 0 vulnerabilities
```

Figure 1.17: Output from 'npm install'

Followed by this:

```
npm start
```

```
> appengine-hello-world@0.0.2 start
> node app.js

App listening on port 8080
Press Ctrl+C to quit.
```

Figure 1.18: Output from 'npm start'

Preview your app with **Web preview**:

Figure 1.19: Location for Web Viewer in Cloud Shell

Your app is now running on Cloud Shell. You can access it by clicking on the web preview button at the top of the Cloud Shell pane and choosing **Preview on port 8080**.

Terminating the preview instance

Terminate the instance of the application by pressing *Ctrl + C* in Cloud Shell.

Step 5. Deploying to App Engine

Create an application

To deploy your app, you need to create an app in a region:

```
gcloud app create
```

> **If you get an error, you may need to set your project_ID for your current workspace by running this command:**

```
gcloud config set project Your Project ID
```

For example:

```
gcloud config set project tidal-advantage-287623
```

Deploying with Cloud Shell

You can use Cloud Shell to deploy your app. To deploy your app, enter the following:

```
gcloud app deploy
```

Visit your app

Click on the URL that is returned in the output. The default URL of your app is a subdomain on appspot.com that starts with your project's ID:

```
Congratulations! Your app has been deployed.
```

Tutorial 1.3: Deploy a Nodejs Container in Cloud Run

Learn how to create a simple Hello World application, package it into a container image, upload the container image to Container Registry, and then deploy the container image to Cloud Run. You can use other languages in addition to the ones shown.

To run this task directly in Cloud Console, click to Activate the Cloud Shell:

Type in the Command Line:

```
cd Chapter 01

teachme tutorial-1.3
```

If you do not wish to use the Google Console—though we strongly recommend that you do—you can watch the video and go through the tutorial steps below:

The following sections take you through the same steps as the interactive tutorial.

Before you begin

1. On the project selector page in the Google Cloud Console, select or create a Google Cloud project.

> **If you don't plan to keep the resources that you create in this procedure, create a project instead of selecting an existing one. After you finish these steps, you can delete the project, removing all resources associated with it.**

2. Ensure that billing is enabled for your Cloud project.

Step 2. Create your web service

For this tutorial, you'll be using the Cloud Shell Editor as your environment for creating your service. The editor comes preloaded with the tools needed for Cloud development. Follow these steps to create your service:

1. Launch Cloud Shell and then click on the **Cloud Shell Editor** button:

Figure 1.20: Location of Cloud Shell editor in terminal

2. Launch the **Cloud Code** menu from the status bar at the bottom of the Editor panel:

Figure 1.21: Location for Cloud Code in Cloud Shell editor

3. When Cloud Code opens, select **New Application**:

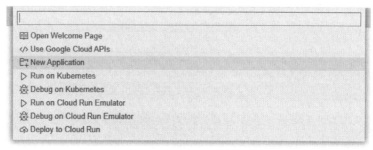

Figure 1.22: Cloud Code initial menu

4. Select the **Cloud Run** application for the type of sample app:

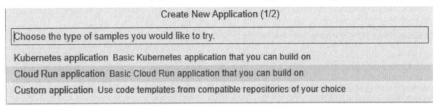

Figure 1.23: Cloud Code – Cloud Run application

5. From the list of sample Cloud Run services, select the **Node.js: Cloud Run** option:

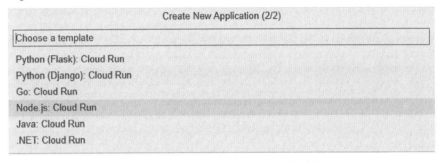

Figure 1.24: Cloud Code – Node.js: Cloud Run

6. Select a folder for your service location and click on **Create New Application**.

    Cloud Shell Editor loads your service in a new workspace. Once it reloads, your service is accessible with the explorer view as **Hello world**. The **readme.md** also opens; you can close this and proceed to step 3.

Figure 1.25: Hello World Workspace (sample)

Step 3. Build and deploy your service to Cloud Run

Now that you've created your Hello-World service, you can deploy it to Cloud Run. To build and deploy your service:

1. Launch the Cloud Code menu from the status bar.

2. Select **Deploy to Cloud Run**. If prompted, Authorize Cloud Shell to make Google Cloud API calls.

3. When prompted, select your Google Cloud project. If prompted, enable your Cloud Run API by clicking on **Enable API**.

4. n the **Deploy to Cloud Run** dialog, under **Service settings**, select an existing service or create a new one.

5. Choose a region to deploy to (e.g., **us-east1**).

6. Select **Allow unauthenticated invocations to make this a public service**.

7. Click **Deploy**.

Cloud Code now builds your image, pushes it to the container registry, and deploys your service to Cloud Run.

Once you see the message **Deployment completed successfully...**, your service is live and accessible via the URL displayed in the Deploy to Cloud Run dialog.

Deployment completed successfully! URL: https://hello-world-1-wmq5mtgo6a-uc.a.run.app

Show Detailed Logs

GCP Project: ultra-evening-331702

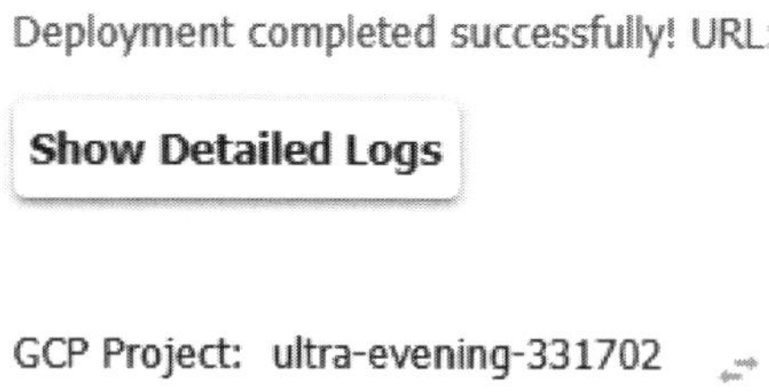

Figure 1.26: Deployment completed successfully

To test the deployment, click on the URL displayed in the 'Deploy to Cloud Run' dialog.

Deployment completed successfully! URL: https://hello-world-1-wmq5mtgo6a-uc.a.run.app

Figure 1.27: Success!

Congratulations! You have just deployed a container image from source code to Cloud Run.

Conclusion

In this chapter, we covered what cloud native apps are and how they are distinguishable from other cloud-based applications. We were then briefly introduced to a topic that will be referred to often in the subsequent chapters of the book: DevOps. However, the main takeaways are that we learned about the Google Cloud's selection of server and serverless platform, what they were for, and how best to use them. We also learned, through hands-on tutorials, how to deploy an app on each of the 3 GCP serverless offerings. This chapter has provided you with the foundation knowledge you will build upon in the subsequent chapters.

In the next chapter, we will cover how to develop cloud native apps using Google Cloud Platform's browser console and its Cloud Shell Terminal.

CHAPTER 2

Developing Cloud Native Apps with Cloud Shell

In this chapter, we will explore the modern approach to software development life cycle and the five principles of cloud-native application design. Understanding and following these concepts help ensure that your designs will take full advantage of the GCP architecture while avoiding the many pitfalls of trying to accommodate old methods and approaches into a new platform. We will discuss automation, state, managed-services, security, and awareness if not acceptance of the need for perennial change in our design and development life cycle.

We will then consider the Agile software development methodology, why it is so important, and how it fits well with cloud native application development. This leads us to specific cloud native development lifecycles, cloud native patterns, components, and the essential pillars of cloud native architecture: microservices, containers, dynamic orchestration (Kubernetes), and DevOps (Continuous Delivery).

Finally, we will consider some best practices when developing cloud native applications and explore GCP development tools and platforms, such as the Cloud SDK, Cloud Code, and Cloud Shell before we get down to some hands-on practical lessons.

Structure

We will be covering the following topics in this chapter:

- A Cloud native approach to SDLC

- Introducing Cloud Code

- Installing and using Cloud SDK

- Working in the Cloud Shell terminal

- Walkthrough:
    - Getting started with Cloud Shell
    - Installing the VScode IDE in the console's browser
    - Installing the SDK Docker image

- Interactive Tutorials:
    - Developing with Cloud code using the Cloud Shell Editor
    - Building a Custom Shell image Docker container

Objectives

After reading this chapter, you will be able to download and install the Cloud SDK, be competent in using the Shell Cloud Terminal, and get familiarized with Cloud code. You will also be able to build your own custom Cloud Shell Docker image and have a basic grounding in developing apps using Cloud code. Moreover, you will have deployed your first serverless app in Cloud Run.

A Cloud native approach to SDLC

The cloud-native approach to developing applications and services has really taken off in the last few years despite the **Cloud Native Computing Foundation** (**CNCF**) only being founded in 2015. The earliest reference to the term cloud native is attributed to *Bill Wilder* in his book, *Cloud Architecture Patterns* (*O'Reilly Media*, 2012). Wilder suggested that a cloud-native application is any application that was architected to take full advantage of cloud platforms. These applications have key characteristics, like they:

- Use cloud platform services

- Scale horizontally

- Scale automatically, using proactive and reactive actions

- Handle nodes and transient failures without degrading

- Feature non-blocking asynchronous communication in a loosely coupled architecture

While these observations were certainly insightful at the time, it would be incorrect to suggest that there are definitive differentiators between traditional and cloud native applications today. The cloud, after all, is not some ethereal structure; it consists of the same hardware, that is, servers, disks, and networks that makes up traditional on-premises data center infrastructure. This means that best practice for on-prem architectural design still applies for cloud-native architecture. However, we have to bear in mind that although the hardware is similar, how it performs can change when you're in the cloud. For instance, provisioning a replacement server can take weeks in an on-prem data center, whereas it can be spun up in seconds in the cloud.

Principles for Cloud Native architecture

The way we approach design for the cloud significantly differs from traditional architecture, which tends to focus on a fixed, high-cost infrastructure that requires manual effort to build and maintain, let alone modify. As a result, the on-prem architecture focuses on the resilience and performance of a relatively static infrastructure, which has been over-provisioned to provide sufficient growth for several years (3-5). In the cloud, however, such a fixed infrastructure with such wasteful provisioning of resources makes much less sense because the cloud can provide additional resources on demand. Additionally, the cloud is charged based on a pay-per-use model and is designed for automation, so it will automatically scale up or down, as required. Consequently, cloud-native designs are more concerned with achieving resilience and scale through mechanisms like distributed processing and automating the replacement of failed components.

Principle 1: Automation by design

Automation of processes should be the goal wherever possible. It has been a best practice for software process design for decades as the root cause of many outages has human error in the mix somewhere. Moreover, the cloud makes automating processes easier as it seamlessly handles the provisioning and building of infrastructure as well as any associated components. The upfront investment will likely be higher, but an automated solution will almost always have a favorable return on investment. This is due to automation solving many of the operational challenges that humans cannot hope to address, such as real-time log analysis. Therefore, in terms of **return on investment (ROI)**, both monetary and in effort, it is a wise investment. This also applies in terms of resilience, availability, and performance,. Not only can automation accelerate repairing, scaling, and deploying of your system, it can also proactively and reactively mitigate issues.

Principle 2: Be wary of Preserving State

The preservation of *'state'* across a user session is problematic in cloud-native architecture if you wish to preserve the benefits of scale, resiliency, and cost. You should try to design your system to be stateless wherever feasible. If this is not an option, then be clear about why, when, and how you store state.

Stateless components are considered to be ideal in cloud architecture as they are easy to:

- **Scale**: To scale up, you just add more clones. To scale down, you can terminate the excess ones after they have finished running their current task.

- **Repair**: The concept of *'repairing'* a failed instance is not practical as it's a waste of time and effort. Simply terminate it gracefully and spin up a replacement.

- **Roll-back**: Stateless components are much easier to roll back as they are not burdened by history. It easier to shut down any new instances and then launch fresh instances of the old version as replacements.

- **Load-balance**: When components are stateless, load balancing is straightforward as any instance can handle any request. However, it becomes very challenging when components are stateful. This is because each instance stores the state, which is the history of the user's recent transactions, effectively forcing that instance to handle all subsequent requests from that user.

Principle 3: Favor managed services

Whether you want to adopt managed services basically comes down to finding an appropriate balance between portability and costs, which is related to budget and the availability of inhouse skills. As such, managed services fall into three broad categories:

- **Managed open source**: This type of a managed service is related to managing open-source services like Kubernetes or offer an open-source compatible interface like Cloud Bigtable. There is little risk of vendor lock-in and many benefits.

- **Managed services with high operational utility**: Some managed services are not open source but are so much easier to use or just do a better job than their alternatives. In this case, a decision is made to accept the risk of vendor lock-in. An example of this type of managed service is Big Query, which is often chosen because it is easy and cheaper to deploy and operate as compared to an on-prem solution.

- **Other use-cases**: This is when product and process knowledge is invaluable in deciding the value of a managed service. There is high risk wherever there is no effortless alternative switch away from the service, especially if there is no real operational benefit. In these use cases, you have to decide whether you are capable and perhaps better off running it yourself or the benefits associated with offloading the burden of managing the service are more. Of course, you have to consider the efforts required to replace the managed service.

However, practical experience shows that there are typically cost effective in terms of money and effort, and there can be significant reduction in operational risk by having the cloud provider manage the service on your behalf.

Principle 4: Practice defense in depth

The traditional approach to network security placed a lot of faith in fortifying the perimeter. With this security model, anything outside the perimeter was untrusted and anything inside the perimeter was trusted. That highly structured and inflexible approach has been discarded by the progress of time and the increasing pressure to provide user mobility. The requirement for flexible and mobile working on the user's own devices has further undermined the network siege mentality.

It has been replaced by the zero-trust security model, best suited for Cloud-native applications and architectures as they were born on the internet. By having their origins in internet-facing services, cloud native apps have always needed to deal with external and internal threats of attacks. Therefore, in the zero-trust model, trust is not an option and mutual authentication between components is mandatory, regardless of their perceived location.

Principle 5: Always be architecting

One key characteristic of a cloud-native system is that it's always undergoing change. As a cloud-native architect, you should always look to simplify and improve the architecture of the system. Change is inevitable, and as organizations undergo change, so do the threat landscape and the IT capabilities of your cloud provider. This approach can be expensive as it requires constant investment, but for IT systems to survive, they need to evolve rapidly to meet the emerging challenges.

What is Agile Development

Traditionally, software development was a regimented process requiring much preplanning, and the specifications and requirements were effectively set in stone at the very onset of the project. Changes were difficult and avoided wherever possible, which sometimes resulted in software being obsolete before the project was even completed. This waterfall model was eventually usurped by the advent of a new software development philosophy called Agile, which introduced flexibility and agility and embraced changes during the SDLC. Agile has since inspired many other software development models, but it was the vanguard for change.

Agile is a cyclical, iterative approach to software delivery that builds software incrementally from the start of the project. Agile works by breaking projects down into little bits of user functionality called user stories, prioritizing them, and then continuously delivering them in short 2-week cycles called iterations. A characteristic of Agile is that development is done in layers instead of trying to deliver it all at once. The development sets out to complete specific targets by the end of each time-constrained cycle, and a working product is always the net result. It may not resemble the desired final product, but it will have earned value as a working model. This means that should the project be terminated early, there is always a product with the earned value to date. This is an essential difference between the iterative development methodology and say the waterfall SDLC, where there is nothing to show for a project's efforts till near the end.

Some other key characteristics of Agile that make it eminently suitable for cloud native apps are:

- **Analysis, design, coding, and testing are cyclical activities**: The project cycle of analysis, design, coding, and testing on an Agile project continues for as long as there are features to build. These activities will continue for the duration of the project.

- **Development is iterative**: Iterative development means starting with something really simple and adding to it incrementally over time. It means evaluating the working model at the end of each cycle period and deciding upon new features and upgrades. This is another major differentiator between Agile and most other SDLC that rely heavily on pre-planning and fixed feature scope. In Agile, accepting that your requirements are going to change and continuously refining and tweaking your product as you go is the plan.

- **Planning is adaptive**: When reality conflicts with the plan, Agilists find it easier to change their plans than try to alter reality. This approach is known as adaptive planning. There can, of course, be many reasons that force a plan to change, such as time, cost, and feature constraints, but the most common solution is to flex on scope.

- **Roles are blurred**: Developers tend to wear several hats during Agile projects as roles are not always strictly defined. This does not mean there is no hierarchy or control but that it's a more collaborative effort where team members pitch in and contribute to make the project successful.

- **Scope can vary**: Agile typically works by defining time, budget, and quality and by being flexible around scope.

- **Requirements can change**: Traditionally, change has been shunned on software projects because of its high perceived cost, especially when it comes late in the project timeframe. Agile reverses this notion and believes that the cost of change can be relatively flat; hence Agilists accept and embrace change even late in the delivery process.

- **Working software is the primary measure of success**: At the end of the day, only working software is of any value to the customer. Therefore, Agilists measure progress by the time taken to deliver the customer's expectations into working software. After all, the customer is paying to get working software, not project plans, test plans, and analysis artifacts.

Understanding the Cloud Native development lifecycle

Cloud Native software development differs significantly from building monolithic software applications as it focuses on producing applications that leverage cloud characteristics, features, and functionality. This new breed of applications is built to benefit specifically from a cloud native architecture.

Cloud native patterns

Cloud architecture patterns are not a requirement for developing cloud native applications. Indeed, cloud native apps can just as readily run on-prem as in the cloud. The 12-factor pattern is often heralded as a core requirement for cloud native apps, but this pattern contemplates the details of application development that are not specifically related to cloud-native development. Indeed, the 12-factor pattern applies just as much to application development in general and how well-behaved software interacts with the infrastructure.

A cloud native approach, on the other hand, requires at least the foundation of the four-core cloud native platform capabilities, which are:

- **Containers**: The capability to handle containers at scale and across heterogeneous platforms is a prerequisite for any cloud native application. Developers need to automate and monitor these tasks so that they can set policies for control, access, and auditability.

- **Continuous delivery**: Cloud platforms should give developers the facility to create automated pipelines for build, verification, policy enforcement, deployment, and the eventual controlled release of applications.

- **Edge management**: A platform should be able to handle the centralized configuration of system defaults, such as security and policy compliance, as well as the decentralized configuration of system defaults.

- **Observability**: This platform feature allows developers to monitor and analyze end-user traffic directly. This allows marketing and product teams to gather market intelligence and set real market priorities and conforming **key performance indicators** (**KPIs**) to suit. Observability is critical in delivering the required **service level objectives** (**SLOs**).

The four pillars of Cloud native

Each cloud native application has four underlying pillars: microservices, containers, dynamic orchestration (Kubernetes), and DevOps (Continuous Delivery). Let's understand these in detail:

- **Microservices**: Microservices are a critical component in cloud-native applications because a services-based design allows for isolation and focus on a specific task. Microservices are loosely coupled with other microservices and the underlying application, which means that they can be disconnected, updated, or replaced without impacting other components or services within the application. This characteristic of microservices allows them to be deployed and maintained more efficiently than monolithic applications.

- **Containers**: Containers are key to scale and resilience in cloud native applications as they allow multiple instances of an app to live on one virtual machine. With containerization, applications are bundled with all their dependencies, such as libraries, configuration files, and binaries, into self-contained bundles called containers. Containers speed up the process of deploying new applications and updating the existing ones.

- **Dynamic orchestration**: Orchestration is a requirement in the software development process as it handles the efficient provisioning and configuration of applications. DevOps relies on dynamic orchestration to manage the automation of provisioning new servers, databases, and other required cloud infrastructure.

- **Continuous delivery**: A goal of DevOps is continuous delivery, which means applications can be easily configured, modified, or upgraded as part of a more efficient deployment workflow. With a continuous integration, continuous delivery/deployment model and autonomous pipeline, which can pull code directly from a source code repository, push it to staging/development servers, and then ultimately have the code pushed to production.

Best practices for cloud native application development

Cloud native architecture has no set of rules; hence, you are free to approach development as you wish. However, there are well established best practices, which are based on well-known business problems or scenarios that you may well be trying to solve.

Nonetheless, the common objective of all cloud native apps is to be designed once and deployed anywhere. Additionally, despite there being no firm ground rules, all cloud-native application designs should dictate how the app will be built, its performance requirements, and how they will be measured as well as the scope for continuous improvement through the application's lifecycle.

Here are the five key best practices for Cloud Native design and development:

- **Automate**: Automation wherever possible as it provides the means for the consistent provisioning of apps across multiple cloud environments. Automation should be deployed throughout the system, such as **infrastructure as code (IaC)**, which is used to rapidly build consistent infrastructure. In DevOps organizations, you should also consider CI/CD automation throughout the dev, stage, and production phases for your application.

- **Monitor**: Monitoring is key to measuring performance, and applications should be monitored for SLO and KPIs across the development environment. Monitoring reveals how an application or service is performing and how it is being used.

- **Document**: There may be many people collaborating in building your cloud native apps, but they may also have limited visibility into what others are doing. Documentation is always important, but docs-as code that follows the same revisioning system as the code allows developers to track changes and helps keeps the docs and the code revisions synchronized.

- **Make incremental changes**: Changes should only be made to the application or the infrastructure, where possible, in incremental and reversible stages. Being able to quickly reverse or roll back a change is critical to system availability. Applying incremental changes that can be easily rolled back also enables developers to build confidence and learn from any mistakes.

- **Design for failure**: Testing is critical in CI/CD pipelines and processes, so the testing stage should be diligently designed for fast and efficient testing. However, tests cannot always uncover bugs in the code, so you need to be prepared for the inevitable as things will go wrong in a cloud environment. This means implementing and updating test frameworks to simulate known causes of failures.

Tools for cloud-native app development

Several software tools are used for each cloud-native application development process. Together, they create a typical cloud native development stack. Here is the software found in a cloud-native development stack:

- **Docker**: The Docker platform is open source and synonymous with containers. Docker creates, deploys, and manages virtualized application containers that can be ported across clouds and OS environments. In addition to portability, Docker containers provide the required isolation of resources that permits multiple containers to share the same host OS without contention.

- **Kubernetes**: The Kubernetes platform was developed to help manage and orchestrate Linux containers; it has proven invaluable in running medium to large scale container deployments.

- **Node.js**: This JavaScript runtime is commonly used for creating real-time applications and other microservices. For example, Node.js is used to create virtual servers and to define the routes that connect microservices to external APIs.

Cloud SDK or Cloud Code is a set of tools that you can use to manage resources and applications hosted on Google Cloud. These tools include the gcloud, gsutil, and bq command-line tools.

What is Google Cloud Code?

You were introduced to Cloud Code in the interactive tutorial 1-3 in *Chapter 1: "Introducing Cloud Native Apps"* where we used a Cloud Code sample app to demonstrate a build and deploy of a node.js app to Cloud Run. In that example, you were perhaps not aware of the role and heavy lifting that Cloud Code was doing on our behalf. We will focus on Cloud Code in the next chapter, but for now, a high-level introduction will suffice.

Cloud Code can be looked upon as being a lightweight native IDE for Google Cloud. It's not really a full-blown IDE but actually a set of plugins for GCP's Cloud Shell as well as the established IntelliJ and Visual Studio Code IDEs, which let developers build cloud native applications from within the cloud itself.

Typically, developers build and test code on their local machines using a locally installed IDE. An **Integrated Development Environment** (**IDE**) is a standalone software application that helps developers write code. An IDE streamlines many of the tasks required to write code, keep code organized, test and debug code, and perhaps even to deploy code to the cloud. Cloud-based IDEs are now in vogue, especially for developing cloud native applications.

In GCP, Cloud Code saves developers from the hassle of having to set up an IDE on their personal computers as they can now run their enhanced IDE, with plugins, from their browser. Moreover, because the code is already developed, tested, and debugged within Google Cloud, it makes deployment much easier. Moreover, developers will use Cloud Code as it simplifies the process of integrating Google

Cloud APIs into an application. The Cloud Code plugins manage things like dependencies in order to make APIs work. Hence, Cloud Code allows developers to use the language that suits them and to catch errors much earlier in the development cycle, when they are easier to fix. Google Cloud currently has Cloud Code plugins for IntelliJ, VSCode, and Cloud Shell.

Selecting a development and operations environment

Google Cloud SDK is the framework we will use in this book. The Cloud SDK is a set of tools that you can use to manage resources and applications hosted on Google Cloud. These tools include the gcloud, gsutil, and bq command-line tools.

Google Cloud SDK

As we are working on the Google Cloud Platform, it makes sense to use the Cloud SDK as it holds all the tools and libraries for interacting with the Google Cloud Platform's products and services.

The tools inherent to Cloud SDK allow us to:

- Orchestrate virtual machine instances directly from your command line.

- Manage Compute Engine networks, firewalls, and disk storage with the gcloud command-line tool.

- Choose your language with Client Libraries for Java, Python, Node.js, Ruby, Go, .NET, and PHP.

- Run and simulate local service emulators for Pub/Sub, Cloud Spanner, Bigtable, and Datastore.

You have a choice when using Cloud SDK: you can install and initialize the SDK locally or you can use Cloud SDK without installation by using Cloud Shell via the GCP Cloud Console.

Either way, we will get the benefits from utilizing the Cloud SDK, which are mentioned in the following section.

The gcloud command-line tool

The gcloud CLI tool helps us manage local configuration, authentication, developer workflow, and interactions with Google Cloud APIs, among other things. With the gcloud command-line tool, it's easier and quicker to perform many common cloud tasks, like building and managing a Google Kubernetes Engine cluster, deploying an

App Engine application, or cloning a code repository by using the command line, in scripts or through other automations.

Client libraries

Cloud SDK comes with a wide range of pre-installed and installable language-specific Cloud Client Libraries. The SDK also has all the preinstalled tools to access the Google API Client Libraries. The Cloud Client Libraries use each supported language's natural conventions and styles, handling authentication, reducing the amount of necessary boilerplate code, and optimizing the developer workflow.

Product-specific command-line tools

A collection of command-line tools comes packaged with Cloud SDK, including gsutil, bq, and kubectl. In addition to the gcloud tool, there is the gsutil tool, which allows you to manage Cloud Storage buckets and objects using the command line. There is also the bq tool, which allows you to run queries and manipulate datasets, tables, and entities in BigQuery through the command line. Furthermore, with kubectl, you can deploy and manage Kubernetes container clusters using the command line.

Cloud Shell

The fastest and most convenient way to get to grips with the Cloud SDK is by initiating it via the Cloud Shell in your browser. When you start Cloud Shell terminal in the console, the Cloud SDK gcloud command-line tool and other utilities are available to you as they come pre-installed. What's more, they are fully authenticated, which saves you from having to authenticate your local system to cloud components.

Additionally, as we will experience first-hand in the interactive tutorials, Cloud Shell comes with a built-in code editor, which allows you to do all your development work as well as build, debug, and deploy your cloud-based apps in the cloud. You can also launch interactive tutorials or preview web apps on a Cloud Shell VM instance.

Nonetheless, many developers prefer to work on their own devices, so you can download and customize the Cloud SDK and then use its full power for local development and testing and also for scripting. Therefore, our first practical lesson from this chapter will be how to download Cloud SDK.

Walkthrough 2.1: Cloud Shell setup

In order to access and use the GCP Console, you will need to initially create a Project and a Billing Account; follow the steps on the previous tutorials to configure these. We will be using the gcloud command-line tool, which is the powerful and unified command-line tool in Google Cloud. There is no need to download and install the SDK locally as gcloud comes preinstalled in Cloud Shell:

1. In the Cloud Console, click on **Activate Cloud Shell**:

Figure 2.1: Activating Cloud shell

It can take a few moments to provision, initialize, and then connect to Cloud Shell as it starts up in a VM.

This virtual machine is preconfigured with all the development tools you'll need, such as the Cloud SDK. In addition, the VM offers a persistent 5GB home directory, so anything you save in the home directory will persist across reboots. Apps loaded into the home directory also run in Google Cloud, which provides typically better network performance and seamless application and device authentication. Once connected to Cloud Shell, you should see that you are already authenticated and that the project is already set to your project ID.

```
Welcome to Cloud Shell! Type "help" to get started.
Your Cloud Platform project in this session is set to tidal-advantage-287623.
Use "gcloud config set project [PROJECT_ID]" to change to a different project.
alasdair_gilchrist@cloudshell:~ (tidal-advantage-287623)$ []
```

Figure 2.2: Set project

2. Run the following command in Cloud Shell to confirm that you are authenticated:

gcloud auth list

```
alasdair_gilchrist@cloudshell:~$ gcloud auth list
Credentialed Accounts

ACTIVE: *
ACCOUNT: alasdair.gilchrist@gmail.com

To set the active account, run:
    $ gcloud config set account `ACCOUNT`

alasdair_gilchrist@cloudshell:~$ █
```

Figure 2.3: Confirm authentication

```
gcloud config list project
```

Command output:

```
alasdair_gilchrist@cloudshell:~ (tidal-advantage-287623)$ gcloud config list project
[core]
project = tidal-advantage-287623

Your active configuration is: [cloudshell-26616]
```

Figure 2.4: List default project

```
[core]
project = <PROJECT_ID>
```

If the project is not set correctly, you can set it with this command:

```
gcloud config set project <PROJECT_ID>
```

Command output:

```
Updated property [core/project].
```

3. Use the command line.

   After Cloud Shell launches, you can use the command line to invoke the Cloud SDK gcloud command, or you can use the other tools available on the virtual machine instance. You can also use your **$HOME** directory to store files across projects and between Cloud Shell sessions as it has persistent disk storage. This is not just convenient; it is also secure as your **$HOME** directory cannot be accessed by other cloud users.

   To get started with using the Cloud Shell terminal, we will take a look at the commands available to you. Type this command to begin exploring the CLI:

   ```
   gcloud -h
   ```

   As an example, simple usage guidelines are available by adding **-h** onto the end of the command. Verbose help can be obtained by appending the **--help flag** or executing the gcloud **help** command.

   Type in the following to demonstrate this:

   ```
   gcloud help config
   ```

   You will see that this command gives a long, verbose, and very detailed help description.

4. Using gcloud commands:

   We can use the command gcloud list to view the list of configurations in our current Shell environment:

```
gcloud config list
```

```
alasdair_gilchrist@cloudshell:~ (tidal-advantage-287623)$ gcloud config list
[accessibility]
screen_reader = True
[component_manager]
disable_update_check = True
[compute]
gce_metadata_read_timeout_sec = 30
[core]
account = alasdair.gilchrist@gmail.com
disable_usage_reporting = True
project = tidal-advantage-287623
[metrics]
environment = devshell

Your active configuration is: [cloudshell-26616]
```

Figure 2.5: To see the list of configurations

You may wonder about whether there are other properties that were not set. You can see all properties by calling the following:

```
gcloud config list --all
```

In this tutorial, you launched Cloud Shell and called some simple gcloud commands to investigate the environment's standard configuration.

Launching Cloud Shell from the Console

To launch a Cloud Shell session from the Cloud Console, use the Activate Cloud Shell button Activate Shell Button in the Cloud Console. This launches a session in the bottom pane of Cloud Console:

Figure 2.6: Launching Cloud Shell

You can also transfer this session to a full screen experience by clicking on the **Open in new window** icon or **Open** in new window button.

Figure 2.7: Full Screen or New Window icon

Launching a standalone session

If you'd prefer a standalone session, you can launch a Cloud Shell session using this browser command:

shell.cloud.google.com.

The Cloud Shell terminal and Cloud Shell Editor are automatically started for you.

You can use this to open just the Cloud Shell Editor:

ide.cloud.google.com.

You can still access the Cloud Shell terminal at any time using the Open terminal button or the **Activate Shell** Button in the Cloud Shell menu bar.

When you click on the Activate Shell button, a Cloud Shell session opens inside a new frame at the bottom of the Console and displays a command-line prompt. It can take a few seconds for the session to be initialized.

Using the Cloud Shell Terminal

The Cloud Shell provides access to the command-line in a terminal window that opens in the Google Cloud Console.

In addition to accessing the gcloud command-line tool and other utilities from the command line, you can use the cloud shell command to launch tutorials, open the Cloud Shell Editor, and download files.

Using the Cloud Shell Editor

There is also a built-in code editor that provides the convenience of viewing and editing files in the same environment where projects are built and deployed. You can launch the Cloud Shell Editor by clicking on the pencil icon Code Editor button on the toolbar of the Cloud Shell window:

Figure 2.8: *Open Cloud Shell editor*

Ephemeral mode

There are two modes that you can run Cloud Shell in; by default, Cloud Shell provides a **$HOME** directory with 5 GB of free persistent disk storage. All the files you store in your home directory persist between sessions when you use the default Cloud Shell experience.

However, if you do not want to have any persistent storage, you can choose to use Cloud Shell in Ephemeral mode. In this mode, you can get started with Cloud Shell faster as there is less work to be done by GCP setting up your environment. However, it means that all the files you create during your Ephemeral mode session are lost when you end the session.

To choose Ephemeral mode, select **Ephemeral** mode from the Cloud Shell three-dotted **More** menu icon. You also have the choice of setting Ephemeral mode as your default Cloud Shell experience by toggling on the **Always start Cloud Shell in Ephemeral mode** option.

Walkthrough 2.2: Running VScode with Cloud Shell in the browser

Developers often prefer to work in the IDE that they have become accustomed to, and one of the most popular is Visual Studio Code. However, if you want, you can run Visual Studio Code in a browser. It works because Visual Studio Code has its own code-server function. In this tutorial, we will be integrating code-server into the Cloud Shell environment:

1. Go to **console.cloud.google.com** and open Cloud Shell:

Figure 2.9: To open Cloud Shell

2. Install code-server:

```
curl -fsSL https://code-server.dev/install.sh | sh
```

```
############################################################## 100.0%##O=#  #
+ mv ~/.cache/code-server/code-server_3.12.0_amd64.deb.incomplete ~/.cache/code-server/code-server_3.12.0_amd64.deb
+ sudo dpkg -i ~/.cache/code-server/code-server_3.12.0_amd64.deb
Selecting previously unselected package code-server.
(Reading database ... 125961 files and directories currently installed.)
Preparing to unpack .../code-server_3.12.0_amd64.deb ...
Unpacking code-server (3.12.0) ...
Setting up code-server (3.12.0) ...

deb package has been installed.

To have systemd start code-server now and restart on boot:
  sudo systemctl enable --now code-server@$USER
Or, if you don't want/need a background service you can run:
  code-server
alasdair_gilchrist@cloudshell:~$ []
```

Figure 2.10: Install code-server

3. Start the code-server from the Cloud Shell terminal:

```
code-server --auth none --port 8080
```

> **Note: You don't need authentication since the Google Cloud Shell proxy already handles that for you.**

4. Click on **Web Preview** → **Preview** on port **8080**:

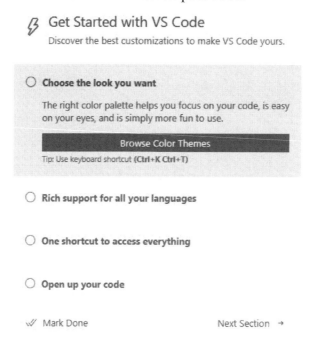

Figure 2.11: *VS code IDE*

Congratulations! That's it. You have the VS Code IDE running in your browser now.

Installing the Cloud SDK locally

Despite all the benefits of the cloud, many developers still prefer to work on their laptop or local devices, in which case they probably will want to download and install the Cloud SDK locally.

You can install the Cloud SDK on Windows, Linux, and macOS. The quick setup guides for each OS are available at **https://cloud.google.com/sdk/docs/install**. For the sake of brevity, we will quickly run through the installation procedure for Windows.

The Cloud SDK installer lets you download, install, and set up the latest version of Cloud SDK quickly in an interactive mode. When you run the installer, it downloads Cloud SDK components and installs them on the local system. It also performs additional setup tasks like adding Cloud SDK components to your PATH and enabling command completion in your shell.

Steps:

1. Download the Cloud SDK installer.

2. Launch the installer and follow the prompts.

3. The installer will download and install all necessary dependencies, including the required Python version.

4. After installation is complete—be very patient, it takes a long time—start the Cloud SDK shell and configure the Cloud SDK.

5. Ensure that you leave the options to start the shell and configure your installation selected.

6. The installer starts a terminal window and runs the **gcloud init** command.

In Windows 10, the installer appears to hang approximately ¾ of the way through, but be patient; it just takes long. It is still working away in the background, but eventually, it loads successfully.

Since this book is all about Cloud Native apps, we also encourage you to use a container to deploy Cloud SDK.

Walkthrough 2.3: Installing Cloud SDK Docker Image

An alternative way to load the SDK locally on your machine is to use the Cloud SDK Docker image. The Docker image is a fully functional Cloud SDK that lets you pull a specific version of the Cloud SDK as a Docker image from the GCP's Container Registry and quickly execute gcloud tool commands in an isolated, correctly configured container.

The Cloud SDK Docker image contains the Cloud SDK installed on top of a Debian-based OS image. The Docker image is hosted on Container Registry, with the repository name **gcr.io/google.com/cloudsdktool/cloud-sdk**.

Docker image options

The Cloud SDK Docker images come in three versions: latest, slim, and alpine. You can specify your preference using the appropriate tag after the host repository name.

Installing a specified Docker image

1. To use the image of the latest Cloud SDK release, **gcr.io/google.com/ cloudsdktool/cloud-sdk:latest**, pull it from Container Registry by running the following command:

   ```
   docker pull gcr.io/google.com/cloudsdktool/cloud-sdk:latest
   ```

2. If you've pulled the latest version, verify the installation by running the following command:

   ```
   docker run --rm gcr.io/google.com/cloudsdktool/cloud-sdk:latest
   gcloud version
   ```

3. List compute instances using these credentials to verify by running the container with **--volumes-from**:

   ```
   docker run --rm --volumes-from gcloud-config gcr.io/
   google.com/cloudsdktool/cloud-sdk gcloud compute instances list
   --project your_project
   ```

> The **gcloud-config** container now has a volume containing your Google Cloud credentials. Do not use the **gcloud-config** volume in other containers.

By default, the latest images (**gcr.io/google.com/cloudsdktool/cloud-sdk:latest** and **gcr.io/google.com/cloudsdktool/cloud-sdk:VERSION**) have all the gcloud tool components installed.

Interactive Tutorial 2.1: Developing with Cloud Code using the Cloud Shell Editor

Learn how to Develop with Cloud Code using the Cloud Shell Editor.

To run this task directly in Cloud Console, click to Activate the Cloud Shell.

Type in the Command Line:

```
cd Chapter 02
teachme tutorial-2.1
```

Step 1. Create and deploy a Cloud Run serverless service

In this interactive tutorial, you will learn how to:

1. Create a simple web service.

2. Build the service and deploy it to Cloud Run.

3. View logs to ensure that the service is running without issues.

4. Clean up to avoid billing charges.

1.1 Create a web service

These steps show you how to work in Cloud Shell Editor. You can use a similar process if you use the Cloud Shell extension in your IDE:

1. Open Cloud Shell Editor.

2. Click on **Cloud Code** in the Cloud Shell Editor status bar.

3. Select **New Application**.

4. Select **Cloud Run** application as the sample type.

5. From the list of sample **Cloud Run services**, select the **Go: Cloud Run** option.

6. Select a folder for your service location and click on **Create New Application**.

Cloud Shell Editor loads your service in a new workspace. Once it reloads, your service is accessible with the explorer view.

The service consists of:

- **main.go**, which responds to requests with "**It's running!**".

  When directly invoked for local use, this code creates a basic web server that listens on the port defined by the **PORT** environment variable.

- **go.mod**, which declares Go dependencies.

- Dockerfile, which Cloud Run uses to build an executable container image.

1.2 Build and deploy the service to Cloud Run:

1. Click on Cloud Code in the status bar.

2. Select **Deploy to Cloud Run**.

3. If prompted, authorize Cloud Shell to make Google Cloud API calls.

4. On the **Deploy to Cloud Run** tab, click on Select **GCP Project** and select a project.

   If you don't already have a Google Cloud project, you'll need to create a new one and enable billing.

5. Click on **Enable API to enable the Cloud Run API**.

   Additional settings appear in the tab after you enable the API.

6. Under **Service settings**, select an existing service or do the following to create a new one:

   - In the **Service** list, select **+Create a service**.

   - For the **Deployment** platform, choose **Cloud Run** (fully managed).

   - For **Authentication**, choose **Allow unauthenticated invocations to make this a public service**.

   - Use Cloud Build.

7. Click on **Deploy**.

   Cloud Code builds an image, pushes it to the container registry, and deploys your service to Cloud Run.

8. When you see the message **Deployment completed successfully! URL: your URL**, visit the service by clicking on the URL at the end of the message.

Step 2: View your service logs

1. Navigate to the Cloud Run Explorer.

2. Right-click on your Cloud Run service and select View Logs.

3. In the **Logs Viewer** tab, click on the refresh button that appears above the logs display.

   The latest logs from your service appear in the logs display.

4. To view more logs, revisit your service's URL, and click on the **Refresh** button in the **Logs Viewer** tab again.

🎉 **Success**

Congratulations! You have successfully created and deployed a service on Cloud Run!

Working with Cloud Run

Beyond the tutorial, Cloud Shell has a lot to offer for Cloud Run development. Here's a snapshot of what Cloud Shell with integrated Cloud Code comes with:

- Support for Go, Node.js, Python, Java, and .NET.

- Fully functional run- and debug-ready starter services.

- Easy creation and editing of configuration files with smart template.

- Add out-of-the-box snippets and context-based completions.

- One-click run of your services from your browser and logging support to monitor the status of your resources.

- "Watch" mode to allow continuous building and real-time editing when you're in run mode.

- Automatic port-forwarding and resource cleanup on service termination.

- Service management with the inbuilt Cloud Run Explorer.

- Cluster creation with Cloud Run for Anthos enabled with inbuilt Kubernetes Explorer.

Workspace management in the Cloud Shell Editor

Another interesting feature of the Cloud Shell Editor is its ability to manage your projects as workspaces. In the GCP, a workspace represents the root folder of your project and includes your project-specific configuration files. A Home workspace is, therefore, based on your $Home directory and is automatically created for you.

What makes working with workspaces useful is that you can specify persistent settings and run and debug configurations and UI states (like open files) for all the folders in your workspace.

In the following short technical walkthrough, we will learn how to create, open, save, and close a workspace as well as configure Cloud Shell Editor to use your workspace settings. We will create a directory and upload code that we will use later to build a project based on Hugo, which is a static website generator.

Walkthrough 2.4: Create a new workspace

1. Using the Cloud Shell terminal, create a new directory to use as your workspace:

    i. Use **mkdir** to manually create a new directory, and change to that **dir**:

    ```
    mkdir hugo ; cd hugo
    ```

    ii. Use curl to copy an existing repository:

    ```
    curl -LO https://github.com/gohugoio/hugo/releases/
    download/v0.88.1/hugo_extended_0.88.1_Linux-64bit.deb
    ```

    iii. Load the Hugo extensions and create the site:

    ```
    sudo dpkg -i hugo_extended*.deb
    ```

```
mkdir sites; cd sites
hugo new site mysite; cd mysite
```

2. Once your directory is ready, you can open it as a new workspace with **File | Open Workspace...**

Opening a workspace

You can open a workspace in one of the following ways:

1. Click on the **Open Workspace** button in the Cloud Shell Editor Explorer view.

   Alternatively, you can access **File | Open Workspace...**

   i. Select a recently opened workspace from the **Recent** section in the Welcome to Cloud Shell window.

   ii. Alternatively, you can access **File | Open Recent Workspace....**

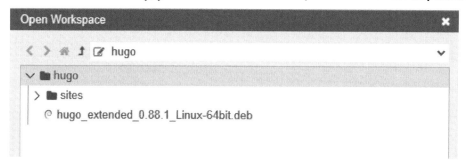

Figure 2.12: Opening a workspace

Opening a Home workspace

To open and work in your Home workspace, all you need to do is open your Home directory as your workspace with **File | Open Workspace...** and choose your Home directory from the folder dropdown menu.

Saving a workspace

If you make changes to a workspace and want to save it under a new name, you can save your workspace by navigating to **File | Save Workspace As...**

Closing a workspace

To close your workspace, navigate to **File | Close Workspace** and click on **OK** when prompted to confirm this action.

Configuring Workspace settings

You can use the **Settings** menu to configure the Cloud Shell Editor's behavior and interface. You can define your preferences for all sorts of things, such as debugging configurations, YAML editing support, and Command Palette history limits, using this Settings editor. The settings are accessible through **File** | **Settings** | **Open Preferences**.

There are two types of settings:

- **User settings**: These are globally applicable settings, and they are applied to all your instances of the Cloud Shell Editor.

- **Workspace settings**: These are workspace-specific settings, and they are only applied to the currently active workspace.

If a conflicting setting is configured in both the user and workspace level, the workspace setting takes precedence and overrides the more general user setting.

Due to there being a vast number of settings, you need to search for a setting. So, you need to have a method for filtering out those that don't relate to your criteria; you can use the **Search Settings** search bar to do this. Using the Search bar, you can search for a category or a specific keyword that returns a match to your query. The settings themselves can be set either by filling in the input field, choosing an option from a dropdown menu, or toggling a checkbox.

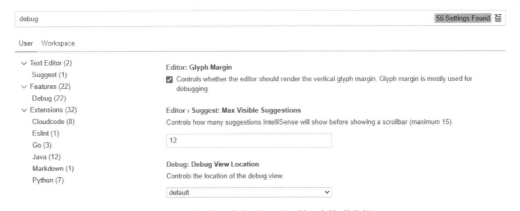

Figure 2.13: Search Settings in Cloud Shell Editor

Debugging with Cloud Shell Editor

Within the Cloud Shell Editor, there is a debugging utility that supports applications written in Go, Node.js, Python, Java, and Ruby. When you use the Cloud Shell Editor for reviewing your code, it allows you to quickly debug your application. The Cloud

Shell Editor's debugging support lets you concentrate on your code as you do not have to concern yourself with any manual setup; it's all handled for you. Within the editor, you can create launch configurations, set breakpoints, and inspect variables.

Debugging actions

To access the Cloud Shell Editor's debugging support, navigate to the Debug view with the **Debug** icon in the **Activity** bar ⬡. When you click on the debug icon, it opens the **Debug View**. You can now select a context and start a debugging session with the **Start** icon.

Once your debugging session starts, you can manage it with the Debugging control action icons: **Pause**, **Step over**, **Step in**, **Step out**, **Restart**, and **Stop**.

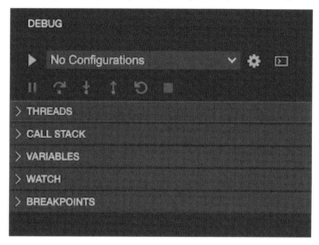

Figure 2.14: Debugging Support

Setting breakpoints

You can set or toggle breakpoints within your code, and all you need to do is click inside the editor margin to set a breakpoint next to the line you'd like to break. A red circle will be placed at the breakpoint at the designations of active breakpoints, while inactive breakpoints are marked with grey ones. If a breakpoint cannot be registered with the debugger when a session starts, it changes to a grey-outlined hollow circle.

You will use breakpoints when you want to inspect the status of your code at that point, For example, when you are running a debugging session, the app will stop running at the breakpoint so that you can inspect the Variables panel in the Debug View. This allows you to inspect the variable values as the app is paused.

Additional Kubernetes debugging support

With the Cloud Shell Editor, there is additional support for you to debug Kubernetes applications on a local cluster (like minikube or Docker Desktop), on a remote cluster on Google Kubernetes Engine, or on any other Cloud provider. You can also attach a debugger to a Kubernetes pod.

Configuration files in your Cloud Shell home directory

By default, Cloud Shell provides you with 5GB of free persistent disk storage mounted as your **$HOME** directory. This means that anything that you install or save in this directory will persist across sessions. Since your shell configuration file **.bashrc** persists across sessions, it's a great way to customize your Cloud Shell behavior. Similarly, you can install packages into your home directory to set up your environment with all your commonly used software.

The way this works is that the Cloud Shell automatically runs the script located at **$HOME/.customize_environment** on bootup. This script runs once as root at boot time, unlike **.profile** or **.bashrc**, which run every time you log in.

This script runs with root privileges, which means you can use it to install any packages that you want available in each Cloud Shell session. You do this by entering standard Debian package management commands in the script.

For example, if you'd like to have erlang installed on Cloud Shell, your **.customize_ environment** file will look like this:

```
01.
02.   #!/bin/sh
03.   apt-get update
04.   apt-get -y install erlang
05.
06.
```

Figure 2.15: Adding an app to the custom Shell Env

The **.customize_environment** script runs as a background process, and it will touch **/google/devshell/customize_environment_done** on successful execution. Execution logs of your **.customize_environment** script can be found at **/var/log/ customize_environment**.

Package installation runs in parallel with you logging in to the shell, so any installed packages will only become available after the login has been completed.

tmux support

Essentially, tmux is a terminal multiplexor and so, is adept at handling several terminals within one program instance. Cloud Shell uses tmux by default, which allows you to tile windowpanes in a command-line environment. This feature helps you run multiple programs within one terminal. Another advantage is that tmux improves persistence across browser tab sessions. For example, you can switch between devices running a Cloud Console in a tab or connect to your Cloud Shell from a different machine and the session state will not be lost.

Another handy feature is that you can leave terminal sessions running and come back later without interrupting the running process. This means that you can start a terminal on a remote computer, run some long installation process in tmux, then go offline and come back later on a different device to see the results.

By default, Cloud Shell supports the native tmux key bindings. For example, if you press *Ctrl + b* and then **%**, tmux splits the current session window into left and right panes, which can be useful for debugging.

Follow these steps to disable tmux in Cloud Shell:

1. Click on the **Terminal Settings** button (wrench icon).

2. Select **Tmux Settings** and deselect the **Enable Tmux Integration** option.

Container image customization

Container image customization allows you to create a Docker image that functions as a custom Cloud Shell environment with your specified additional packages and custom configurations. Your Docker image must be based on the base Cloud Shell image and hosted in Container Registry.

Unlike environment customization, container image customization doesn't affect your default Cloud Shell experience. You can use and share your custom image with open in Cloud Shell links.

Customizing Cloud Shell container images

If you were wondering how the interactive tutorials work, then here is where most of the magic is revealed. In order to run a tutorial on your GCP console, we need to have you working on a clone of my environment. Otherwise, we would experience dependencies and version issues, and it would fall into the too difficult to be bothered with category; just show them a video. Instead, we can use a cloned Shell image in a container that is activated by the user via the Open in Cloud Shell button. To witness this in action, let's go through a tutorial to create an interactive tutorial.

Interactive tutorial 2.2: Creating a custom Cloud Shell Docker Image

Cloud Shell supports the customization of the default Cloud Shell experience by creating a Docker image that functions as a custom Cloud Shell environment with your specified additional packages and custom configurations. The only caveats are that the custom Docker image must be based on the base Cloud Shell image and hosted in GCP's Container Registry.

Creating the Docker Image

Create your own custom Cloud Shell Docker image by following these instructions:

1. In Cloud Shell terminal, run the following command to create a boilerplate custom image in a repository hosted by Cloud Source Repositories:

   ```
   cloudshell env create-custom-image NEW_REPO_NAME
   ```

2. Open your new Dockerfile by following the instructions printed to your command line:

   ```
   cd $HOME/NEW_REPO_NAME && cloudshell edit Dockerfile
   ```

3. Add any additional packages you want made available in your Cloud Shell experience below the first line. Consider this example:

   ```
   FROM gcr.io/cloudshell-images/cloudshell:latest
   RUN apt-get -y install *name of package*
   ```

The first line in your Dockerfile, **FROM gcr.io/cloudshell-images/cloudshell:latest**, references the base Cloud Shell image and should not be removed.

1. Build your image locally by running this:

   ```
   cloudshell env build-local
   ```

2. Test your image locally, and verify that your installed packages are present by running the following:

   ```
   cloudshell env run
   ```

3. To exit testing, type this:

   ```
   exit
   ```

4. Commit your code changes locally:

   ```
   git commit -a -m "Initial custom environment check-in."
   ```

5. Push your code changes to Cloud Source Repositories:

```
git push origin master
```

6. Finally, push your custom image to Container Registry:

```
cloudshell env push
```

Congratulations! You have just created your own code repository, cloned your shell image, and created a docker container and pushed it into Google Registry. We will build upon this tutorial in the upcoming chapters.

Conclusion

In this chapter, you learned about the fundamentals of developing cloud native apps using SDLC. You were then introduced to the Google Cloud developer tools that you will most commonly use throughout this book, namely, Cloud Code, Cloud Shell, and the Cloud SDK. You also learned, through practical walkthroughs, how to set up and configure the development tools and how to get started using them. In the Interactive Tutorials, you understood how to build our own custom shell Environment in a Docker container and how to use Cloud Code for developing cloud native apps. You also learned how to deploy a simple app to Cloud Run, which is a GCP Serverless platform.

In the next chapter, we will build upon what you learned here by discussing how we go about building our code into viable working cloud native applications in the Google Cloud Platform.

## CHAPTER 3

Preparing Source Code with Cloud Build

In the previous chapter, you learned how to use the GCP's inbuilt tools like Cloud Shell and Cloud Code to leverage the Google Cloud SDK in order to make some simple cloud native code. That said, writing basic code snippets is one thing, but transforming that code into a working app requires many other steps. In this chapter, we will learn how modern SDLC practices drive the way we develop, build, and deploy cloud native apps into production. We will also learn about the DevOps lifecycle and architecture and understand what building an app entails before we get hands-on practice configuring the tools we need, such as building Docker images, source code repositories, and pushing our built Docker images to Artifact (Container) Registry.

Structure

We will cover the following topics in this chapter:

- Cloud native approach to DevOps
- Software Configuration Management (SCM)
- Introduction to Cloud build
- Interactive tutorials:
    - Creating a Cloud repository
    - Creating a Docker image and pushing it to a repository

Objectives

After going through this chapter, you will understand the nature of and architecture associated with cloud native applications. You will also understand the build process and how we create cloud source repositories to store our code, containers, and other artifacts. By the end of the chapter, you will have created your own Docker image and pushed it to the artifact registry using everything you have learned so far.

A Cloud native approach to DevOps

Development and operations have essential roles in the design and deployment of cloud native applications. The development responsibilities include analyzing the requirements and collecting the specifications and requirements before proceeding to the designing, developing, and testing.

The operations functions consist of the administrative processes, services, and support for the software, such as deploying, releasing, monitoring, and operating the application or its software components in the production *'live'* environment.

Today, there is a tendency to combine the development and operations or at least to have them closely collaborating in what is termed the DevOps. Closer collaboration is seen as the solution to fix the gap between development and operation teams and processes, theoretically making delivery faster as the team is more in-sync.

Agile development, as you learned in the previous chapter, is used to accelerate the designing, testing, and deployment cycle. However, an Agile approach requires DevOps or at least tightly coupled development and operations to provide the required process/system integration ensuring that delivery can be contiguous.

The following figure illustrates the various components that are used in the DevOps architecture:

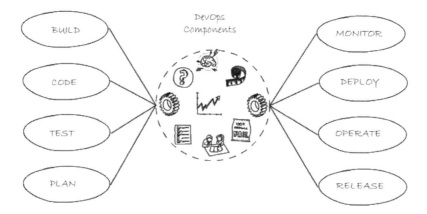

Figure 3.1: DevOps architecture

- **Plan:** DevOps uses the Agile methodology to plan the development project. One of the key benefits of an Agile approach is that it keeps the operations and development teams in sync. It also helps you organize the work and plan accordingly to boost productivity.

- **Build:** With a cloud native approach to DevOps, the usage of cloud platforms and managed services and the sharing and provisioning of resources make the build dependent upon the user's requirements, which, in turn, controls the usage of resources or capacity.

- **Code:** Collaboration requires coordination between the parties, especially if teams are working parallelly. A shared repository for the code, which will be the single source of truth, such as Git, is essential. A repository can be centralized or distributed; either way, it enables the code to be shared, reused, and updated, and changes and versions are tracked. Change and version control are critical to ensure that code can be reverted to the *'last working code'* developed, if necessary. The ubiquitous Git is the most popular code repository, but Google Cloud Platform also hosts its own Cloud Repository and Container Registries.

- **Test:** The application will only be ready for production after undergoing stringent testing. A key objective of DevOps is to continually test via integration and automation. Basically, any changes to the code in the Git or Cloud Repositories will trigger the testing processes. Integrating the development systems with the testing phases enables continuous testing, which reduces the amount of time needed for unit testing and for ratifying errors. Essentially, the time to deploy the code to production is reduced as automating the running of the test scripts accelerates the build-test process.

- **Deploy:** DevOps is all about automating everything, so systems and processes are developed to support the scheduler for automated deployment onto the testing environment. Deployment in the development world follows the build to accelerate the build-test cycle. Once it is deemed ready for production, it will be deployed to the live production servers.

- **Release:** Deployment to the development/testing environment is typically done by automation. However, the final deployment into production is critical at the later production stage, so it is usually done by manually triggering the deployment. At the production stage, the deployment is called a Release.

- **Operate:** Operating the release was purely down to the operations team earlier, but DevOps has changed the traditional approach of developing and operation in separate silos. With DevOps, the new approach is to abandon silos and for the teams to operate in a collaborative way. This means that both the teams actively participate throughout the service or applications lifecycle. Therefore, in today's DevOps environments, the operations team will collaborate with the developers throughout the SDLC, and together they will come up with a suitable monitoring plan for the latest release that serves the IT and business requirements.

- **Monitor:** Continuous monitoring of the release is necessary to identify any potential risk of failure or to surface any unforeseen threats. The monitoring service provided by the cloud management platform provides the team with the capability to capture accurate insights into how the application or service is performing. Monitoring allows the operations team to view or capture analytics on trends and view potential optimization scenarios through the deployment of dashboards. Additionally, monitoring the application helps track the system performance accurately so that the health of the application can be checked against KPIs and any performance issues remedied so that SLOs are maintained.

DevOps lifecycle

Throughout the DevOps lifecycle, there is a clearly defined agile relationship between Operations and Development. This is because DevOps is a process that is practiced by the development team as well as by operational engineers from the very beginning to the final stage of the product. Today, software development is truly cyclical, and there are continuous development and releases throughout a product's lifetime. Indeed, the era of releasing major product upgrades annually is long gone. Today, it's not uncommon for releases to occur on a daily basis. This business-driven requirement means DevOps have had to come up with practices based on Continuous Integration and Continuous Deployment CI/CD.

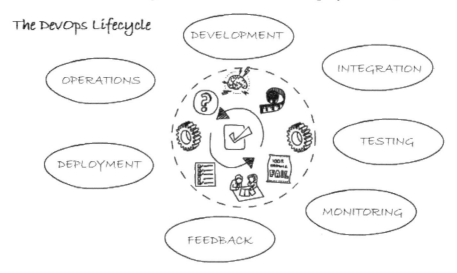

Figure 3.2: *The DevOps lifecycle*

- **Continuous integration**

  This stage is fundamental to the entire DevOps lifecycle. Developers are encouraged to commit their changes to the source code more frequently as every commit is built and tested; this allows for early detection of bugs or errors. When we refer to building code, it doesn't mean simply compiling the code; it also includes unit testing, integration testing, code review, and packaging.

  The premise behind continuous integration is that the fresh code developed is continuously integrated with the existing code stored in the Repository. Therefore, there is continuous development of the software. The updated code needs to be integrated continuously and smoothly with the systems to reflect changes to the end users.

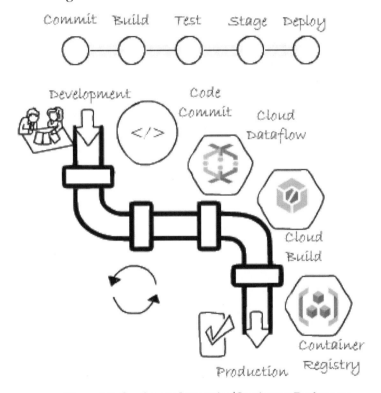

Figure 3.3: Continuous Integration/Continuous Deployment

Jenkins is an example of a continuous integration tool, and it is a popular technology used in this phase. Whenever there is a change in the Git repository, it triggers Jenkins to fetch the updated code and prepare an automated build of that code. The output is an executable file that is forwarded to the test server. In GCP, we can use Cloud Build to perform the same task.

- **Continuous testing**

  The testing phase is where the developed software is continuously tested for bugs. Automating the testing phase saves a lot of time and effort, and it makes it simpler to evaluate the test cases that failed in a test suite. Additionally, we can schedule the execution of the test cases at predefined times. After testing, the code is continuously integrated with the existing code.

- **Continuous feedback**

  A critical step in application development is harnessing feedback in order to drive improvement. By employing feedback mechanisms into the output of a stage in the pipeline, the products are consistently improved by analyzing and moving to rectify any differences between actual and target levels. This form of continual adjustment toward the target ensures that the quality of the product is maintained, and there is no operational drift over time.

- **Continuous deployment**

  In contrast to continuous development, where the tested code is deployed manually into production, in the continuous deployment phase, the modified code is deployed automatically to the production servers. In continuous deployment, the goal is to automatically and rapidly deploy any new or modified code as soon as it is available. Deployment is, therefore, done continuously. Configuration management tools play an essential role in executing the required tasks as frequently and quickly as necessary. Containerization tools also play an essential role in the deployment phase. Docker is almost synonymous with building containers, which helps ensure consistency across development, staging, testing, and production environments. Containerization tools deliver consistency across environments as they package and replicate the same dependencies, libraries, and packages used in the testing, development, and staging environments.

Software Configuration Management (SCM)

Recently, there has been a shift toward deploying a microservice approach to software design. Theoretically, using microservices to decompose monolith applications functionality into individual, independent, and isolated services seems like a good idea. However, when you start having too many microservices, the development gets more complex and the monitoring and logging becomes extremely complicated in terms of logic, size, and difficulty, especially when handling diverse languages and technologies that they may be built upon. For example, you had one or two discrete applications to operate and monitor previously, such as a frontend and a backend, and maybe a middle-tier. However, with microservices, you could feasibly have six or seven discrete components all built on different languages that somehow need to be monitored simultaneously.

If monitoring is problematic, consider the upgrade process where each diverse microservice may need a simultaneous upgrade. In every organization, upgrades to production code happen more often, sometimes even daily. Every new fix/enhancement added to the project makes the software management more complex, but the CI/CD process guarantees that products are subject to constant changes even after release. This is where **Software Configuration Management (SCM)** comes into the picture.

The need for SCM is to bring some measure of control to the software development and management process. SCM's purpose is to enhance productivity, accelerate delivery to market, increase application quality, and boost profits.

The overarching goal of SCM is to improve software development via accountability, auditability, reproducibility, traceability, and coordination. However, SCM is not just a management, tracking tool; it also benefits developers. For example, it makes working as a team, even remotely, feasible. It enables teams to develop in parallel to create complex business processes that deliver auditable software every time. By enforcing the use of code repositories, it provides the team with a 'single source of truth' for our code. Of course, parallel development isn't without risk, but SCM is our basis for version control, which has the ability to go back to the last working stage if necessary.

In the context of cloud native application design, the SCM process encourages developers to adhere to the following best practices:

- Identify and store all their artifacts in the repository.
- Control and audit all changes for all their artifacts.
- Require adherence to Change Requests and audit Change Packages.
- Organize all their versioned artifacts into correctly versioned components.
- Create baseline versions of the code at all the project milestones.
- Record and track change requests in an auditable log.
- Use activities to organize consistent versions of code.
- Ensure thar workspaces are maintained in a stable and consistent manner.
- Support concurrent changes to code in all your artifacts and to all components.
- Integrate the code and test it early and often.
- Perform continuous code build, test, and deployment.
- Ensure that all artifacts are reproducible.

Probably, the most valued element by developers of SCM in software development is version control management. Strict code version control is essential in any development environment, no matter how small the team may be. Version control, also known as revision or source control, is a process that manages a collection of similar program code as individual versions. It provides you with many capabilities: several developers can work concurrently or in parallel on the same code repository. Apart from this, it enables you to do the following:

- Maintain multiple concurrent versions of code.

- Roll back changes to any previous version.

- Track the details of the changes, such as who, which, when, where, and what the changes were.

- Synchronize the code across several repositories.

- Copy/Merge/Undo any code changes.

- Compare code versions.

- Review the history of all the changes in a repository.

- Share, collaborate, and work in parallel on the code across teams around the globe.

In summary, a Version Control System stores all your project code in a repository, which allows you to manage and track all your source code, along with the history of all the changes. Consequently, a version control system ensures that all the previous versions of all your code are stored and can be retrieved and changes reverted later on if required. From an audit perspective, it enables all changes to the code to be traced over time. A version control system is also beneficial for comparing files at specific releases or milestones and highlighting the differences in the code. This is often a quick step in troubleshooting as configuration changes are often the root cause of failures.

Types of Version Control Systems

Under the umbrella of Software Configuration Management, there are two broad types of Version Control Systems, namely, Centralized Version Control and Distributed Version Control. We will briefly compare the merits of the two systems before moving on to discussing their very important mutual purpose: version control.

A centralized version control system is designed to work on a client-server model. This means that there is one central sole repository, which is the hub located at one place, and it provides access to the code repository for many directly connected clients. A centralized system has the advantage of being a single source of truth, but it can also be a single source of failure.

On the other hand, in a Distributed Versioning System, every user holds a local copy of the repository cloned on their local system in addition to having access to the central repo on the server side. This is advantageous because it allows for offline working on the local repository and syncing changes and any modifications from other users later. Distributed versioning requires strict controls to ensure that the integrity of the repository is never compromised, so it is a bit more awkward to get to grips with at first.

Git is, by far, the most popular code repository, and it is a distributed version control system. Git works by locally storing a clone of the master repository, and developers push changes to the master by commits. Git is popular as it provides you with the ability to work as a globally distributed team with full collaboration, saving time and effort while accelerating development.

Version Control Systems – Best Practices

You need to follow some basic guidelines to get the most out of a version control system like Git:

- Store all the project artifacts, such as code, documents, configuration files, etc., in the repository in the version control system.

- When working on an artifact, ensure that you sync your updates regularly in order to incorporate your own and others' changes into your local working copy and to get the latest working version.

- After modifying code, you need to test it in your local area before committing it to the main repository to ensure that it's working as planned.

- Commit any self-contained changes that you have made frequently, but don't commit partial incomplete code work that is untested and may break any functionality.

- When committing a change, ensure that you include a descriptive commit message so that others team can understand the reason for this change and how it differs from the previous version.

- Always remember that the tools are line-based, and ensure that you don't change the file format while updating your code.

- When working as a team, always use a common project structure and naming convention to avoid confusion.

- Set up change notifications and alerts to be distributed by email whenever any commit is made.

- Perform regular backups of your repository.

Cloud Source Repositories

In the **Google Cloud Platform (GCP)**, the Cloud Source Repositories are fully-managed private Git repositories. These repositories are tightly integrated with other GCP tools, making it easy for developers to source code and automatically build, test, deploy, debug, and post the modified code back to the repository. You can also extend Cloud Source Repositories to other GCP tools to perform additional tasks as a part of your development workflow. Some of the GCP tools that are integrated and available for use with Cloud Source Repositories and simplify your development workflows are discussed in the following sections.

Simplified Continuous Integration (CI) with Container Builder

If you are looking to implement continuous integration and validate each check-in to a shared repository with an automated build and test, then Cloud Source Repositories may be the answer. Cloud Source Repositories are tightly integrated with Container Builder, which will come in handy here as it will simplify setting up a CI on a branch or tag. Indeed, there are no CI servers to set up or repositories to configure here. In fact, you can enable a CI process on any existing or new repo present in Cloud Source Repositories. Simply specify the trigger on which Container Builder should build the image.

Pre-Installed tools and languages in Cloud Shell and Cloud Shell Editor

Cloud Source Repositories is integrated out-of-the-box with Cloud Shell and the Cloud Shell Editor. Cloud Shell provides browser-based command-line access, giving you an easy way to build and deploy applications. It is already configured with common tools like MySql client, Kubernetes, and Docker as well as Java, Go, Python, Node.js, PHP, and Ruby, so you don't have to spend time looking for the latest dependencies or installing software. Cloud Editor, meanwhile, acts as a cross-platform IDE to edit code with no setup.

Cloud Source Repositories and App Engine

The integration of Cloud Source Repositories and App Engine makes publishing applications a breeze. It provides a way to deploy apps quickly and lets developers focus just on writing code, without the worry of managing the underlying infrastructure or even scaling the app as its needs grow. You can deploy source code stored in Cloud Source Repositories to App Engine with the gcloud app deploy command, which automatically builds an image and deploys it to the App Engine flexible environment.

The Software Build process

In software development, the term build can be somewhat confusing as it is also used to refer to compiling code in languages such as Java. However, in the context of continuous integration and continuous deployment, we are referring to the process by which code is pulled from a source repository before being built (transformed), along with its dependencies, libraries, and configuration files, into an executable program.

What is a Build?

Basically, Build is the entire process of creating the application program for a software release by taking all the relevant source code files from the repository, compiling them, and then creating a build artefact, such as binaries or an executable program.

Software Build is an essential process in software development, especially in cloud native applications. If we consider how we develop an application, first we write the code, then we test, and if we're happy, we commit the code to the repository and build it through build tools.

The term build is often misunderstood as it is confused with the term build in compiled languages such as Java, where we build or compile the code before we run it.

In the software build process, we are doing several processes in steps, such as:

- Pulling the code from the source code repository.
- Compiling the code along with its dependencies and modules.
- Checking and running the automated unit tests on the build.
- Collecting and linking the libraries, code, config files, etc. accordingly.
- Building the artefacts and storing them securely in the artifact register.
- Viewing and archiving the recent build logs.
- Distributing successful build notification emails to stakeholders.

Types of Software Build

There are two basic types of builds:

- **Full Build:** A full build is where you perform a build from the ground up. When a full build is initiated, the process always starts from an empty work area. The build process will take a full project as the input, work out and source the required dependencies, and then set about compiling all the source files in your project. It then builds all the components in steps before assembling them and pushes the product into the build artifact.

- **Incremental Build:** An incremental build uses the product known as a *last build state*, which is the result of a previous build that has been maintained internally by the build server/tool. When undertaking an incremental build action, the system performs the build process based upon the last build state and on any changes in the project since then.

  Consequently, with an incremental build, the process checks and compares every source file against the last build state. The target will be rebuilt if any dependency has been modified after the last build, otherwise the file from the previous build will be reused.

  Since incremental builds only rebuild any incremental changes, they are usually much faster than full builds and use fewer resources.

Automating the Build

So far, we have only considered manually running the build process. However, there are ways to automate it as we can initiate a build using Build Triggers. Build triggers are simply event triggers that initiate the build process. There are several approaches/methods for triggering the build:

- **Manual build trigger:** This is probably the most used software build trigger. A manual trigger is initiated when you are happy with the code/change, so you go to the build server console and manually trigger the build.

- **Scheduled build trigger:** A scheduled build trigger is automated and, as the name suggests, is pre-configured to run the build at a specific time of the day or when a specific event occurs.

- **Source code repository build trigger:** This type of build trigger is essential in CI/CD environments as it initiates the build process based upon a change in committed code. This trigger fires when it detects any source code change in the repository. For example, when a developer commits a change in the version control system, this trigger gets initiated and fires the build process. However, it can be configured to be more granular and only trigger when a particular file gets changed or any specific set of file(s) get changed/checked-in.

- **Post-Process build trigger:** The post-processing build triggers listen for post-processing events. When a post-processing event is detected, it initiates the trigger, which, in turn, initiates other events or an upstream or downstream build.

Interactive Tutorial 3.1: Creating a Cloud Repository

To run this task directly in Cloud Console, click to Activate the Cloud Shell.

Type in the Command Line:

```
cd Chapter 03

teachme tutorial-3.1
```

1. In the Google Cloud Console, on the project selector page, select or create a Google Cloud project.

2. Ensure that billing is enabled for your Cloud project.

3. Enable the Cloud Source Repositories API.

4. Enable the App Engine Admin API.

Step 1: Create a Cloud Source Repository

1. In a Cloud Shell terminal window, use the **gcloud source repos create** command to create a Google Cloud repository named **hello-world - Type** in:

    ```
    gcloud source repos create hello-world
    ```

Step 2: Clone a repository

Use the gcloud source repos clone command to clone the contents of the Google Cloud repository into a local Git repository:

```
gcloud source repos clone hello-world
```

*   Create a "**Hello, World!**" script.

    In order to create a Python script that prints Hello, World! in a browser window follow the next steps

    1. Go to your Cloud Shell terminal and navigate to the same directory as your new hello-world repository.

2. Using a text editor to create a file named **main.py**, and then enter the following code:

```
01.
02.  #!/usr/bin/env python
03.
04.
05.  import webapp2
06.
07.  class MainHandler(webapp2.RequestHandler):
08.      def get(self):
09.          self.response.write('Hello, World!')
10.
11.  app = webapp2.WSGIApplication([
12.      ('/', MainHandler)
13.  ], debug=True)
14.
15.
```

Figure 3.4: "Hello, World!" main.py script

Step 3: Create an app.yaml file

Create an **app.yaml** file that contains the configuration information you need to deploy your code to App Engine. Using a text editor, create a file named **app.yaml**, and then enter the following configuration information:

```
01.  runtime: python27
02.  api_version: 1
03.  threadsafe: yes
04.
05.  handlers:
06.  - url: .*
07.    script: main.app
08.
09.  libraries:
10.  - name: webapp2
11.    version: "2.5.2"
12.
```

Figure 3.5: app.yaml

Step 4: Push to Cloud Source Repositories

Push the files you just created into Cloud Source Repositories:

1. In a terminal window, go to your **hello-world** directory, as shown here:

    ```
    cd hello-world
    ```

2. Add the files, as follows:

   ```
   git add .
   ```

3. Commit the files to the repository with a comment describing the history of this action, as shown here:

   ```
   git commit -m "Add Hello World app to Cloud Source Repositories"
   ```

4. Use the git push command to add the contents of the local Git repository to Cloud Source Repositories, as shown here:

   ```
   git push origin master
   ```

       i.   Git pushes the files from the master branch to the origin remote; output similar to the following is displayed:

   ```
   Counting objects: 21, done.

   Delta compression using up to 6 threads.

   Compressing objects: 100% (20/20), done.

   Writing objects: 100% (21/21), 9.76 KiB | 0 bytes/s,
   done.

   Total 21 (delta 5), reused 0 (delta 0)

   remote: Storing objects: 100% (21/21), done.

   remote: Processing commits: 100% (6/6), done.

   To https://source.developers.google.com/p/example-
   project-1244/r/repo-name

   * [new branch]      master -> master
   ```

Step 5: View files in the repository

1. In the Google Cloud Console, open **Cloud Source Repositories**.

2. Click on the name of the **hello-world** repository that you created.

3. Go to the files that you pushed to the repository.

   The GCP Console shows the files in the master branch at the most recent commit.

4. In the **Files** list, click on a file to view its contents:

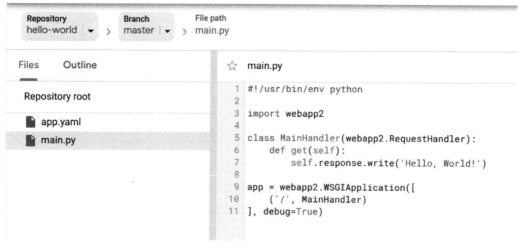

Figure 3.6: *Cloud Source Repositories*

1. Deploy your app. In a terminal window, go to the directory containing the **cd hello-world** repository.

2. Deploy the sample app, as shown here:

```
gcloud app deploy app.yaml
```

3. Verify that your app is running:

```
gcloud app browse
```

4. The browser displays the message **Hello, World!**.

Step 6: Update your app

1. In a terminal window, use a text editor to update the main.py file by entering the following code:

```
01.   #!/usr/bin/env python
02.   import webapp2
03.
04.   class MainHandler(webapp2.RequestHandler):
05.       def get(self):
06.           self.response.write('Goodbye, Moon!')
07.
08.   app = webapp2.WSGIApplication([
09.       ('/', MainHandler)
10.   ], debug=True)
11.
```

Figure 3.7: *Modified main.py*

2. Add the file to Git so that it can commit it:

   `git add main.py`

3. Commit the file along with a comment describing the reason for this action:

   `git commit -m "Update main.py to say Goodbye Moon"`

4. Push the modified file to the Cloud Source Repositories:

   `git push origin master`

Now, try to run it in your browser. What message does it display? You should still see Hello, World because despite our edit and commit, we have not triggered a build and deploy. Continue with the next steps to do that.

Step 7: Redeploy your app

1. Enter the following command in a terminal window:

   `gcloud app deploy app.yaml`

2. Open your app:

   `gcloud app browse`

3. The browser will now display the modified message **Goodbye, Moon!**.

Clean up

Follow these steps to avoid incurring charges to your Google Cloud account for the resources used in this page.

Disabling your app stops all serving requests, but your data and state are retained. You're still billed for applicable charges, such as Compute Engine instances. Shut down your project to release all the resources used within a Google Cloud project.

Disable your app

1. In the Google Cloud Console, go to the **App Engine Settings** page.

2. Click on **Disable application** and follow the instructions.

3. Disabling your app takes effect immediately.

4. Confirm that your app is disabled by visiting the URL of your app; for example, **http://[YOUR_PROJECT_ID].appspot.com/, where [YOUR_PROJECT_ID]** is the name of your Google Cloud project ID. If your app is disabled, an **HTTP 404 Not Found** status code is returned.

Delete the repository

1. In the GCP Console, open the All-repositories page for Cloud Source Repositories.

2. Hold the pointer over the repository you want to delete, and click on **Settings**.

   The **General settings page** opens.

3. Click on **Delete**.

   The **Remove repository** dialog opens.

4. Type the name of the repository you want to delete.

5. Click on **Delete**.

Cloud Build

Cloud Build is a GCP service that allows you to execute and automate your builds on Google Cloud Platform's infrastructure for a CI/CD pipeline. Cloud Build can import source code from a variety of repositories or cloud storage spaces, execute a build to your specifications, and produce artifacts like Docker containers or Java archives, making it ideal for building DevOps pipelines.

Build configuration and the build steps

When you use Cloud Build, you write a build config that is used to provide instructions to Cloud Build on what tasks to perform. This enables you to configure builds to do a lot more than a simple build, as Cloud Build will go and fetch dependencies, install software and run unit tests, static analyses, and integration tests. It will also create artifacts with build tools such as docker, Gradle, maven, bazel, and gulp.

Cloud Build executes your build as a series of build steps, where each build step is run in a Docker container. Executing the build steps is analogous to executing commands in a script.

You can either use the build steps provided by Cloud Build and the Cloud Build community or write your own custom build steps.

When the build step is run with its container, it will be attached to the local Docker network named CloudBuild. As this is a local network, this allows each component within the build steps to communicate with each other and share data.

You can use standard Docker Hub images in Cloud Build, such as Ubuntu and Gradle.

Starting builds

Cloud Build is very flexible, and you can initiate a build either manually, for example, starting a build in Cloud Build using the gcloud command-line tool, or by using the Cloud Build API. You can also use Cloud Build's build triggers feature to create an automated **continuous integration/continuous delivery (CI/CD)** workflow. In this scenario, Cloud Build uses its build triggers to initiate new builds in response to code changes.

You can integrate build triggers with many code repositories, including Cloud Source Repositories, GitHub, and Bitbucket.

Viewing build results

You can view your build results using the gcloud tool, the Cloud Build API, or the Build History page in the Cloud Build section in Cloud Console, which displays the details and logs for every build that Cloud Build executes.

How do builds work?

The following steps describe, in general, the lifecycle of a Cloud Build process:

1. Prepares your application code, config files, and any required dependencies or assets.

2. Creates a build config file in YAML or JSON format, which contains the build steps instructions for Cloud Build to follow.

3. Submits the build process to the Cloud Build service.

4. Cloud Build then executes your build based on the config YAML file that you provided.

5. If applicable, any resultant-built artifacts are pushed to the Artifact Registry.

Overview of Artifact Registry

Artifact Registry is an updated successor to Container Registry, and it enables you to centrally store artifacts and build dependencies as part of an integrated Google Cloud experience.

Introduction

The purpose of the Artifact Registry is to provide a single location for storing and managing all your packages and Docker container images. You can do the following using the Artifact Register:

- Integrate Artifact Registry with Google Cloud CI/CD services or your existing CI/CD tools.

- Store artifacts from Cloud Build.

- Deploy artifacts to Google Cloud runtimes, including Google Kubernetes Engine, Cloud Run, Compute Engine, and App Engine flexible environment.

- Identity and Access Management provides consistent credentials and access control.

- Secure your container software supply chain.

- Manage container metadata and scan for container vulnerabilities with Container Analysis.

- Enforce deployment policies with Binary Authorization.

- Protect repositories in a VPC Service Controls security perimeter.

- Create multiple regional repositories within a single Google Cloud project. Group images by team or development stage and control access at the repository level.

Artifact Registry is used to store containers, packages, and other artifacts resulting from Cloud Build. You can also store any required or trusted dependencies that you use for builds and deployments in the artefact registry.

Artifact registry and container registry

Artifact Registry expands on the capabilities of Container Registry and is the recommended successor to the container registry for Google Cloud.

Cloud Build and Docker

Cloud Build uses Docker to execute builds. For each build step, Cloud Build executes a Docker container as an instance of docker run.

Cloud Build interfaces

You can use Cloud Build with the Google Cloud Console, gcloud command-line tool, or Cloud Build's REST API.

As with other Cloud Platform APIs, you must authorize access using OAuth2 before you can use the API to start new builds, view build status and details, list builds per project, and cancel builds that are currently in process.

Running builds locally

If you want to test your build before submitting it to Cloud Build, you can run your build locally using the cloud-build-local tool.

** The local builder works only on Linux or macOS **

Differences between the local builder and Cloud Build

The local builder is designed to mimic Cloud Build. A build that runs successfully on the local builder should run with the same behavior on Cloud Build.

Here are some of the differences that exist between the two builders:

- The local builder executes on your local machine, while Cloud Build executes on Google Cloud Platform.

- To run the build, the local builder uses your personal account, and the Cloud Build uses the **cloudbuild** service account **[PROJECT_ID]@cloudbuild. gserviceaccount.com**. If you set any permissions on your personal account for the local builder, you may need to replicate these permissions on the **cloudbuild** service account.

- The version of Docker used by the builders could be different. During execution, the local builder prints a warning whenever the Docker version installed is different from the one used in Cloud Build. It's a best practice to use the same Docker version as the one used in Cloud Build.

In the following tutorial, you will learn how to get started with Cloud Build by building a Docker image and pushing the image to Artifact Registry. Artifact Registry provides a single location for managing private packages and Docker container images.

You will first build the image using a Dockerfile, which is the Docker configuration file, and then build the same image using the Cloud Build configuration file.

Interactive Tutorial 3.2

To run this task directly in Cloud Console, click to Activate the Cloud Shell:

Type in the Command Line:

```
cd Chapter 03
teachme tutorial-3.2
```

You will first build the image using a Dockerfile, which is the Docker configuration file, and then build the same image using the Cloud Build configuration file.

> **This quickstart shows you how to build an image with docker, but Cloud Build supports most build tools and programming languages.**

Enable the Cloud Build and the Artifact Registry APIs.

If you've already installed Cloud SDK previously, ensure that you have the latest available version by running the following:

```
gcloud components update
```

Step 1: Prepare your source files

In this tutorial, you will need some sample source code to package into a container image. In this section, you'll create a simple shell script and a Dockerfile. A Dockerfile is a text document that contains instructions for Docker to build an image:

1. Open a terminal window.

2. Create a new directory named **tutorial-docker** and navigate to it:

    ```
    mkdir tutorial-docker
    cd tutorial-docker
    ```

3. Create a file named **tutorial.sh** with the following contents:

    ```
    echo "Hello, world! The time is $(date)." > tutorial.sh
    ```

4. Create a file named Dockerfile with the following contents:

    ```
    FROM alpine
    COPY tutorial.sh /
    CMD ["/tutorial.sh"]
    ```

5. Run the following command to make tutorial.sh executable:

    ```
    chmod +x tutorial.sh
    ```

Step 2: Create a Docker repository in Artifact Registry

1. Create a new Docker repository named **tutorial-docker-repo** in the location **us-central1** with the description "**Docker repository**":

    ```
    gcloud artifacts repositories create tutorial-docker-
    repo --repository-format=docker \  --location=us-central1
    --description="Docker repository"
    ```

2. Verify that your repository was created:

    ```
    gcloud artifacts repositories list
    ```

Step 3: Build using Dockerfile

Cloud Build allows you to build a Docker image using a Dockerfile. You don't require a separate Cloud Build config file.

Follow these steps to build using a Dockerfile:

1. Get your Cloud project ID by running the following command:

   ```
   gcloud config get-value project
   ```

2. Run the following command from the directory containing **quickstart.sh** and Dockerfile, where **project-id** is your Cloud project ID:

   ```
   gcloud builds submit --tag us-central1-docker.pkg.dev/project-id/
   quickstart-docker-repo/quickstart-image:tag1
   ```

If your project ID contains a colon, replace it with a forward slash.

After the build is complete, you will see an output similar to the following:

```
DONE
---------------------------------------------------------------------
-----------------------------------------------------------
ID                                    CREATE_TIME
DURATION   SOURCE     IMAGES      STATUS
545cb89c-f7a4-4652-8f63-579ac974be2e  2020-11-05T18:16:04+00:00
16S        gs://gcb-docs-project_cloudbuild/source/1604600163.528729-
b70741b0f2d0449d8635aa22893258fe.tgz  us-central1-docker.pkg.dev/gcb-
docs-project/quickstart-docker-repo/quickstart-image:tag1  SUCCESS
```

Congratulations!

You've just built a Docker image named tutorial-image using a Dockerfile and pushed the image to Artifact Registry (but you are not done yet).

Step 4: Build using a build config file

In this section, you will use a Cloud Build config file to build the same Docker image as above. The build config file instructs Cloud Build to perform tasks based on your specifications.

In the same directory that contains tutorial.sh and the Dockerfile, create a file named **cloudbuild.yaml** with the following contents. This file is your build config file. At build time, Cloud Build automatically replaces **$PROJECT_ID** with your project ID:

```
steps:
- name: 'gcr.io/cloud-builders/docker'
  args: [ 'build', '-t', 'us-central1-docker.pkg.dev/$PROJECT_ID/
```

```
quickstart-docker-repo/quickstart-image:tag1', '.' ]
images:
- 'us-central1-docker.pkg.dev/$PROJECT_ID/quickstart-docker-repo/
quickstart-image:tag1'
```

Start the build by running the following command:

```
gcloud builds submit --config cloudbuild.yaml
```

When the build is complete, you will see an output similar to the following:

```
DONE
--------------------------------------------------------------------------
------------------------------------------------------------
ID                               CREATE_TIME
DURATION   SOURCE           IMAGES         STATUS
046ddd31-3670-4771-9336-8919e7098b11  2020-11-05T18:24:02+00:00  15S
gs://gcb-docs-project_cloudbuild/source/1604600641.576884-8153be22c94d
438aa86c78abf11403eb.tgz  us-central1-docker.pkg.dev/gcb-docs-project/
quickstart-docker-repo/quickstart-image:tag1  SUCCESS
```

Congratulations! You've just built a tutorial-image using the build config file and pushed the image to Artifact Registry.

Step 5: View build details

1. Open the Cloud Build page in the Google Cloud Console.

2. Select your project and click on **Open**. You will see the Build history page, as shown here:

Figure 3.8: Build history

3. Click on a particular build. You will see the **Build details** page.

4. To view the artifacts of your build, click on **Build Artifacts** under **Build Summary**. You will see output similar to the following:

Figure 3.9: Build artifacts

You can download your build log and view your image details in the Artifact Registry from here.

Clean up

Follow these steps to avoid incurring charges to your Google Cloud account for the resources used:

1. Open the Artifact Registry page in the Google Cloud Console.

2. Select your project and click on **Open**.

3. Select **tutorial-docker-repo**.

4. Click on **Delete**.

You have now deleted the repository that you created as part of this quickstart.

Conclusion

In this chapter, we learned about the DevOps lifecycle, its architecture, how it drives through its overarching principles of CI/CD, and how modern software is deployed into production. You learned about the fundamental processes that underpin DevOps such as Git, code versioning, source code repositories, and you also learned about building docker and configuration files as well as Container and Artifact Repositories.

In the interactive tutorials, you got the experience of building a source code repository and then creating a docker image of an application before you completed the build process by deploying the container to both the Artifact Registry and to Cloud Run.

In the next chapter, we will move from handling code snippets and functions to handling real applications using a microservices architecture. This is when you will start to use everything you have learned so far to truly develop cloud native apps.

CHAPTER 4

Create and Deploy Microservices

In the previous chapter, you learned about developing code in the Google Cloud Platform and building and deploying your apps to run in Google App Engine or Cloud Run. These are the skills that we will build upon as we move up to developing real-world applications that are functional and do more than just output a text string. However, to do that, we have to learn something important about software and modern application architectures. Therefore, in this chapter, we will be learning about code segmentation, services, and an architecture that is commonly used for building modern applications: the microservices architecture.

Microservices architecture came to the fore only around 2011, but it has since been on the verge of going mainstream. A recent survey from Nginx showed that 36 percent of enterprises surveyed are currently using microservices, with another 26 percent in the research phase. However, microservices architecture is still often misunderstood. Is microservices architecture right for your organization's culture, skills, and needs? Well, let's see.

In this chapter, we will take a deep dive into microservice, the microservices architecture, and some reasons why you should consider microservices for your next application development project, Additionally, we'll take a look at some obstacles you'll have to navigate to be successful.

Structure

We will cover the following topics in this chapter:

- Microservices architecture

- Interactive tutorial 4.1: Demonstrating the Monolith and microservice architectures

- Deploying microservices in Cloud Functions

- Walkthrough: Deploying microservices using Cloud Functions

- Deploying Microservices in App Engine

- Interactive tutorial 4.2: Build and deploy microservices in App Engine

Objectives

After going through this chapter, you will be able to describe microservice architecture, its benefits and best use cases, and some caveats where it is best avoided. You will also be able to deploy your microservices into functions that can be run in Cloud Functions or as containers that can be deployed to Google App Engine. You will also have picked up the required practical skills to allow you to handle and deploy microservices using GCP's Cloud Function and APP Engine.

The case for microservices architecture

Microservices architecture can be considered a close relative of **Service-Oriented Architecture** (**SOA**). The overarching concept is similar as microservices is an architectural style in which applications are decomposed into loosely coupled services. A microservice architecture focuses on building fine-grained services and lightweight protocols. As a result, microservices deliver code modularity, making applications easier to develop, test, deploy, and more importantly, understand, change, and maintain.

Organizations for most of the 2000s preferred a client-server architecture where clients, typically desktop PCs, accessed web-served applications. These generally three-tier systems, comprising a web server, application server, and a database, dominated the data center at the time. What is interesting about their architecture is that they were built as monolithic applications. These centralized, multi-tier architectures were used to create entire applications using a single codebase; hence, the term monolithic. The architecture worked well, and the client-service model was the dominant architecture for the time.

However, times change, and there was a significant shift towards mobility by the end of the 2000s, driven by advancements in mobile devices and emerging technologies. Mobility shook up the way architects and security practitioners went about designing enterprise architectures. There was now a need for mobile users to remotely have access to back-end data, which must always be available for a wide range of devices. Applications needed to be changed to meet these new working demands, but the monolithic architecture makes that difficult. Having a single codebase now becomes a huge problem as it isn't going to make changes easy. The dilemma is that everything is tied into a single codebase, so you can't scale a specific function or service; you have to scale up the entire application, leading to escalating costs.

Rising costs demand change, but whenever a change is made, the entire application's code has to be rigorously examined and understood as individual functions would need to be updated, without breaking something else. Changing monolithic always opens the possibility of inadvertently introducing complexity or new bugs every time you try to add or refactor code for a new feature.

Microservices seems to be the answer, albeit with a hindsight approach. With microservices, the application code is built using independent services like building-blocks that run as self-contained and isolated processes. These functional building blocks are then arranged so that the output from one service is used as an input to another in an orchestration of independent, communicating services. This makes identifying and isolating specific functions easy and makes adding, scaling, upgrading, or replacing them easier.

Microservices architecture requires a rethink in the way applications are developed, but they are very useful for businesses that do not have a pre-set idea of the array of devices that its applications will need to support or the scale of the traffic and demands on its resources. By being highly scalable and device- and platform-agnostic, microservices enables businesses to develop applications that provide consistent user experiences.

It is for these reasons the *born on the Internet* scale companies like Netflix, PayPal, Amazon, eBay, and Twitter are just a few enterprises currently using microservices architecture. That said, you don't need to be an internet behemoth to benefit from microservices as they are ideal for startups and the like. When combined with the power of the cloud and APIs, they make software development of cloud native applications rapid and agile.

Here are some other benefits of a microservices architecture:

- **Increased resilience:** With microservices, an application is designed to be decentralized and decoupled into self-contained independent services. This means that unlike monolithic architecture, wherein a failure in the code could well affect several services or functions, the extent of the failure is restricted to that specific service with microservices.

- **Improved scalability:** The ease of scalability is the key aspect of microservices. Each service is a separate component, so you can scale up a single function or service without having to scale the entire application. Horizontal scaling allows you to simply deploy and load balance across a farm of microservices on multiple VMs or servers without impacting the performance of other services. By doing so, you can take several systems down for maintenance and your users won't notice it. This type of scaling makes cloud deployment very attractive for increased availability and optimized performance.

- **A best of breed approach:** With microservices, you don't have to get tied up with a single vendor, coding language, framework, or tool. Instead, you have the flexibility to use the right tool for the right task. As they work like a black box where only the format and status of the inputs and output is of interest, each service can use its own language, framework, or functions and still integrate and communicate with the application's other services.

- **Faster time to market:** Microservices design demands loosely coupled services, so you only need to rewrite the particular microservices code to add or modify a feature. Unlike with a monolith, you make changes only to a specific service. Moreover, by developing applications in smaller functional building-blocks that are independently testable and deployable, you will get your application and services to market and to profit quicker.

- **Easier testing and deployment:** Microservices also makes it easy to upgrade, test, and deploy applications. With smaller modules going through continuous delivery and testing, such as a DevOps CI/CD process, your ability to rapidly deliver and deploy consistently error-free applications is vastly improved.

- **Improved ROI with reduced TCO:** Microservices also allow you to optimize resources and reduce costs. By decoupling services, you won't have to operate on large expensive servers. Cloud VMs are sufficient as is on-prem basic x86 machines, just about anything will suffice. The increased efficiency of microservices not only reduces infrastructure costs but also minimizes downtime.

- **Ongoing development:** The microservices approach of incremental development results in code being continuously developed, integrated, tested, and deployed. Additionally, you can reuse code from the existing libraries instead of reinventing the wheel.

- **So, what can go wrong?** After reading the last section, you may well be sold on the microservice architecture, but it doesn't suit every business. You need to understand that some businesses that have embraced microservices have realized significant benefits, but not all businesses have benefitted as microservice is not some magical panacea.

While microservices look promising, not every business can capitalize on the architecture. Ensure that your business is capable enough to manage it. Here are some organizational caveats you should take note of:

- **A DevOps mindset:** With incremental development and continuous integration and continuous delivery CI/CD, microservices demands a DevOps way of thinking.

  To work in cross-functional teams, your business should incorporate DevOps practices and culture. In DevOps, everyone is responsible for service provisioning.

- **Live on the Cloud:** Many organizations deploy a microservices architecture while being on-prem and working in their own data centers and on their own applications and servers.

  However, there are some questions to consider: do you really need continuous integration and development? If you don't, you should consider whether your staff are able to provision resources quickly enough to keep up with the pace required to make the most of microservices. Therefore, the Cloud makes much more sense as infrastructure, services, and functions can be deployed in seconds. Similarly, you should have the desire, need, and the capability to be able to quickly deploy new services or applications if you hope to benefit from on-prem deployment of microservices.

- **Robust monitoring is a must:** A big problem potentially with microservices is that application developers start to build the frontend and backend using a variety of languages and frameworks. As each service relies on its own language, framework, platform, and APIs, you will be juggling multiple skill sets. Supporting a mix of languages and frameworks, let alone cloud platforms, requires orchestrating multiple teams that will be working simultaneously on different entities of your microservices project. This requires robust monitoring of diverse services. To effectively monitor and manage the entire infrastructure, if you don't know when a service fails or a machine goes down, it may be impossible to track down issues when they arise, which is no easy task.

- **Monitoring and testing can be complex:** Scale is a problem with microservices, which is ironic as it is a key characteristic. The problem is that we start out with a few microservices, but they soon propagate everywhere till there are microservices spread all over. If not checked, they become a virulent plague. This is a big problem as monitoring and testing isn't straightforward with microservices. Each service can have its own language, framework, and assorted dependencies, some direct, others transitive. As features are added, new dependencies pop up. Keeping tabs on all this quickly becomes impractical. Plus, as your number of services increases, so does the complexity. The input/output relationships between microservices within the application soon resemble a spider's web. This makes monitoring extremely difficult, so your microservices architecture better be able to handle a reasonable level of faults. Whether it's database errors, network latency, caching issues, or service unavailability, resiliency testing and fault injection are must.

- **You need to design with failure in mind:** Following on from resiliency testing, you also need to be designing for failure. You should be prepared to handle multiple failure issues, such as system downtime, slow service, and unexpected responses. Load balancing is important here, but you must have a coherent plan for when a failure arises, where the troubled service should still run in degraded functionality mode without crashing the entire system.

Interactive tutorial 4.1: Demonstrating the Monolith and Microservice architectures

To run this task directly in Cloud Console, click to Activate the Cloud Shell.

Type in the Command Line:

```
cd Chapter 04

teachme tutorial-4.1
```

In this tutorial, we will simply demonstrate the core difference between a monolith and a microservices architecture. This simple demonstration will show you some tangible behavior by both these architectures. In the tutorial, we will construct two versions of the same application: one architected as a monolith and the other as a set of microservices.

In this simplistic demonstration, we will look at the difference between architectural approach to monolithic and microservices architecture. In the first case, we will build both versions and then run them to see what services are running. In the case of the monolith, we should expect to see only the main application up and running and awaiting connections. However, when we run the microservices application, we should see three decomposed function specific services: namely Products, Orders and Frontend, up and running and awaiting connections.

The code for this tutorial is available here:

Step 1: Set up the environment

git clone `https://github.com/papa107/monolith-to-microservices.git`

`cd monolith-to-microservices`

`./setup.sh`

```
alasdair_gilchrist@cloudshell:~/monolith-to-microservices (ultra-evening-331702)$ ./setup.sh
Checking for required npm version...Completed.
Installing monolith dependencies...Completed.
Installing microservies dependencies...Completed.
Installing React app dependencies...Completed.
Building React app and placing into sub projects...Completed.

Script completed successfully!
alasdair_gilchrist@cloudshell:~/monolith-to-microservices (ultra-evening-331702)$ []
```

Figure 4.1: To set up the environment

Build the Monolith

Use the following commands from the top-level directory to build the monolith version of the application:

`cd monolith`

`npm start`

You should see output similar to the following:

```
> monolith@1.0.0 start
> node ./src/server.js

Monolith listening on port 8080!
```

Figure 4.2: To build monolith

That's it! You now have a perfectly functioning monolith running on your machine!

Type: `^C` to exit

Build the Microservice

Use the following commands from the top-level directory to run the microservices project:

`cd ..`

`cd microservices`

`npm start`

You should see output similar to the following:

```
Products microservice listening on port 8082!
Orders microservice listening on port 8081!
Frontend microservice listening on port 8080!
```

Figure 4.3: To run microservices

Type: ^C to exit

That's it! You now have a perfectly functioning set of microservices running on your machine!

Microservices deployed on Cloud functions

Now that we have a high-level understanding of why we might use a microservices architecture, let's look at ways to implement it in practice on the GCP. One way is to take advantage of the wide range of VMs that are available to us via Compute Engine to deploy our microservices. Compute Engine VMs will enable us to replicate our on-prem architecture if we already have one in what is called a lift and shift method.

Another method we could use is to take advantage of Google's serverless platforms, which are ideally suited for the purpose of running small apps, Microservices, and functions. The obvious choice if we just want to run our microservices as code is to use Cloud Functions.

Cloud Functions is a serverless platform that abstracts the complexities of the underlying hardware from the user. With Cloud Functions, we can deploy code and let Cloud Function manage how the code runs and scales for us.

Cloud Functions run your code based on specific events that allow you to trigger your code from Google Cloud, Firebase, and even from Google Assistant or call it directly from any web, mobile, or backend application via HTTP.

A great feature of deploying in a serverless platform like Cloud Functions is that you only pay for your function's execution time. Cloud Functions are billed and metered to the nearest 100 milliseconds. However, you pay nothing when your function is idle. This means you can deploy your code to Cloud Functions, and it automatically spins up and backs down in response to your specified configurable events.

Technical walkthrough 4.1: Under the Bonnet with Cloud Function Microservices

Let's examine a use case to understand how Cloud Function triggers your code, whether it is a code snippet, function, mobile app, or a microservice.

It is often the case that businesses end up with multiple scattered systems that are not connected and therefore, have siloed data. It would be hugely advantageous to somehow integrate these systems so that data can be used and shared across all these systems, such as the CRM and the Help-Desk systems. However, there seems to be no easy way to achieve this. That is, until now.

By using serverless microservices, we can effectively stitch these disparate systems together to exchange data. Additionally, you can integrate even enterprise software systems if you can code in JavaScript.

By using Google Cloud Functions as our serverless event-driven framework, we will demonstrate how you can easily integrate with a variety of standard tools, APIs, and Google products. So, where shall we start?

Let's consider a basic and fundamental issue: how do we extract data from a source using Cloud Functions running a microservice? In this use case, we want to extract a selection of documents that correspond to particular books published in the Cloud, Cloud Native, or JavaScript categories:

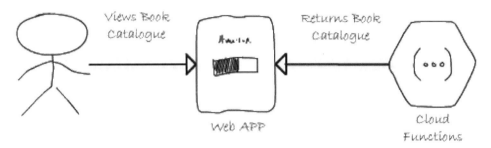

Figure 4.4: *Application use case model*

One way is to write a function to create a URL that extracts and then lists all the relevant documents and lets the user look up a simple web app to find the right one.

The microservice, which we can call **booksetdocs**, should return a JSON array where each element is a set of books belonging to a category. Then, we will need a simple web app that will interact with our microservice.

Let's start up code editor and write some code for the **booksetdocs** microservice using Cloud Functions:

```
01.  exports.booksetdocs = (req, res) => {
02.    handleCors(req, res);
03.    res.status(200).type('text/json').end(JSON.stringify(getBooksetDocs()));
04.  };
05.
```

Figure 4.5: *'booksetdocs' functions code*

This is the first code that runs when the service's URL is accessed. The first line sets up **Cross-Origin Resource Sharing (CORS)**, which we'll explain in further detail later. The second line of the function calls our **getBooksetDocs()** function, which is responsible for returning the response to the service call.

Now, we need to deploy the **getBooksetDocs()** function in the same file as **booksetdocs** above. The draft function uses a simple hard-coded list of documents:

```
function getBooksetDocs() {
  return [
    {'Category': 'Cloud', Title: 'Developing Cloud Native Apps in GCP', url: '...'},
    {'Category': 'Cloud', Title: 'Building Serverless Apps with Azure Functions and Cosmos DB', url: '...'},
    {'Category': 'Cloud', Title: 'Cloud Computing', url: '...'},
    {'Category': 'Python', Title: 'Python Made Simple', url: '...'},
    {'Category': 'Python', Title: 'Python for Beginners', url: '...'},
    {'Category': 'JavaScript', Title: 'Learning Node.js', url: '...'},
    {'Category': 'Go', Title: 'Go Programming', url: '...'},
    {'Category': 'Go', Title: 'Hands-on Go Programming', url: '...'},
    {'Category': 'Python', Title: 'Quick Interview Guide', url: '...'},
  ];
}
```

Figure 4.6: Deploying the getBooksetDocs

A known issue with functions is when you try to work across domains as it is not permitted. A solution to this issue is called CORS in Cloud Functions, which allows applications running on one domain to access content from another domain. This lets us write web pages that run on the company's internal domain but make requests to the **booksetdocs** microservice running on cloudfunctions.net, Cloud Functions' default hosting domain:

```
01.  handleCors = (req, res) => {
02.    res.set("Access-Control-Allow-Origin", "*");
03.    res.set("Access-Control-Allow-Methods", "GET");
04.    res.set("Access-Control-Allow-Headers", "Content-Type");
05.    res.set("Access-Control-Max-Age", "3600");
06.    if (req.method == 'OPTIONS') {
07.      res.status(204).send('');
08.    }
09.  }
```

Figure 4.7: CORS script

We will put all three functions above into a file called **index.js**, and this deploys the **booksetdocs** microservice as a cloud function:

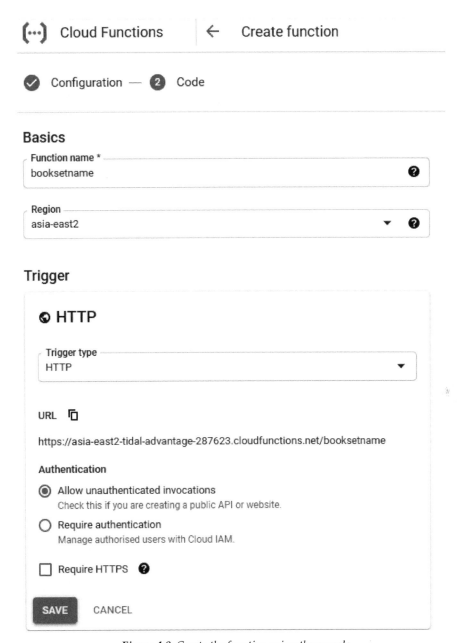

Figure 4.8: Create the function using the console

The steps are as follows:

1. Enter a name for your Function: **booksetname**.

2. Select a **Region** for your Function: **asia-east2** (select a region closest to you).

3. Select **HTTP**.

4. Select **Allow unauthenticated users**.

5. Deselect **Require HTTPS**.

6. **Save** and **Next**.

Step 2.

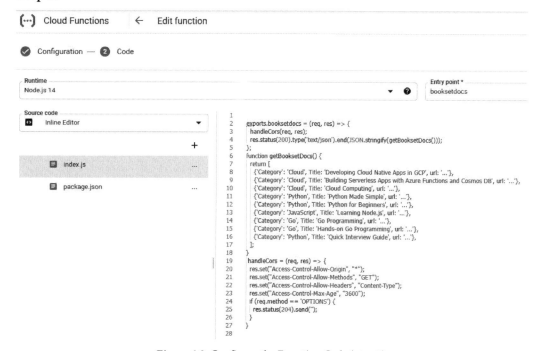

Figure 4.9: Configure the Function Code (step 2)

1. Select a **Runtime** - Pick the latest your code supports (Node js 14).

2. Select an Entry point - **booksetdocs** (Function name).

3. Copy and paste your function code into the in-line editor.

4. Click on **Deploy**.

Figure 4.10: Test the Function

Test the function with the following steps:

1. Click on the **Actions** menu (3-dots).

2. Select **Test function**.

3. On the next page, click on **Test the Function** (big blue button).

4. Check the **Output** and the log entries.

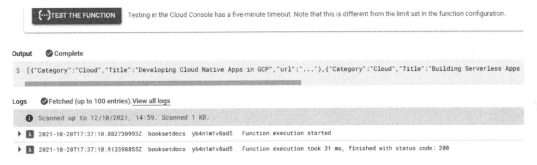

Figure 4.11: Log entries

That's the Function containing our microservices deployed and ready, and we can invoke it by going to the **Functions Details** page, selecting the **Trigger** tab, and clicking on **HTTP trigger**:

Figure 4.12: HTTP trigger

Web app

We have a function and a trigger. Now, we need to rustle up a web app to display our books. We will need some HTML, which consists of two empty lists. The first list will display all the book categories, but when an entry in that list is clicked on, the second list will be populated with all the corresponding books in the selected category.

We will call this file **books.html**:

```
01.  <html>
02.   <head>
03.    <title>
04.      Booksets   </title>
05.    <script type="text/javascript" src="script.js"></script>
06.   </head>
07.   <body>
08.    <h1>Categories</h1>
09.    <ul id="bookset_list">
10.    </ul>
11.    <hr/>
12.    <h1>Books</h1>
13.    <ul id="doc_list">
14.    </ul>
15.   </body>
16.  </html>
```

Figure 4.13: Web app HTML (sample)

How does it work?

To populate each list, the function calls the **booksetdocs** microservice from the app's JavaScript file. When the web page first loads, it runs the JavaScript in **script.js** and duly hits the microservice URL or HTTP trigger to get the list of **Categories** and populates the first list of the page. When a user browses the list and clicks on a category, the books that correspond to that category are displayed in the second list on the page:

```
01.  const URL_BASE = 'https://<REGION>-<PROJECT ID>.cloudfunctions.net/';
02.  const BOOKSET_URL = URL_BASE + 'booksetdocs';
03.  let docs;
04.  fetch(BOOKSET_URL).then(function(response) {
05.    return response.json();
06.  }).then(function(responseJson) {
07.    docs = responseJson;
08.  const booksetNames = [...new Set(docs.map(doc => doc.bookset))];
09.    let ul = document.querySelector('#bookset_list');
10.    booksetNames.forEach(booksetName => {
11.      let li = document.createElement("li");
12.      let a = document.createElement("a");
13.      a.setAttribute('href', '#');
14.      a.onclick = () => { populateDocList(booksetName) };
15.      a.appendChild(document.createTextNode(booksetName));
16.      li.appendChild(a);
17.      ul.appendChild(li);
18.    })
19.  });
20.  function populateDocList(booksetName) {
21.    let ul = document.querySelector('#doc_list');
22.    ul.innerHTML = '';
23.    docs.forEach(doc => {
24.      if (doc.bookset == booksetName) {
25.        let li = document.createElement("li");
26.        let a = document.createElement("a");
27.        a.setAttribute('href', doc.url);
28.        a.appendChild(document.createTextNode(doc.name));
29.        li.appendChild(a);
30.        ul.appendChild(li);
31.      }
32.    })
33.  }
```

Figure 4.14: Script.js

This completes the Walkthrough lesson. We have set up a service using a microservice to demonstrate how we can trigger functions to perform real tasks. The code, albeit primitive, solves a real business need in a fairly simple manner.

Microservices architecture on Google App Engine

So far in this chapter, we have introduced microservices architecture and its benefits and drawbacks. However, now we need to take a deeper dive and look at microservices through the technical lens of Google Cloud Platform.

When we work with microservices on Google App Engine, we consider microservices to refer to an architectural style for developing applications. In a microservices architecture, a large application is decomposed into independent functional blocks, with each having its own area of responsibility. A microservice, when initiated to serve a single user or API request, works by running its own internal function code, but it can also call other microservices in order to get the data it requires to collate and compose its response.

A properly implemented microservices-based application can achieve the following goals:

- Strong contracts between the various microservices

- Independent deployment and rollback

- Concurrent, A/B release testing on subsystems

- Minimal test automation and quality-assurance overhead

- Better clarity of logging and monitoring

- Fine-grained cost accounting

- Better overall application scalability and reliability

From this list, it is clear that a microservices architecture will require a bit more thought and preparation than we initially thought. Fortunately, Google App Engine has several features that are well-suited for a microservices-based application, so let's explore them.

App Engine Services as Microservices

App Engine is a serverless platform that is ideal for running software, applications, and microservices. You can deploy multiple microservices on App Engine as separate services. These services will be independent and their code fully isolated. Indeed, once we have provisioned our microservices, the only way to execute the code in these services is through an HTTP trigger, such as a user request or via a RESTful API call.

Project isolation

When designing GCP projects for microservices, some developers want to guarantee that there is isolation of code between services. A simple way to do this is to deploy services on their own project. While that is probably overkill, it would certainly be effective. The recommended approach is to use a single Google App Engine project with multiple services.

Unless you have a specific need for multiple projects, it's best to start with using multiple services within a single project because performance will be better and the administrative overhead will be minimized. Of course, you can also choose some hybrid of the two approaches if your design requires it.

As you learned earlier, the code is isolated between services, so one service can't directly call code in another service. Isolation of the code also means that the code can be deployed to services independently. Therefore, different services can be written in different languages, such as Python, Java, Go, and PHP. Moreover, autoscaling, load balancing, and machine instance types are all managed independently for each service.

Figure 4.15: Service isolation

Versions within services

When we deploy multiple services within a single GAE project, each service can have multiple versions deployed simultaneously. Only one of the versions can be active and default to serving requests at a given time, though it is possible to directly access any deployed version of a service as each version of each service has its own address. The App Engine framework allows versions to co-exist, which provides many possibilities, such as for A/B testing between different versions, or testing a new version, and also simplified upgrades and rollback operations.

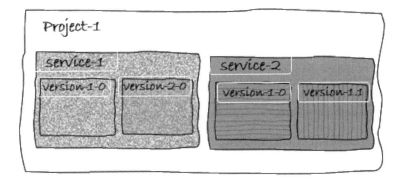

Figure 4.16: Service version isolation

Service isolation

Though the code is considered to be isolated, interestingly, services share some App Engine resources. For example, microservices within the same App Engine project will share resources like Cloud Datastore, Memcache, and Task Queues. While this seems to go against everything we have learned about microservices, there are ways to help mitigate unwanted sharing. Of course, sharing has some advantages in some situations, but it's important for a microservices-based application to maintain code- and data-isolation between microservices:

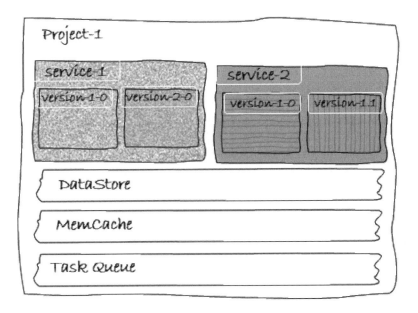

Figure 4.17: Isolated services with shared resources

Interactive tutorial 4.2: Build and deploy Microservices in App Engine

What makes the Google serverless platform **Google App Engine (GAE)** ideal for microservices is that it is very easy and cheap to develop, deploy, test, and run microservices in various language runtimes. In the App Engine, each microservice can run as code as an app or function in the standard edition or in run in its own isolated Docker container. A microservice in a container is again isolated only to a point as it can also use shared resources.

This tutorial will take you through the process required to deploy three microservices, one each in Node, Python, and Go in a single GAE project, and run them on a single GAE instance.

1. Clone the following repository from Git:

   git clone **https://github.com/bpbpublications/Cloud-Native-Apps-on-Google-Cloud-Platform**

   This will create the following directory structure:

   - `Chapter 04\chapt-4-1\app-microservices\`: This is the root directory for all three microservices:

     o `\app-microservices\node`: The root directory for Node microservice.

     o `\app-microservices\python`: The root directory for Python microservice.

     o `\app-microservices\go`: The root directory for Go microservice.

   Open Cloud Shell and enter the following from your $Home directory on the CLI.

2. Build a Node Microservice:

   Here, we are going to build and launch a very simple service written in Node.js and packaged as a microservice on App Engine. In this tutorial, we will use Express to serve any incoming HTTP requests on port 8080.

   i.   Open Cloud Shell and change to the Node.js the working directory:

   ```
   cd /Chapter 04/chapt-4-1/app-microservices/node
   ```

   This is where we have created and stored the files; we will execute all our commands from this directory for the Node.js microservice.

ii.   Open Cloud Editor. Browse to **File** and then **Open Workspace** and
      select the **Chapter 04** directory as the root of our workspace. Click
      Open and your new workspace should open in the left-side column.
      Navigate to the **hello.js** file, view the following code, and click on
      Save.

```
01.
02.   const express = require('express');
03.
04.   const app = express();
05.
06.   app.use('/', (req, res) => {
07.       res.json({ 'Congratulations': '' });
08.   });
09.
10.   const port = process.env.PORT || 8080;
11.   app.listen(port, () => {
12.       console.log(`Node server listening on port ${port}`);
13.   });
14.
```

Figure 4.18: hello.js

> The const port - **process.env.PORT** variable sets the listening
> port for the web server to **8080**.

iii. Open the Terminal and type the following:

      npm init

> Select the default values provided to create the **package.json**
> file.

iv.   Run this:

      npm install --save express

> This command will install Express.

v. Navigate to the start script and view the Node version and the NPM version in the **package.json** file. Your final **package.json** file should look similar to this:

```
01.  {
02.    "name": "node",
03.    "version": "1.0.0",
04.    "description": "",
05.    "main": "hello.js",
06.    "scripts": {
07.      "start": "node hello.js",
08.      "test": "echo \"Error: no test specified\" && exit 1"
09.    },
10.    "author": "",
11.    "license": "ISC",
12.    "dependencies": {
13.      "express": "^4.17.1"
14.    },
15.    "engines": {
16.      "node": ">=17.0.0",
17.      "npm": "8.1.0"
18.    }
19.  }
```

Figure 4.19: package.json

vi. View the **node-app.yaml** file and check the following code. The runtime param lets GAE know that we want to use the Node.js runtime, the **env: param** lets GAE know that we want to use the GAE flexible environment, and the service param lets GAE know the name of the service, default in this case. The service param is optional for the default service, but we have specified it anyway.

```
01.
02.  runtime: nodejs
03.  env: flex
04.  service: default
05.
06.  manual_scaling:
07.    instances: 1
08.  resources:
09.    cpu: 1
10.    memory_gb: 0.5
11.    disk_size_gb: 10
```

Figure 4.20: Node.js runtime

Furthermore, to reduce costs during development, we have specified the use of bare minimum computing resources on Google App Engine. However, these would be unacceptable in production environments, so you would obviously want to increase their values and look into auto scaling for real-world workloads.

vii.   Open the Terminal and enter the gcloud command on the CLI to deploy Node microservice. This should take a few minutes:

```
gcloud app deploy node-app.yaml
```

```
Deployed service [default] to [https://ultra-evening-331702.et.r.appspot.com]

You can stream logs from the command line by running:
  $ gcloud app logs tail -s default

To view your application in the web browser run:
  $ gcloud app browse
```

Figure 4.21: Deploying Node microservice

viii.   When the build is successful, enter the following:

```
gcloud app browse
```

You will be shown a link similar to this. Click on the link: **https://[your-project-id].appspot.com/**; the page will open in your default browser, and you should see the Node.js microservice that is deployed to App Engine -Flex in action.

3.   Build and deploy a Python microservice

In this tutorial, we will configure and deploy a Python microservice that uses Flask and Gunicorn to serve HTTP requests.

i.   Open Terminal and change the directory:

```
cd Chapter 04/chapt-4-1/app-microservices/python
```

We will create, store, and execute all commands for our Python microservice from this directory.

ii.   Next, install Flask and gunicorn:

```
pip install flask
pip install gunicorn
```

Open Shell Editor, view the **hello.py** file, and note the following code:

```
01.
02.    from flask import Flask
03.    from flask import jsonify
04.
05.    app = Flask(__name__)
06.
07.    @app.route('/')
08.    def hello():
09.        dictionary = {'Welcome to Developing Cloud Native Apps on GCP': ''}
10.        return jsonify(dictionary)
11.
12.    if __name__ == '__main__':
13.        app.run(debug=True)
14.
```

Figure 4.22: *hello.py file*

iii. Next, open and view the **python-app.yaml** file taking note of the following code:

```
01.
02.    runtime: python
03.    runtime_config:
04.      python_version: 3
05.    env: flex
06.    service: python
07.    entrypoint: gunicorn -b :$PORT hello:app
08.    .
09.
10.    manual_scaling:
11.      instances: 1
12.    resources:
13.      cpu: 1
14.      memory_gb: 0.5
15.      disk_size_gb: 10
16.
17.
```

Figure 4.23: *app.yaml*

The **python_version** param lets GAE know that we want to use the latest supported Python 3.x release, which is currently 3.7. The **entrypoint** param lets GAE know that we want to have Gunicorn listen on port 8080, as defined by the environment variable **$PORT**, which is set by the GAE runtime.

iv. Now, create a **requirements.txt** file and enter the following code to list the latest versions we wish to install of our two dependencies, that is, Flask and gunicorn:

```
01.   Flask==2.0.2
02.   gunicorn==20.1.0
03.
```

Figure 4.24: requirements.txt

v. Open the Terminal and deploy the Python microservice on the CLI. This should take a few minutes:

```
gcloud app deploy python-app.yaml
```

vi. Run this command:

```
gcloud app browse -s python
```

> **You can safely ignore comments about the default browser. Instead, click on the link you have been given, i.e., https://python-dot-[your-project-id].appspot.com/; the page will open in your default browser, and you should see your Python microservice in action.**

{"Welcome to Developing Cloud Native Apps on GCP":"Congratulations you have launched a microservice on python!"}

Figure 4.25: Command browser output

4. Building and Deploying Microservices on Go

In this tutorial, we will use a Go microservice that uses the built-in **net/http** module to serve HTTP requests.

a. Open the Terminal and change the working directory to **\go**:

```
cd /Chapter 04/chapt-4-1/app-microservices/go
```

You will use this as the working directory and execute all commands for Go microservice from this directory.

b. Open Editor and view the **hello.go** file using the following code:

```
01.
02.
03.  package main
04.
05.  import (
06.    "encoding/json"
07.    "log"
08.    "net/http"
09.  )
10.
11.  func main() {
12.
13.    http.HandleFunc("/", hello)
14.
15.    log.Print("Go server listening on port 8080")
16.    log.Fatal(http.ListenAndServe(":8080", nil))
17.
18.  }
19.
20.  func hello(w http.ResponseWriter, r *http.Request) {
21.
22.    if r.URL.Path != "/" {
23.      http.NotFound(w, r)
24.      return
25.    }
26.
27.    dictionary := make(map[string]string)
28.    dictionary["Welcome to Developing Cloud Native Apps on GCP"] = ""
29.
30.    json, _ := json.Marshal(dictionary)
31.
32.    w.Header().Set("Content-Type", "application/json")
33.    w.Write(json)
34.
35.  }
36.
37.
38.
```

Figure 4.26: *To view the hello.go file*

c. Next, open and view the **go-app.yaml** file; note that the code is similar to the following:

```
01.
02.   runtime: go
03.   env: flex
04.   service: go
05.
06.
07.
08.   manual_scaling:
09.     instances: 1
10.   resources:
11.     cpu: 1
12.     memory_gb: 0.5
13.     disk_size_gb: 10
14.
```

Figure 4.27: go-app.yaml

The runtime is Go, the env: flex, and the service: go.

d. Run the following command to deploy Go microservice. This should take a few minutes:

```
gcloud app deploy go-app.yaml
```

e. Run gcloud app browse **-s go**. You will be redirected to https://go-dot-[your-project-id].appspot.com/ in your default browser and should see Go microservice in action.

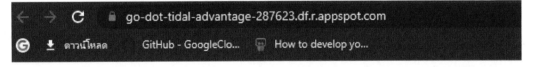

{"Welcome to Developing Cloud Native Apps on GCP":"Success you have just completed the tuorial!!"}

Figure 4.28: Browser output

Congratulations! You completed all the tasks in deploying microservices in the Google App Engine.

Conclusion

In this chapter, we have examined the purpose and value of microservices architecture. Furthermore, we learned how to build a working application using just a few simple code functions as microservices and then building and deploying them as a microservices architecture application. We explored building an application using microservices running in Cloud Function. We also contemplated deploying and working with microservices in Google App Engine. Furthermore, through the interactive tutorials, we gained valuable experience deploying apps in Go, Python, and Nodejs as microservices and deploying them into App Engine as containers.

In the next chapter, we will concentrate more on containers and how we can best utilize this pervasive technology.

CHAPTER 5

Building and Deploying Containers in Cloud Build

In the previous chapter, we discussed how we use microservices architecture in modern software design. Today, microservices architecture is not discussed as much as it was earlier because it has been usurped in the fashion stakes by containers, Docker containers to be precise. Microservices still exist and are still the architectural pattern utilized today when building cloud native applications of all sizes. However, the code is now bundled in self-contained units called containers, so we don't tend to hear so much about them these days. However, they are still as important to cloud native design as they ever were.

In this chapter, we will turn our attention to containerization, which is the modern trend to package software and all its dependencies and libraries into a container. If you are unfamiliar with containers, we will briefly introduce you to the basics, such as what they are; how they are relevant to cloud native development; and how we build, manage, and deploy them on the Google Cloud Platform. We will also review some of our options for building containers such as Cloud Build and Docker and for deploying and running containers. You will also be introduced to Cloud Run, which is a Google serverless offering that is the go-to tool for running containers in GCP.

Structure

We will cover the following topics in this chapter:

- What are Containers?

- Containerization

- Walkthrough 5.1 – Exploring the Artifact Registry Repositories

- Interactive tutorial 5.1 – Build and deploy a Container in Cloud Run

- Working with Cloud APIs

- Interactive tutorial 5.2 – Running a Google Translate API on Cloud Run

Objectives

After completing this chapter, you will have learned all about containers and the recent trend of containerization. You will have learned, through a practical lesson, how to create and deploy a container to Cloud Run. You will also have understood how to explore and push containers to the Artifact Registry in GCP. A practical tutorial will also teach you to build your own application using a Google API, host your translation app to artifact registry, and deploy it to Cloud Run.

What are Containers?

A simple explanation of a container is that it is a software bundle that we package up as code, along with all its dependencies. By doing so, the application can run quickly and reliably on any computer. This defeats the age-old problem - *well it works on my laptop.*

Containers are designed to be extremely portable as the container image is a very lightweight, self-contained, and executable software bundle. These images include everything needed to run an application, such as the code, a specific runtime, any required system tools, and the necessary system libraries and settings. When we create a container, we ensure that we will have the same user experience regardless of the system it is run on. This is because containers will run the same across any computer, platform, cloud, or device.

The container images transform into a container at runtime when it is initiated to run on a Container Engine. Docker is the most popular tool for building containers; it is a name practically synonymous with containerization. Docker developed containers to be portable and used anywhere, and they have become the industry standard now.

In business, organizations favor a container approach as they solve many of the previous software inconsistencies across the development, testing, and staging environments. As a solution, containers ensure that code works uniformly despite differences in the environment. Additionally, containers provide a standard way to have an OS and infrastructure-independent architecture that offers ease of code distribution and service availability.

Perhaps, the most compelling reason why businesses like containers is portability. This is because they only need to create one generic product and not a range of platform-specific versions of the same product. VMs were once considered the answer to the question of portability, but containers are more lightweight than VM as they share the machine's OS system kernel. As a container does not require an OS per application, it results in better server efficiency, reduces server count, and, in some cases, perhaps lowers or eliminates licensing costs. In addition, containers are secure as containerized applications are isolated from their environment.

There are two broad categories of Containers:

- **System Containers:** These are the oldest container type and are very similar to virtual machines. System containers are stateful and OS dependent, and they are used to run multiple processes. Typically, they will have supporting tools embedded, which enables you to use them with traditional or monolithic applications. There are different implementations of system containers, like LXC/LXD, Linux vServer, etc.

- **Application Containers:** These are a relatively new container type that are typically deployed to host and run only a single process. This type of streamlined container is typically best suited to hosting stateless microservice-centric services that scale horizontally. Application containers are best suitable for hosting a microservices architecture, even on ephemeral infrastructures, as their agility aligns them well with cloud native architectures. Application Containers are utilized heavily by modern business where computing requires portability, agility, and scalability, as containerization and cloud-native systems are the best way to achieve these goals. Cloud developers are combining containers, microservices, and Agile development techniques because they are a convenient way to create agile, fast, and powerful cloud native applications.

Container architecture

A fundamental dilemma in cloud computing was: How do we create an application-neutral method for portability among cloud platforms?

The concept of virtualization of software has been around for many decades as an approach to componentize whole computer systems. It allowed one to abstract applications from reliance on the physical platform, allowing one to move them around from platform to platform (or cloud to cloud). The most common approach on-prem and in the cloud was to run individual components as services running on their native OS in VMs on a host server.

Docker, the most famous of them all, takes a different approach and does away with the VM as the middleman. Docker builds a container using the Linux kernel, which provides the resource isolation (CPU, memory, I/O, network, etc.) for the containerized application, but it doesn't require starting any virtual machines. Instead, Docker uses what is known as **Linux Containers (LXC)** with an API. This combo provides a lightweight solution that runs the application processes in isolation. Docker also provides other Linux style tools, such as namespaces, which can be used to further hide an application's view of the operating environment. Namespaces can also hide process trees, network, user IDs, and file systems, making them an ideal way to segregate a shared workspace.

Docker technology is a breakthrough because although the same workloads could just as well be run in virtual machines, containers are a much more efficient approach. Additionally, containers are readily transportable between clouds. In many cases, containers provide a viable alternative to virtualization, particularly when moving workloads within and between cloud environments without having to modify the application.

Containers have a few basic features and advantages, including the ability to:

- **Reduce interaction with the host through container abstractions:** Applications have their own dependencies.

- **Leverage automation:** Build Process automation replaces manual scripting to ensure quality.

- **Provide better security and governance:** These issues fall out with the container, significantly reducing any complexity.

- **Provide flexible designs for distributed computing:** An application can be divided and executed as individual containers across different cloud platforms.

To make the most of distribution and portability, containers need to be available for teams to use. This requires version-control and a software-control system similar to Git to ensure that everyone is using the most up-to-date version or at least the correct version.

DockerHub

Docker has established and compiled a public registry for storing applications available as Docker images: DockerHub. This can be understood as similar to

GitHub but for containers. DockerHub is also a community, which provides a vast repository of public facing Docker container images and also a support community. The repository provides many jumping off points for downloading, building, and running your own container-based applications.

Running a Docker Container

If you have Docker installed on your local system, you can run a Docker application image by entering the following:

```
sudo docker run --rm -p 3000:3000 docker_image_name
```

Note that the **docker run** command we used is for running an image called **docker_image_name**. If Docker can't find the image on your local file system, it will check the public registry DockerHub and invoke it there if found. The **-rm switch** allows us to launch multiple isolated instances of the app as containers on a single host.

The Docker container is simply an instance of a Docker image, much like applications are instances of executables that exist in memory. This allows us to launch multiple instances that helps us scale. Furthermore, when the Docker container closes, the image remains cached but is removed from working memory, thereby revoking any changes to the local environment that the application may have made during its runtime. However, because the image remains in cache, it can be quickly restarted if required.

Roll your own Container

Building a Docker image for an application requires starting with a base Docker image for the core OS you want the application to run on. Next, you must collect, install, and configure all the dependencies, such as libraries and any necessary tools. Once you have everything, you can use the Docker **commit** command to save the container as an image. Finally, if you wish to share the image, you can push it to the public Docker image registry.

To automate this process and ensure that we have consistent build quality and reliability, we can script the build steps in a Dockerfile. This is simply a script of steps that automates the process of installing and configuring the application, creating a reliable process that can be repeated.

Docker created the industry standard for containers and is synonymous with the technology, but on the GCP, we can use Docker or Cloud Build to build and deploy our own containerized applications.

Containerization – Suitable GCP Engines

Container images include a runtime, but they still need to be run on a compatible container engine. Support for Docker images is ubiquitous, but GCP can also run Linux and Podman, among others. The solutions for running containers in GCP vary essentially with regard to how much of the underlying infrastructure will be revealed by the platform.

The first way to run a container on GCP is to use Google Kubernetes Engine, or GKE. Google invented Kubernetes, so it is no surprise that even though they released it to the open-source community, they offer a fully managed Kubernetes service called **Google Kubernetes Engine** (**GKE**). The GKE platform in GCP takes care of provisioning, scheduling, and scaling your containers while also monitoring their health and state. Getting your code to production on GKE can be as simple as creating a container deployment with the cluster being provisioned on the fly. However, for many situations, a full-fledged container orchestrator like Kubernetes is potentially not only intimidating but also overkill. This leads us to the second way you can deploy your containers on Google Cloud: with Google App Engine.

When we deploy to App Engine (GAE), we simply deploy and run our containers on the Google App Engine - Flexible Edition as it supports containers. Building and deploying containers onto App Engine is something we have done in the earlier tutorials, so you already know that App Engine is an easy and affordable way to run applications in containers. In App Engine, building an image of your application requires a dockerfile and an **app.yaml** configuration file. Then, you can deploy using either Docker or Cloud Build to App Engine - flexible edition. However, there is a third way, and that is with Cloud Run.

Cloud Run is the latest serverless offering available on the GCP. In essence, Cloud Run is an abstraction that runs on top of a Kubernetes cluster, giving you the benefits of working with both containers and cloud native architectures. With Cloud Run, you no longer need to write those troublesome YAML build files as creating a container only requires you to select a location, give it a name, and set any authentication credentials you may require. You do not need to set up or provision your own Kubernetes; there is no cluster or infrastructure to provision or manage as that is done in the background. Monitoring and management of the underlying Kubernetes cluster is also hidden from the user as Cloud Run automatically monitors and scales any of your stateless containers. A notable characteristic of Cloud Run is its ability to scale both up and down to match traffic and load, but it can do this with the ability to scale to zero or scale to infinity. What this means in practice is if your application is not is use, Cloud Run will scale to zero, i.e., it will effectively shut down and hibernate, awaiting new traffic. This can be extremely cost effective in certain use cases.

Furthermore, Cloud Run is very flexible in its usage:

- It natively supports multiple requests per container

- It works with any language, runtime, library, and binary

- It can use any base Docker image

- It is a fully managed service with pay-for-usage

- It comes with built-in Cloud Monitor, Cloud logging, error reporting, and automated fault handling

The fourth option for deploying your containers is straight to Google Compute Engine (GCE). This means you can leverage your familiar virtual machine environment to run your containers using your existing workflow and tools without requiring your team to learn cloud native architectures.

When going down the Compute Engine route to host containers, you will need to create a specific type of GCE virtual machine. This is straightforward because when you create the VM, there is a configuration area called the container section that will let you specify the container image as well as a few other important options. You also need to select and configure the VM in the boot disk section; here, the suggested virtual machine OS is called a Container-Optimized OS, which is an operating system that has been optimized by Google for running Docker containers.

You will need to select this as the boot OS image as it comes prepacked with a Docker Runtime pre-installed. Without this, you will not be able to bring up your Docker container at the same time you create your virtual machine. So, you can containerize your VM to support containers with just a few clicks during VM creation.

However, there are a few caveats that you should be aware of. The Container OS is specialized to run Docker, so the trade-off is the loss of many standard Linux OS tools and packages. However, you could view this as a bonus as it effectively locks down and hardens your environment, ensures a smaller attack surface, and keeps your container runtime as safe from threats as possible.

The great thing about running your containers on Compute Engine is that you can still create scalable services using managed instance groups as they offer auto scaling, auto healing, rolling updates, multi-zone deployment, and load balancing for the compute instances.

Google Artifact Registry (formerly Google Container Registry)

When you first transition from learning about containers to building and deploying them, many questions arise, such as:

- Where do I get these container images?

- Where do I store the images for private use or for sharing?

- How do I control the versions?

- And how do I secure them?

The answer to each of the questions lies in the Google Artifact Registry, which was formerly known as Container Registry, or GCR. The Artifact Registry is an evolution from GCR as it is no longer just a private-by-default Container Registry that runs on GCP but a universal package manager. Artifact Registry expands on the capabilities of Container Registry and is the recommended container registry for Google Cloud. You can still do everything you could earlier, such as push, pull, and manage images in the Artifact Registry from any system, VM instance, or your own hardware, and maintain control over who can access, view, and download those images.

Artifact Registry also still works with popular continuous delivery systems, such as Cloud Build, Spinnaker, or Jenkins, to automatically build containers on code or tag changes to repository.

Working with repositories and registries

You are probably familiar with Git and GitHub as a distributed versioning system. Well, GCP has its own source code repository that works just like Git. Developers can use the source code repository for storing and tagging their code revisions. Storing working code in a repository allows you to readily identify which version is still in development, which version of a build is currently being worked upon or which version is being tested in staging, and which build version is the current stable production version. Version tagging our code allows us to follow the same best practices to ensure that each environment is running its own version of code.

The beauty of a source code repository is that it's a safe place to make changes to our development version of code without changing the current version or impacting our staging or production environments until we are ready to update the code versions there.

Since we are working with GCP, we will leverage the Google Cloud Source Repositories, although Git is still a popular alternative for local development. However, in the cloud, Source Repositories will be a convenient alternative to Git to track our code revisions and edits. We can also use the cloud-based repo to store all the project source code and share it with our team. From a security perspective, this is beneficial as we don't have to publish to the public repo GitHub. In addition, if you know how to work with Git, then working with Cloud Source Repositories will be easy as it's essentially a private Git repository but with some built-in integrations with other Google Cloud services.

Cloud Source Repositories is also very flexible as it can connect to GitHub or Bitbucket, with GitLabs in the pipeline. So, even if you have decided to host your code elsewhere, such as on GitHub, you can leverage the automated cloud deployment features in Google Cloud source repositories.

Branching with Git is also a viable option when we want to keep our code synchronized between local and cloud environments. You can trigger automation events in your deployment process if you want. However, with larger development teams, it may be better to use a combination of both code branches and tagging to keep your code revisions synchronized.

Creating a Cloud Source Repository is easy. You just need to go to your GCP account, navigate the left menu to find `Source Repositories`, and then click on `Add repository`.

When you start by clicking on `Create new repository`, you will be prompted to give the repository a name and assign it to a GCP project. At this stage, you can also add a connection to an external Git repository or Bitbucket repository.

Now that we have a Cloud Source Repository, we can run Google Cloud Build using the code stored in the new repository to build and deploy our application to production automatically, for example, as the basis for a CI/CD pipeline.

There have been some changes in GCP lately, with the Artefact registry replacing the Container Registry. However, creating a new repository on Artifact Registry is much the same as using Cloud Source Repository. Artifact Registry is a replacement for Google Container Registry as it can support several build types.

Exploring artifact registry

For quite some time, the Container Registry has provided us with a single place for storing and managing our Docker images. Through its fine-grained access control, it has also provided a handy location for performing vulnerability analysis and for either storing images privately or for sharing images with our team. Container Registry was also fundamental in helping us support our CI/CD integrations, which, in turn, let us set up fully automated Docker pipelines to get fast build quality feedback. However, everything is evolving rapidly these days, and it was Container Registry's turn to get a makeover to build upon its very powerful foundation. As such, Google Cloud released the next generation of container management tools: Artifact Registry.

With Artifact Registry, you can now manage your container images, along with all your other stuff like language packages, Cloud Build files, **customer-managed encryption keys** (**CMEK**), build dependencies, support for VPC-SC, and custom Pub/Sub notifications.

There are also much more improved and granular IAM permissions in comparison to Container Registry. These allow you to control access at the Artifact Registry level and at the project level. Additionally, within a single Google Cloud project, you can now create multiple regional repositories that have their own independent Artifact Registry-specific permissions. This gives you much focused control over where artifacts are stored and who can access them.

So, let's take a closer look at Artifact Registry to see what it is about. In the following brief tutorial, you will learn how to create a new repository, list the existing repositories, and configure access controls.

Walkthrough 5.1: Exploring the artifact registry repositories

Step 1. The first thing we need to do is to enable the Artifact Registry API in the console. Then, we will create a new repository by following these steps:

    i.   Open Cloud Shell and create a new repository:

```
gcloud beta artifacts repositories create REPOSITORY \
— repository-format=FORMAT [ — location=LOCATION] \
[ — description="DESCRIPTION"] [ — async]
```

The switches we use in this command are as follows:

- **REPOSITORY** is the name of the new repository.

- **FORMAT** is the repository format.

- **LOCATION** is the regional or multi-regional location for the repository. You can omit this flag if you set as default. Run the following command to view the list of supported locations:

  ```
  gcloud beta artifact's locations list
  ```

- **DESCRIPTION** is a description that you can give the repository.

- The **--async** flag uses background mode and returns the cursor without waiting for the operation in progress to complete. This is a hint that it might take a while.

Without waiting for the new repository to complete, let's continue:

Step 2. To view a list of repositories, you''ll run this command:

```
gcloud beta artifacts repositories list [ — project=PROJECT] \
[ — location=LOCATION]
```

The switches associated with this command are as follows:

- **PROJECT:** This is your project ID. If this flag is omitted, the current or default project will be used.

- **LOCATION:** This is a regional or multi-regional location for the repository. You will use this flag to view repositories in a specific location. You can also **use--location=all**, and this will list all the repositories across all regions.

  If you omit this flag, the command uses the default location if configured. Else, it defaults to '**all**' and lists repositories across all the regions.

Step 3. View the Current Access Policy.

i. Run the following command to get the currently configured policy:

```
gcloud projects get-iam-policy <PROJECT_ID>
```

A quick guide to some essential technologies

You cannot really understand the utility of repositories, version control, and how it makes collaboration possible without a basic understanding of Git. We are not going into too much detail on Git; we will discuss it just enough so that you can develop a basic understanding of what we are doing in the tutorials and why we are doing it.

Git is a free and open-source version control system originally created by *Linus Torvalds*, who wrote Linux; he released Git around 2005. Git immediately became popular among developers because it was free, open-source, and distributed, unlike the other version control systems of the time, which were SVN and CVS.

When we say Git is distributed, it means that every user or developer has their own local repository with a full history of their code on their local disk. Although this makes the initial clone of the repository slower, it has many advantages to compensate for this, like portability, privacy, and the ability to work offline. Subsequent Git operations such as commit, blame, diff, merge, and log are also faster.

Git is as much a collaboration tool as it has excellent support for branching, merging, and rewriting repository code history, which has led to many innovative and powerful workflows and tools. However, the problem with Git is that it is not so much difficult as unintuitive; learning the terms does not come easily for most people. Nonetheless, Git is the most widely used version control system in the world today and is considered the modern standard for software development.

How does Git work?

To get to grips with Git, we need to first try to understand the opaque language and terms. Here is a basic overview of the most common Git tasks and their associated terms, which also gives us a glimpse into how Git works:

- You need to create a *repository* (project) with a Git.

- You Clone (copy) the remote repository to your local machine.

- You then add files to your local repo (repository) and "`Commit`" (save) the changes.

- To advertise your local changes to the team, you `Push`" your changes to the main branch in the Git repo.

- You make a change to your file with a Git and commit the change.

- You `Pull` other people's code or changes to your local machine from the Git repo.

- You Create a *branch* (a new version of the code tree), make a change, and commit the change to prevent damaging the master tree.

- You Open a `pull request` (propose changes to the main branch).

- When the team agrees that the code is good, they `Merge` your branch with the main branch.

At its core, Git is a valuable code source control system, but it has changed the way we think about code. It is the inspiration behind the latest development and operations initiatives, such as code-based infrastructure and operational procedures that rely on Git as the single source of truth. Git has also inspired GitOps, which is an evolution of **Infrastructure as Code (IaC)** and DevOps best practices, which are based upon Git's practice of using pull requests to verify and automate the deployment of system infrastructure. However, at the heart of Git or any other software versioning or control system is the trust in the integrity of the repository, and this requires strict access control from the ground up.

Access controls

Although you can use the primitive Owner, Editor, and Viewer roles to grant access to source code and container repositories, more granular and role-specific access control is a requirement in most businesses. Artifact Registry uses a roles-based approach to access control, which enables you to apply the security principle of least privilege. This means that users and service accounts only have the permissions that are required for them to do their job. For example, the primitive roles of `viewer` give the holder the ability to view all artifacts and resources in all the repositories across the project. However, the more stringent role-based **artifactregistry.reader** role only allows a user to view and get artifacts from a specific project's repositories.

Configuring permissions

When you want to grant a user permission to the Artifact Registry, you will typically want to grant them a project role that already includes the required permission. This is the concept of **role-based access control (RBAC)**, and it is the easiest way to manage user permissions on a large scale. However, there may be situations where it is more appropriate to use the Artifact Registry roles to control access to your repositories rather than project roles.

You can assign the following Artifact Registry roles:

- **Artifact Registry Reader:** Grants permission to View and Get artifacts.

- **Artifact Registry Writer:** Grants permission to Read and Write artifacts.

- **Artifact Registry Repository Administrator:** Grants permission to Read, Write, and Delete artifacts.

- **Artifact Registry Administrator:** Grants permission to Create and Manage repositories and artifacts.

If you are assigning roles using the gcloud command, you will need to include them in a policy configuration file (YAML). The following reference policy template can be used when constructing your own **policy.yaml** file as it shows the template and some example user and service account names.

Here is an example **policy.yaml** file:

```
01.  bindings:
02.  - role: roles/owner
03.  members:
04.  - user: jenperson@thisemailisfake.com
05.  - role: roles/artifactregistry.reader
06.  members:
07.  - serviceAccount: repo-readonly@iam.gserviceaccount.com
08.  - user:fakeuser2@thisemailisfake.com
09.  - role: roles/artifactregistry.admin
10.  members:
11.  - serviceAccount: ar-admin@iam.gserviceaccount.com
12.
```

Figure 5.1: Policy YAML template

Use this to add a team member to a project and grant them an Artifact Registry role:

```
gcloud projects set-iam-policy <PROJECT_ID> /PATH/TO/policy.yaml
```

Where the **PROJECT_ ID** is the GCP project ID or fully qualified identifier for the project, and the **/PATH/TO/policy.yaml** is the path and file name of the policy file.

Customizing Cloud Shell containers

An interesting thing about when you start Cloud Shell is that GCP is busy provisioning an ephemeral, pre-configured VM to run the Cloud Shell session in the background. Therefore, Cloud Shell is running on a Debian-based Linux operating system in a Docker container. This means that Cloud Shell instances can be provisioned on a per-user, per-session basis by customizing the container. This is often an attractive proposition as the Cloud Shell instance persists by default only as long as your Cloud Shell session is active; your session terminates after an hour of inactivity, and its VM is automatically discarded. This means everything that is not directly under your **$Home** directory will be lost, including installed applications. You can, however, customize your environment automatically on VM boot to load your own custom container for your Cloud Shell instance, which includes your preferred tools.

Persistent storage for $HOME

By default, Cloud Shell provisions 5GB of free persistent disk storage mounted as your **$HOME** directory on the virtual machine instance. However, this persistent storage is on a per-user basis and is shared across all projects. However, this storage is persistent and will not be lost if the session times out due to inactivity. Consequently, all of your files stored in your home directory, including installed software, scripts, and user configuration files, like **.bashrc** and **.vimrc**, will persist between sessions. In addition, your **$HOME** directory is private to you and cannot be accessed by other users.

Interactive tutorial 5.1: Building a custom Cloud Shell Docker Container

In this tutorial, you will learn how to build and customize a Docker image of your custom Cloud Shell environment. Having a custom Shell environment can come in handy as you can preconfigure it to have all the tools you often require loaded at boot time.

You will also learn how to create a Source Code Repository and how to push and commit changes to the code using Google's Git commands.

Customizing Cloud Shell container images

Cloud Shell supports the customization of the default Cloud Shell environment by the user, which can positively affect your user experience. Customizing the Shell environment requires us to rebuild the Docker image using a custom shell Docker image. The image must be based on the standard Docker shell image and subsequently hosted in the Container Registry (now contained within the Artifact Repository).

To create a custom Cloud Shell with all our favorite tools and styles, you need to first create a Dockerfile that acts as a configuration list for the custom Cloud Shell environment. It is in the docker file that you will tell Docker what additional packages and custom configurations you want installed during the container build process.

To run this task directly in Cloud Console, click to Activate the Cloud Shell.

Type in the Command Line:

```
cd Chapter 05

teachme tutorial-5.1
```

Creating a custom Shell Docker image

Step 1. Follow these steps to create your own custom Docker image:

i.   In a Cloud Shell terminal tab, run the following command to create a boilerplate custom image in a repository hosted by Cloud Source Repositories:

```
cloudshell env create-custom-image NEW_REPO_NAME
```

ii. Open a new empty Dockerfile using the following command:

```
cd $HOME/NEW_REPO_NAME && cloudshell edit Dockerfile
```

This convoluted command simply changes the working directory to our new source repository and opens a new dockerfile.

iii. Now, you can edit the Dockerfile and add any additional packages you want made available in your Cloud Shell container. For example, the following snippet required Codeserver and Higo to be installed at startup:

```
FROM gcr.io/cloudshell-images/cloudshell:latest

ENV CODESERVER_VERSION="2.1665-vsc1.39.2"

ENV HUGO_VERSION="0.88.1"
```

> The first line in your Dockerfile, `FROM gcr.io/cloudshell-images/cloudshell:latest`, references the base Cloud Shell image and should not be removed.

Step 2. Once you have finished editing, you can Build your image locally by running the following:

```
cloudshell env build-local
```

i.   Once the build completes, you can proceed to Test your image locally and verify that your installed packages are present by running the following:

```
cloudshell env run
```

ii.   Run this to exit testing:

```
exit
```

Step 3. You now want to Commit your code changes locally by checking-in your code:

```
git commit -a -m "Initial custom environment check-in."
```

i.   Push your code changes to Cloud Source Repositories:

```
git push origin master
```

ii.   Finally, push your custom image to Container Registry:

```
cloudshell env push
```

Step 4. Use the Console Browser to open Artifact Repository and click on Container Registry to view your new customized Container:

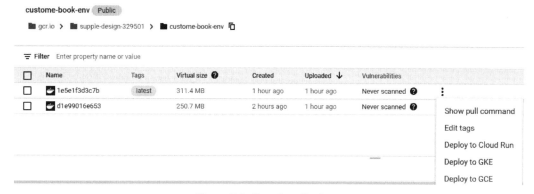

Figure 5.2: Container Registry

Note that the menu options in Container Registry allows us to deploy to Cloud Run, GKE, and GCE. So, let's see how we can deploy to Cloud Run by putting everything we have learned so far in the book to the test.

Interactive tutorial 5.2: Build and deploy a Container in Cloud Run

To run this task directly in Cloud Console, click to Activate the Cloud Shell:

Type in the Command Line:

```
cd Chapter 05
teachme tutorial-5.2
```

In this tutorial, we will be learning how to build and deploy an application container to Cloud Run.

Cloud Run is a serverless managed compute platform that can run stateless containers initiated via HTTP requests. This tutorial aims to teach you to build a container image and deploy it to Cloud Run.

Step 1. Setup and requirements

Set up your Project and environment.

i.   Sign in to Cloud Console and create a new project or reuse an existing one.

ii. Next, you'll need to enable billing in Cloud Console to use Google Cloud resources.

iii. Open Cloud Shell and enable the APIs.

From Cloud Shell, enable the Cloud Build and Cloud Run APIs:

```
gcloud services enable cloudbuild.googleapis.com run.googleapis.com
```

This should produce a successful message similar to this one:

```
Operation "operations/acf.cc11852d-40af-47ad-9d59-477a12847c9e"
finished successfully.
```

Step 2. Write the sample application

In this step, you'll build a simple Flask-based Python application responding to HTTP requests:

i.   To build your application, use Cloud Shell to create a new directory named **helloworld-python** and change directory into it:

```
mkdir ~/helloworld-python
cd ~/helloworld-python
```

ii. Use the Cloud Shell web editor (click on the **Open Editor** pen-shaped icon), create a file named **app.py**, and paste the following code into it:

```
from flask import Flask, request


app = Flask(__name__)


@app.route("/", methods=["GET"])
def hello():
    """ Return a friendly HTTP greeting. """
    who = request.args.get("who", "World")
```

```
        return f"Hello {who}!\n"

if __name__ == "__main__":
    # Used when running locally only. When deploying to Cloud
Run,
    # a webserver process such as Gunicorn will serve the app.
    app.run(host="localhost", port=8080, debug=True)
```

The purpose of this tutorial is to create code that builds a basic web server app that will respond to HTTP **GET** requests with a friendly message. Once you have done this, your app will be ready to be packaged up as a container, tested, and uploaded to the Google Cloud Container Registry.

Step 3. Containerize your app by uploading or pushing it into the Container Registry

   i.   In order to containerize your sample app, you will need to create a new file named **Dockerfile** in the same directory as the source files, this is the instructions as to how to build the container, to do this, copy the following content into a new file:

```
# Use an official lightweight Python image.
# https://hub.docker.com/_/python
FROM python:3.9-slim

# Install production dependencies.
RUN pip install Flask gunicorn

# Copy local code to the container image.
WORKDIR /app
COPY . .

# Service must listen to $PORT environment variable.
# This default value facilitates local development.
ENV PORT 8080

# Run the web service on container startup. Here we use the
gunicorn
# webserver, with one worker process and 8 threads.
# For environments with multiple CPU cores, increase the number
of workers
# to be equal to the cores available.
CMD exec gunicorn --bind 0.0.0.0:$PORT --workers 1 --threads 8
--timeout 0 app:app
```

ii. Define the **PROJECT_ID** and **DOCKER_IMG** environment variables, which will be used throughout the next steps, and ensure that they have the correct values:

```
PROJECT_ID=$(gcloud config get-value project)
DOCKER_IMG="gcr.io/$PROJECT_ID/helloworld-python"

echo $PROJECT_ID
echo $DOCKER_IMG
```

iii. Now, build your container image using Cloud Build by running the following command from the directory containing the Dockerfile:

```
gcloud builds submit --tag $DOCKER_IMG
```

Cloud Build is a service that executes your builds on GCP. It executes a series of build steps, where each build step is run in a Docker container to produce your application container (or other artifacts) and push it to Cloud Registry all in one command.

Once pushed to the registry, you will see a **SUCCESS** message containing the image name. The image is stored in the Artifact Registry and can be reused if desired.

iv. You can use this command to list all the container images associated with your current project:

```
gcloud container images list
```

v. Before deploying, run and test the application locally from Cloud Shell; you can start it using these standard docker commands:

```
docker pull $DOCKER_IMG

docker run -p 8080:8080 $DOCKER_IMG
```

vi. If the docker command cannot pull the remote container image, try running this:

```
gcloud auth configure-docker
```

In the Cloud Shell window, click on the **Web preview** icon and select **Preview on port 8080**:

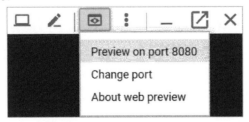

Figure 5.3: *Web preview in Cloud Shell*

This should open a browser window showing the **Hello World!** message. You can also simply use **curl localhost:8080** from another Cloud Shell session. When you're done, you can stop your docker run command with *Ctrl + c.*

Step 4. Deploy to Cloud Run

When you deploy an app to Cloud Run, you are deploying it regionally. What this means is that the infrastructure that runs your Cloud Run services will be available across all the zones within that region. Perform the following steps to define the region that you'll use for your deployment, for example, **REGION="asia-south2"**.

i. Deploy your containerized application to Cloud Run with the following command:

```
gcloud run deploy helloworld-python \
    --image $DOCKER_IMG \
    --platform managed \
    --region $REGION \
    --allow-unauthenticated
```

> **Note:**
>
> - **You can also define a default region with gcloud config set run/region $REGION.**
>
> - **The --allow-unauthenticated option makes the service publicly available. To avoid unauthenticated requests, use --no-allow-unauthenticated instead.**

Use **gcloud run deploy –help** to check all options. Then, wait for a few moments until the deployment is complete. On success, the command line displays the service URL:

```
Deploying container to Cloud Run service [helloworld-python] in
project [PROJECT_ID...

✓ Deploying new service... Done.

 ✓ Creating Revision... Revision deployment finished. Waiting for
health check...

 ✓ Routing traffic...

 ✓ Setting IAM Policy...

Done.

Service [helloworld-python] revision [helloworld-python-...] has
been deployed

and is serving 100 percent of traffic.
```

```
Service URL: https://helloworld-python-....a.run.app
```

You can also retrieve your service URL from Vloud Shell command line with this command:

```
SERVICE_URL=$( \
  gcloud run services describe helloworld-python \
  --platform managed \
  --region $REGION \
  --format "value(status.url)" \
)
echo $SERVICE_URL
```

It should display something like this:

https://helloworld-python-....a.run.app

ii.   You can now visit your deployed container by opening the service URL in a web browser. You can also call your service from Cloud Shell:

curl $SERVICE_URL?who=me

You should see your **helloworld** service listed:

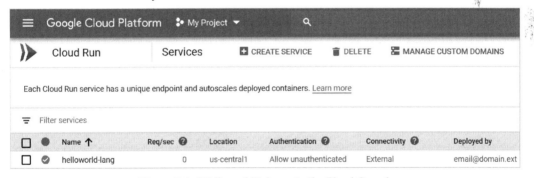

Figure 5.4: "Helloworld" shown in the Cloud Console

You can also use the console to deploy Cloud Run services.

Congratulations! You have just built your application, packaged it inside a container image, and deployed it to Cloud Run.

Working with APIs

In the last section and in the interactive tutorial, we saw that you can easily run code from your web browser and deploy it to the cloud. We were using simple standalone code, but what if you want to extend your application to use the extended functionality available to us through Google Cloud APIs?

Well, Cloud Shell Editor's plug-in, Cloud Code integration, makes it very easy. As you learned in *Chapter 2: Developing Cloud Native Apps with Cloud Shell*, Cloud Code is available to you as a set of IDE plugins. Cloud Code helps develop your cloud-native applications as it integrates well with many other GCP services, such as Cloud Run and Kubernetes.

However, you can do a lot more with Cloud Code as it has a Cloud API section that enables you to use the long list of Google Cloud APIs. Indeed, Cloud Code lets you select them, enable them, and add any associated API client libraries to your project.

Interactive tutorial 5.3: Running a Google Translate API on Cloud Run

To run this task directly in Cloud Console, click to Activate the Cloud Shell:

Type in the Command Line:

```
cd Chapter 05

teachme tutorial-5.3
```

Step 1: Enable the translation API

In this section, you'll learn how to enable the Cloud Translation API, the Cloud Run API, and the Cloud Artifact Registry API.

Option 1: From the Cloud Console

You can enable the translate API in the console under API and Services from the Cloud Console, and then go to **API Manager** and select **Library**.

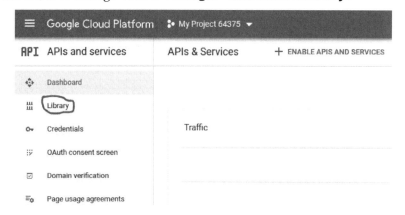

***Figure 5.5**: API Library location in Cloud Console*

Alternatively, you can click on the **ENABLE APIS** and **SERVICES** links; they will take you to the same location. If you want to enable the Cloud Translate API, start by entering **Translate** in the search bar, and anything that matches what you've entered so far will appear:

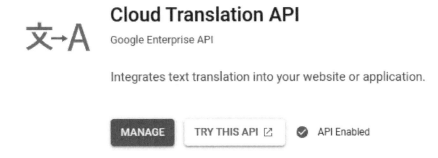

Figure 5.6: Enabling the Cloud Translation API

Click on the button to enable the API.

Option 2: From Cloud Shell or your command-line interface

While enabling APIs from the Cloud Console is easy, it can be a bit cumbersome to navigate if you want to enable several APIs at once. Additionally, developers are notoriously keen on sticking to the shell command line. That might be fine for experienced developers, but it is not ideal for beginners using the command line to activate the APIs as they will need to look up an API's **service name**.

The API's Service name looks like a URL: **SERVICE_NAME.googleapis.com**. You can find it in the Supported products chart, or you can query for it using the Google Discovery API.

For example, this command enables the Cloud Translate API:

```
gcloud services enable translate.googleapis.com
```

1. Enable all four APIs you require for the tutorial. Type the following in the Cloud Terminal:

   ```
   gcloud services enable translate.googleapis.com run.googleapis.
   com cloudfunctions.googleapis.com appengine.googleapis.com
   ```

```
alasdair_gilchrist@cloudshell:~ (ultra-evening-331702)$ gcloud services enable translate.googleapis.com
Operation "operations/acf.p2-725961719554-d99df401-0388-485c-b7ec-9e08a1371112" finished successfully.
```

Figure 5.7: The output of enabling the API command

> **If this command results in errors, ensure that the current Project ID matches your own Project ID. Use the following command to find the current Project ID being used by Cloud Shell:**

```
gcloud config list
```

If the project ID is not correct, issue the following command to specify the correct project ID:

```
gcloud config set project <PROJECT_ID>
```

Replace **<PROJECT_ID>** with the correct project ID.

2. Copy the files from the GitHub repository:

   git clone **https://github.com/papa107/cloud-translation-serverless-python**

3. Open Cloud Editor and navigate to Dir **/cloud-translation-serverless-python** directory.

Step 2: View the Code

In this tutorial, the app is a simple Google Translate derivative that prompts users to enter text in English and receive the equivalent translation of that text in Spanish.

1. Open the Shell Editor, highlight the **Cloud-translation-serverless-python** folder in **File**, click on **Open Workspace**, and select **Cloud-translation-serverless-python**. This will readjust your workspace to remove all the clutter.

2. Open the Python **main.py** file so that we can view its contents and explore how the Python code works. The code will look as follows, with the commented lines about licensing, etc. cropped:

```
from flask import Flask, render_template, request
import google.auth
from google.cloud import translate

app = Flask(__name__)
_, PROJECT_ID = google.auth.default()
TRANSLATE = translate.TranslationServiceClient()
PARENT = 'projects/{}'.format(PROJECT_ID)
SOURCE, TARGET = ('en', 'English'), ('es', 'Spanish')
```

```python
@app.route('/', methods=['GET', 'POST'])
def translate(gcf_request=None):
    """

    main handler - show form and possibly previous translation
    """

    # Flask Request object passed in for Cloud Functions
    # (use gcf_request for GCF but flask.request otherwise)
    local_request = gcf_request if gcf_request else request

    # reset all variables (GET)
    text = translated = None

    # form submission and if there is data to process (POST)
    if local_request.method == 'POST':
        text = local_request.form['text'].strip()
        if text:
            data = {
                'contents': [text],
                'parent': PARENT,
                'target_language_code': TARGET[0],
            }
            # handle older call for backwards-compatibility
            try:
                rsp = TRANSLATE.translate_text(request=data)
            except TypeError:
                rsp = TRANSLATE.translate_text(**data)
            translated = rsp.translations[0].translated_text

    # create context & render template
    context = {
        'orig':  {'text': text, 'lc': SOURCE},
        'trans': {'text': translated, 'lc': TARGET},
    }
    return render_template('index.html', **context)
```

```
if __name__ == '__main__':
    import os
    app.run(debug=True, threaded=True, host='0.0.0.0',
        port=int(os.environ.get('PORT', 8080)))
```

    i.   The imports section of the code brings in Flask functionality, such as the **google.auth** module and the Cloud Translation API client library.

    ii.   The additional global variables within the script represent the Flask app, the Cloud project ID, and the Translation API client, along with the parent **location path** for Translation API calls and the optional source and target languages. In this case, it's English (**en**) and Spanish (**es**), but you can feel free to change these languages to other any other language codes that are supported by the Cloud Translation API.

    iii.   The last section of code is that large **if** block at the bottom. You need to review this as it is used in the tutorial for running this app locally; in short, it utilizes the Flask development server to serve your app.

Step 3: Cloud Run (Python 3 via Cloud Buildpacks)

1. Navigate to the **/cloud-translation-serverless-python** directory (if you are not already there) and **DELETE** the **Dockerfile**, **credentials.son**, and **lib** files.

2. Open **requirments.txt** and make the following changes:

```
gunicorn>=19.10.0
flask>=1.1.2
google-cloud-translate>=2.0.1
```

3. Open Procfile and make the following changes:

```
#web: python main.py
web: gunicorn -b :$PORT -w 2 main:app
```

Step 4: Deploy your translation service to Cloud Run

1. Run the following command:

```
gcloud run deploy translate --source . --allow-unauthenticated
--platform managed
```

Remember, with Cloud Run, there is no need to write YAML build files or Dockerfiles. The output should look as follows and should provide some prompts for the next steps:

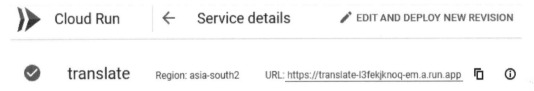

```
Building using Buildpacks and deploying container to Cloud Run service [translate] in project [supple-design
OK Building and deploying new service... Done.
  OK Uploading sources...
  OK Building Container... Logs are available at [https://console.cloud.google.com/cloud-build/builds/5d8b0e
  OK Creating Revision...
  OK Routing traffic...
  OK Setting IAM Policy...
Done.
Service [translate] revision [translate-00001-nag] has been deployed and is serving 100 percent of traffic.
Service URL: https://translate-13fekjknoq-em.a.run.app
alasdair_gilchrist@cloudshell:~ (supple-design-329501)$ []
```

Figure 5.8: Service URL the output from Cloud Build

Now that your app is available globally, you should be able to reach it at the URL containing your project ID, as shown in the deployment output: **Service URL**.

Step 5: Open Cloud Run to verify that the service is deployed and active, and note the URL

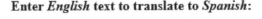

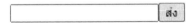

Figure 5.9: Cloud Run Service details

Translate something to see it work!

My Google Translate (1990s edition)

Previous translation

- **Original**: the cat chased the mouse (*en*)
- **Translated**: el gato persiguió al ratón (*es*)

Enter *English* text to translate to *Spanish*:

[   ] ส่ง

Figure 5.10: Translation app page

Congratulations! You have just built a Cloud Native App that calls an API. You have containerized it, posted it to the Container Registry, and then successfully deployed it to production using Cloud Run.

Now that we have seen how to build, deploy, and run containers, it is time to move on to learn how to manage them.

Managing Containers

Containers are now a standard way to divide applications into distributed objects or self-contained software packages. Splitting up monolithic applications this way allows us to place them on different physical and virtual machines, in the cloud or in-prem. This flexibility in deployment offers more advantages around workload management and allows us to make fault-tolerant systems if, and it's a big IF, we manage the container environment.

Containerization is quick and easy but can rapidly get out of control. Containers can propagate everywhere and soon become the problem rather than the solution. To help overcome this issue, a well-defined container management layer that provides the capabilities for the use of clustering, scheduling, and orchestration technology, and for the direct control and version management of many containers through container registries came into the picture. Indeed, it's difficult to build container applications without these management layers and tools like the Kubernetes Engine and Container Registry.

Conclusion

In this chapter, we learned about containers and the trend towards containerization in application development. Containers like microservices are fundamental to the concept of cloud native, so they are of relevance to us. Therefore, we have learned about the underlying technologies that make working with containers possible. We also got hands-on experience building our own applications into containers and deploying them to the artifact registry through the interactive tutorials. We understood how we can have your containerized apps interact with Google APIs to provide us with a vast range of out-of-the-box functions. Finally, we briefly covered container management and identified a pressing need for a method of managing and orchestrating containers.

In the next chapter, we will focus on our interaction with APIs to include external functions to build automated pipelines. Automation allows your cloud native apps to fully integrate with their environment using event triggers and schedulers to stop and start autonomous processes.

CHAPTER 6
Create a Serverless Pipeline with Pub/Sub, Dataflow, and BigQuery

In this chapter, we will build upon what we have learned about the various serverless platforms, Cloud Run, and App Engine to explore the world of automation. A key characteristic of Cloud Native applications is their ability to automate processes such as code upgrades and integrating with real-time streaming data. Indeed, streaming real-time video and IoT data streams is now the norm for Cloud Native applications, and in this chapter, you will learn how to do this in the Google Cloud Platform.

You will learn about the key components needed to build automation and understand how you can build an event-driven pipeline to automate a process.

Structure

We will cover the following topics in this chapter:

- Introducing Pub/Sub
- Interactive tutorial 6.1 – Getting familiar with Cloud Pub/Sub
- Cloud tasks
- Interactive tutorial 6.2 – Building a task queue
- Introducing Cloud Scheduler

- Introducing BigQuery

- Interactive tutorial 6.3 – Building a Serverless Pipeline with Pub/Sub, Functions, and BigQuery

- Introducing Cloud DataFlow

- Interactive tutorial 6.4 – Stream processing with Cloud Pub/Sub and Dataflow

Objectives

After going through this chapter, you will have good knowledge of the component and services that you can use to build automated pipelines in GCP. You will know what Pub/Sub is, how it works, and how you can deploy it in practice. You will also have learned how to initiate and schedule automated tasks using both Cloud Task and Cloud Scheduler. Additionally, you will have learned how to handle streaming data in a pipeline by using Cloud Dataflow and BigQuery. You will also be proficient in deploying BigQuery and using its bigdata capabilities.

Cloud Pub/Sub

When it comes to ensuring efficient and reliable communications between applications, we use Cloud Pub/Sub as it enables reliable messaging between applications. Cloud Pub/Sub is designed to provide reliable, many-to-many, asynchronous messaging between applications. For example, if you have a Publisher application, then it can send messages to a "*topic*", and other interested applications can subscribe to that topic to receive the messages.

Cloud Pub/Sub is used as a messaging-orientated service, but it is equally adept at handling streaming data for analytics. As a result, Cloud Pub/Sub is commonly found in data integration pipelines where it is used to ingest and distribute data. However, it is also effectively deployed as a queue to parallelize tasks.

Pub/Sub can handle these diverse roles because it works by interconnecting event producers and subscribers, respectively; hence the name. If there are lots of subscribers and a few publishers in networks, communications require direct connections, which are managed by synchronous **remote procedure calls** (**RPCs**). These can be wasteful if there are many subscribers and inefficient if there are only rarely topic updates. In the Pub/Sub model, the Publishers communicate with subscribers asynchronously by broadcasting events. Using a broadcast bus method allows subscribers to listen in to topics they are interested in, and they can pull messages from a subscriber queue whenever they want.

A Publisher has no need for knowledge of the subscribers as it simply sends events to the Pub/Sub service and forgets about them. The Pub/Sub service then takes the responsibility as to when and how that event will be delivered to all the subscribed services. This is far more flexible and efficient from a network perspective than the RPC synchronous method, where publishers make a connection with each subscriber and must wait for the subscribers to acknowledge that they have received the data. Instead, with Pub/Sub, a topic queue means that subscribers can connect or receive topic updates whenever they come online, so its asynchronous integration increases the flexibility and robustness of the overall system.

How does Pub/Sub work?

Google Cloud Pub/Sub is designed to provide reliable, one-to-many, many-to-many, or many-to-one asynchronous messaging patterns between applications. Publisher applications send messages to a "*topic*", and other applications can subscribe to that topic to receive the messages. By decoupling senders and receivers via a subscription queue, Google Cloud Pub/Sub allows applications to communicate more reliably and efficiently. Pub/Sub also provides the way for developers to communicate between independently written applications:

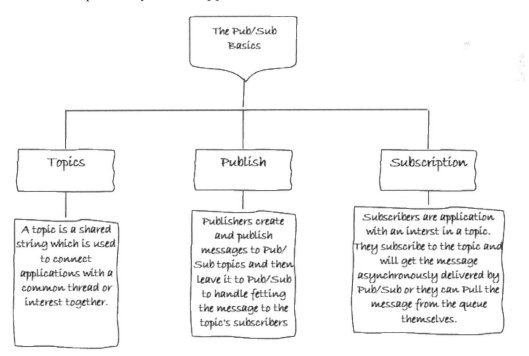

Figure 6.1: Cloud Pub/Sub model

- **Topic:** This is a named resource for a specific category of interest, an alias to which the publishers send messages.

- **Publisher:** This is an application (Producer) that creates and distributes a message to a Pub/Sub topic.

- **Subscriber:** This is an application that is interested in receiving some type of messages from the producer. So, it registers itself to a specific topic of interest in order to filter the appropriate messages.

- **Subscription:** This is the mechanism that represents a request for messages related to a specific topic that are to be delivered to the subscriber.

- **Message:** This is the data of interest that a subscriber wants; it can be a combination of data and other attributes. It is product sent by a publisher to a topic that is of interest to the subscribers.

- **Message attribute:** This is a key-value pair used by a publisher to define a message.

The following diagram explains the key components of the Google Cloud Pub/Sub messaging system and the flow of messages between publishers and subscribers:

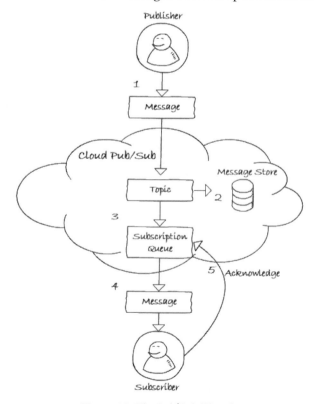

Figure 6.2: The Pub/Sub lifecycle

1. In the Pub/Sub lifecycle, a publisher application will create a topic in the Cloud Publisher/Subscriber service. It then sends, publishes, a message to the topic. The message comprises a payload and optional attributes that will describe the payload content.

2. The Pub/Sub service will ensure that messages published by the publishers are stored and retained. This is necessary to fulfil the obligation to the subscribers. The message published is retained for a particular subscription until it is acknowledged by a subscriber that has received the message or until it times out.

3. Pub/Sub forwards messages from the subscriber queue to subscribers by pushes or by broadcasting messages individually or collectively from a topic to all of its subscriptions.

4. A subscriber can receive the messages if they are online and active either by Pub/Sub pushing them to the subscriber's chosen endpoint or by broadcast. However, if they are offline at the time, the subscriber can pull them from the service queue.

5. An acknowledgment needs to be sent by the subscriber to the Pub/Sub service for each received message.

6. The Pub/Sub service will then remove all the acknowledged messages from the subscription's message queue.

Common use cases

Some common use cases are as follows:

- Pub/Sub allows you to gather events from many clients to simultaneously capture and store user interaction events from end-user apps, network events, or server events from your system. With Pub/Sub, you can then forward them using a stream processing tool (such as Dataflow) to deliver them to be stored in BigQuery.

- **Real-time event distribution:** In this case, events whether raw or processed, may be delivered or made available as a topic to multiple applications across your organization for real-time processing. This supports an "enterprise event bus" and event-driven application design patterns.

- **Replicating databases:** A common use of Pub/Sub is to distribute change events from databases. These events can be used to construct a view of the database state and state history in BigQuery and other data storage systems.

- **Parallel processing and workflows:** By using Pub/Sub messages to connect and trigger Cloud Functions, you can efficiently distribute a large number of tasks among multiple workers, such as compressing text files, sending email notifications, evaluating AI models, or reformatting images.

- **Enterprise event bus:** Establish an enterprise data sharing bus by distributing application and server events, database updates, and analytics events across your organization.

- **Data streaming from IoT devices:** Pub/Sub has many use cases in IoT, such as streaming data from sensors to backend servers hosted in the cloud.

- **Refreshing distributed caches:** For example, an application can publish invalidation events to update the IDs of objects that have changed.

- **Load balancing for reliability:** For example, instances of a service may be deployed on Compute Engine in multiple zones, but they subscribe to a common topic. When the service fails in any zone, the others can pick up the load automatically.

Limitations

Pub/Sub is intended for service-to-service communication rather than communication with end users or IoT clients. For those types of use cases, other patterns are better supported by other products:

- **Client-server:** Use solutions such as Firebase Realtime Database and Firebase Cloud Messaging to send messages between a mobile/web app and a service.

- **IoT-client-service:** Use Cloud IoT Core to send messages between an IoT app and a service.

- **Asynchronous service calls**: Use Cloud Tasks.

Let's get some hands-on practice to understand this better.

Interactive tutorial 6.1: Getting familiar with Cloud Pub/Sub

An overview

Cloud Pub/Sub is a messaging service for the asynchronous exchange of messages between data producers, known as Publishers, and data consumers, known as Subscribers. A publisher publishes messages to a Cloud Pub/Sub topic, and a subscriber enrolls to receive messages from that topic. Subscribers can pull message from a subscription queue but must acknowledge each message within a certain period.

Tutorial objectives:

- Create a topic to hold the message
- Create a subscription to a topic to access the message
- Publish and then consume messages with a pull subscriber

Setting up Pub/Sub

You use the Cloud Console to perform operations in Google Cloud Pub/Sub. Enter https://console.cloud.google.com into your browser.

Navigate to the Pub/Sub item in the GCP Services menu.

Step 1: Create a Pub/Sub topic to hold the messages

Click on **Navigation** menu | **Pub/Sub** | **Topics**.

1. Click on **Create topic**.

2. The topic must have a unique name. For this tutorial, name it **MyTopic**.

3. In the **Create a topic** dialog:
   - For **Topic ID**, type: **MyTopic**
   - Leave the **Encryption** option set at the default value
   - Click on **Create Topic**

Step 2: Create a corresponding subscription to allow you to access **MyTopic**

1. Click on **Topics** in the left panel to return to the **Topics** page. Search for **MyTopic** on the list of topics and click on the three-dot icon; then, click on **Create subscription**.

2. In the **Add subscription to topic** dialog:
   - Type a subscription name, such as **MySub**
   - Set **Delivery Type** as **Pull**
   - Leave other options set to their default values
   - Click on **Create**

   Your subscription is listed in the Subscription list:

Subscription details

Subscription name	projects/supple-design-329501/subscriptions/My-Sub
Topic name	projects/supple-design-329501/topics/my-topic

Figure 6.3: Subscription list in Cloud Pub/Sub

Step 3: Publish a message to the topic

1. Navigate to the bottom of the **Topics details** page and click on the **MESSAGES** tab; then, click on **PUBLISH MESSAGE**.

2. In the **Message field**, type in the text **Hello World** and then click on **Publish**.

Step 4: View the new Pub/Sub message

In order to view the message, you can use the Pub/Sub subscription (**MySub**) to pull the message (**Hello World**) from the topic (**MyTopic**).

1. Open Cloud Shell and enter the following command in the command line:

   `gcloud pubsub subscriptions pull --auto-ack MySub`

   The message appears in the **DATA** field of the command output:

```
alasdair_gilchrist@cloudshell:~ (supple-design-329501)$ gcloud pubsub subscriptions pull --auto-ack My-Sub
DATA: Hello World!
MESSAGE_ID: 3349830949395370
ORDERING_KEY:
ATTRIBUTES:
DELIVERY_ATTEMPT:
alasdair_gilchrist@cloudshell:~ (supple-design-329501)$ []
```

Figure 6.4: Output from the Pub/Sub Subscription Pull

Congratulations! You have completed the Pub/Sub Tutorial where you created a topic and a subscription for that topic and then published a message to the topic before retrieving (pulling) the message via the subscription.

Cloud Task Queues

With the trend in developing applications using a microservices architecture comes the need to break up large monolithic applications into smaller chunks of services that are easy to build, maintain, and upgrade. However, these services need a way to communicate, so there has been a shift in interaction across the services within an application. Previously, functions within an application would use RPC synchronous calls and would have to wait for a response and for acknowledgement that the work was completed. However, services allow you to offload work to the background, which, in turn, can be consumed later by another service. This ensures quicker response and smoother interaction across a mesh of services. Google Cloud Tasks provides developers with a tool that enables them to offload long-running asynchronous operations, thereby facilitating point-to-point collaboration and interaction across these microservices.

On the Google Cloud Platform, this asynchronous job handling service, Cloud Tasks, is a fully managed service that allows you to manage the execution, dispatch, and delivery of a large number of distributed tasks. Using Cloud Tasks, you can perform work asynchronously outside of a user or service-to-service request. In practice, the utility of Cloud Tasks is that it lets you fork from the main application flow some activities that can be performed independently. Splitting out these individual activities and sending them off to be processed, asynchronously elsewhere, lets you offload time-consuming processes that can be performed by other handlers.

These independent pieces of work are called tasks. For example, if you need to update a database as a step or a detail in processing a user request, it can result in long delays. However, offloading that detail as a task allows you to return from the request much more quickly.

The way it works is that the offloaded task is added to a queue, which keeps track of the task until it is successfully executed. The queue is managed by the Cloud Tasks service.

Once tasks are added to a queue, the queue persists and dispatches them, and it ensures that they are reliably processed. The tasks consist of a unique name and a payload. The payload is some configuration information and any data necessary to process the request. As the payload is sent in the request body, tasks that include payloads must use **POST** or **PUT** as their **HTTP** method.

Interactive tutorial 6.2: Working with Cloud tasks

In this tutorial, you will learn how to create tasks and a task queue. You need to prepare your environment before you begin:

1. Create or select a **GCP project** and enable the Cloud Tasks API.

2. The samples use the Google Cloud Client Libraries to interact with App Engine, so you need to set an environment variable to point to the key you downloaded earlier, which the library uses to authenticate your requests. You can create your requests without using the client libraries, but they can help you manage the details of low-level communication with the server, including authentication.

Step 1: Download and install the code sample

The Node.js sample consists of two files: one (**createTask.js**) run locally as a command-line tool to create and add tasks to the queue, and one (**server.js**) deployed on App Engine as a worker to **process** the task. The queue itself runs on App Engine.

To download and install the sample:

1. Clone the sample application repository to your local machine:

   git clone **https://github.com/googleapis/nodejs-tasks.git**

2. Navigate to the directory that contains the sample code:

   ```
   cd nodejs-tasks/samples
   ```

3. Install all dependencies; you can use npm:

   ```
   npm install
   ```

   Alternatively, you can use yarn:

   ```
   yarn install
   ```

4. Deploy the worker service (server.js) to App Engine standard environment:

   ```
   gcloud app deploy app.yaml
   ```

5. Check to ensure that the app containing the service is running:

   ```
   gcloud app browse
   ```

Your browser opens **https://{YOUR_PROJECT_ID}.appspot.com/** and displays **Hello, World!**.

Cloud Task Queues

With the trend in developing applications using a microservices architecture comes the need to break up large monolithic applications into smaller chunks of services that are easy to build, maintain, and upgrade. However, these services need a way to communicate, so there has been a shift in the nature of interaction across the services within an application. Previously, functions within an application would use RPC synchronous calls and have to wait for a response and acknowledgement that the work was completed or not. However, with services you can now offload work to the background, which can in turn be consumed later by another service. This helps in quicker response times as well as smoother interaction across a mesh of services. Google Cloud Tasks provides developers with a tool that enables offloading long-running asynchronous operations, thereby facilitating point-to-point collaboration and interaction across these microservices.

On the Google Cloud Platform, this asynchronous job handling service, Cloud Tasks, is a fully managed service that allows you to manage the execution, dispatch, and delivery of a large number of distributed tasks. Using Cloud Tasks, you can perform work asynchronously outside of a user or service-to-service request. In practice, the utility of Cloud Tasks is that it lets you fork from the main application flow some activities that can be performed independently. Splitting out these individual activities and sending them off to be processed, asynchronously elsewhere, lets you offload time-consuming processes that can be done by other handlers.

These independent pieces of work are called tasks. For example, if you need to update a database as a step, a detail, in processing a user request this can result in long delays but offloading that detail as a task allows you to return from the request far more quickly.

The way it works is that the offloaded task is added to a queue, which keeps track of the task until it is successfully executed. The queue is managed by the Cloud Tasks service.

Once tasks are added to a queue, the queue persists and dispatches them and makes sure they are reliably processed. The tasks consist of a unique name and a payload. The payload is some configuration information and any data necessary to process the request. As the payload is sent in the request body, tasks that include payloads must use **POST** or **PUT** as their **HTTP** method.

Interactive tutorial 6.3: Working with Cloud tasks

In this tutorial, you will learn how to create tasks and a task queue. You need to prepare your environment before you begin:

1. Create or select a **GCP project**.
2. Enable the Cloud Tasks API.

Step 1: Download and install the code sample

The Node.js sample consists of two files, one (**createTask.js**) run locally as a command-line tool to create and add tasks to the queue and one (**server.js**) deployed on App Engine as a worker to **process** the task. The queue itself runs on App Engine.

To download and install the sample:

1. Clone the sample application repository to your local machine:

    git clone **https://github.com/googleapis/nodejs-tasks.git**

2. Navigate to the directory that contains the sample code:

    cd nodejs-tasks/samples

3. Install all dependencies; you can use npm:

    npm install

    Alternatively, you can use yarn:

    yarn install

4. Deploy the worker service (server.js) to App Engine standard environment:

    gcloud app deploy app.yaml

5. Check to ensure that the app containing the service is running:

    gcloud app browse

Your browser opens **https://{YOUR_PROJECT_ID}.appspot.com/** and displays **Hello, World!**.

Step 2: Create a Cloud Tasks Queue

In this tutorial, you will use the Cloud Shell with its inbuilt Cloud SDK gcloud queue management function to create your queue in the environment you prepared earlier:

1. Enter the following at the command line:

   ```
   gcloud tasks queues create my-queue
   ```

   Wait a bit for the queue to initialize and then proceed to the next step.

2. Check whether the Task queue is built successfully:

   ```
   gcloud tasks queues describe my-queue
   ```

   Verify that the output is similar to this:

   ```
   name: projects/supple-design-329501/locations/us-central1/queues/my-queue
   rateLimits:
     maxBurstSize: 100
     maxConcurrentDispatches: 1000
     maxDispatchesPerSecond: 500.0
   retryConfig:
     maxAttempts: 100
     maxBackoff: 3600s
     maxDoublings: 16
     minBackoff: 0.100s
   state: RUNNING
   ```

Figure 6.5: Cloud Task Queue sample output

Step 3: Add a task to the Cloud Tasks queue

Create a task locally, add it to the queue you set up, and deliver that task to an asynchronous worker:

1. Set the following environment variables on your machine manually, in the code in your sample app, or via an alias. The client uses this information to create the request:

   ```
   export PROJECT_ID=PROJECT_ID # The project ID from above
   ```

   ```
   export LOCATION_ID=LOCATION_ID # The region in which your queue
   is running
   ```

   > You can find the location ID using the following gcloud command: gcloud task's locations list

   ```
   export QUEUE_ID=my-queue # The queue you created above
   ```

2. Create a task with a payload of hello and add it to your queue. The payload can be any data from the request that the worker needs to complete processing:

```
node createTask.js $PROJECT_ID $QUEUE_ID $LOCATION_ID hello
```

```
Sending task:
{
  appEngineHttpRequest: { httpMethod: 'POST', relativeUri: '/log_payload', body: 'aGVsbG8=' }
}
Created task projects/supple-design-329501/locations/us-central1/queues/my-queue/tasks/5199750
```

Figure 6.6: Create Cloud Task output

3. Verify that the payload was received by displaying the logs of the worker service:

```
gcloud app browse
```

Congratulations! you have successfully completed the Cloud Task tutorial.

Cloud Scheduler

Cloud Scheduler is useful in automation chains and pipelines as it lets you set up scheduled units of work, known as cron jobs. If you are familiar with Unix or Linux, you will understand cron jobs here, but for the benefit of Windows users, a cron job is a Linux tool often used for scheduling tasks to be executed at a specific time. Typically, a cron task is used to schedule a job that is executed at desired times or is sent to targets depending on a schedule, also called the job interval or frequency. When considering deploying cron jobs, remember that its best to run a single instance of a job; if you want to run repeatable jobs, use the Cloud Scheduler as it is meant for this. If you want to run a job only once, then consider using Cloud Tasks, which can schedule a task up to 30 days in advance.

Each cron job created using Cloud Scheduler is sent to a target according to a specified schedule, where the work for the task is accomplished. The target must be one of the following types:

- HTTP/S endpoints
- Pub/Sub topics
- App Engine applications

You can create cron jobs using either the Cloud Console or the gcloud command line tool.

BigQuery

Google BigQuery is a cloud-based analytics web service for processing very large read-only data sets. BigQuery was designed for analyzing data on the order of billions of rows, using SQL-like syntax. It runs on the Google Cloud Storage infrastructure, and it is a fully managed, serverless, highly scalable, multi cloud data warehouse designed to be cost effective at a massive scale. You can query streaming data in real-time and get up-to-date information on all your business processes such as logs and events. BigQuery's high-speed streaming insertion API provides a powerful foundation for real-time analytics; you can also leverage Pub/Sub and Dataflow to build pipelines that stream data into BigQuery for immediate analysis.

Working with data in BigQuery typically involves three steps: creating a store for the data (storage), inputting the data into the store, (ingestion), and then retrieving the data (querying).

Unlike most database, BigQuery is easy to use as it is a fully managed Google service. This means that all you have to do is log in to your Google Cloud project from a browser and then set up your storage, configure the ingestion, and handle the querying. Google will handle everything else.

The other big plus for BigQuery is that it natively supports vast capacity, but the data is stored in a structured table. This means that although you are dealing with vast amounts of big data, you can still use standard SQL for querying and data analysis. However, the initial problem is, how to get the data in there in the first place?

Fortunately, there are easy ways to upload and input your data, such as upload data from Cloud Storage or pipe streaming data from Cloud Dataflow, build an ETL pipeline, import data from a variety of file formats, or use a combination of all of these things.

Once your data is in BigQuery, you are ready to perform the analytics to get answers to those big questions.

Interactive tutorial 6.4: Building a Serverless Pipeline with Pub/Sub, Functions, and BigQuery

In this tutorial, we will step through a simple process to build a serverless data pipeline that obtains data from an API/service and loads it into BigQuery, which is an analytics engine, so that the data can be explored further.

The technology stack that we will use comprises some of Google Cloud Platform's serverless offerings, such as:

- **Cloud Scheduler**: Using this cron service, we may schedule the intervals of the execution of our Cloud Function, which will be able to invoke the Cloud Pub/Sub trigger that is required to import data from the weather API.

- **Cloud Pub/Sub**: This is our weather topic that will trigger our Cloud Function.

- **Cloud Function**: This is the function we have created so that our code will be subscribed to our execution topic of Pub/Sub, run and obtain data from the weather API/service, and then load it into BigQuery.

- **BigQuery**: The data will be loaded and stored here. It is our analytics engine, allowing us to make simple or complex queries and data processes.

Along with GCP, the role of API/service will be covered by the current weather API by OpenWeatherMap. The next image outlines our reference architecture:

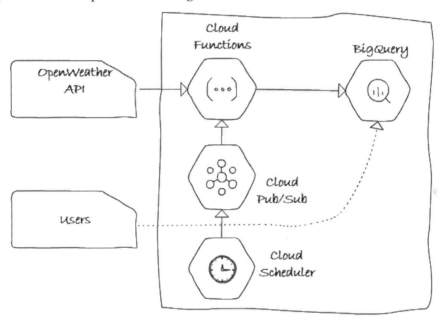

Figure 6.7: *Serverless data pipeline reference architecture*

Step 1: Clone the repo

You must clone the repo that contains the function code:

git clone https://github.com/jovald/gcp-serverless-data-pipeline.git

```
cd gcp-serverless-data-pipeline
```

Step 2: Setting up environmental variables

You will be using the Cloud Shell terminal to run most of your commands, so it is a good practice to plan out your data model beforehand as that will let you preconfigure your environment with the required variable names rather than making them up as you go along.

Therefore, we will export some core variables in this step:

PROJECT_ID: Your project ID,

REGION_ID: Your Region

ZONE_ID: Your Zone

Now, we want to expand on this methodology and export some of the other core variables we have already decided upon:

Variable	Value	Description
TOPIC_NAME:	weather	This is the Pub/Sub topic
JOB_NAME:	getWeather-job	This is the Cloud Scheduler job
FUNCTION_NAME:	loadDataIntoBigQuery	This is the name of the function
SCHEDULE_TIME:	"every 1 hours"	This is the frequency of execution
BQ_DATASET:	weather_dataset	This is the BigQuery dataset
BQ_TABLE:	open_weather_data	This is the BigQuery table

Table 6.1: Core variable to be exported

Run the following commands in the Cloud Shell Terminal:

```
export TOPIC_NAME= weather

export JOB_NAME= getWeather-job

export FUNCTION_NAME= loadDataIntoBigQuery

export SCHEDULE_TIME="every 1 hours"

export BQ_DATASET= weather_dataset

export BQ_TABLE= open_weather_data
```

Step 3: Get the API key for the Open-weather service

To do this, you will need to go and register with OpenWeather and download the API Key. Once you copy and paste the API default-key from their site, you can export it into the Cloud Shell environment.

OPEN_WEATHER_MAP_API_KEY: Sign up on OpenWeather, and then you will have access to copy and paste the default API key using this link **https://openweathermap. org/**.

```
export OPEN_WEATHER_MAP_API_KEY="the API key"
```

Step 4: Activate the GCP project

Activating the project helps execute the next commands more quickly:

```
gcloud config set project $PROJECT_ID
```

Step 5: Create the Cloud Pub/Sub topic

```
gcloud pubsub topics create $TOPIC_NAME
```

Step 6: Create the Cloud Scheduler job

This command will create a Cloud Scheduler job, named **JOB_NAME**, that is going to send a message through the Pub/Sub **TOPIC_NAME** every **SCHEDULE_TIME** (frequency).

```
gcloud scheduler jobs create pubsub $JOB_NAME --schedule="$SCHEDULE_
TIME" --topic=$TOPIC_NAME --message-body="execute"
```

Step 7: Create the BigQuery dataset and table

```
bq mk $BQ_DATASET
```

Step 8: Create the BigQuery table

The **BQ_TABLE** will contain our data:

```
bq mk --table $PROJECT_ID:$BQ_DATASET.$BQ_TABLE
```

Step 9: Deploy the function

```
gcloud functions deploy $FUNCTION_NAME --trigger-topic $TOPIC_NAME
--runtime nodejs10 --set-env-vars OPEN_WEATHER_MAP_API_KEY=$OPEN_
WEATHER_MAP_API_KEY,BQ_DATASET=$BQ_DATASET,BQ_TABLE=$BQ_TABLE
```

Step 10: Go to Cloud Functions and check whether the service is running with no errors

Test the function execution by clicking on the three dots and select **Run Test** and then **Test Function**:

Figure 6.8: Test the BigQuery function

Step 11: Test if the Scheduler is executing

Go to Cloud Scheduler in the Console and click on **Run Now!**

Target	Last run	Result	Logs	Run
Topic : projects/supple-design-329501/topics/weather	29 Oct 2021, 04:37:00	Success	View	RUN NOW

Figure 6.9: Test the scheduler is running

Step 12: Check whether BigQuery's data table is being populated

Go to BigQuery and click on **Open**.

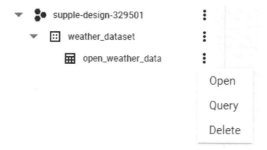

Figure 6.10: Check BigQuery tables

When the **Schema page** opens, click on **Preview** to see whether the data that has been loaded. **Congratulations!** You have successfully built a serverless data pipeline.

Clean Up!

- Delete the instance of Cloud Scheduler
- Delete the instance of Cloud Function
- Delete the Topic in Cloud Pub/Sub
- Delete the Dataset in BigQuery
- Delete the Cloud Storage Buckets

Cloud Dataflow

Cloud Dataflow is one of Google's serverless data processing services to perform **Extract Transform and Load** (ETL) operations for both streaming and batch data processing. You will certainly want to use Dataflow when you need a serverless, fast, streaming data pipeline with low data latency. Dataflow simplifies building pipelines as it is a fully managed, serverless approach that eliminates the need for any technical and operational overhead such as clusters and reduces cost due to on-demand resource auto-scaling to match demand.

When you initiate Cloud Dataflow, in the background, it creates the infrastructure that it needs to run on by spinning up a cluster of virtual machines in Compute Engine. It then silently distributes the tasks in your job to the cluster of VMs. As the job progresses, Dataflow monitor the performance and health of the cluster and dynamically scales the cluster if needed based on how the job is performing. Indeed, it can even make intelligent decisions such as shifting the order of operations in your processing pipeline in order to optimize your job.

Dataflow fits many use cases, not just as an ETL; for example, you can use Cloud Dataflow to build data pipelines, monitor their execution and transform and analyze that data. More importantly, the same pipelines work both for batch data and streaming data.

Moreover, Cloud Dataflow is often used in automating cloud pipelines as it fully automates operational tasks such as resource management and to ensure performance optimization as all resources are provided on-demand and then automatically scaled to match the process requirements.

The Cloud Dataflow API also integrates with Cloud Shell for CLI programming, Cloud Storage, Cloud Pub/Sub, Cloud Datastore, and BigQuery for seamless data processing. It's the glue that can hold it all together and can also be extended to interact with other sources and sinks.

Interactive tutorial 6.5: Stream processing with Cloud Pub/Sub and Dataflow

Task 1. Create Project Resources

1. In Cloud Shell, create variables for your bucket, project, and region:

   ```
   PROJECT_ID=$(gcloud config get-value project)
   BUCKET_NAME=$PROJECT_ID
   TOPIC_ID=my-id
   REGION=us-central1
   ```

2. Cloud Storage bucket names must be globally unique. Your Project ID is always unique, so that is used for your bucket name in this lab. Create a Cloud Storage bucket owned by this project:

   ```
   gsutil mb gs://$BUCKET_NAME
   ```

3. Create a Pub/Sub topic in this project:

   ```
   gcloud pubsub topics create $TOPIC_ID
   ```

4. Create a Cloud Scheduler job in this project. The job publishes a message to a Pub/Sub topic at 1-minute intervals.

   If an App Engine app does not exist for the project, this step will create one.

   ```
   gcloud scheduler jobs create pubsub publisher-job --schedule="* *
   * * *" \
       --topic=$TOPIC_ID --message-body="Hello!"
   ```

   If prompted to enable the Cloud Scheduler API, press *Y* and *Enter*. If prompted to create an App Engine app, press *Y* and select **us-central** for its region.

If you get an error about your project not having an App Engine app after this, run the gcloud scheduler jobs' create command again.

5. Start the job:

```
gcloud scheduler jobs run publisher-job
```

6. Use the following commands to clone the **quickstart** repository and navigate to the sample code directory:

```
virtualenv env

source env/bin/activate

git clone https://github.com/GoogleCloudPlatform/python-docs-samples.git

cd python-docs-samples/pubsub/streaming-analytics

pip install -U -r requirements.txt  # Install Apache Beam dependencies
```

Task 2: Stream messages from Pub/Sub to Cloud Storage

Review the code sample. This sample code uses Dataflow to:

- Read Pub/Sub messages
- Window (or group) messages into fixed-size intervals by publishing timestamps
- Write the messages in each window to files in Cloud Storage

You can download it here:

Task 3: Start the pipeline

1. To start the pipeline, run the following command:

```
python PubSubToGCS.py \

    --project=$PROJECT_ID \

    --region=$REGION \

    --input_topic=projects/$PROJECT_ID/topics/$TOPIC_ID \

    --output_path=gs://$BUCKET_NAME/samples/output \

    --runner=DataflowRunner \

    --window_size=2 \

    --num_shards=2 \

    --temp_location=gs://$BUCKET_NAME/temp
```

The preceding command runs locally and launches a Dataflow job that runs in the cloud. When the command returns **JOB_MESSAGE_DETAILED**: Workers have started successfully, exit the local program using *Ctrl + C*.

```
JOB_MESSAGE_DETAILED: Pub/Sub resources set up for topic 'projects/supple-design-329501/topics/my-id'.
JOB_MESSAGE_DETAILED: Autoscaling: Raised the number of workers to 1 so that the pipeline can catch up

JOB_MESSAGE_DETAILED: Workers have started successfully.
JOB_MESSAGE_DETAILED: Workers have started successfully.
```

Figure 6.11: Job message details

Task 4: Observe job and pipeline progress

You can observe the job's progress in the Dataflow console. Go to the Dataflow console and open the job details view to see:

- Job structure

- Job logs

- Stage metrics

You may have to wait for a few minutes to see the output files in Cloud Storage. You can see the output files by navigating to the **Navigation** menu > **Cloud Storage**. Click on your bucket name and then click on **Samples**:

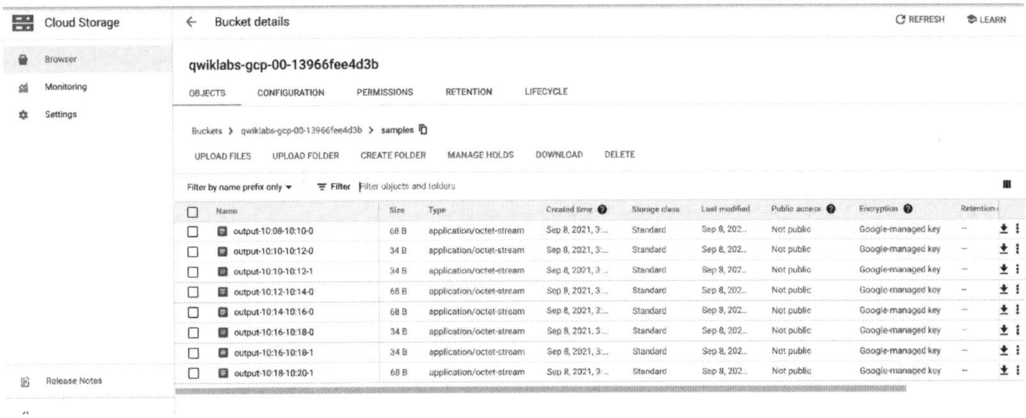

Figure 6.12: Cloud Storage Buckets List

Alternatively, use the following command line to check which files have been written out:

```
gsutil ls gs://${BUCKET_NAME}/samples/
```

The output should look like as follows:

```
gs://supple-design-329501/samples/output-04:12-04:14-1
gs://supple-design-329501/samples/output-04:14-04:16-1
gs://supple-design-329501/samples/output-04:16-04:18-1
gs://supple-design-329501/samples/output-04:18-04:20-0
gs://supple-design-329501/samples/output-04:18-04:20-1
gs://supple-design-329501/samples/output-04:20-04:22-1
gs://supple-design-329501/samples/output-04:22-04:24-0
gs://supple-design-329501/samples/output-04:22-04:24-1
```

Figure 6.13: Output

Congratulations! You have completed the tutorial.

Clean up!

Delete the Cloud Scheduler job:

```
gcloud scheduler jobs delete publisher-job
```

If prompted with **Do you want to continue**, press *Y* and *Enter*.

Press *Ctrl + C* in your Cloud Shell if it's still busy printing the output of your Dataflow job. In the Dataflow console, stop the job. With your job selected from the Dataflow Console, click on the **Stop** button. Select the Cancel bubble to cancel the pipeline without draining.

Delete the topic:

```
gcloud pubsub topics delete $TOPIC_ID
```

Delete the files created by the pipeline:

```
gsutil -m rm -rf "gs://${BUCKET_NAME}/samples/output*"
gsutil -m rm -rf "gs://${BUCKET_NAME}/temp/*"
```

Remove the Cloud Storage bucket:

```
gsutil rb gs://${BUCKET_NAME}
```

Conclusion

In this chapter, you were introduced to the concept of automation through serverless architecture pipelines. You learned about some of the key components used in automating pipelines, such as the messaging service Cloud Pub/Sub and Cloud Tasks for event-driven queues. You also learned about the streaming service Dataflow and its close integration with both cloud storage and BigQuery. The massive capacity of the latter makes it uniquely suitable for big data and streaming applications. Cloud scheduler allows us to trigger our pipelines and processes based on date and time rather than an event, so it completes the automation toolkit.

In the next chapter, we will discuss how to scale up our operating environment and introduce you to the answer to the containerization dilemma: Kubernetes, an open source, enterprise class, container orchestration and management solution.

## CHAPTER 7

Container Orchestration with Google Kubernetes Engine

In this book, Developing Cloud Native Apps in GCP, we have so far focused on the trend towards running containerized applications. Sometimes, these containerized apps run on serverless platforms such as Cloud Run and App Engine, but your application consists of multiple, independent services, and you need to host them at scale other times. Managing these applications with hundreds of containers is not a trivial task. Luckily, there's a solution. You need a container management and orchestration solution like Kubernetes, which makes managing these applications easy as it is a dedicated **Container as a Service (CaaS)** platform. With Kubernetes, you have access to the container management layer via the Kubernetes API, which lets you automate a lot of tasks related to resource provisioning and management. Furthermore, Kubernetes Engine is a managed service that eliminates most of the administration burden and the complexity of running a large scalable application. However, why the need for Kubernetes at all? Is running containers even at scale that difficult?

In this chapter, we will explain why you need a container management solution and why Kubernetes Engine is an ideal choice.

Structure

We will cover the following topics in this chapter:

- Scaling containers

- Kubernetes and GKE

- Kubernetes architecture

- Cluster orchestration with Google Kubernetes Engine

- Interactive tutorial 7.1 – Building your first Kubernetes Cluster

    o Building our first Kubernetes App

Objectives

After going through this chapter, you will have a good understanding of the underlying issues with managing containers at scale. You will also have been introduced to the need for container orchestration and the leading solution: Kubernetes. Through practical exercises, you will have learned how to create a Kubernetes cluster and deploy an application to it.

Scaling Containers

Scaling containers is not simply a matter of using clusters and cluster managers as there are processes and procedures we need to follow. An issue with all technologies is the surrounding hype that accelerates way beyond the product's reality, and containers is no exception. Therefore, we need to contemplate some significant limitations of scaling.

Clusters, specifically cluster management, is the simple go-to solution that many developers and application architects go with, but they often don't understand the limitations of emerging technologies. If you're not fully aware of these limitations and take steps to mitigate them, your container-based applications could either fail to scale or fail to provide the resiliency required.

In this chapter, we will consider clustering and managing containers by studying the emerging best practices that make container clustering work reliably.

Clustering basics

In the last chapter, we examined containers and saw how we could run several containers concurrently to solve issues with workload scaling. This is referred to as horizontal scaling as we are spinning up another instance to run in parallel, which works great for stateless applications. Nonetheless, to be able to automate this process so that we can scale up and down automatically in response to demand requires that we have control over each and every container. Therefore, we use the concept of clustering to group similar containers together under a central control.

However, when you group containers together to meet a specific workload's demand, you need a way to monitor and manage those individual container workloads. This requires a management layer that lets you view and share resources, schedule tasks, and handle the many running processes across all the individual workloads as one unified process.

This is what compute clusters and compute cluster managers do as they form a shared computing environment made up of servers (nodes), where resources have been aggregated (clustered) together to support all the individual workloads and processes running within the cluster as a group. The combined processes are called tasks. and combined tasks are called a **job**.

Cluster management architecture

To be able to manage the cluster, we will need a cluster management framework that runs, among others, a resource manager service that will track individual node resources (memory, CPU, and storage). Therefore, when a task is running but is lacking a resource, the resource manager will automatically detect this and provision the required resources. Consequently, the job is executed using a well-behaved cluster with well-managed access to resources, which can scale on demand, either virtually or physically.

However, there are other components of the cluster manager you need to understand, such as the task manager. In a cluster manager, the task manager is responsible for task execution and state management. This is hugely important if we wish to support stateful applications as the task manager handles state. The cluster managers also contain schedulers, which are core components of a cluster manager solution. A scheduler assigns tasks to a node, but it also handles all the dependencies between individual tasks that make up the job.

Now that you understand what cluster managers are—combined resource, task, and schedule management services at a high level—let's consider Google's Kubernetes.

Google Kubernetes

When most people think of containers, they think of Docker, but when they consider cluster managers, they think of Kubernetes and not Docker Swarm. This is because Google delivered Kubernetes as open-source, and it was the first container cluster manager. As a result, Kubernetes set the standard and benchmark for container managers.

However, containers and cluster managers still aren't fully mature technologies, and there's some areas that need improvement, such as:

- Networking and storage lack portability and scalability, which is a problem as these are defining characteristics to the true value of containers and cluster managers.

- Security services are incomplete. Many cluster managers that were introduced failed to address security as they didn't even have basic services to address the pressing policy compliance concerns for cluster management at an enterprise level.

- Identity and access management services also need to be more granular and scale down to apply a presence inside the cluster itself; instead, most cluster managers today operate at the project level.

From a security and enterprise perspective, containerized applications need to be security-focused, resilient to threats, highly scalable, and manageable to be viable, and Kubernetes is the popular solution for that. However, Kubernetes comes with its own issues; it is not for the faint-hearted as it is challenging to install, configure, and run.

Whenever you hear talk of cloud native, containers, CI/CD, or DevOps, you will hear the name Kubernetes. It has become pervasive and tightly coupled if not synonymous with modern DevOps, so what makes Kubernetes so dominant in this field? To understand why Kubernetes is so popular for cluster management and the container orchestrator of choice, we must understand the concepts that make it so crucial to cloud native development.

Kubernetes was developed by Google but released as an open-source platform for managing containerized workloads and services that enables both declarative configuration and automation. These core characteristics allow you to run an application on distributed systems resiliently, with scaling and failover.

Basically, Kubernetes is a container manager and orchestrator. We know what a container manager does, but what about the orchestrator? The function of an orchestrator is to track and control each container and its processes so that the containers can perform together as a well-behaved group. There's a lot of things going on behind the scenes when a scalable application is running, so Kubernetes ensures that all the required services are run as the developer intended.

That is not as straightforward as it may first seem. Traditionally, developers designed applications to be monoliths, which means they put all the functionality, like transaction and third-party integration, into a single deployable artifact. This has its own distinct advantages, and monoliths are still a common way to build applications.

That said, monoliths have a few important weaknesses. The most obvious one is that their deployments can take a long time since everything has to roll out altogether. Synchronizing all those different components and dependencies, which are perhaps managed by different teams, makes for a lot of additional complexity and project management when preparing the final version for testing, let alone a deployment to production.

A monolith also suffers from scaling issues arising from the same problem. Having such tightly coupled functional components means that development teams have to explore and refactor the whole application, even if the work required is specific to a single function.

Decomposing the Monolith

Around 2010, there was a significant shift away from building monolith applications back to a service orientated approach, but this time using microservices. In a microservices architecture, each piece of functionality is split into smaller individual artifacts called microservices.

Developers use these microservices as functional modules or building blocks to construct their application. The advantage is that if there's an update, only that exact service has to be replaced.

Furthermore, the microservice model has scaling benefits as the individual services can be scaled to match their traffic, so it's easier to avoid bottlenecks without over-provisioning.

This is all great, but having one machine or even a VM for each service would require a lot of resources; that's why containers are the preferred choice. Unfortunately, microservices and containers came with their own set of problems: as containers sprawled throughout the application, they became unmanageable. Therefore, we've come to need a conductor of our container orchestra: Kubernetes.

Kubernetes is all about automating the managing of these containers on virtual machines or nodes. The nodes in the containers they run are grouped together as a cluster, and each container has endpoints, DNS, storage, and scalability. Kubernetes automates most of the complexity, repetition, and inefficiencies of doing things by hand. It is declarative as the app developer tells Kubernetes what it wants the cluster to look like, and Kubernetes makes it happen.

Kubernetes is a container orchestrator and, in our cloud, native context containers are built to deploy smaller services with isolation and consistency. These two concepts are all about giving a process isolation, protecting it from interfering with other processes and protecting itself from others.

There are quite a few container runtimes, but Docker is one of the most popular.

The Docker container runtime has a built-in API that lets the app developer define what they want the runtime to look like instead of spending time messing around with the kernel. This is all done in a configuration script called a Dockerfile.

If you were working on a simple Flask app, for example, your Docker file might look like this:

```
$cat Dockerfile
FROM ubuntu:16.04

RUN apt update && apt install python -y
RUN app install python-pip -y
RUN pip install flask

COPY app.py /opt/app.py

ENTRYPOINT FLASK_APP=/opt/app.py flask run --host=0.0.0.0
```

Figure 7.1: *A sample Dockerfile*

The first line, `'From ubuntu:16.04'` is the base image that the app should use, and ideally, you would choose one that has exactly what you need with less overhead, making your container smaller.

Next, the **RUN** line states what commands to run when being initialized. As your Flask app is definitely going to need Python, the script installs Python, Pip, and Flask.

The Copy command will grab files from your local environment and copy them into the container. In this case, your local **app.py** file gets copied to **/opt/app.py**. Finally, the Entry Point command is set, which lets your container run as an executable, starting up the Flask application.

With just a few lines, you've created a container, which we can manually deploy, manage, and handle situations. For example, we can restart the container if it goes down, or we can roll out an upgrade to your app code if you want, but the more containers we have, the more complex this becomes. That is why we need Kubernetes.

Kubernetes automates managing your containers, regardless of the number of containers; it could be 1 or 1,000. All you need to do is tell Kubernetes what you want your container to do, and it will take care of it. Just like with the Dockerfile, you configure Kubernetes for the desired state, that is, what you want your whole cluster to do, and it automates everything from provisioning pods and nodes to configuring load balancers and much more.

Kubernetes essentials

Kubernetes is a complex system that consists of an architecture, control and management layers, and a set of services.

Kubernetes architecture

The Kubernetes architecture consists of several functional components such as, pods, nodes, labels, replication controllers, and services:

- **Pods:** The smallest Kubernetes entities are the Pods, which are ephemeral units that manage one or more tightly coupled containers. Containers that run inside a pod "share fate," meaning that if one container dies, they all die.

- **Nodes:** A node is a virtual or physical machine that you run your workloads on. Each node contains the services necessary to run pods. A node consists of a container runtime for running containers, a kubelet for ensuring that everything that should be running is, and the kube-proxy for handling networking.

- **Labels:** These are metadata that's attached to objects, including pods, for identification. The use of well-constructed labels lets you run queries, such as *What is the load on nodes labeled Test*, or perform actions, such as upgrading to a new version of the web home page only for containers marked *web front-end*.

- **Replication controllers:** These are what makes Kubernetes a declarative system as they control the desired state from a pod template to ensure that the desired number of pods are up and running. To ascertain this, the replication controllers' poll each of the pods to see how many are alive and responding. They determine the identity of each pod within the container cluster to ensure that the specified number of Pods with a given set of labels are running.

- **Services:** These are required to be able to route requests towards a group of pods in a cluster. This is a mechanism designed to route requests to a set of pods with the same labels in the cluster. Services are necessary because pods are not immutable as clusters shrink and grow, terminating and creating pods as they go. Additionally, pods can even migrate across new nodes within the cluster manager. This means that IP addresses change, as do physical location, so the job of Services is to keep track of the pods for you and route requests automatically for any application components held in a pod within a cluster instance.

Deployment

Deployment is a commonly used term when discussing clusters. A deployment, much like an instance group, represents a group of multiple and identical pods. When a deployment is configured, it runs multiple replicas of your application and monitors the health of each one to ensure that any instances that fail or become unresponsive are replaced. In this way, Deployments help ensure that there is always at least one or more instances of your application that is alive and available to serve user requests. You do not need to manage deployments as they are a fully managed service run autonomously by the Kubernetes Deployment controller.

You declaratively configure a deployment by using a Pod template, a YAML file, that contains the specification for each Pod. The Pod specification determines the desired state for each Pod, that is, what it should look like, what applications should run in the containers, and which volumes the Pods should mount, its labels, and the type of health checks, among others.

An important thing to note about deployment templates is that if it changed, the old pods will be torn down and new Pods automatically created to replace them one at a time. Now, if we had to manually manage all the pods on each node, it would be impossible to handle. That's one of the most important reasons why Kubernetes exists.

So how do we make a pod?

A pod is the smallest execution unit in Kubernetes. A pod can contain one or more containers running one or more applications. Pods are temporary *ephemeral* by nature, so if a pod (or the node that it executes on) fails, Kubernetes can automatically create a new replica to continue operations.

Pods also provide a place to store configuration data needed to run the container(s) within the pod as well as the environmental dependencies, including the shared persistent storage volumes available to all pods in the cluster. Also, if we limit a pod to run just a single process, and, as we know, Kubernetes can report on the health of each pod, then we can determine the health of the process running in the cluster as they are directly related. Moreover, pods have a unique IP address that allows them to communicate with each other, so we can locate closely-related processes in their own pod.

Although it is a common design for the reasons just given to have a pod contain containers with the same service, some pods will have several containers with different services running that work closely together to execute a desired function. Therefore, you have the flexibility to choose which model you prefer.

You must instruct Kubernetes to create a pod using the configuration file. All you have to do to put, for example, a flask container into a desired state of being a pod, is to tell Kubernetes to make it happen. We use a configuration file using YAML to do that.

Here's a YAML file that gives the desired state for a pod. This metadata section gives a way for Kubernetes to group pods and other resources together:

```
apiVersion: v1
kind: Pod
metadata:
  name: static-web
  labels:
    role: myrole
spec:
  containers:
    - name: web
      image: nginx
      ports:
        - name: web
          containerPort: 80
          protocol: TCP
```

Figure 7.2: *A Sample POD Configuration file*

For now, the key part is this Spec section. Here's where you name the pod and tell it which image to use. In this simple example of a pod, the container is the only one running an image nginx.

The YAML configuration file also has a port section, so the container can be accessed through the web on the default network HTTP port **80**. By configuring Kubernetes using the YAML file, it knows what you want to do and is in charge of ensuring that your actual state matches your desired state.

Kubernetes Control Plane

Kubernetes manages the pods through the control plane API. The control plane is where Kubernetes can define, deploy, and manage the lifecycle of our pods. The API server, which handles data validation and configuration for all the API objects, makes up the control plane.

Then, there is the **etcd**, which is a local data key-value store for holding on to all the important data that Kubernetes uses, and the Scheduler, where the important decisions are made about where exactly a pod will run. The Scheduler looks at the available resources for all the nodes and ensures that a pod goes to a node that can handle it.

And then there is the Controller Manager, where the core Kubernetes logic happens with regard to lifecycle management; it ensures that all the various pieces are working correctly.

Similarly, there is the Cloud Controller Manager, which lets Kubernetes hook into cloud providers. So, if you're running Google Kubernetes Engine, the Cloud

Controller Manager is what speaks to Google Cloud when something is needed, like a new virtual machine for a node.

That's where the Kubernetes API comes in.

At a high level, the Kubernetes API lets you tell it how you want the cluster to look and what you want it to do. Kubernetes is a declarative system, and the API allows you to declare your intentions. The steps to configuring Kubernetes are straightforward. First, if you're going to deploy a container, you make a pod that will use your container. Second, you ensure that Kubernetes has nodes available, and it figures out the rest.

How does this work? The kubelets on the nodes are tracking all the activity and key resources on the node itself, so when the control plane needs to schedule a pod on that node, both the control plane and the node have enough information to ensure that it happens flawlessly. Additionally, if a pod runs into an issue, the control plane will work with the kubelet to remove the unhealthy pod and replace it with a new one.

That's at a high level of understanding, but to move forward, we need to take a deeper dive into the Kubernetes API and understand how it makes modeling the application lifecycle easier. In order to run a fully scalable application, we need to know a lot more than just about clusters, pods, and nodes; that's where the Kubernetes API comes in. It offers some really convenient primitives that make managing cloud native applications a lot easier.

We've already talked about a few API objects, like pods and nodes, but there's also services, deployments, secrets, and many more, which we will discuss later.

Kubernetes on Google Cloud

When you deploy and run a GKE cluster, you also gain the benefit of all the advanced cluster management features that Google Cloud provides as part of its fully managed **Kubernetes Engine service** (**GKE**). These management features include the following:

- Load balancing across all the Compute Engine VM instances

- Configuration of Node pools to designate subsets of nodes within a cluster

- Automatic horizontal scaling of your cluster (adds or deletes instances)

- Automatic upgrades of the cluster's node software

- Auto-repair of Nodes to maintain health and availability

- Logging and monitoring with Cloud Monitoring for cluster observability

Cluster orchestration with Google Kubernetes Engine

Google Kubernetes Engine (GKE) is a fully managed platform for clusters of containers powered by the Kubernetes open-source cluster management system. Clusters are constructs of grouped VMs nodes, and Compute Engine Kubernetes provides the API, service, and the mechanisms through which you interact with your cluster. You can use Kubernetes commands and resources to deploy containerized applications, which enables you to manage them, perform administrative tasks, set policies, and monitor the health of your deployed container workloads.

In this chapter, we will explore Kubernetes Engine and demonstrate how it provides your container clusters with automatic management, monitoring, health and liveness probes, automatic scaling, rolling updates, and more.

Interactive tutorial 7.1: Building your first Kubernetes Cluster

In this introductory tutorial, we will explore GKE and gather hands-on knowledge of how it provides a managed environment for deploying, managing, and scaling your containerized applications using Google Cloud infrastructure. The Kubernetes Engine environment consists of multiple machines (specifically Compute Engine VM instances) grouped to form a container cluster. In this tutorial, you will get hands-on practice with container creation and application deployment with GKE.

Step 1: Set defaults – Project_ID, compute zone

The first thing you must do is export to the Cloud Shell your default **Project_ID**, compute zone, and region. For example, **us-central1-a** is a zone in the **us-central1** region.

1. To set your default compute zone to asia-south2-a, start a new session in Cloud Shell and run the following command:

```
gcloud config set compute/zone asia-south2-a
```

Expected output (Do not copy):

Updated property [compute/zone].

Step 2: Create a GKE cluster

When you create your cluster, be aware that a minimum size cluster must consist of at least one cluster master VM. The worker instances are called **Nodes**, and these are additional Compute Engine virtual machine (VM) instances. The VMs will run the

Kubernetes processes necessary to make them part of the cluster.

1. To create a cluster, run the following command, replacing **[CLUSTER-NAME]** with the name you choose for the cluster (for example: **my-cluster**):

```
gcloud container clusters create [CLUSTER-NAME]
```

2. You can ignore any warnings in the output. It might take several minutes to finish creating the cluster.

Step 3: Get authentication credentials for the cluster

After creating your cluster, you need to obtain authentication credentials in order to interact with it.

1. To authenticate the cluster, run the following command, replacing **[CLUSTER-NAME]** with the name of your cluster:

```
gcloud container clusters get-credentials [CLUSTER-NAME]
```

Step 4: Deploy an application to the cluster

Now that you have a cluster built, you can go ahead and deploy a containerized application to the cluster. For this lab, you'll run hello-app in your cluster. GKE uses Kubernetes objects to create and manage your cluster's resources. Kubernetes provides the Deployment object for deploying stateless applications like web servers. Service objects define rules and load balancing for accessing your application from the internet.

1. Run the following command to create a new deployment **hello-server** from the **hello-app** container image:

```
kubectl create deployment hello-server --image=gcr.io/google-
samples/hello-app:1.0
```

This Kubernetes command creates a Deployment object that represents **hello-server**. In this case, **--image** specifies a container image to deploy. The command pulls the example image from a Container Registry bucket. **gcr.io/google-samples/hello-app:1.0**, and this indicates the specific image version to pull. If a version is not specified, the latest version is used.

2. Run the following command to create a Kubernetes Service, which is a Kubernetes resource that lets you expose your application to external traffic:

```
kubectl expose deployment hello-server --type=LoadBalancer --port
8080
```

In this command:

```
--port specifies the port that the container exposes.
```

```
type="LoadBalancer" creates a Compute Engine load balancer for
your container.
```

3. Run the following command to inspect the **hello-server** service:

   ```
   kubectl get service
   ```

   > **It might take a minute for an external IP address to be generated. Try running the command again.**

4. To view the application from your web browser, open a new tab and enter the following address, replacing **[EXTERNAL IP]** with the **EXTERNAL-IP** for **hello-server**:

   ```
   http://[EXTERNAL-IP]:8080
   ```

Congratulations! You have just created your first KGE Cluster and deployed an application.

Interactive tutorial 7.2: Building your first Kubernetes App

Launch Cloud Shell.

In this tutorial, you will use Cloud Shell as it comes preinstalled with the gcloud command-line tool and the kubectl command-line tool. The gcloud tool provides the primary command-line interface for Google Cloud, and kubectl provides the primary command-line interface for running commands against Kubernetes clusters.

To launch Cloud Shell, type the following in the browser:

```
console.cloud.google.com
```

From the upper-right corner of the console, click on the **Activate Cloud Shell** button:

A Cloud Shell terminal session opens inside a frame in the bottom half of the console. This is the terminal we will configure to use to run gcloud and kubectl commands.

Set default settings for the gcloud tool

To make entering some of the commands easier, you can configure your Cloud Shell terminal session to use the following default settings: your default project, compute zone, and compute region. Configuring these default settings makes it easier to run gcloud commands because gcloud requires you to specify the project and location in which you want to work. If you do not configure your own default settings, you would have to specify these settings with flags, such as **--project**, **--zone**, **--region**, and **--cluster**, in your individual gcloud commands.

When you create GKE resources after configuring your default project, zone, and region, the resources are automatically created in that project, zone, and region.

In Cloud Shell, perform the following steps:

Step 1: Configure the Cloud Shell environment

1. **Set the default project:** Replace **PROJECT_ID** with your project ID:

   ```
   gcloud config set project PROJECT_ID
   ```

2. **Set the default zone:** Replace **COMPUTE_ZONE** with your compute zone, such as **asia-south2-a**:

   ```
   gcloud config set compute/zone COMPUTE_ZONE
   ```

3. **Set the default region:** Replace **COMPUTE_REGION** with your compute region, such as **asia-south2**:

   ```
   gcloud config set compute/region COMPUTE_REGION
   ```

4. **Enable the APIs:** Go to the Cloud Console and enable the APIs for:

   - Compute Engine
   - Kubernetes Engine

Step 2: Create a GKE cluster

A cluster consists of at least one cluster control plane machine and multiple worker machines called nodes. You will use Compute Engine virtual machine (VM) instances as the nodes that will run the Kubernetes processes. Additionally, you will build the nodes that run the processes necessary to make them part of the cluster, and then you will deploy your application to the cluster.

To create clusters in GKE, you need to choose a mode of operation: Standard or Autopilot. If you use the Standard mode, your cluster is zonal (in this tutorial). If you use the Autopilot mode, your cluster is regional.

1. Create a one-node Standard cluster named hello-cluster:

   ```
   gcloud container clusters create hello-cluster --num-nodes=1
   ```

It might take several minutes to finish creating the cluster.

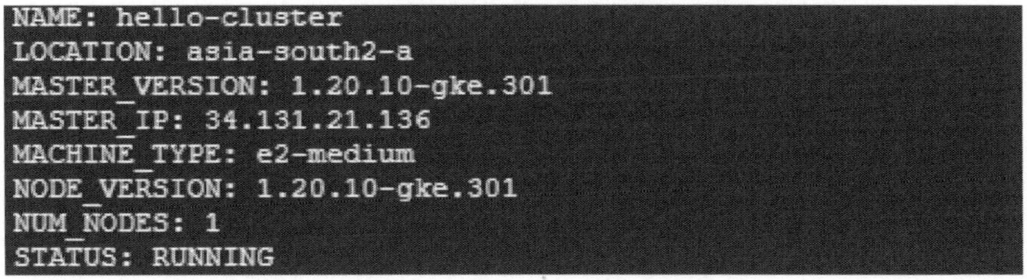

```
NAME: hello-cluster
LOCATION: asia-south2-a
MASTER_VERSION: 1.20.10-gke.301
MASTER_IP: 34.131.21.136
MACHINE_TYPE: e2-medium
NODE_VERSION: 1.20.10-gke.301
NUM_NODES: 1
STATUS: RUNNING
```

Figure 7.3: Create Cluster command output

2. After creating your cluster, you need to get authentication credentials to interact with the cluster:

    gcloud container clusters get-credentials hello-cluster

    This command configures kubectl to use the cluster you created:

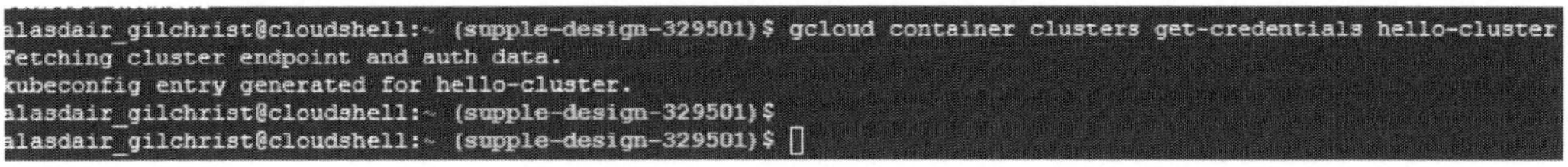

```
alasdair_gilchrist@cloudshell:~ (supple-design-329501)$ gcloud container clusters get-credentials hello-cluster
Fetching cluster endpoint and auth data.
kubeconfig entry generated for hello-cluster.
alasdair_gilchrist@cloudshell:~ (supple-design-329501)$
alasdair_gilchrist@cloudshell:~ (supple-design-329501)$ []
```

Figure 7.4: Get Cluster credentials

3. Deploy an application to the cluster

    The cluster is now available, so you can deploy a containerized application to it. For this tutorial, you can deploy the example web application, **hello-app**.

However, there are two parts to this, one is creating the deployment where GKE uses the Deployment object to create and manage your cluster's resources, for example, when deploying stateless applications like web servers. Then, there is the second part where you create a service. A service object defines the rules and load balancing for accessing your application from the internet. You will use kubectl to configure these via the Kubernetes API.

Step 3: Create the deployment   .

To run **hello-app** in your cluster, you need to deploy the application by running the following command:

```
kubectl create deployment hello-server \
    --image=us-docker.pkg.dev/google-samples/containers/gke/hello-
app:1.0
```

The kubectl create deployment command creates a Deployment named **hello-server**. The Deployment's Pod runs the hello-app container image.

In this command, **--image** specifies a container image to deploy. In this case, the command pulls the example image from an Artifact Registry repository, and **us-docker.pkg.dev/google-samples/containers/gke/hello-app**. **:1.0** indicates the specific image version to pull. If you don't specify a version, the image with the default tag latest is used:

```
alasdair_gilchrist@cloudshell:~ (supple-design-329501)$ kubectl create deployment hello-server \
>     --image=us-docker.pkg.dev/google-samples/containers/gke/hello-app:1.0
deployment.apps/hello-server created
alasdair_gilchrist@cloudshell:~ (supple-design-329501)$ []
```

Figure 7.5: Create Deployment

Step 4: Expose the Deployment

After deploying the application, you will need to expose it to the internet. This is so that external users can access it. You will expose your application by creating a Service, which is a Kubernetes resource that exposes your application to external traffic on the internet.

To expose your application, run the following kubectl expose command:

kubectl expose deployment hello-server --type LoadBalancer --port 80 --target-port 8080

- Passing in the **--type LoadBalancer** flag creates a Compute Engine load balancer for your container.

- The **--port** flag initializes public port **80** to the internet.

- The **--target-port** flag routes the traffic to port **8080** of the application.

  This command creates a Kubernetes API object called a deployment that manages the lifecycle of an application. You will set the desired number of app instances for the deployment to manage, and it will ensure that number of instances, or replicas, are kept running and available.

In the tutorial, if we increase the number of replicas that we want, the deployment will automatically detect that there's currently not enough replicas and spin up another one. It works the same way when a node crashes. If the node goes down, the current state will differ from the desired state and Kubernetes will spin up another replica to restore the correct order.

Step 5: Inspect and view the application

1. Inspect the running Pods by using kubectl get pods:

   kubectl get pods

You should see one **hello-server** Pod running on your cluster.

```
service/hello-server exposed
alasdair_gilchrist@cloudshell:~ (supple-design-329501)$ kubectl get pods
NAME                         READY    STATUS     RESTARTS    AGE
hello-server-5bd6b6875f-pt597  1/1      Running    0           2m16s
```

Figure 7.6: Get Pods status

2. Inspect the **hello-server** Service by using **kubectl get service**:

   kubectl get service hello-server

```
alasdair_gilchrist@cloudshell:~ (supple-design-329501)$ kubectl get service hello-server
NAME          TYPE          CLUSTER-IP    EXTERNAL-IP    PORT(S)       AGE
hello-server  LoadBalancer  10.3.244.133  34.131.209.53  80:30960/TCP  2m28s
```

Figure 7.7: Get Service output

The service that you just created provides an endpoint that we can use to access the running app instances. In this case, we have multiple app instances. So, this service will **loadbalance** incoming requests between the two running pods.

Any container inside of the cluster can connect to the **hell-server** service using the service's name (**hello-server**). Regardless of where you connect from, the service keeps track of wherever the pod is actually running so that you don't need to keep track of a changing IP address.

A good example of how Kubernetes eliminates the need to manually keep track of where your containers are running is if a pod goes down, a new one comes online; the service will automatically update its list of endpoints to target the new pod.

So, deployments and services automatically ensure that your clusters have the right number of app instances running by maintaining the availability of the pods and ensuring that you can always reach them.

3. From this command's output, copy the Service's external IP address from the **EXTERNAL-IP** column.

> You might need to wait for several minutes before the Service's external IP address populates. If the application's external IP is <pending>, run the **kubectl** command again.

4. View the application from your web browser by using the external IP address with the exposed port:

   Note: In my case, the IP is **34.131.209.53**; yours will be different, so use your IP address.

http://34.131.209.53

Hello, world!
Version: 1.0.0
Hostname: hello-server-5bd6b6875f-pt597

Figure 7.8: *Success!*

Congratulations! You have just deployed a containerized web application to GKE.

Clean up!

Follow these steps to avoid incurring charges to your Google Cloud account for the resources used in this page:

1. Delete the application's Service by running **kubectl delete**:

    kubectl delete service hello-server

    This command deletes the Compute Engine load balancer that you created when you exposed the Deployment.

2. Delete your cluster by running gcloud container clusters delete:

    gcloud container clusters delete hello-cluster

```
alasdair_gilchrist@cloudshell:~ (supple-design-329501)$ kubectl delete service hello-server
service "hello-server" deleted

alasdair_gilchrist@cloudshell:~ (supple-design-329501)$
alasdair_gilchrist@cloudshell:~ (supple-design-329501)$ gcloud container clusters delete hello-cluster
The following clusters will be deleted.
 - [hello-cluster] in [asia-south2-a]

Do you want to continue (Y/n)?  y

Deleting cluster hello-cluster...done.
Deleted [https://container.googleapis.com/v1/projects/supple-design-329501/zones/asia-south2-a/clusters/hello-cluster]
```

Figure 7.9: *Delete cluster*

In *tutorial 7.2*, we used some of the Kubernetes features that removed much of the administrative burden by automating things that were manually coded earlier. Building and maintaining container clusters just become afterthoughts when using Kubernetes as it does all the heavy lifting behind the scenes.

The Kubernetes API makes it easy to manage and control the basic primitives -- pods, service, deployments. Additionally, it allows sysadmins and developers to focus on the app without having to worry about managing it at scale. However, in tutorial 6.1 and 6.2, we used imperative commands via the API, that is, you told Kubernetes exactly what you wanted it to do, and it did it, but that isn't really scalable. We need a declarative approach for scalability and support for cloud-native apps.

Difference between imperative and declarative

An imperative approach is to directly instruct the program via defined steps, whereas a declarative approach just states what it wants done and leaves it to the program to figure out the best way to accomplish this. Fixing your car is an example.

The imperative approach:

1. Kick the tyres

2. Lift the hood

3. Stare sadly at the engine

4. ....

A declarative approach:

1. Tell the garage to fix it

2. Go and delegate another task

3. ....

To get the best out of Kubernetes and get it to work the way it was intended to, we should use declarative commands and update the config files. In the next tutorial, we will configure and deploy an app to Kubernetes using the declarative method of updating the config files.

Interactive tutorial 7.3: A declarative approach to configuring and deploying to Kubernetes

In this lab, we want to do things declaratively by having a file that describes what we want the desired state to be. Then, we will let Kubernetes do all the hard work. This means that Kubernetes will figure out how to make that desired state work.

Having our state defined declaratively in files allows us to make changes to our deployments by just editing the file describing it. We can also track those changes through source control and use great tools for deploying applications at scale, like continuous integration and continuous deployment tools.

In this tutorial, you will set up the Cloud Shell environment just like you did in *tutorial 7.1* and export the **project_id**, **zone**, and **region** into Cloud Shell as defaults.

Step 1: Create the Kubernetes cluster

1. Create a one-node Standard cluster named hello-cluster:

    ```
    gcloud container clusters create hello-cluster --num-nodes=1
    ```

    It might take several minutes to finish creating the cluster.

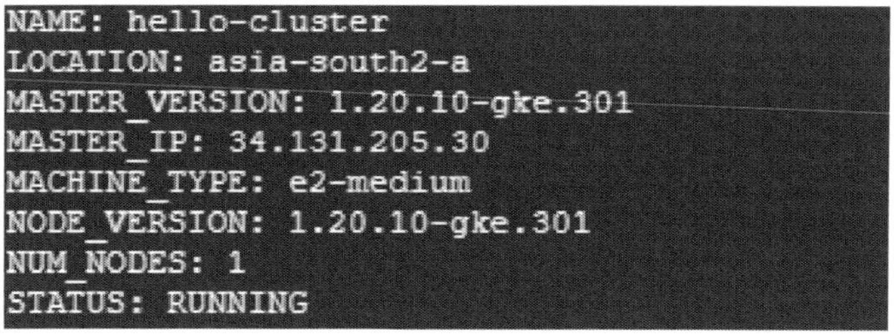

    ```
    NAME: hello-cluster
    LOCATION: asia-south2-a
    MASTER_VERSION: 1.20.10-gke.301
    MASTER_IP: 34.131.205.30
    MACHINE_TYPE: e2-medium
    NODE_VERSION: 1.20.10-gke.301
    NUM_NODES: 1
    STATUS: RUNNING
    ```

    Figure 7.10: Creating cluster

2. After creating your cluster, you need to get authentication credentials to interact with the cluster:

    ```
    gcloud container clusters get-credentials hello-cluster
    ```

    This command configures **kubectl** to use the cluster you created.

3. Make a working **dir** and download the source files:

    ```
    git clone https://github.com/papa107/declarative-patterns.git
    ```

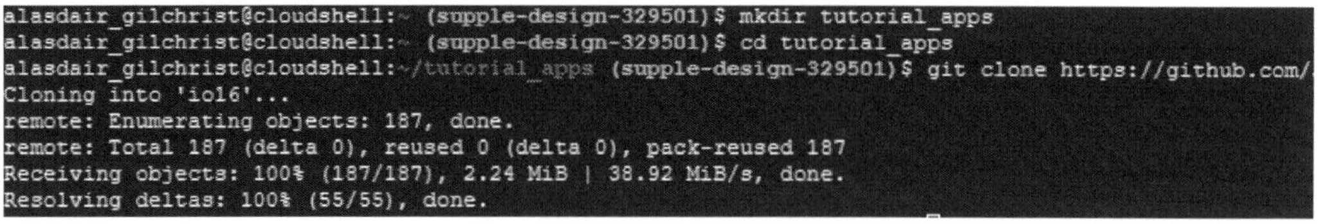

    ```
    alasdair_gilchrist@cloudshell:~ (supple-design-329501)$ mkdir tutorial_apps
    alasdair_gilchrist@cloudshell:~ (supple-design-329501)$ cd tutorial_apps
    alasdair_gilchrist@cloudshell:~/tutorial_apps (supple-design-329501)$ git clone https://github.com/
    Cloning into 'io16'...
    remote: Enumerating objects: 187, done.
    remote: Total 187 (delta 0), reused 0 (delta 0), pack-reused 187
    Receiving objects: 100% (187/187), 2.24 MiB | 38.92 MiB/s, done.
    Resolving deltas: 100% (55/55), done.
    ```

    Figure 7.11: Clone repository

    Use the Cloud Shell terminal to navigate to the new directory **tutorial_apps**, and run LS here to list the files; you will see some subdirectories that hold the files you will need to create that microservice application in Kubernetes. Navigate to the **tutorial_apps/io15/kubernetes** directory. You will work from this directory for all exercises in the tutorial.

4. Open **deployments/hello.yml** in Cloud Shell Editor:

```
01.  apiVersion: apps/v1
02.  kind: Deployment
03.  metadata:
04.    name: hello
05.  spec:
06.    replicas: 3
07.    selector:
08.      matchLabels:
09.        app: "hello"
10.    template:
11.      metadata:
12.        labels:
13.          app: hello
14.          track: stable
15.          version: 1.0.0
16.      spec:
17.        containers:
18.          - name: hello
19.            image: "tut_6.2-/hello:1.0.0"
20.            ports:
21.              - name: http
22.                containerPort: 80
23.              - name: health
24.                containerPort: 81
25.            resources:
26.              limits:
27.                cpu: 0.2
28.                memory: "10Mi"
29.            livenessProbe:
30.              httpGet:
31.                path: /healthz
32.                port: 81
33.                scheme: HTTP
34.              initialDelaySeconds: 5
35.              periodSeconds: 15
36.              timeoutSeconds: 5
37.            readinessProbe:
38.              httpGet:
39.                path: /readiness
40.                port: 81
41.                scheme: HTTP
42.              initialDelaySeconds: 5
43.              timeoutSeconds: 1
```

***Figure 7.12**: Deployment – Hello-yaml*

This is the configuration file we will edit to deploy our app to kubernetes:

i.   You are giving that deployment a name.

ii.   You are telling Kubernetes the number of replicas of the pods that will be in this deployment.

iii. You are defining the container image.

iv.   You have defined a liveness probe and a readiness probe.

The liveness and readiness probes are health check tools that Kubernetes provides to help ensure that your application is up and ready to receive traffic. All the information about what we want this deployment to look like is here in this file, and this is what we mean by declaring our desired state. If we wanted to make a change, like changing the image that we're going to be running in this deployment, we could do that in this file and track that change through source control.

5. Open **services/hello.yaml** in Cloud Shell Editor:

```
01.  kind: Service
02.  apiVersion: v1
03.  metadata:
04.    name: "hello"
05.  spec:
06.    selector:
07.      app: "hello"
08.    ports:
09.      - protocol: "TCP"
10.        port: 80
11.        targetPort: 80
```

Figure 7.13: Service – hello-yaml

In *tutorial 7.1*, you had to create a service to be able to connect to our app; this is what you are doing in this file: you are creating a Kubernetes service. This is creating another Kubernetes service that will provide server connections to your **Hello** application, which will be deployed in its own deployment.

If you consider the **service.yml** contents, you see that the service definition is pretty simple.

i.   It has a name for the service.

ii.   It has a selector that tells the service how to find the backends that it is serving.

iii.   It has some port information that tells us how to reach the application.

Step 2: Deploy the hello microservices to Kubernetes cluster

`kubectl apply -f deployments/hello.yaml -f services/hello.yaml`

```
deployment.apps/hello created
service/hello created
```

Figure 7.14: Service created

You can run several deployments at the same time by just adding another **-f** and the deployment files' name.

1. Deploy the frontend microservice to Kubernetes cluster.

    This application uses a Nginx server, which will act as your frontend. However, we will first need to create a service for it using the same template for the hello service. You give it a name and a selector and define the ports:

```
01.   kind: Service
02.   apiVersion: v1
03.   metadata:
04.     name: "frontend"
05.   spec:
06.     selector:
07.       app: "frontend"
08.     ports:
09.       - protocol: "TCP"
10.         port: 443
11.         targetPort: 443
12.     type: LoadBalancer
```

Figure 7.15: Code snippet for service 'frontend'

Run the following command when you have finished:

`kubectl apply -f deployments/frontend.yaml -f services/frontend.yaml`

```
deployment.apps/frontend created
service/frontend created
```

Figure 7.16: Service created

2. Examine the rest of the Frontend Configuration File:

```
16.         containers:
17.           - name: nginx
18.             image: "nginx:1.9.14"
19.             lifecycle:
20.               preStop:
21.                 exec:
22.                   command: ["/usr/sbin/nginx","-s","quit"]
23.             volumeMounts:
24.               - name: "nginx-frontend-conf"
25.                 mountPath: "/etc/nginx/conf.d"
26.               - name: "tls-certs"
27.                 mountPath: "/etc/tls"
28.         volumes:
29.           - name: "tls-certs"
30.             secret:
31.               secretName: "tls-certs"
32.           - name: "nginx-frontend-conf"
33.             configMap:
34.               name: "nginx-frontend-conf"
35.               items:
36.                 - key: "frontend.conf"
37.                   path: "frontend.conf"
```

Figure 7.17: *Frontend config file*

Note the volumes being mounted in line 23. You should see that two external volumes are being mounted: **ng-frontend-conf** and **tls-certs**. Starting at line 28, you should find these volumes identified as being a **secret (tls-certs)** and a **configMap (nginx-frontend-conf)** volumes, respectively.

In Kubernetes and Docker containers, we can think of a volume as an external directory, possibly with some data in it, that is accessible to the containers in a pod. Volumes are a convenient way to access data that is external to the container.

To use a volume, you need to specify the volumes to provide for the Pod in the **frontend.yaml** file in **.spec.volumes** (see line 28) and also declare where to mount those volumes into containers in **.spec.containers[*].volumeMounts** (see line 23).

A process in a container sees a filesystem view that is made up of their Docker image and any mounted volumes. The Docker image is at the root of the filesystem hierarchy with volumes mounted at the specified paths within the image. Volumes cannot be mounted onto other volumes or have hard links to other volumes. Each Container in the Pod's configuration must independently specify where each volume should be mounted.

Now, let's see what these volumes are used for.

Step 3: Configure the Nginx Container

You now have a frontend consisting of a container running Nginx, but there is some configuration information that you want to pass into your Nginx server. We can do this using a Kubernetes tool called **ConfigMaps**.

1. Create a ConfigMaps for the nginx frontend.

   A config map lets you map your configuration information to your application running in a Kubernetes deployment. The configuration information that is needed for your Nginx frontend is located in **nginx/frontend.conf**.

   Here, you can see that there is a bunch of configuration information for my Nginx frontend.

   However, this config file is not in YAML format, so we will need to create a ConfigMap that uses this as an input:

   ```
   kubectl create configmap nginx-frontend-conf –from-file=nginx/
   frontend.conf
   ```

   In this command, Configmap is the type of Kubernetes object that you want to create. You have given it a name and provided a source file, which is **nginx/frontend.conf**.

   ```
   configmap/nginx-frontend-conf created
   ```

   Figure 7.18: Nginx frontend created

2. Pass confidential information into the container using secrets.

   If we wanted to run this application in production, we would need to use SSL/TLS to enable HTTPS; however, we need to pass some TLS certificates to do that.

Figure 7.19: TLS file location

You don't want to use a **configMap** for this config map because that information is passed in plain text. You need the certs to be passed encrypted, and Kubernetes has a tool for this called **secrets**:

```
kubectl create secret generic tls-certs –from-file tls/
```

```
secret/tls-certs created
```

Figure 7.20: Secrets created

We use the **kubectl** command to create a secret just like creating a ConfigMaps, except they're for secret information. To create a secret, we provide a secrets type; in this case, we have chosen the all-purpose generic type, given it the name **tls-certs**, and provided a source file location, **tls/**.

Step 4: Deploy the Auth microservice

The **auth** module is the last piece of the microservice application. Of course, I'm going to need a **service/auth.yml** service and something for that service to serve, which will be a deployment once again; it's going to be **deployment/auth.yml** as well.

```
kubectl apply -f deployments/auth.yaml -f services/auth.yaml
```

That is the whole microservice architecture for the app deployed to Kubernetes:

```
deployment.apps/auth created
service/auth created
```

Figure 7.21: auth created

Step 5: Test that the app is deployed in Kubernetes

Run the following to test whether the app has deployed okay in Kubernetes:

```
kubectl get services
```

To test the app, we can **run kubectl get services**, or just svc for short:

```
alasdair_gilchrist@cloudshell:~/tutorial_apps/io16/kubernetes (supple-design-329501)$
NAME         TYPE           CLUSTER-IP     EXTERNAL-IP      PORT(S)         AGE
auth         ClusterIP      10.3.244.1     <none>           80/TCP          50s
frontend     LoadBalancer   10.3.245.116   34.131.209.53    443:32697/TCP   29m
hello        ClusterIP      10.3.247.5     <none>           80/TCP          32m
kubernetes   ClusterIP      10.3.240.1     <none>           443/TCP         52m
```

Figure 7.22: Get Service for External IP

1. Get the External IP address

   You want to obtain the Kubernetes **EXTERNAL_IP** address in this step, so you need to get this information for the frontend. In this case, Kubernetes has created an actual load balancer resource in Google Cloud, and that external load balancer resource has created an external IP for you so that anyone can use it to reach the application that you created.

2. Export the **EXTERNAL_IP**

   Copy and export that IP as a variable just to make the following commands a little bit easier.

   Export EXTERNAL_IP

   So, now I can run a **curl** command to test to ensure that my application is running correctly. And if you remember, we incorporated some security capabilities into this application earlier.

Step 6: Test the App from the Public IP

We set up TLS and some security measures, so we have to connect to this application using HTTPS. Run the following to do this:

curl -k https://$EXTERNAL_IP

```
alasdair_gilchrist@cloudshell:
{"message":"Hello"}
```

Figure 7.23: Success!

Step 7: Examine the health of the cluster

In the step, we will examine the health checks we configured in the YAML config file:

```
29.        livenessProbe:
30.          httpGet:
31.            path: /healthz
32.            port: 81
33.            scheme: HTTP
34.          initialDelaySeconds: 5
35.          periodSeconds: 15
36.          timeoutSeconds: 5
37.        readinessProbe:
38.          httpGet:
39.            path: /readiness
40.            port: 81
41.            scheme: HTTP
42.          initialDelaySeconds: 5
43.          timeoutSeconds: 1
```

Figure 7.24: Code snippet for Liveness and Readiness

We configured Liveness and a Readiness Probes in the YAML config, so let's see if they are working as planned. Follow these steps:

1. Examine the logs by running this command:

```
kubectl logs deployments/hello -c hello
```

2. Note the output from the logs and then close using *Ctrl + c*:

Congratulations! You now know the application is up and running properly on Kubernetes.

In this tutorial, you learned how to create deployments with config maps and secrets. You learned how to accomplish this for both the deployments and the services in a declarative way. Running things declaratively is useful in the real world as running your deployments based on a file makes it easy to set up CI/CD, source control, and other processes that are useful for running applications at scale on Kubernetes.

Troubleshooting Kubernetes

We have learned about the Kubernetes core primitives such as pods, containers, nodes, and services, among other things, and we have deployed our app to a cluster; everything works just fine. However, now that we are routinely going to be building and deploying apps to containers and are going to do a lot more over the next few chapters, we need to get some basic troubleshooting skills.

Not everything is going to work straight away. We might make typos or just not enter commands fully; then, what do you do when things aren't working? When things go wrong, we need to find out why. So, learning how to debug Kubernetes is very useful, especially in real-world situations. This is particularly true as troubleshooting applications on Kubernetes clusters can be a daunting task just because of the sheer size. In addition, the fact that Kubernetes does such a good job of abstracting away the underlying infrastructure means it can be very difficult to know what's going on under the hood at any given time.

What we need is some basic analytical steps and tools that we can apply in a logical manner to quickly get to the root cause of a failure.

Using the kubectl CLI for debugging issues

Kubectl has some useful tools for debugging problems or at least to get us started. These include the following:

- **kubectl explain**: This is useful when you need to know what a particular entity does; it's like a very specific help file for that resource.

- **kubectl describe**: This gives you verbose technical and configuration details about a resource, such as a pod or a node.

- **kubectl logs**: This lets you see what's going on inside a pod as it logs events from the containers.

- **kubectl get -o flag**:

Let's see what these do, for starters, on our Kubernetes cluster. Running the - **kubectl get pods** - command will provide the following output:

```
alasdair_gilchrist@cloudshell:~ (supple-design-329501)$ kubectl get pods
NAME                           READY   STATUS    RESTARTS   AGE
auth-5798bf4589-gqr6b          0/1     Pending   0          129m
frontend-6869899d96-jkm5v      1/1     Running   10         158m
hello-5f69ddb5df-45nrr         0/1     Pending   0          161m
hello-5f69ddb5df-48rrb         1/1     Running   0          161m
hello-5f69ddb5df-d4qwl         0/1     Pending   0          161m
```

Figure 7.25: Get Pods status

The output from the - **kubectl get pods** – command can tell you a lot. For instance, in our example, you can see that there are several pods stuck in the pending state. That could mean that you have insufficient resources available to establish a running pod, which prevents the pod from getting scheduled onto a node.

To test this theory, we will run the - **kubectl describe pods** - command to get a verbose output on each pod's status and configuration. The output is very long, and we are unable to show it here, but here's a small but relevant snippet from the first pod on the above-mentioned list:

```
Name:           auth-5798bf4589-gqr6b
Namespace:      default
Priority:       0
Node:           <none>
Labels:         app=auth
                pod-template-hash=5798bf4589
                track=stable
Annotations:    <none>
Status:         Pending
IP:
IPs:            <none>
Controlled By:  ReplicaSet/auth-5798bf4589
Containers:
  auth:
    Image:          kelseyhightower/auth:2.0.0
    Ports:          80/TCP, 81/TCP
    Host Ports:     0/TCP, 0/TCP
    Limits:
      cpu:     200m
      memory:  10Mi
    Requests:
      cpu:          200m
      memory:       10Mi
    Liveness:       http-get http://:81/healthz delay=5s timeout=5s period=15s #success=1 #failure=3
    Readiness:      http-get http://:81/readiness delay=5s timeout=1s period=10s #success=1 #failure=3
    Environment:    <none>
    Mounts:
      /var/run/secrets/kubernetes.io/serviceaccount from default-token-497cr (ro)
Conditions:
  Type           Status
  PodScheduled   False
Volumes:
  default-token-497cr:
    Type:          Secret (a volume populated by a Secret)
    SecretName:    default-token-497cr
    Optional:      false
QoS Class:         Guaranteed
Node-Selectors:    <none>
Tolerations:       node.kubernetes.io/not-ready:NoExecute op=Exists for 300s
                   node.kubernetes.io/unreachable:NoExecute op=Exists for 300s
Events:
  Type      Reason            Age                   From                Message
  ----      ------            ---                   ----                -------
  Warning   FailedScheduling  3m43s (x110 over 129m) default-scheduler  0/1 nodes are available: 1 Insufficient cpu.
```

Figure 7.26: Describe Pods snippet

Take note of the name: **auth-5798bf4589-gqr6b**:

The status: Pending

IP: none assigned

PodScheduled: False

Events:

Warning: Failed Scheduling

Message: 0/1 nodes are available: 1 Insufficient cpu.

Therefore, it looks like we have insufficient CPU resources available to launch the desired state of No of Pods. Let's check that out using the - **kubectl get nodes** - command and check the node status:

```
alasdair_gilchrist@cloudshell:~ (supple-design-329501)$ kubectl get nodes
NAME                                         STATUS   ROLES    AGE     VERSION
gke-hello-cluster-default-pool-a7078adf-n0c3 Ready    <none>   3h19m   v1.20.10-gke.301
```

Figure 7.27: *Get Node status*

The current status is Ready, so let's run - **kubectl describe nodes** - to get more details. Again, the output from the common is very verbose and long, so we have only included a snippet here:

```
Allocated resources:
  (Total limits may be over 100 percent, i.e., overcommitted.)
  Resource                    Requests       Limits
  --------                    --------       ------
  cpu                         761m (80%)     353m (37%)
  memory                      555Mi (19%)    1275Mi (45%)
  ephemeral-storage           0 (0%)         0 (0%)
  hugepages-1Gi               0 (0%)         0 (0%)
  hugepages-2Mi               0 (0%)         0 (0%)
  attachable-volumes-gce-pd   0              0
Events:                       <none>
```

Figure 7.28: *Describe Nodes status*

If we go to the Kubernetes console and view our cluster, we immediately see that there is an unschedulable pods notification due to a resource problem:

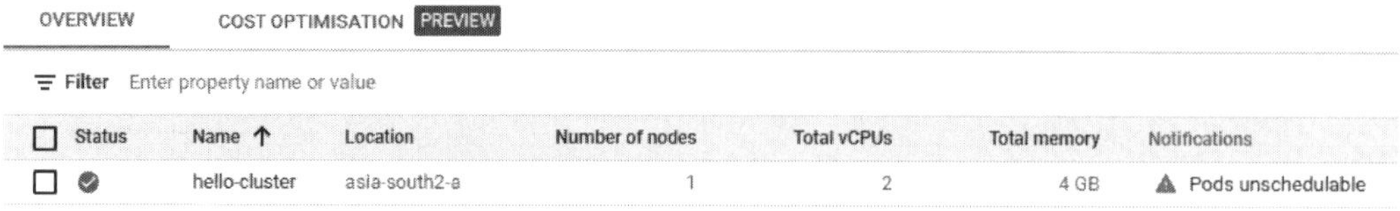

	Status	Name ↑	Location	Number of nodes	Total vCPUs	Total memory	Notifications
☐	✔	hello-cluster	asia-south2-a	1	2	4 GB	⚠ Pods unschedulable

OVERVIEW   COST OPTIMISATION PREVIEW

⇌ Filter   Enter property name or value

Figure 7.29: *Kubernetes Console View - unschedulable*

By clicking on the Notification link:

Cluster hello-cluster has unschedulable pods

Problem

Your cluster has 3 unschedulable pods

Details

Unschedulable pods

- hello-5f69ddb5df-45nrr
- auth-5798bf4589-gqr6b
- hello-5f69ddb5df-d4qwl

Possible actions

- Enable auto-scaling in one or more node pools that have auto-scaling disabled.
- Increase size of one or more node pools manually.

Figure 7.30: *Unschedulable Pods error*

Another common state that a pod can be in is the waiting state. This can happen when a pod has been scheduled onto a node, but it can't run. For instance, in this case, there are sufficient resources as it has been successfully scheduled but perhaps cannot find the required container image. So, even though there's space to run the app, it just won't work.

Another scenario is when there's sufficient space and resources to run the append and the image is accessible and working, but the app itself is broken. In this case, we can use the **kubectl command - kubectl exec** - as it lets you open a shell terminal and execute commands inside the container.

This comes in handy when you want to examine the contents, state, and/or explore the environment of a container. Let's first list the pods with the **- kubectl get pods** - command and choose one as the target for the exec command (in the following example, the **frontend-6869899d96-jkm5v** pod is the target). Now, you want to get the cluster IP of your service (for example, using **kubectl get svc**):

```
alasdair_gilchrist@cloudshell:~ (supple-design-329501)$ kubectl get svc
NAME         TYPE           CLUSTER-IP      EXTERNAL-IP     PORT(S)          AGE
auth         ClusterIP      10.3.244.1      <none>          80/TCP           3h4m
frontend     LoadBalancer   10.3.245.116    34.131.209.53   443:32697/TCP    3h33m
hello        ClusterIP      10.3.247.5      <none>          80/TCP           3h35m
kubernetes   ClusterIP      10.3.240.1      <none>          443/TCP          3h55m
```

Figure 7.31: *List Pods*

When running the following commands, be sure to replace the pod name and the service IP with your own:

```
kubectl exec frontend-6869899d96-jkm5v -- curl -k https://10.3.245.116
```

We will discuss troubleshooting, along with monitoring and logging, in greater detail in the later chapters.

Clean Up!

1. Delete all deployments:

   ```
   kubectl delete deployments auth frontend hello
   ```

2. Delete the secrets volume:

   ```
   kubectl delete secrets tls-certs
   ```

3. Delete the ConfigMap Volume:

   ```
   kubectl delete configmaps nginx-frontend-conf nginx-proxy-conf
   ```

4. Delete your cluster by running gcloud container clusters delete:

   ```
   gcloud container clusters delete hello-cluster
   ```

Conclusion

In this chapter, you were introduced to Kubernetes, an open-source cluster management and orchestrator that is native to Google Cloud Platform. You learned why Kubernetes is critical for scaling containerized apps and how it is the answer to many of the container sprawl issues that many organizations are experiencing today. The pervasiveness and wild propagation of unmanaged containers throughout enterprises is a real concern, and it is down to the lack of good business processes. Kubernetes enforces best practices and, in the case of GKE, is a fully managed service that relieves you of much of the administrative burden. You also learned how to build a Kubernetes cluster and how to deploy an app to that Kubernetes cluster. Up until now, we have built our cluster and deployed our app imperatively, but that doesn't scale well, so you learned how to declaratively configure Kubernetes, which is how you release its full potential.

In the next chapter, we will stay with Kubernetes and contemplate how to deploy and manage Kubernetes at scale in the real world, in the workplace.

CHAPTER 8

Deploying and Managing Kubernetes Applications

In the previous chapter, you were introduced to Kubernetes and learned how to configure and build clusters both imperatively and declaratively. You also learned how to deploy apps to your cluster. That's all very well when working with tutorials and in the console, but what about designing your Kubernetes environment for the real world?

In this chapter, we will look at designing practical, real-world clusters and consider some of the best design patterns. We will also look under the hoof to see that features and tools are at our disposal to help us manage and maintain our Kubernetes cluster.

Structure

We will cover the following topics in this chapter:

- Cluster Design patterns
- Managing Cluster resources
- Interactive tutorial 8.1: Migrating a Monolith to Microservices on Kubernetes Engine

Objectives

After going through this chapter, you will have a good understanding of cluster design patterns and what designs are best suited to scenarios. You will also understand resource management and how to go about transforming a monolith application into microservices architecture for deployment on a Kubernetes cluster.

Cluster Design patterns

The first thing you need to do when considering deploying apps to Kubernetes is to sit down and consider just how you intend to structure your clusters and what the most effective model for your organization is. What you have to consider is the need for a standard model throughout the organization as there are several approaches you can take when building clusters when hosting containers. You can, for instance, host a single or multi-cluster setup where you have several workloads running on a single large cluster, or you can run many clusters with only a few workloads deployed in each cluster or is sometimes the case a cluster per application.

Here is what we should consider when selecting the best model:

- Should we have a single or multi cluster model?

- In either case, how large should we make it?

However, we also need to consider the design constraints, such as:

- Performance

- Security

- Reliability

- Cost

In the first part of this chapter, we will consider these questions and analyze some of the pros and cons regarding cluster sizing and app deployment.

The age-old dilemma

Most organizations, regardless of size, will develop, deploy, test and then operate multiple applications concurrently in production. Furthermore, if they are into software development, then they are likely to run multiple versions of each instance of these applications across several dedicated platforms; for example, they will have siloed dev, test, and prod environments.

This results in a lot of duplication of applications within segregated environments. In the preceding example, there are two applications and three environments, dev, test, prod, which results in six concurrent instances of the applications.

To complicate matters, in a microservices architecture, an application instance may consist of multiple microservices and containers, each with a specific purpose such as the frontend, backend, database, etc. In a microservices application, an instance will likely consist of one or more of each type of microservices.

Hence, in an organization, there tends to be a lot of duplication even before we consider high-availability designs. However, importantly, each of these applications has self-contained deployment instances that can be operated independently from one another, so they could just as easily run on one cluster in a single environment.

As a Kubernetes architect, this raises some concerns for me:

- Should you run all your application on a single cluster?
- Or should you have a separate cluster for each application instance?
- Or would it be best to use a combination of the two?

This brings us back full circle to the days of metal servers and data center provisioning of applications. Then, there were differing approaches with some wanting only one application per server and others wanting to collocate tightly coupled apps together on a single server. Then, just as now, all of these are valid approaches. Kubernetes may well be flexible enough to handle each scenario, but the system architecture and deployment rules within an organization rarely are.

Let's take a look at some of the different approaches:

- A single large, shared cluster
- Multi single-purpose clusters

The single cluster model

The most common starting point, especially on-prem, is to build and run all your workloads on a single cluster. This makes a lot of sense when you are commissioning and deploying hardware servers in your cluster. Building and maintaining several hardware clusters would soon become expensive and time consuming, so going with a single general-purpose cluster would seem like a sensible solution.

With this approach, the cluster is a single all-purpose server platform, so you deploy whatever you need to run to this Kubernetes cluster. The trouble with this approach is that you will likely need to over-provision to ensure that you can manage the required current and future workloads.

The problem of workload isolation can be an issue as concurrently running different workloads may be considered a security risk. To work around this, Kubernetes provides namespaces, which are used to logically segregate areas of a cluster. Therefore, to create the necessary segregation, you could use the Linux trick of using a separate namespace for each workload instance.

Let's look at some of the positives and negatives when adopting this approach.

- **Efficient resource usage**: Running a single large cluster for all your workloads is certainly going to be resource efficient. When it comes to resource usage, all the workloads share the same resources to run and manage the Kubernetes cluster, such as the master nodes, control planes, load balancers, and ingress controllers, among many other services and functions. By using the same cluster for multiple workloads, you effectively reuse these services for all your workloads.

- **Cheap**: As a result of reusing resources, a single cluster will be cheaper to build and run because the costs of the overheads associated with the resources is shared among all the workload owners. This is particularly true when you consider running multiple master nodes, which can be expensive both in terms of time and money, regardless of whether it is on-premises or in the cloud.

- **Easier administration**: Administering a single cluster is always going to be easier than administrating many clusters. A single cluster effectively reduces the administrative burden by limiting many tasks to single one-time activities; for example, you only need to perform tasks like these once for all workloads:

  - Rolling out a Kubernetes version upgrade
  - Configuring a new CI/CD pipeline
  - Setting up the users

Many admin tasks will only need to be run once for all your workloads if you have a single cluster. On the other hand, if you run specific clusters per workload, you will eventually have many clusters, which would mean applying the same task multiple times. However, this can create problems with consistency and would become tiresome very quickly without some automated processes and tools to assist you in keeping all the clusters consistent with the organizational policy.

However, it's not all blue water sailing; here are the negatives:

- **Troubleshooting apps**: Just like in the on-prem days, troubleshooting a server with many different applications running is very difficult. Hence, data centers traditionally insisted on one app per server. The problem is that it becomes very difficult to isolate the failure domain when multiple apps are running on the same cluster. Indeed, it's not always the workload that is causing concern and is the root of the problem, so attributing responsibility is also an issue when multiple workloads co-exist. For example, an intermittently failing workload may be getting starved of resources because another greedy workload is using up all the available resources at peak load times. Isolating the failure domain and locating the root cause is always going to be more complex in a shared workload cluster.

- **Single point of failure**: A single cluster is also a single point of failure, even if it has high availability and redundancy mechanisms preconfigured. Typically, the cluster will be built to support redundant configuration, but not always. If you have only one cluster with a single master node and if that cluster should fail, then all your workloads that reside on that cluster are going to fail! The obvious solution is to build redundancy into the design and have three master-nodes, preferably running on different power sources and at different locations, so that a single node failure isn't going to be catastrophic. However, that negates many of the advantages of running a single cluster.

  Hardware failures are the most commonly considered cause for failure, but there are many ways in which something can bring your cluster down:

  - o   A software upgrade goes wrong
  - o   A configuration error is applied to the cluster
  - o   Kubernetes controller crashes after an upgrade
  - o   An administrative error shuts down the cluster
  - o   An application misbehaves and consumes more resources than it should

  Any of these common incidents can bring down the cluster and cause considerable damage to all your workloads if you have them all running on that single shared cluster.

- **Maintenance and support costs**: The costs of supporting a cluster that hosts many different applications will escalate as the app count rises.

- **A lack of hard security segregation**: When you have multiple apps running in the same Kubernetes cluster, they are sharing the hardware, network, and operating system running on the underlying cluster nodes. This may be an issue from a security perspective—it theoretically isolates the apps but does allow unrelated apps to share common resources, such as a database.

  Furthermore, talk of isolation is a bit hazy as workloads in a Kubernetes cluster are theoretically isolated as they cannot communicate with each other directly. Of course, they do participate in using shared services, for example DNS, which allows apps to discover and connect to other services running in the cluster.

- **No hard multi-tenancy**: Given that applications can use many shared resources in a cluster, there is always the noisy neighbor issue. This is where an app monopolizes a shared resource, such as CPU cycles or available working memory, and starves the other apps running on that cluster node.

There are ways to curb this behavior and support multi-tenancy; for example, you could configure appropriate resource requests and resource limits. In addition, you could apply **ResourceQuotas** and **LimitRanges** to limit the consumption of resources. However, be aware that multi-tenancy does not come out-of-the-box.

- **Clusters have a finite practical size**: If you decide upon a single cluster for all your workloads, this cluster will probably grow to be large (in terms of nodes and Pods). You need to be realistic about how large you want this cluster to scale - do you usually run everything on one massive supercomputer - probably not; so, why try now?

Kubernetes has published some theoretical limits for cluster size, which are defined at a recommended maximum of 5000 nodes, 150,000 Pods, and 300,000 containers, respectively.

Multi-cluster model

With the opposite approach, you can use single-purpose cluster for every application or even microservice. This is similar to the old on-prem model of one app/ microservice per server. With this strategy, Kubernetes is used as a dedicated server per application runtime.

The positives:

- **Reduced blast radius**: If a cluster fails, the damage is contained and limited to only the workload that is running on that cluster; all the other clusters and their workloads will be unaffected.

- **Segregation**: There is a good degree of segregation as applications run on separate isolated clusters. As a result, workloads running in their own isolated clusters cannot share any resources. This means they have their own dedicated CPU, memory, storage, and network resources.

  This model delivers strong isolation between unrelated applications, which is a big plus mark for security.

- **Cluster can be customized for an app**: Having a dedicated cluster per application also means that you can customize it to perfectly match the specifications and requirements of the application. If an app has specific resource requirements, such as GPU nodes, a service mesh, or any other specialized service, then its cluster can be configured to suit those without affecting any of the other clusters.

Let's look at the negatives:

- **Expensive**: More clusters will be reflected in the bill. For example, if you run 100 clusters instead of 1 for the same compute power, this will be reflected in your monthly bill.

- **Higher administration burden**: Increasing the number of clusters with undoubtedly increase the administrative burden as managing many clusters is going to be more time-consuming than administering a single Kubernetes cluster.

For example, you will need to configure the authentication and authorization services for each cluster, which can be a pain. Furthermore, upgrading to the latest Kubernetes version will require you to do this many times, and this repetition can be tedious and is likely to introduce errors.

Maintaining a multi-cluster model will need you to have automated processes and software to do this efficiently, and this adds to the cost and complexity.

On deciding on the ideal cluster size to app deployment model, a lot will depend on your own particular organizational policy and needs; there is no one correct way it depends on your circumstances. It is, however, interesting to note that as you start to build more and more apps on top of a Kubernetes cluster, even those routine tasks will begin to get troublesome. For example, developers are unable to use the same name when creating Kubernetes Services or Deployments. This might not seem important, but it does show there will need to be a policy or communication structure in place to resolve these minor issues. Also, the more the cluster grows, the more pods you will end up with, and you could end up with potentially thousands of pods; viewing them would take some time, let alone managing them.

Managing Kubernetes resources

There are some inbuilt tools that are available to you for managing and administering Kubernetes resources. Using Kubernetes namespaces is one very effective and simple solution that can make managing your Kubernetes resources much easier.

What is a namespace?

The concept of namespace come from Unix, where, in a multi-user environment, Namespaces were used to allow the reuse of names in different contexts. In Kubernetes, the use of namespaces segregates the cluster, so you can think of a Namespace as a virtual cluster inside your Kubernetes cluster. Configuring namespaces is easy and effective as each namespace is isolated from the others. Furthermore, you can configure as many namespaces as you want within a single Kubernetes cluster. Moreover, the namespaces are all logically isolated from each other. Namespaces can help you separate teams and work areas and allow autonomous administration of each namespace, which lowers the administrative burden on you.

The "default" namespace

A Kubernetes cluster comes with a set of predefined namespaces: default, kube-system (used for Kubernetes components), and kube-public (used for public resources). The last two are reserved and not of much use to you, but you can use the default namespace as that is where your services and apps are created.

The problem with the default namespace is that it lumps everybody and everything together in the one namespace. Therefore, there will be the inevitable conflicts between teams in naming resources and files, for example. However, it is also easy to make mistakes that propagate across the entire cluster. You do not need to use the default namespace and are advised to set up your own namespaces for your teams.

Creating namespaces

To create namespaces to segment your services, you don't need to be concerned about any performance penalty as the Kubernetes API will actually have a smaller set of objects to work with. Creating a namespace is done with a single **kubectl** command in Cloud Shell, so if you wanted to create a namespace called **test**, you would type in:

```
kubectl create namespace test
```

Alternatively, you can do this declaratively using a YAML configuration file and apply it just like any other Kubernetes resource.

```
01.   test.yaml:
02.   kind: Namespace
03.   apiVersion: v1
04.   metadata:
05.     name: test
06.     labels:
07.       name: test
08.   kubectl apply -f test.yaml
```

Figure 8.1: Creating a YAML file

Viewing namespaces

You can view all the Namespaces in the cluster by typing the following command:

```
kubectl get namespace
```

The expected output from this command will be the three built-in namespaces as well as the new namespace you created called **test**.

> **You cannot delete the Default namespace.**

Creating resources in the namespace

Viewing the code of a simple YAML to create a Pod:

```
01.   apiVersion: v1
02.   kind: Pod
03.   metadata:
04.     name: mypod
05.     labels:
06.       name: mypod
07.   spec:
08.     containers:
09.     - name: mypod
10.       image: nginx
```

Figure 8.2: nginx YAML file

You will probably see that there is no mention of namespaces anywhere in the script. Nonetheless, if you were to run the **kubectl apply** command on this file, it will create the Pod in the current active namespace. This will, of course, be in the **default** namespace unless you change it. Therefore, you are probably going to want to explicitly instruct Kubernetes of the Namespace you want to create your resources in rather than keeping track of the current namespace.

There are two ways to explicitly tell Kubernetes which namespace to use. The first is to set the "namespace" flag when creating the resource; so, you type in:

```
kubectl apply -f pod.yaml --namespace=test
```

This command will instruct Kubernetes to create the resource in the namespace **test**. You can also specify a namespace in the YAML config file declaration.

```
01.   apiVersion: v1
02.   kind: Pod
03.   metadata:
04.     name: mypod
05.     namespace: test
06.     labels:
07.       name: mypod
08.   spec:
09.     containers:
10.     - name: mypod
11.       image: nginx
```

Figure 8.3: nginx YAML with namespace

When a namespace is specified in the YAML declaration, the resource is always produced in that namespace. This implies that you can't use the **namespace** flag to set a different namespace afterward; the command will fail. To rectify this, you would need to remove the entry from the YAML file and reapply the file.

Viewing resources in the namespace

A common problem when using namespaces is that users cannot find their resources. This is because all commands are conducted against the presently active namespace. To find your Pod, you need to use the correct **namespace** flag. For example, no resources are found if you type in the following:

```
kubectl get pods
```

However, suppose you specify the namespace:

```
kubectl get pods --namespace=test
```

Then, the expected output is shown as follows:

```
NAME      READY     STATUS      RESTARTS    AGE
mypod     1/1       Running     0           10
```

Namespace communication

By default, namespaces are **hidden** rather than isolated from each other. You need to be aware of an anomaly with namespaces as they are hidden from others' view but are not isolated. As an example, a service in one namespace can talk to a service in another namespace. There is nothing preventing this, and often, this can be very useful.

Resources within namespaces can communicate with other Kubernetes services by using the built-in DNS service discovery to resolve to an IP address by simply pointing to the service's name. However, as we have seen, you can freely create resources and a service with the same name in other Namespaces. That, however, can work in your favor by specifying the namespace in the DNS lookup request. You can then communicate across Namespace borders.

Kubernetes services use a standard DNS pattern to expose their endpoints. It looks like this:

```
<Service Name>.<Namespace Name>.svc.cluster.local
```

Normally, when you communicate with another service, you just need to know the service's name, and then you ask DNS to reconcile that name to an IP address. DNS will automatically resolve to the registered IP address for you. However, if you need to access a service in a different Namespace, then DNS is once again your friend as you use the Service name plus the namespace name.

For example, if you want to connect to the **storage** service in the **development** namespace, you use the following address format: **storage.development**.

Therefore, there is no actual isolation between namespaces as services and resources are just hidden from view. If you want to isolate Namespaces, you need to use Network Policies to accomplish this.

Namespace granularity

Previously, we discussed how large should clusters be or how many apps per cluster we should have. There is a similar dilemma for architects when considering Namespaces. The recurring theme is: how many Namespaces should we create and for what purpose? The answer to the dilemma is just like sizing clusters: it depends. Create too many Namespaces, and you will find that they work against you and become **the** problem, but make not enough, and you will miss out on the benefits.

The answer, infuriatingly, depends on the stage of your project or company policy and whether it's a small team or a mature enterprise as each will have its own organizational structure. You should adopt the relevant Namespace strategy based on your situation.

It's probably a reasonable rule of thumb to say, start out small. If you are a small organization, use the default namespace on a single cluster as most work will be done on developers' local machines anyway. As your DevOps team grows and development demands outstrip working on local machines, perhaps introduce a cluster and namespaces for dev, test, and prod; that said, it's not a requirement. When the organization becomes large enough that teams are diverse and working on different projects, perhaps with third parties, then each team will certainly need its own namespace and perhaps even its own cluster. At the enterprise-level where there is no interaction between teams, and services are consumed through well-documented APIs, namespaces should be deployed and locked down. At this point, it will make sense to have a multi-cluster model. As we learned earlier, a multi-cluster model will reduce the blast radius of a failure and will also make billing and resource management granular at a project level.

Liveness and readiness checks

Google Kubernetes Engine is a managed system, which means it is required to ensure that your applications keep running at the desired state. Indeed, many of Kubernetes features and functions, even in on-prem deployments, require Kubernetes to have a deep understanding of the applications status at any given time. To provide that insight into an application's performance, Kubernetes uses some enhanced health checks, such as readiness and liveness probes. Configuring these can help you build a more robust app.

Readiness

Readiness is a measure that your app is, as the name suggests, ready to receive and handle a workload. This is not the same state as being alive. The difference is that not only is the app or service up and alive but also in a fit condition to process work. For example, by default, Kubernetes will start to send a service its workload traffic as soon as the process running in the container responds to a ping. However, if your app takes a minute or so to ramp up and get started, then your service, despite showing to be alive, won't work even though the process has started. This is important as Kubernetes is scaling up and down instances all the time, so it needs to know when a newly spun app is, in fact, ready to work. By using a readiness probe, Kubernetes knows to wait until the app is fully started and responds to the readiness probe before it sends the service any traffic.

Liveness

Another scenario that takes us beyond keep-alive probes is where your app is running on a pod that is alive but has stopped serving requests. The process, or rather the pod, is showing its state as running, so Kubernetes thinks that everything is fine. As a result, it continues to send requests to the unresponsive app. However, Kubernetes can mitigate this issue by using a liveness probe. With a Liveness probe, Kubernetes will detect that the app is no longer responding and serving requests, and it will restart the pod.

Type of Probes

Readiness and liveness can use three types of probes: HTTP, Command, and TCP:

- **HTTP**: HTTP probes are the most commonly used type of liveness probe. With HTTP probes, Kubernetes pings a URL or path. The app will send an HTTP response as a 200 or 300 response code, which means the app is considered healthy. Otherwise, it is marked as unhealthy.

- **Command probes**: Sometimes, an app does not have the capabilities to handle an HTTP probe; in this case, you will likely go for command probes. The way that the command probe works is that Kubernetes runs a command inside the container, and if the command returns with an exit code 0, then the container is considered healthy. Otherwise, it is marked unhealthy.

- **TCP**: A TCP probe is used when Kubernetes wants to establish whether a service is alive and ready on a specific port. It tries to establish a TCP connection every 10 seconds to the specified port. If it can establish a TCP connection, the container is considered healthy; if it can't, it is considered unhealthy.

With all Liveness probes, there is one critical setting that you need to configure: - `initialDelaySeconds` - `setting`. Remember that with a liveness probe, a failure will cause Kubernetes to restart the pod. Therefore, you will want to ensure that Kubernetes doesn't start sending the probe until the app is ready. Otherwise, Kubernetes will get caught in a loop whereby it constantly restarts a pod, which never gets the chance to be ready.

A rule of thumb is to use the **p99** startup time as the `initialDelaySeconds` -- the **p99** latency is a good representative of practically the worst case. Additionally, our goal, almost always, is to reduce the **p99** latency, or you could just take the average startup time and then add to it a safety buffer. However, as systems age, your app's startup time will typically get slower, so ensure that you update this number.

Exploring some key Kubernetes features

Zero-downtime upgrades

When upgrading your clusters, you must bear in mind that there are masters and nodes in a cluster and both need to be updated, but in different ways. The masters need to be updated first, and then the nodes can follow. With the masters, there is a need to upgrade using the Kubernetes Engine with zero downtime. This is essential today as a cluster cannot be down for any time if it is at all avoidable.

With Kubernetes Engine, seamless upgrades occur because the KGE automatically upgrades the master as point releases become available; however, it usually won't upgrade to a new version (for example, 1.7 to 1.8) automatically. For this type of upgrade, you are provided with the means to run the upgrade to a new version when you are ready. At that time, you can just click on the upgrade master button in the Kubernetes Engine console to initiate the master's upgrade.

However, take note of what it says in the dialog box:

Changing the master version can result in several minutes of control plane downtime. During that period, you will be unable to edit this cluster.

Now, we have to be very careful here and fully understand what state the master and the cluster will be in and what services or apps will be affected by the loss of the master, even for a short time.

When the master is taken down for the upgrade, all the deployments, services, apps, etc. that are running on the cluster will continue to work as expected. However, that is not the full story because there is a catch. Anything that requires interaction with the Kubernetes API stops working. Let's be clear, this is a big deal as everything you do when you interact with the cluster goes through that API. This means the CLI kubectl will not work for the duration that the master is down. What this means is that any tools or applications that use the Kubernetes API to get information about the cluster will stop working, such as dashboards and monitoring and logging tools. Obviously, you also can't make any CLI or Console changes to the cluster while it is being upgraded.

This is, by no means, a zero-downtime upgrade; even if the app keeps working, the cluster is severely compromised. The way you can get zero-downtime is by having **Highly Available (HA)** master-nodes by deploying a Kubernetes Engine regional cluster. This is because the standard `zonal` Kubernetes Engine clusters only have one master node, so they are a single-point-of-failure. If your apps are production or are critical, you should create `regional` clusters as these provide multi-zone, highly available master-nodes. Therefore, if zero-downtime is a necessity, be sure to select the `regional` option when creating your cluster.

As a result of selecting regional, Kubernetes Engine will automatically create your nodes and masters in three zones, putting each of the masters behind a load-balanced IP address. This enables the Kubernetes API to continue to work during an upgrade.

Upgrading nodes with zero downtime

When you contemplate upgrading nodes within a cluster, there are a few different strategies you can use for zero-downtime. There are two that are commonly used and we will want to focus on:

- Rolling updates
- Migration with node pools

Rolling update

You have likely heard of the term rolling updates as it applies to software upgrades. It is one of the most convenient ways to update your cluster nodes with zero-downtime. Indeed, this is the default upgrade mechanism that Kubernetes Engine deploys to update your cluster nodes.

A rolling update works by upgrading each node in a round robin way, one by one. To do this, each node is drained and cordoned; this ensures that there are no active pods running or attempting to connect on that node. In the background, Kubernetes will be concurrently spinning up replacement nodes so that they are prepared to take over. Once drained and cordoned, the node to be replaced is then deleted. The prepared node is then initiated with the updated software version. Once that replacement node is up and running, the next node is drained, cordoned, and updated. This sequence continues until all nodes are replaced with updated ones.

While perform a rolling update is the default method on Kubernetes Engine, it has limitations. One notable thing that is lacking with this procedure is that you have one less active node available to serve requests in your cluster during the upgrade process, but this is easily resolved by pro-actively scaling up your node pool prior to the upgrade. By scaling up with an additional node, you will effectively maintain the normal capacity and scale the node pool back down once the upgrade is done.

The second issue is that although the automated rolling update makes it convenient to use, you don't have any actual control over the process. Similarly, should something go wrong, it can take time to roll back the updates to the last-working-version. This is because you will need to first stop the rolling update and then reverse it using a last-known-working version.

Migration with node pools

A node pool is a group of nodes within a cluster, all of which have the same configuration. When you initially create a cluster, the number of nodes and type of nodes that you specify becomes the default node pool. All nodes in any given node pool are identical to one another. You can create, upgrade, and delete node pools individually without affecting the whole cluster. A single node in a node pool cannot be configured; any changes to the node pool's configuration affect all nodes.

The benefit of using node pools is that you are not working on the *live* node pool to upgrade it as you do with a rolling update. Instead, you create a fresh replacement node pool that has the upgrade. Then, when all the nodes are running, you start shifting workloads over one node at a time. If something goes wrong, you can easily roll back by simply shifting the workloads back. In the following tutorial, we will learn how to do a node-pool migration upgrade.

Tutorial 8.1: Migrating a Monolith to Microservices on Kubernetes Engine

Introduction

Why migrate from a monolithic application to a microservices architecture? Breaking down an application into microservices has the following advantages, and most of these stems from the fact that microservices are loosely coupled:

- The microservices can be independently tested and more easily deployed.

- Microservices can be implemented in different languages and frameworks.

- Microservices can be managed by specialist teams.

- By moving to microservices, each team only needs to know about the APIs of the microservices they are responsible for.

- You can easily design for failure as there are clear boundaries between services.

Some of the disadvantages when compared to monoliths are:

- As a microservice-based app becomes a web of different interconnecting services, the workings of the system can become opaque.

- Unlike the internals of a monolith, microservices communicate over a network, which means they are susceptible to network conditions.

- On a network, it is hard to achieve consistent high levels of performance because of latencies between services.

- The behavior of your system is determined by how well the services mesh together.

Interactive tutorial 8.1: Running Microservices in Google Kubernetes Engine (GKE)

Overview

In this tutorial, we will deploy and run microservices in **Google Kubernetes Engine** (**GKE**). GKE is a fully managed platform to host, scale, and deploy containers. As containers are a handy and portable way of packaging, deploying, and running apps across diverse environments, they are well suited to the microservices architecture, where each microservice can run within its own dedicated container.

For this tutorial, we will start by deploying an existing monolithic sample application to a GKE cluster. Then, we will decompose this monolith one service at a time and deploy these as individual microservices components.

Architecture diagram of the Microservices

The services of interest in our monolith application are the orders, products, and frontend. We will segment the service code and build a Docker image for each microservice using Cloud Build. After that, we will deploy and expose our microservices one at a time on GKE. During this transition process, we will have both our monolith and our microservices running simultaneously. This state will continue until the very end when we are able to switch over completely and delete our monolith.

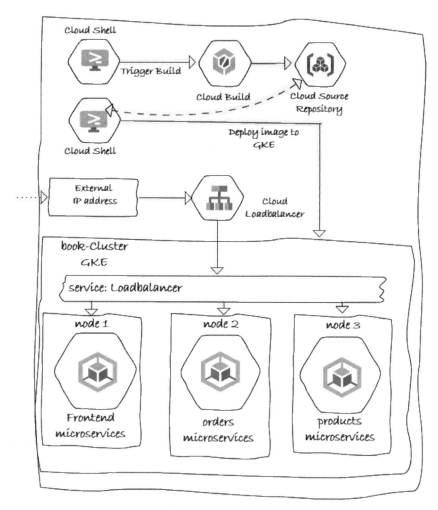

Figure 8.4: *Architecture Diagram of the Microservices*

What you'll learn:

- How to decompose a Monolith to individual Microservices?

- How to create your own Google Kubernetes Engine cluster?

- How to create Docker images using Cloud Build?

- How to deploy Docker images to our Kubernetes cluster?

Step 1: Open Cloud Shell and some environment variables as default; this will make entering commands easier as you will not have to keep entering your **Project_ID**, **Zone**, and **Region**.

```
echo $GOOGLE_CLOUD_PROJECT
```

Command output:

`<PROJECT_ID>`

Step 2: Next, set the default region and zone for your project; use your own or use the US default details:

`gcloud config set compute/zone asia-south2-a`

You can choose your own or use the US defaults as this isn't going to be testing the latency of our app in any way.

Step 3: Clone Source Repository

In this tutorial, we will use a sample monolithic application of a typical e-commerce website. The sample app has a basic landing page, a products page, and an order transaction and history page. To load the monolith application, we will simply clone the source from our Git repo. Then, we can focus on decomposing it into individual microservices and deploying it to GKE.

Run the following commands to clone the git repo to your Cloud Shell instance and change to the appropriate directory. We will also install the NodeJS dependencies so that we can test our monolith before deploying. It may take a few minutes for this script to run:

`cd ~`

`git clone https://github.com/googlecodelabs/monolith-to-microservices.git`

`cd ~/monolith-to-microservices`

`./setup.sh`

This command will clone our GitHub repo, change to the directory, and install the dependencies needed to run our application locally. It may take a few minutes for this script to run.

Step 4: Create a GKE Cluster

1. Before we do anything else, we have to enable the APIs that we will use in this tutorial. In order to ensure the proper APIs are enabled, we run the following command:

   `gcloud services enable container.googleapis.com`

   This command enables the containers API so that we can use Google Kubernetes Engine.

2. Next, we need to build a GKE cluster in which to deploy our monolith and eventually, our microservices. Run the command below to create a GKE cluster named book-website with 3 nodes:

```
gcloud container clusters create book-website  --num-nodes 3
```

It can seem like it takes forever for the cluster to be created, but be patient and when the command has completed, run the following command; and see the cluster's three worker VM instances:

```
gcloud compute instances list
```

You can view your Kubernetes cluster and any related information by navigating to the Kubernetes Engine page in the Google Cloud console. To do this simply, click on the menu button in the top left, then scroll down to find Kubernetes Engine and select and click on **Clusters**. You should see your cluster listed and named book-website.

> **If you have been following along and have created a cluster with the gcloud container clusters create command listed above, the next step is not necessary.**

3. If you have created your cluster using the GCP console or are using an existing Google Kubernetes Engine cluster, you will need to run the following command to retrieve cluster credentials and configure the **kubectl** command-line tool with them:

```
gcloud container clusters get-credentials book-website
```

Step 5: Deploy the Existing Monolith

1. We are first going to deploy our monolith website app as we need to get a monolith application up and running before we can start to demonstrate how to break it down into microservices architecture. Run the following script to deploy a monolith application to our GKE cluster:

```
cd ~/monolith-to-microservices
./deploy-monolith.sh
```

Accessing the Monolith

2. To find the external IP address for our monolith application, run the following command:

```
kubectl get service monolith
```

You should see output similar to the following:

NAME	CLUSTER-IP	EXTERNAL-IP	PORT(S)	AGE
monolith	10.3.251.122	203.0.113.0	80:30877/TCP	3d

> **Behind the scenes, an external load balancer and IP are being provisioned for this, so it will take a few moments. If your output lists the external IP as <pending>, give it a few minutes and try again.**

Once you've determined the external IP address for your monolith, copy the IP address. Point your browser to this URL (such as **http://203.0.113.0**) to check if your monolith is accessible.

You should see the welcome page for the monolithic website, just like in the picture above. The welcome page is a static page that will be served up by the Frontend microservice later. You now have your monolith fully running on Kubernetes!

> **Take a note of the IP or benchmark the link in your browser as you will continue to use it throughout this tutorial. Nonetheless, it saves you from having to run this same command again.**

Rebuild Monolith Config Files

3. Now, we have to rebuild the monolith app as we have changes to be applied:

   ```
   npm run build:monolith
   ```

Step 6: Create Docker Container with Google Cloud Build

In order to deploy our app to our Kubernetes cluster, we have to first put it into a container:

```
cd ~/monolith-to-microservices/monolith
gcloud builds submit --tag gcr.io/${GOOGLE_CLOUD_PROJECT}/monolith:2.0.0
.
```

When the cloud build process is complete and it has been pushed to the Container Registry, we are ready to deploy our app.

- **Deploy Container to GKE**

  To deploy container from the Container Registry to KGE, we use the following command:

  ```
  kubectl set image deployment/monolith monolith=gcr.io/${GOOGLE_
  CLOUD_PROJECT}/monolith:2.0.0
  ```

You can verify that your application is now servicing requests using the new **Orders** microservice by going to the monolith application in your browser and navigating to the **Orders** page. The expected result is that now all the order IDs should end in a suffix **-MICROSERVICE**, as shown here:

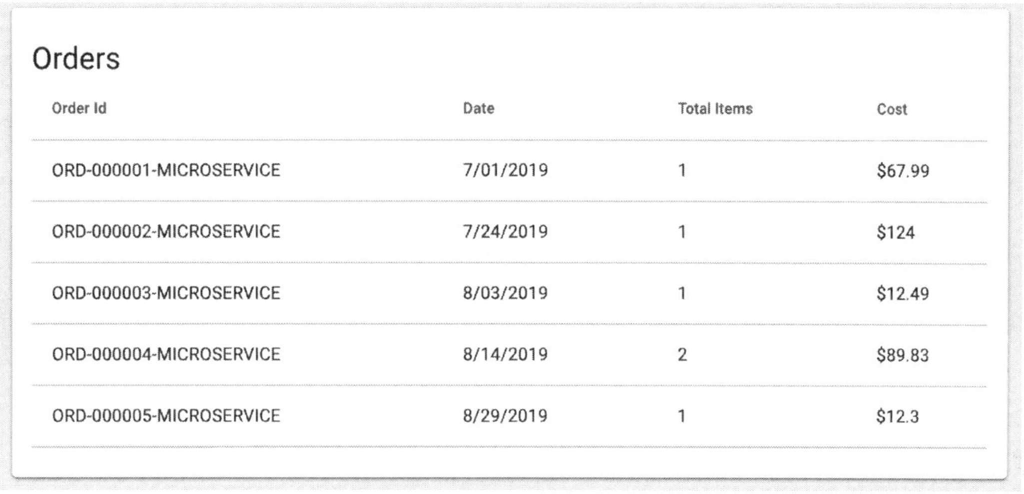

Orders

Order Id	Date	Total Items	Cost
ORD-000001-MICROSERVICE	7/01/2019	1	$67.99
ORD-000002-MICROSERVICE	7/24/2019	1	$124
ORD-000003-MICROSERVICE	8/03/2019	1	$12.49
ORD-000004-MICROSERVICE	8/14/2019	2	$89.83
ORD-000005-MICROSERVICE	8/29/2019	1	$12.3

Figure 8.5: Order Microservice output

Step 7: Migrate Products to Microservice

1. Create `New Products Microservice`

   The next step is to repeat the process by migrating the `Products service`. You will follow the same broad process we used for the orders microservice.

   Run the following commands to build a Docker container using Cloud Build for the products microservice, and then deploy your container and expose it to via a products Kubernetes service.

2. Create Docker Container with Google Cloud Build:

   ```
   cd ~/monolith-to-microservices/microservices/src/products
   gcloud builds submit --tag gcr.io/${GOOGLE_CLOUD_PROJECT}/
   products:1.0.0 .
   ```

3. Deploy the products Container to the GKE cluster:

   ```
   kubectl create deployment products --image=gcr.io/${GOOGLE_CLOUD_
   PROJECT}/products:1.0.0
   ```

4. Expose the GKE Products Container:

   ```
   kubectl expose deployment products --type=LoadBalancer --port 80
   --target-port 8082
   ```

5. Discover the newly assigned public IP of our products service. You will do this the same way we did for our orders service, by typing in the following command:

   ```
   kubectl get service products
   ```

Output:

```
NAME          CLUSTER-IP        EXTERNAL-IP       PORT(S)           AGE
products      10.3.251.122      203.0.113.0       80:30877/TCP      3d
```

Make sure to take a note of the external IP address for the next step when we reconfigure our monolith to point to our newly deployed Products microservice.

6. Reconfigure the Monolith

Use the nano editor to replace the local URL with the IP address of our new Products microservices:

```
cd ~/monolith-to-microservices/react-app
nano .env.monolith
```

When the editor opens, your file should look like this:

```
REACT_APP_ORDERS_URL=http://<ORDERS_IP_ADDRESS>/api/orders
REACT_APP_PRODUCTS_URL=/service/products
```

Replace the **REACT_APP_PRODUCTS_URL** to the new format while replacing with your Product microservice IP address so that it matches the following:

```
REACT_APP_ORDERS_URL=http://<ORDERS_IP_ADDRESS>/api/orders
REACT_APP_PRODUCTS_URL=http://<PRODUCTS_IP_ADDRESS>/api/products
```

Press *Ctrl + O*, press *Enter*, and then press *Ctrl + X* to save the file in the nano editor.

You can now test your new microservice by navigating to the URL you just configured in this file. The web page launched should display a JSON response from our Products microservice.

Next, we will:

1. Rebuild our monolith to decompose the frontend code.

2. Repeat the cloud build process to build the container for the frontend microservice.

3. Redeploy it to our GKE cluster.

Run the following commands to complete these steps.

7. Rebuild Monolith Config Files to decompose the frontend code:

```
npm run build:monolith
```

8. Create Docker Container with Google Cloud Build:

```
cd ~/monolith-to-microservices/monolith
```

```
gcloud builds submit --tag gcr.io/${GOOGLE_CLOUD_PROJECT}/
monolith:3.0.0 .
```

9. Deploy Container to GKE:

```
kubectl set image deployment/monolith monolith=gcr.io/${GOOGLE_
CLOUD_PROJECT}/monolith:3.0.0
```

You can now verify that your microservice enabled application is servicing the new Products microservice by going to the monolith application in your browser and navigating to the Products page. All the product names should be prefixed by MS.

Step 8: Migrate frontend to Microservice

The final stage in the migration process will be to move the Frontend code out of the monolith and into a container that contains the frontend microservice; only then will we be in a position to shut down the monolith app. After this step is completed, we will have successfully migrated our monolith to an all-microservices architecture.

1. Create New Frontend Microservice

You will follow the same procedure as the last two steps, but this time you will create a new frontend microservice. When we rebuilt our monolith app, we updated our config to still point to our monolith application, but now we will need to reuse that same config for our Frontend microservice. To be able to handle this transition, we will have to copy across the config so that the service transitions seamlessly.

To do this, run the following commands to copy the monolith config files to the Frontend microservice codebase:

```
cd ~/monolith-to-microservices/react-app
```

```
cp .env.monolith .env
```

```
npm run build
```

Once this command completes successfully, you should be pointing to the new microservice frontend. With that step completed, you can follow the same process as the previous steps to build, deploy, and expose the frontend microservice.

Run the following commands to build a Docker container, deploy your container, and expose it to via a Kubernetes service.

2. Create Docker Container with Google Cloud Build:

```
cd ~/monolith-to-microservices/microservices/src/frontend
gcloud builds submit --tag gcr.io/${GOOGLE_CLOUD_PROJECT}/
frontend:1.0.0 .
```

3. Deploy Container to GKE:

```
kubectl create deployment frontend --image=gcr.io/${GOOGLE_CLOUD_
PROJECT}/frontend:1.0.0
```

4. Expose GKE Container:

```
kubectl expose deployment frontend --type=LoadBalancer --port 80
--target-port 8080
```

Delete the Monolith.

5. Now that all our microservices are up and running and serving requests, we can proceed to shut down and then delete our monolith application. Note that in an actual real-world migration, this would not be so easy as we would also have to propagate the DNS changes, etc. to get our existing domain names to point to the new frontend microservices for our application.

Run the following commands to delete our monolith:

```
kubectl delete deployment monolith
kubectl delete service monolith
```

Step 9: Test your work

To verify that everything is working, check that your old IP address from your monolith service is not working and that your new IP address from your frontend service hosts the new application. To see a list of all the services and IP addresses, use the following command:

```
kubectl get services
```

The expected output should look similar to the following:

NAME AGE	TYPE	CLUSTER-IP	EXTERNAL-IP	PORT(S)
frontend TCP 12m	LoadBalancer	10.39.246.135	35.227.21.154	80:32663/
kubernetes 18d	ClusterIP	10.39.240.1	<none>	443/TCP
orders TCP 31m	LoadBalancer	10.39.243.42	35.243.173.255	80:32714/
products TCP 21m	LoadBalancer	10.39.250.16	35.243.180.23	80:32335/

Once you've determined the external IP address for your Frontend microservice, copy the IP address. Point your browser to this URL (such as **http://203.0.113.0**) to check if your frontend is accessible.

Step 10: Migration with node pools

Instead of upgrading the *active* node pool as you would with a rolling update, you can create a fresh node pool, wait for all the nodes to be running, and then migrate workloads over one node at a time.

For example, suppose a Kubernetes cluster has three VMs and you can see the nodes with the following command: **kubectl get nodes**

NAME	STATUS	AGE
gke-cluster-1-default-pool-7d6b79ce-0s6z	Ready	3h
gke-cluster-1-default-pool-7d6b79ce-9kkm	Ready	3h
gke-cluster-1-default-pool-7d6b79ce-j6ch	Ready	3h

1. Then, you would need to create a new node pool. To create the new node pool with the name **pool-two**, you would run the following command:

    ```
    gcloud container node-pools create pool-two
    ```

    You can also use the Console GUI to create a new node pool if you prefer. Now, if you check the nodes, you will notice that there are three more nodes with the new pool name:

NAME	STATUS	AGE
gke-cluster-1-pool-two-9ca78aa9-5gmk	Ready	1m
gke-cluster-1-pool-two-9ca78aa9-5w6w	Ready	1m
gke-cluster-1-pool-two-9ca78aa9-v88c	Ready	1m
gke-cluster-1-default-pool-7d6b79ce-0s6z	Ready	3h
gke-cluster-1-default-pool-7d6b79ce-9kkm	Ready	3h
gke-cluster-1-default-pool-7d6b79ce-j6ch	Ready	3h

    However, the pods are still on the old nodes! Let's move them over.

2. Drain the old pool

    The first thing we have to do is to drain the old pool so that there is a graceful transition when we move work to the new node pool. To do this, we will move over one node at a time in a rolling fashion.

    First, we will cordon off each of the old nodes. This will prevent new pods from being scheduled onto them; to do this, we use the command:

    ```
    kubectl cordon <node_name>
    ```

3. Once all the old nodes are cordoned, they can no longer receive scheduled pods; so, any new pods can only be scheduled onto the new node pool. This means that it is safe for you to start to remove pods from the old node pool, and Kubernetes will automatically schedule them to migrate over to the new node pool.

> **Warning: Make sure your pods are managed by a `ReplicaSet`, `Deployment`, `StatefulSet`, or something similar. Standalone pods won't be rescheduled.**

Run the following command to drain each node. This deletes all the pods on that node:

```
kubectl drain <node_name> --force
```

After you drain a node, make sure the new pods are up and running before moving on to the next one.

If you encounter any issues during the migration, simply uncordon the old pool and then cordon and drain the new pool. The pods will automatically get rescheduled back to the old pool.

4. Delete the old pool

When all the pods have been successfully rescheduled onto the new node pool, you can tidy up and safely remove the old node pool. Replace **default-pool** with the pool you want to delete:

```
gcloud container node-pools delete default-pool
```

You have successfully updated all your nodes!

Congratulations! You have completed the tutorial.

By using Kubernetes Engine, you can keep your Kubernetes cluster up to date with just a few kubectl commands. In production, the recommended way is to use Kubernetes Engine regional clusters for their high-availability masters and their automatic node upgrades for a hassle-free upgrade experience. If you need the extra control for your node updates, using node pools gives you that control without foregoing the advantages of a managed Kubernetes platform that Kubernetes Engine provides.

Conclusion

In this chapter, we looked at potential cluster design patterns and compared big clusters with little ones. We also compared multi-purpose vs specific clusters and compared their operational characteristics. You learned that there is no best practice. Each deployment is different, and you should design your clusters to fit your requirements. You were also introduced to key cluster features such as health checks and autoscalers. Finally, you learned, through the interactive tutorial, how to decompose a monolith application and deploy it as microservices on your Kubernetes cluster. You learned about many things during this challenging exercise, such as building, deploying, and exposing services as containers. You also learned how to push these new containers to the container registry and roll out revisions in a zero-downtime process.

In the next chapter, we will build upon the good work and progress you made today and use the knowledge gained here to investigate how to optimize and automate the scaling of the Kubernetes cluster for both performance and cost-optimization.

CHAPTER 9

Optimizing Kubernetes Cluster and Apps in GKE

Kubernetes clusters in Google Kubernetes Engine are fully managed in auto-pilot multi-region mode and to a lesser extent, you retain some flexibility over node and node pool configuration in the standard single region deployment. Nonetheless, regardless of which mode you choose, Google retains control of the all-important Kubernetes control plane, leaving only access to the GKE API for the customer. This is normally a good thing as GKE can abstract much of the administrative complexity away from the customer, allowing them to concentrate on their application. That's the theory, but that's not always how it works in practice.

In this chapter, we will look at ways to run GKE to leverage its performance and resiliency features so that you can get the most from your cloud native applications. We will look at preparing and optimizing the application for GKE as well as many of the performance and resiliency techniques that enable you to efficiently execute your workloads on GKE in a high-performance, cost-optimized way. You will learn about application design and optimization, application health checks, scalability, and auto-recovery, among other tips and tricks to help you cost-optimize your GKE applications.

Structure

We will cover the following topics in this chapter:

- Analyzing and matching your application's capabilities to Kubernetes
- Optimizing Kubernetes applications on GKE
- The four Kubernetes scaling dimensions
- Disruption budgets
- Interactive tutorial 9.1: Autoscaling deployments with GKE workload metrics

Objectives

When you have finished going through this chapter, you will have gained all the knowledge and skills required to optimize your application to run on a Kubernetes Engine. You will know how to analyze and if necessary, refactor your applications to get the best from Kubernetes performance and scalability. You will also know how to identify metrics and apply disruption budgets.

Optimization starts with the application

An issue with fully managing any service, but particularly true in the case of GKE, is that it is so effective in removing the complexity of the technology away from the customer that it leaves them in a state of willful ignorance. They now expect GKE, as if by magic, to run any applications they throw at it, flawlessly and in an optimal state.

The reality, however, is that GKE is only as good as the application it is being asked to run. GKE can only run an application that is mot optimized for running on a cluster in a best effort but sometimes haphazard manner. On the other hand, you can be confident that a Kubernetes optimized application will be seamlessly and transparently run in close to an optimized state.

The reason for this is that GKE, especially if constructed using autopilot mode, is designed to do all the heavy lifting and let you focus on your application. However, you are not handing over management control completely as GKE still expects you to configure the details of how your app can run. Therefore, best results on application performance occur when you fine-tune your application and your GKE configuration to work together. Interestingly, unlike most systems where application performance and cost optimization are found at opposite ends of the scale, they are tightly entwined with GKE. Setting up Kubernetes for the best performance for your application will also deliver the most value and reduce resource wastage.

Running Cloud Native apps on GKE

It's often the case that developers think that GKE will manage their application autonomously and flawlessly. However, when the application doesn't perform as expected on the cluster in production, they start looking at optimizing GKE through monitoring GKE metrics, health-check responses, adjusting node machine types, tinkering with autoscaling, and more. They rarely, if ever, start with a ground up review of the application; that is where you should always start.

Understanding apps and resources

To understand application design, you need to start with the resource side and then progress toward getting the application and Kubernetes working well together.

The best way to start is to understand the details of your application and how it is designed to respond to increased or fluctuating demand. Monitoring can help understand what resources are used as demand increases, but only in a realistic model. Therefore, test your application in a GKE cloud deployment, not on your laptop. Additionally, ensure that the app under test is stable and that the measurement tools are consistent before you start testing. A suggested test lab scenario would look something like this:

1. Ideally, start running your app as a single pod replica in the same zone and region as production.

2. Test the application under load without any autoscaling.

3. Monitor and benchmark its responses to fluctuating traffic and how it responds under high and low loads.

4. Run multiple iterations of tests to verify the consistency of each result.

5. Use that data to configure resource requests and limits.

6. Test your app again with cluster autoscaling and horizontal or vertical autoscaling.

7. Now, test large, rapid spikes in demand to see how your app responds.

8. Monitor, analyze, and store the test data; there is a lot you can do with this information.

*No matter which tool you use to stimulate demand, always test in the region or zone where your app will be running in production. Not only does it replicate the real-world latency conditions, but it also lets you understand all the performance and timing details of how your app scales under those conditions.

Setting resource requests and limit ranges

Earlier in step 4 of our test plan, we mentioned setting the resource requests and limit ranges.

You want to set resource requests so that the required amounts are always available, and you want to use limit ranges to control resources so that you don't overshoot and consume too many. When setting these, remember that a resource request defines the lower boundary; it sets how many resources your application requires to run. On the other hand, a resource limit, sets the upper boundary, i.e., the maximum number of resources that your app is permitted to use.

Setting the correct requests and limits on resources will help Kubernetes figure out how to schedule your pods. This alone ensures that they don't use up all the host node's resources. To complicate matters, you will also need to understand how individual resources, being different technologies, may respond to requests and limits; this will take some research on your part.

An example of setting resource requests and limits to different strategies is when you set your memory limit equal to your memory requests, bringing the lower and upper boundaries at the same level. That said, you may set your CPU limit to be much higher than your CPU requests, maybe even leave it unbounded.

The reason for two different strategies is based on how GKE and the underlying technologies work together. For example, Kubernetes can always throttle the CPU that your pods are using down to the requested amount if the CPU resources are in high demand elsewhere. However, it cannot use this approach for memory. Instead, Kubernetes will need to take the drastic action of shutting down pods if there's too much demand on the memory.

Autoscaling

Another heavily relied upon but poorly understood feature of GKE is its ability to auto scale to meet fluctuating demands. However, as we just learned, autoscaling has to work within the configured resource availability range set by the lower and upper boundaries, i.e., the resource requests and limits. Therefore, autoscaling will not happen if you do not have sufficient resources available.

In addition, any form of autoscaling might not be very useful if your application isn't designed to be capable of scaling in response to demand. If we consider how Kubernetes uses auto scaling in practice, we can see whether an app is suitable. Hence, vertical autoscaling will only prove to be effective if your application can actually use the node's increased resources. Similarly, horizontal autoscaling is only effective if your app can make effective use of the additional instances now running concurrently on the new pod replicas.

Moreover, indiscriminate horizontal auto scaling can make matters worse. If the actual performance bottleneck is on something like a shared back-end database, then spinning up more pods will likely worsen the problem rather than making it better:

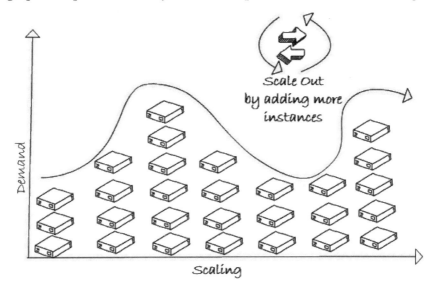

Figure 9.1: *Autoscaling vs variation of demand*

However, if you find that your app can't scale, for example, single-threaded apps or apps that can only run a limited number of concurrent processes may not get much value out of the extra resources, then you might need to consider refactoring to a microservices architecture or another structure that works well with Kubernetes. On the other hand, if your app can scale, the next step is to look at optimizing the spinning up and spinning down times.

Autoscaling has another obvious constraint when you think about it, and that is how it handles spinning up new containers. Whenever the cluster autoscaler creates a new node, that node must download the base image for each app that it'll run. Obviously, the smaller your image is, the faster a node can download it and get started. However, that is often overlooked when developers are building containers for their app. Instead of using the smallest available image and adding only dependencies that are strictly required, they often take the safer top-down approach and bundle everything into the container. However, the increase in the startup tasks like loading libraries, classes, and caches can significantly increase the amount of time between creation and when it is ready. This will almost always cause some disruptions to service as requests will fail while your app is spinning up.

Conversely, you may also want to make sure that your app can shut down gracefully. You may think shutdown is easy, but it's not. If your workload has issues when shutting down, it can again lead to unacceptable delays and disruptions in service.

Technically, when a pod is going to be shut down, it should receive a **SIGTERM**, which is a signal to do some cleanup tasks in preparation for shutdown. This is because, to fail gracefully, your pod must still finish all the active requests and any new ones that come in. However, since it can take a bit of time for Kubernetes to update where those requests are going to be delivered, you will want to update your readiness probe to fail quickly to prevent further requests from coming into the pod.

In addition to all that, your pod should run any cleanup steps like persisting in-memory state. If you're not handling **SIGTERM** or can't because your app is using a system that you don't actually have control over, like a web server or a reverse proxy, you can even put a sleep command in for a few seconds to postpone the **SIGTERM**.

There's also a configuration to give your pods a bit more time to shut down, called **terminationGracePeriodSeconds**, but it's not advisable to change this unless you feel you really need it. By default, it's set to 30 seconds, but it can go all the way up to 10 minutes before the cluster autoscaler forcibly terminates it.

We will discuss these techniques in detail later in the chapter, but for now, it's enough to understand that quick startups and proper shutdowns let your autoscalers work more reliably and efficiently. The more specific you configure GKE to match your application's requirements, the better it will work.

Pod disruption budgets

Setting a pod disruption budget is a technical (fancy) term for when you set the minimum number of pod replicas to keep your app running. Kubernetes will try to respect that number as it handles rollouts, upgrades, and autoscaling. Setting a pod disruption budget ensures that your app will almost always have enough replicas to keep running effectively. However, take note of the almost in the previous sentence. Be aware that it's not a guarantee as unexpected things can happen. That said, it's still a best practice to define pod disruption budgets for every application.

Liveness and readiness probes

In addition to pod disruption budgets, you'll want to make sure that you're correctly setting readiness and liveness probes for your app. We have covered liveness and readiness probes in earlier chapters, but let's take a quick recap.

Kubernetes will use the readiness probe to know if each pod is not just alive but in a state where it is ready to handle traffic. The readiness probe is used to mitigate the issue with race conditions between traffic delivery and the setup time.

Liveness probes are used to tell if the pod is still alive and working. This allows GKE to know if your application is working correctly and when it gets stuck or deadlocked, in which case Kubernetes knows to restart it. However, working out the correct values for these probes requires deep knowledge about and testing of your application.

Using these probes in your application is critical as they are key features that you can configure so that Kubernetes can optimize working with your app. Readiness ensures the quickest startup condition, whereas liveness ensures efficient, responsive, and speedy autoscaling.

The following are some best practices for working with liveness and readiness probes:

- Always define readiness probes for every container.

- Know when your application is actually ready. For example, if your app depends on a cache being loaded, the readiness probe should say the pod is ready only after that cache has been loaded.

- If your app doesn't need any startup time, define a simple readiness probe, such as just returning - **HTTP 200**.

- Make sure the code for your probes is as simple and isolated as possible so that there are no blockers when Kubernetes is requesting the status.

- Your probe logic should try to avoid remote services. Additionally, if you have to use something remote, try to test against the simplest and hopefully fastest one.

- Configure retries.

The last of those best practice tips considers configuring retries. This is a useful tip for all services, especially in a full microservices environment. A service call could fail for any number of reasons, like a network failure or rate limits. When there's a failure, it usually makes sense to retry the request in case there was some glitch in the network. However, if it's persistent, you may end up sending lots of useless requests and potentially, even overwhelming the destination. Therefore, always use exponential backoff to protect against retries overwhelming the service when working with or designing your own services.

Exponential back off just adds a bit of time, a penalty, after each failure and then increments the size of the penalty on subsequent failures; this continues exponentially. It might seem complicated, but when calling a service in your app, you can implement exponential backoff logic yourself, use a library, or even use Istio or Anthos Service Mesh, which support a proxy level retry that handles it all for you. On the other hand, if your application has the service being called, you can rate limit requests from the same caller to force exponential backoff.

You'll also want to prepare your application for handling retry requests so that you don't end up duplicating the handling of identical requests, say in a financial transaction, for example. Of course, the specific details of how to implement that will depend on your application.

Nonetheless, these are some things to keep in mind when working with your application, and the key here is to have your application and GKE work together as efficiently as possible.

Batch and serving applications

The best way to maximize cost/performance optimization for Google Kubernetes Engine is to make sure your app and GKE are configured for each other. Here are some suggestions for achieving that goal, but as always, it's the deep knowledge about your application that can help you focus on which cost-optimization techniques will give you the most impact.

Applications can be categorized broadly into two groups: batch and serving.

Batch apps

A general definition of a Batch application is that it has predefined and scheduled work to do. As a result, batch applications tend to be less concerned about startup time and usually aren't time-sensitive overall. Examples of batch apps are monthly payroll calculations or low-priority data transformations.

The advantage of batch jobs is that these jobs are scheduled, so the cluster autoscaler can spin up new nodes when required and remove them when the job is done. Even better, node auto provisioning will work best with batch workloads since it can figure out optimal resources and then create a new node pool. Additionally, it doesn't need to worry as much about spikes in demand as data volume may differ from one job to another but data ingress delivery can remain constant.

Here's some other tips for working with batch workloads:

- The cluster autoscaler can delete empty nodes faster when it doesn't need to also restart the pods on those nodes.

- Splitting up your applications into dedicated node pools and using labels and selectors or taints and tolerations can help the cluster autoscaler scale quicker and avoid resource wastage.

- There's even an optimize-utilization profile for the cluster autoscaler that focuses on maximizing utilization rather than keeping spare resources ready. It scales down a lot quicker, which can help aggressively minimize extra resources.

- Plus, you can separate different applications with node auto-provisioning, along with using taints and tolerations.

- Node pools will then be better sized for each application, once again, optimizing your resource usage.

- Don't forget that preemptible VMs are much cheaper to use, but only if your apps are fault-tolerant and much less time-sensitive.

Serving apps

The opposite of batch applications are serving apps. A serving app, unlike a batch app, needs the ability to scale rapidly in response to spikes in demand; for example, a retail website on major shopping holidays.

In order to handle the sudden increases in demand, it's good for serving workloads to be lean and optimized to work best with GKE. The quicker GKE can respond to resource levels and the quicker the pods can start up, the more efficient autoscalers are at responding to demand.

If you have a serving app that requires resources with a long provisioning time, like GPUs, it makes sense to overprovision and have resources at the ready before the demand spikes. Indeed, you might want to consider using pause pods to help you scale ahead. Overprovisioning and keeping your apps lean may seem like a contradiction to basic cloud practice. Nonetheless, optimizing both of those will give you the most cost-efficient way to handle high-demand spikes.

There are other tips available for handling spikey traffic in GKE, such as using **NodeLocal DNSCaching**. If you're running a version with **kube-dns**, it responds to increased demand by creating new instances, but that takes time. Instead of just increasing the **kube-dns** replicas in your configuration, add the NodeLocal DNSCache add-on so that each node will store a DNS cache, which helps **kube-dns** require less resources and saves the overall time for lookups.

Another network config tip is to try to optimize round-trip request time. One tip for lowering this is to use container-native load balancing. Rather than sending requests to instance groups and then pods, container-native load balancing allows requests to go directly to the pod by creating what's called a **Network Endpoint Group**.

When these are configured, GKE Ingress will handle the creation of the L7 load balancer, along with forwarding rules, healthchecks, firewalls, and more. However, if you go down the container-native load balancing path, you'll want to start failing your readiness probe as soon as you receive a **SIGTERM**. This way, the load balancers will know to stop forwarding new requests to your app immediately.

Not only does container-native load balancing provide improved load balancing and more efficient autoscaling, but it can also enable you to use other tools, like Traffic Director and other Google Cloud services.

Optimizing Kubernetes applications on GKE

In the remainder of this chapter, we will take a deep dive into the technical aspects of the tools we discussed in the overview. We will look into all the **Google Kubernetes Engine (GKE)** features and options, and we will discuss the best practices for running cost-optimized applications on GKE and to take advantage of the elasticity provided by Google Cloud.

As Kubernetes gains widespread adoption, a growing number of enterprises are using multi-tenant Kubernetes clusters for their workloads. What this means is that a single cluster might be running multiple applications that belong to different teams, departments, or environments. We discussed the pros and cons of this in the previous chapter and learned how the multi-tenancy model provided by Kubernetes lets companies manage a few large clusters instead of many smaller ones. As a result, they get benefits such as more appropriate resource utilization, simplified management control, and reduced fragmentation.

However, the multi-tenancy model is not without its drawbacks; for example, fast-growing Kubernetes clusters tend to experience a disproportionate increase in cost. This happens due to the companies overlooking their lack of cloud readiness in their rush to embrace cloud-based solutions like Kubernetes. This inevitably leads to their legacy applications becoming unstable during autoscaling. The common fix was considered throwing resources at the problem. Such over-provisioning of their clusters, which was necessary in an elastic environment, unavoidably leads to considerably higher CPU and memory allocation than required.

A cloud native approach to this conundrum would have been a more appropriate response based upon the foundation of building cost-optimized cloud native applications that forces you to better understand the environment that your applications are running in, in this context, the GKE environment.

A cost-optimized Cluster

In order to achieve low cost, high performance, and application stability, you must correctly set or tune some features and configurations (such as autoscaling, health-checks, and readiness and liveness probes). However, all that is for nothing if your application cannot leverage these features. Therefore, depending on the workload type and your application's requirements, you must apply different configurations in order to gain benefits from hosting on the GKE platform.

GKE cost-optimization features and options

Optimizing GKE and cloud native applications for performance and cost relies heavily on understanding and correctly configuring and fine-tuning GKE autoscaling.

Autoscaling is the strategy that GKE uses to let applications scale to meet the demands of fluctuating traffic and unpredictable loads. In GKE, a correctly configured and matched application will seamlessly grow and shrink with demand. When matched, GKE and the application will work together to optimize performance and bolster resilience even against the most challenging spikey loads. However, there is another benefit to autoscaling, which comes in the billing. Google Cloud customers pay only for what they need by minimizing infrastructure uptime. In other words, autoscaling saves costs by:

- Making workloads and their underlying infrastructure start before demand increases.

- Shutting them down when demand decreases.

Four Kubernetes scaling dimensions

In Kubernetes, your workloads are containerized applications that are running inside Pods, and the underlying infrastructure, which is composed of a set of Nodes, must provide enough computing capacity to run the workloads.

A Kubernetes environment has four scalability dimensions:

- Infrastructure
- Workload
- Pods
- Nodes

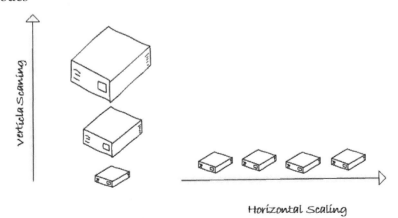

Figure 9.2: Vertical vs Horizontal Scaling

Essentially, the workload and infrastructure scale horizontally by adding and removing Pods or Nodes, and they can scale vertically by increasing and decreasing Pod or Node size. GKE handles these autoscaling scenarios by using the following techniques:

- **Horizontal Pod Autoscaler (HPA)** for adding and removing Pods based on utilization metrics.

- **Vertical Pod Autoscaler (VPA)** for sizing your Pods.

- Cluster Autoscaler for adding and removing Nodes based on the scheduled workload.

- Node auto-provisioning for dynamically creating new node pools with nodes that match the needs of users' Pods.

None of these techniques should be new to you, but we still need to discuss these GKE autoscaling capabilities in detail and cover other useful cost-optimized configurations for both serving and batch workloads.

Horizontal Pod Autoscaler (HPA)

The **Horizontal Pod Autoscaler (HPA)** is meant for scaling applications. A common belief is that it works automatically and autonomously, running in Pods based on metrics that express load. However, the reality is that HPA needs to be configured and set up to match your application. To trigger HPA, you can configure it to respond to either CPU utilization or other custom metrics (for example, requests per second). When configured correctly and if resource request and resource limits allow, HPA adds and deletes Pods replicas. As HPA creates additional identical pods, it is called horizontal scaling; this strategy is best suited for stateless workers that can spin up almost instantaneously to react to usage spikes and then shut down gracefully to avoid workload instability and unnecessary costs.

HPA setting the thresholds

To get HPA to kick into action, you must configure a target utilization threshold, expressed in percentage. There are many custom metrics on which you can base when to automatically trigger scaling. In this example, let's set the target CPU utilization to 80%. That leaves our workload with a 20% CPU buffer for handling the existing and new requests that arrive while the new replicas are spinning up. There are a couple of points to consider here:

- A small buffer prevents early scale-ups, but it can overload your application during spikes.

- A large buffer causes resource waste, increasing your costs.

- As always, it's a trade-off and the best target is application-specific.

- You must consider the buffer size to be enough for handling requests for 2 or 3 minutes during a spike.

- Even if you can guarantee that your application can start up instantaneously, this extra time is required when Cluster Autoscaler adds new nodes to your cluster or when Pods are throttled due to a lack of resources.

The following are a few best practices for enabling HPA in your application:

- Ensure size-appropriate resource requests and limits that match your applications needs.

- Set your target utilization to provide enough buffer so that it can handle requests during a spike.

- Make sure your application starts as quickly as possible and shuts down according to Kubernetes expectations.

Vertical Pod Autoscaler (VPA)

In comparison to HPA, which adds and deletes Pod replicas for rapidly reacting to usage spikes, **Vertical Pod Autoscaler (VPA)** observes Pods over time and gradually finds the optimal CPU and memory resources required by the Pods. By setting the right resources to match your application, VPA can provide stability and cost efficiency. However, if your Pod resources are too small, your application can either be throttled or can fail due to out-of-memory errors. If your resources are too large, you will inevitably create waste and unnecessary larger bills. The benefits of VPA are that it can be used when you don't know the application's actual resource requests. In addition, VPA is meant for both stateless and stateful workloads, which are not suitable for handling by HPA.

In practice, the VPA monitors and detects that the Pod's target resource is consistently running at its limits, so it recreates the Pod with larger resources. Fortunately, the opposite also happens when the Pod is consistently underutilized—a scale-down is triggered.

VPA can work in three different modes:

- **Off**: In this mode, also known as the recommendation mode, VPA does not apply any change to your Pod, but recommendations are calculated and can be inspected in the VPA object.

- **Initial**: VPA assigns resource requests only at Pod creation and never changes them later.

- **Auto**: VPA updates CPU and memory requests during the life of a Pod. That means, the Pod is deleted and CPU and memory are adjusted, and then a new Pod is started.

If you plan to use VPA, the best practice is to start with the Off mode for pulling VPA recommendations. Make sure it's running for 24 hours, ideally one week or more, before pulling recommendations. Then, consider switching to either Initial or Auto mode only when you feel confident.

Follow these best practices for enabling VPA, either in **Initial** or **Auto** mode, in your application:

- Don't use VPA if you need to handle sudden spikes in traffic; use HPA instead.

- Make sure your application can grow vertically.

- Set minimum and maximum container sizes in the VPA objects to prevent the autoscaler from making significant changes when your application is not receiving traffic.

- Don't make abrupt changes, all at once. Some changes may require a new deployment, new label set, and new VPA object.

When considering using Auto mode, make sure you also follow these practices:

- Make sure your application can be restarted while receiving traffic.

- Add a **Pod Disruption Budget** (**PDB**) to control how many Pods can be taken down at the same time.

Some best practices common to both HPA And VPA

- Make sure your application can start as quickly as possible and can shut down gracefully.

- Set meaningful readiness and liveness probes.

- Make sure that your Metrics Server is always up and running.

- Inform clients of your application that they must consider implementing exponential retries for handling transient issues.

- Consider using node auto-provisioning along with VPA so that if a Pod gets large enough to fit into the existing machine types, Cluster Autoscaler provisions larger machines to fit the new Pod.

*Important Note: Do not mix HPA and VPA in initial or auto mode. You can safely mix them when VPA is running in recommendation mode (OFF).

Cluster Autoscaler

The **Cluster Autoscaler (CA)** automatically resizes the underlying computer infrastructure. The purpose of the CA is to provide additional nodes for Pods that don't have a place to run in the cluster and then remove any failing or under-utilized nodes. CA is cost-optimized for infrastructure, so if there are two or more node types in the cluster, CA chooses the least expensive one that fits the given demand.

CA, unlike HPA and VPA, does not rely on load metrics or configurable thresholds. Instead, CA is based on scheduling simulation and declared Pod requests. It's considered to be a best practice to always enable CA whenever you are using either HPA or VPA. Doing this will ensure that if your Pod autoscaling needs more capacity, your underlying infrastructure can grow accordingly.

Additionally, CA can automatically add and subsequently remove compute capacity to handle traffic spikes. However, to do this, you must define a PDB for all your applications. This is particularly important at the CA scale-down phase as PDB controls the number of replicas that can be taken down at a time.

Some specialist Pods, such as the metrics-server or kube-dns, cannot be restarted by any autoscaler even when they cause some temporary disruption, so CA cannot delete the node they are hosted on. For example, Pods using local storage won't be restarted. However, you can change this behavior by defining PDBs for these system Pods and by setting the annotation: `"cluster-autoscaler.kubernetes.io/safe-to-evict": "true"` - for Pods using local storage that are safe for the autoscaler to restart. Moreover, consider running long-lived Pods that can't be restarted on a separate node pool so that they don't block scale-down of other nodes.

If your workloads are resilient to nodes restarting inadvertently and to capacity losses, you can save more money by creating a cluster or node pool with preemptible VMs. For CA to work as expected, Pod resource requests need to be large enough for the Pod to function normally. If resource requests are too small, nodes might not have enough resources, and your Pods might crash or have troubles during runtime:

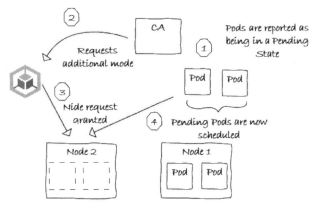

***Figure 9.3**: Autoscaling at work with Cluster Autoscaler (CA)*

The following is a summary of the best practices for enabling CA in your cluster:

- Use either HPA or VPA to autoscale your workloads.

- Make sure you are following the best practices described in the chosen Pod autoscaler.

- Size your application correctly by setting appropriate resource requests and limits or use VPA.

- Define a PDB for your applications.

- Define PDB for system Pods that might block your scale-down, for example, kube-dns. To avoid temporary disruption in your cluster, don't set PDB for system Pods that have only 1 replica (such as metrics-server).

- Run short-lived Pods and Pods that can be restarted in separate node pools so that long-lived Pods don't block their scale-down.

- Avoid over-provisioning by configuring idle nodes in your cluster. For that, you must know your minimum capacity—for many companies, it's during the night—and set the minimum number of nodes in your node pools to support that capacity.

- If you need extra capacity to handle requests during spikes, use pause Pods, which are discussed in Autoscaler and over-provisioning.

Node auto-provisioning

Node auto-provisioning (**NAP**) is a mechanism of Cluster Autoscaler that has the job of automatically adding new node pools and managing their size. Without node auto-provisioning, GKE starts new nodes only from within the set of user-created node pools. However, with node auto-provisioning, GKE can now create and delete new node pools automatically.

A characteristic of Node auto-provisioning is that it tends to reduce resource waste by dynamically creating node pools that best fit with the scheduled workloads. However, the autoscale latency can be slightly higher when new node pools need to be created.

The following are best practices for enabling node auto-provisioning:

- Follow all the best practices of Cluster Autoscaler.

- Set minimum and maximum resource sizes to prevent NAP from making significant changes in your cluster when your application is not receiving traffic.

- When using Horizontal Pod Autoscaler for serving workloads, consider reserving a slightly larger target utilization buffer because NAP might increase autoscaling latency in some cases.

Choose the right machine type

Beyond autoscaling, other configurations can help you run cost-optimized kubernetes applications on GKE. This section discusses choosing the right machine type.

Preemptible VMs

Preemptible VMs (PVMs) are Compute Engine VM instances that last a maximum of 24 hours and provide no availability guarantees. PVMs are up to 80% cheaper than standard Compute Engine VMs, but we recommend that you use them with caution on GKE clusters. PVMs on GKE are best suited for running batch or fault-tolerant jobs that are less sensitive to the ephemeral, non-guaranteed nature of PVMs. Only use PVMs for stateless apps. Be warned that stateful and serving workloads must not use PVMs.

Whatever the workload type, you must deploy PVMs with caution and due diligence, and you must pay attention to the following constraints:

- Pod Disruption Budget might not be respected because *preemptible nodes can shut down inadvertently*.

- There is no *guarantee that your Pods will shut down gracefully* once node preemption ignores the Pod grace period.

- It might take several minutes for GKE to detect that the node was *preempted and that the Pods are no longer running*, which delays rescheduling the Pods to a new node.

Finally, PVMs have no guaranteed availability, meaning that they can stock out easily in some regions.

- **E2 machine types**: E2 machine types (E2 VMs) are cost optimized VMs that offer you 31% savings as compared to N1 machine types. E2 VMs are suitable for a broad range of workloads, including web servers, microservices, business-critical applications, small-to-medium sized databases, and development environments.

- **Select the appropriate region**: Where you run your GKE clusters affects both performance and cost. Due to many factors, cost varies per computing region, so make sure you are running your workload in the least expensive option but close enough so that latency doesn't affect your customer. Also consider whether your workload needs to copy data from one region to another as that will be an additional networking charge.

- **Review small development clusters**: For small development clusters, such as clusters with three or fewer nodes or clusters that use machine types with limited resources, you can reduce resource usage by disabling or fine-tuning a few cluster add-ons. This practice is especially useful if you have a cluster-per-developer strategy and your developers don't need things like autoscaling, logging, and monitoring. However, because of the cost per cluster and simplified management, we recommend that you start using a multi-tenancy cluster strategy.

- **Review inter-region egress traffic in regional and multi-zonal clusters**: The types of available GKE clusters are single-zone, multi-zonal, and regional. The best cost-optimization comes with single zone clusters. However, because of the high availability benefits of having nodes across zones, regional and multi-zonal clusters are well suited for production environments. However, you are charged by the egress traffic between zones. For production environments, you should monitor the traffic load across zones and improve your APIs to minimize it.

- **Batch workloads**: Batch workloads are concerned with eventual work that is commonly tolerant to some latency at job startup time. This tolerance gives Cluster Autoscaler space to spin up new nodes only when jobs are scheduled and take them down when the jobs are finished.

  The first recommended practice is to separate batch workloads in different node pools by using labels and selectors and taints and tolerations. The rationale is the following:

  o Cluster Autoscaler can delete empty nodes faster when it doesn't need to restart pods. As batch jobs finish, the cluster speeds up the scale-down process if the workload is running on dedicated nodes that are now empty. Consider configuring CA's optimize-utilization profile to further improve the speed of scale-downs.

  o Some Pods cannot be restarted, so they permanently block the scale-down of their nodes. These Pods, which include the system Pods, must run on different node pools so that they don't affect scale-down.

The second recommended practice is to use node auto-provisioning to automatically create dedicated node pools for jobs with a matching taint or toleration. This way, you can separate many different workloads without having to set up all those different node pools.

Serving workloads

Serving workloads must respond to bursts or spikes in traffic as quickly as possible. Your application must be prepared to handle them. Problems in handling such spikes are commonly related to one or more of the following:

- Applications not being ready to run on Kubernetes, for example, apps with large image sizes, slow startup times, or non-optimal Kubernetes configurations.

- Applications dependent on infrastructure that takes a long time to be provisioned, like GPUs.

- Autoscalers and over-provisioning not being appropriately set.

Prepare cloud-based Kubernetes applications

Some of the best practices in this section can save money by themselves. However, because most of these practices are intended to make your application work reliably with autoscalers, we strongly recommend that you implement them.

Understand your application capacity

When you plan for application capacity, you will need to discover how many concurrent requests your application can handle, how much CPU and memory it requires, and how it responds under heavy load. Most developers don't know these capacities, so we recommend you to test how your application behaves under pressure.

Make sure your application can grow vertically and horizontally

Ensure that your application can grow and shrink so that you can choose to handle traffic increases either by adding more CPU and memory or adding more Pod replicas. Unfortunately, some applications cannot grow as they are single threaded or limited by a fixed number of workers or subprocesses, which makes scaling impossible without a complete refactoring of their architecture.

Set appropriate resource requests and limits

To set your application capacity, you can set what to configure in your container resources. Resources in Kubernetes are mainly defined as CPU and memory (RAM). When you've correctly set resource requests, Kubernetes scheduler can use them to decide which node to place your Pod on. This guarantees that Pods are being placed in suitably sized nodes so that you experience better stability and less resource waste. Moreover, defining resource limits helps ensure that these applications never use all the available underlying infrastructure provided by the computing nodes.

A good practice for setting your container resources is to use the same amount of memory for requests and limits and a larger or unbounded CPU limit. You can also use VPA in recommendation mode to help you determine CPU and memory usage for a given application. VPA provides such recommendations based on your application usage, so we recommend that you enable it in a production-like environment to face real traffic. VPA status then generates a report with the suggested resource requests and limits, which you can statically specify in your deployment manifest.

Make sure your container is as lean as possible

When you run applications in containers, it's important to follow some practices for building those containers. When running those containers on Kubernetes, some of these practices are even more important because your application can start and stop at any moment. This section focuses mainly on the following two practices:

- **Have the smallest image possible**. It's a best practice to have small images because every time Cluster Autoscaler provides a new node for your cluster, the node must download the images that will run in that container. The smaller the image, the faster the node can download it.

- **Start the application as quickly as possible**. Some applications can take minutes to start because of class loading, caching, and so on. When a Pod requires a long startup, your customers' requests might fail while your application is booting.

Consider these two practices when designing your system, especially if you are expecting bursts or spikes. Having a small image and a fast startup helps you reduce scale-ups latency. Consequently, you can handle traffic increases better without worrying too much about instability.

Understand the metrics server

Metrics server is the source of the metrics used by autoscaler. Metric server retrieves metrics from kubelets and exposes them through the Kubernetes metrics API. In turn, both HPA and VPA use these metrics to determine when to trigger autoscaling.

For the health of GKE autoscaling, you must have a healthy Metrics server. With GKE metrics-server deployment, a resizer nanny is installed, which makes the Metrics Server container grow vertically by adding or removing CPU and memory according to the cluster's node count. In-place update of Pods is still not supported in Kubernetes, which is why the nanny must restart the metrics-server Pod to apply the new required resources.

Follow these best practices when using metric server:

- Pick the GKE version that supports metrics-server resize delays. You can confirm it by checking whether the metrics-server deployment YAML file has the scale-down-delay configuration in the metrics-server-nanny container.

- Monitor metrics-server deployment. If metrics server is down, it means no autoscaling is working at all. You want your top-priority monitoring services to monitor this deployment.

Consider using Anthos Policy Controller

Anthos Policy Controller (APC) is a Kubernetes dynamic admission controller that checks, audits, and enforces your clusters' compliance with policies related to security, regulations, or arbitrary business rules. The APC uses constraints to enforce your clusters' compliance. For example, you can install, in your cluster, constraints for many of the best practices already discussed. This way, deployments are rejected if they don't strictly adhere to your Kubernetes practices. Enforcing such rules helps avoid unexpected cost spikes and reduces the chances of workload instability during autoscaling.

Design your CI/CD pipeline to enforce cost-saving practices

APC helps you avoid deploying non-compliant software in your GKE cluster. However, you should be enforcing such policy constraints much earlier in your development cycle. You should check during pre-commit checks, pull request checks, or in delivery workflows as this practice lets you find and fix misconfigurations quickly. It also helps you understand what you need to pay attention to by creating guardrails.

Spread the cost-optimization culture

Many organizations create abstractions and platforms to hide infrastructure complexity from you. This is a common practice in companies that are migrating their services from virtual machines to Kubernetes. Sometimes, these companies let developers configure their own applications in production. However, it's not uncommon to see developers who have never touched a Kubernetes cluster.

The practices we recommend in this section don't mean that you should stop doing abstractions at all. Instead, they help you view your spending on Google Cloud and train your developers and operators on your infrastructure. You can do this by creating learning incentives and programs where you can use traditional or online classes, discussion groups, peer reviews, pair programming, CI/CD and cost-saving gamifications, and more. For example, in the Kubernetes world, it's important to understand the impact of a 3GB image application, a missing readiness probe, or an HPA misconfiguration.

Interactive tutorial 9.1: Autoscaling deployments with GKE workload metrics

This tutorial demonstrates how to automatically scale your GKE workloads based on custom metrics emitted by your application (for instance, the number of accounts actively logged in or the number of HTTP requests).

You use the GKE workload metrics pipeline to collect metrics emitted by your application, send them to Cloud Monitoring, and then use them to power the HPA.

Objectives

This tutorial covers the following tasks:

1. How to deploy an example application that emits Prometheus-style metrics?

2. How to deploy a PodMonitor resource to scrape the metrics from your application and publish them to Cloud Monitoring?

3. How to deploy the Custom Metrics Adapter?

4. How to query workload metrics using the Kubernetes Custom Metrics API?

5. How to deploy a HPA resource to scale your application based on the workload metrics scraped from your application.

Before you begin

Take the following steps to enable the Kubernetes Engine API:

1. Visit the Kubernetes Engine page in the Google Cloud Console.

2. Create or select a project.

3. Wait for the API and related services to be enabled. This can take several minutes.

4. Make sure that billing is enabled for your Cloud project.

Step 1. Setting up your environment

1. To create a new cluster with workload metrics enabled, use the following command but replace the following:

   o **CLUSTER_NAME**: The name of your cluster.

   o **PROJECT_ID**: The ID of your Google Cloud project.

   o **ZONE**: Choose a zone that's closest to you.

```
gcloud beta container clusters create CLUSTER_NAME \
  --project=PROJECT_ID \
  --zone=ZONE \
  --monitoring=SYSTEM,WORKLOAD
```

Step 2. Deploying an example application that emits Prometheus-style metrics

Download the repository containing the application code for this tutorial:

```
git clone https://github.com/papa107/kubernetes-engine-samples.git
cd kubernetes-engine-samples/workload-metrics
```

The example application for this tutorial generates two metrics and exposes them via a built-in Prometheus endpoint at **localhost:1234/metrics**:

- **example_requests_total**: A counter of requests generated by the application polling itself.

- **example_random_numbers**: A histogram of randomly generated numbers.

The repository contains a Kubernetes manifest to deploy the application to your cluster:

workload-metrics/manifests/workload-metrics-deployment.yaml

Deploy the application on your cluster:

```
kubectl create namespace gke-workload-metrics
kubectl apply -f manifests/workload-metrics-deployment.yaml
```

After waiting a moment for the application to deploy, all Pods reach the Ready state:

```
kubectl -n gke-workload-metrics get pods
```

Output:

```
NAME                                READY   STATUS    RESTARTS   AGE
workload-metrics-74fb6c56df-9djq7   1/1     Running   0          1m
```

Step 3. Deploying a PodMonitor resource to scrape the metrics from the example application

To collect the metrics emitted from the example application, you need to create a PodMonitor custom resource. The repository contains a Kubernetes manifest to deploy the PodMonitor to your cluster:

workload-metrics/manifests/workload-metrics-podmon.yaml

Deploy the PodMonitor on your cluster:

```
kubectl apply -f manifests/workload-metrics-podmon.yaml
```

Step 4. Deploying the Custom Metrics Adapter

The Custom Metrics Adapter lets your cluster send and receive metrics with Monitoring.

1. Grant your user the ability to create required authorization roles:

```
kubectl create clusterrolebinding cluster-admin-binding \
  --clusterrole cluster-admin --user "$(gcloud config get-value
  account)"
```

2. Deploy the new resource model adapter on your cluster:

```
kubectl apply -f manifests/adapter_new_resource_model.yaml
```

3. Check that the custom metrics adapter is deployed and in the ready state:

```
kubectl -n custom-metrics get pods
```

Output:

```
NAME                                          READY  STATUS   RESTARTS  AGE
custom-metrics-stackdriver-adapter-6d4fc94699-zqndq  1/1 Running 0     2m
```

Querying workload metrics using the Kubernetes Custom Metrics API

You can use the Kubernetes Custom Metrics API to check whether your workload metrics are visible to GKE. GKE workload metrics are exported to Monitoring with the prefix workload.googleapis.com. The Kubernetes Custom Metrics API server does not support the **/** character in metrics paths, so you need to replace all **/** characters with **|**.

Therefore, you must use **workload.googleapis.com|example_request_total** for the metric name. After waiting a few moments for the applications metrics to be sent to Monitoring, run the following command to query for the **workload. googleapis.com|example_request_total** metric:

```
kubectl get --raw   "/apis/custom.metrics.k8s.io/v1beta2/namespaces/
gke-workload-metrics/pods/*/workload.googleapis.com|example_requests_
total"
```

Expected output - Similar to this:

```
{"kind":"MetricValueList","apiVersion":"custom.metrics.k8s.io/v1beta2",

  "metadata":{"selfLink":"/apis/custom.metrics.k8s.io/v1beta2/
namespaces/

  gke-workload-metrics/pods/%2A/workload.googleapis.com%7Cexample_
requests_total"},
```

```
  "items":[{"describedObject":{"kind":"Pod","namespace":"gke-workload-
metrics",

  "name":"prom-example-74fb6c56df-9djq7","apiVersion":"/__
internal"},"metric":

  {"name":"workload.googleapis.com|example_requests_
total","selector":null},"timestamp ":

  "2021-08-23T10:48:45Z","value":"1199m"}]}
```

Deploying a HorizontalPodAutoscaler object

Once you see the **workload.googleapis.com|example_requests_total** metric in the response payload of the Custom Metrics API in the previous step, you can deploy a HPA to resize your deployment based on that metric.

The repository contains a Kubernetes manifest to deploy the HPA to your cluster:

workload-metrics/manifests/workload-metrics-hpa.yaml

This HPA sets the minimum pod replicas to 1 and the maximum to 5. It scales your deployment to ensure that the average value of **workload.googleapis. com|example_request_total** across all pods is 1.

Deploy the **HorizontalPodAutoscaler** on your cluster:

```
kubectl apply -f manifests/workload-metrics-hpa.yaml
```

Observing HorizontalPodAutoscaler scaling up

You can periodically check the number of replicas in your deployment and watch it scale to 5 replicas by running the following command:

```
kubectl -n gke-workload-metrics get pods
```

Output:

```
NAME                                READY   STATUS    RESTARTS   AGE
  workload-metrics-74fb6c56df-9djq7   1/1     Running   0          5m
  workload-metrics-74fb6c56df-frzbv   1/1     Running   0          7m
  workload-metrics-74fb6c56df-h26rw   1/1     Running   0          8m
  workload-metrics-74fb6c56df-kwvx9   1/1     Running   0          10m
  workload-metrics-74fb6c56df-vvtnn   1/1     Running   0          11m
```

You can also inspect the state and activity of the HPA by running the following command:

```
kubectl -n gke-workload-metrics describe hpa workload-metrics-hpa
```

Clean up

To avoid incurring charges to your Google Cloud account for the resources used in this tutorial, either delete the project that contains the resources, or keep the project and delete the individual resources.

Summary of optimization's broad steps

Let's take a quick look at the summary and start with the culture before we move the cost discussion toward the architecture:

- The idea is that we want to help teams understand how their work affects cost, even if you've built an abstraction layer between teams and their clusters.

- Use monitoring to better understand how applications use resources, and then implement quotas, requests, and limits that make sense for your apps while also minimizing any wasted costs.

- From machine families to preemptable, you can optimize your infrastructure to improve performance and save money.

- The cloud's dynamic resources help make autoscaling an efficient strategy, but configuring it correctly for your applications is vital to handling spikes in demand while also balancing performance with cost.

- Make sure that you spend time to increase your application's compatibility with Kubernetes and configure GKE for your application for the best results.

- Cost optimization is all about increasing the business value for what you get out of what you're spending on the cloud.

- Saving costs can be a part of that, but these tips are more about getting the maximum return out of costs and optimizing your usage when building, scaling, and deploying on GKE.

Conclusion

In this chapter, you learned about optimization of the Kubernetes cluster for performance and cost. You learned that performance and cost are often coupled as an efficient finetuned cluster is also a high performance and cost-effective solution. You also understood that the heart of optimization lies with matching your application to Kubernetes and making sure it is Kubernetes ready. You looked at several scaling mechanisms and performance probes to determine which ones best suit what purpose. Finally in the interactive tutorial, you learned how to automate the scaling of clusters depending on the workload metrics.

In the next chapter, we will look at scaling up to support a fully automated modern CI/CD process on our Kubernetes platform.

## CHAPTER 10

Deploying a CI/CD Pipeline With Kubernetes and Cloud Build

In the previous chapters, you learned about Kubernetes and clusters. In this chapter, we will build upon the Kubernetes platform for what has become one of the modern-day purposes for such a resilient platform: **Continuous Integration and Continuous Deployment (CI/CD)**.

Structure

We will cover the following topics in this chapter:

- Why CI/CD?
- GitOps
- Understanding Continuous Integration
- Understanding Continuous Delivery/Deployment
- Interactive tutorial – GitOps-style CI/CD with Cloud Build

Objectives

After going through this chapter, you will be familiar with the DevOps practice of continuous integration and continuous delivery, which is also process automation in action. You will be able to describe each stage in the CI/CD process and also be able to design and deploy your own pipeline in GCP.

Why CI/CD?

Kubernetes reinforces DevOps goals of a fully automated CI/CD pipeline while also supporting and enabling new workflows that align with microservices architectures. Indeed, containers, VMs and microservices architectures were the solution to many problems, but ironically, they also became a problem in themselves. Subsequently, Kubernetes became the platform solution to many of the new management and administration problems that arose with container and microservices-based application architectures, i.e., the container swarm.

DevOps seemed to be the organizational solution as it brought with it the advent of containerization and Kubernetes. It didn't just blur the boundaries between development and operations, it literally tore them down.

The adage *"you wrote it you support it"* became commonplace, which led to software-driven tooling and automation processes. This brought the software engineers kicking and squealing into the deployment process. However, there was still a disconnect between developers and operators due to their incentives.

Developers are incentivized by finding new features and functions, which drives rapid deployments of new versions of code. Operators, on the other hand, are incentivized by stability and predictability, and the fewer upgrades, the better.

Development teams have never wanted visibility into operations deployments; they are happy to work on their laptops with all the latest SDKs and libraries. Operations have always worked to a strict data center rule book: one app per server and standard builds per server OS. Consequently, developers and operations teams have always been troublesome due to missing dependencies, incorrect versions, or the wrong platform. Consequently, everyone is nervous about deployments due to inconsistent environments, versions, and dependencies causing maintenance windows to shift, leading to downtime, and in the worst cases, causing projects to fail.

DevOps had a trick up its sleeve though: automation of Continuous Integration and Continuous Deployment or, as its better-known, CI/CD. As a result of the huge success of the automated CI/CD pipelines, Kubernetes and DevOps have become synonymous with CI/CD. Indeed, it has been CI/CD that has removed much of the friction between Development and Operations. Strict control of the automation process and the enforcement of policy has enabled developers to focus on application coding rather than building infrastructure, and it also introduces Operations engineers into the world of development, giving both a taste of life on the other side of the wall.

Why Kubernetes?

Well, there are eight key features that make Kubernetes an ideal platform for DevOps engineers, enabling them to set up, configure, and manage their containerized applications through **Continuous Integration and Continuous Delivery (CI/CD)** pipelines:

- **Use building blocks**: When you are designing your application, you will be planning for each function to be represented as a self-contained logical block. This method works well with microservices architecture and Kubernetes. This is because in Kubernetes, you can deploy your app using these preconfigured blocks (functions) to Pods. As the smallest programmable unit within Kubernetes, Pods represent a group of one or more containers, typically of the same type and function, that will share storage and network resources. Assigning logical functionality as a building-block to a Pod allows you to build out your application by interconnecting pods at the Kubernetes level. Developers typically build out pods that contain only single-purpose containers, there have been use cases where closely-related or coupled containers have been housed together in a pod to take advantage of the close connectivity and build a type of service mesh.

  By using building blocks along with a service mesh approach, it becomes easier to visualize and map services and functions into multiple containers running in the same pod. In theory at least, this should deliver efficiency and performance gains.

- **Simplified service discovery**: A big differentiator between microservice approach and the monolith is the speed of inter-service communication or rather, the lack of it. In a monolithic and microservices application, all the different services will have their own single purpose, so they need to intercommunicate to perform any complex task. The monolith, however, has all their services self-contained within the application and running on the same physical platform. This means that services are readily discovered, and communication is via internal RPC application calls, which facilitates fast and efficient communication. In a microservices architecture, on the other hand, microservices that need to talk to each other will typically have to do so across a network—this is particularly true with Kubernetes. The way around this is for you to use the same Kubernetes namespace. This can help performance as discovering and then requesting a service is faster since Kubernetes figures out how to route the request for you; this makes managing microservices in Kubernetes easier.

- **Centralized and declarative model**: Despite the fact that, in most of our tutorials, we have used imperative methods like kubectl to instruct

Kubernetes what we want it to do, it is recognized that the best way to work with Kubernetes is via declarative methods. A Declarative model gets the best out of Kubernetes as it is designed to operate on the concept of the desired state. For example, you describe a desired state and then pass that to Kubernetes, which will then try to work out how to achieve that state for you. Consequently, Kubernetes is best when working with configuration (YAML) files. These config files will describe the desired state you want Kubernetes to achieve. The config files are best stored in a Git repository; this way, you can control revisions and see any time the configuration changes.

Kubernetes can also help with configuration management as it does the heavy lifting when configuring your application containers that are running in your cluster or their network endpoints. Moreover, Kubernetes can also set up and configure your environment for you. It does this using a ConfigMap, which you use to define environment variables and any specific dependencies such as configuration files needed by your application. Similarly, Kubernetes has a method for managing confidential objects, which it calls secrets. These secrets will typically contain confidential information that is required to allow your application to run.

- **Real-time source of truth**: Traditionally, prior to DevOps and the CI/CD pipeline, deploying new apps or versions was a stressful and difficult manual process. Today's automated CI/CD pipelines make continuous delivery of products seem very easy. Running manual scripts could be tricky, especially if something went wrong and you had to try to troubleshoot the failed process. However, deploying apps to Kubernetes can be done by anybody. Furthermore, you can deploy and check on the delivery status using Kubernetes' *Run on Kubernetes* with just a few clicks. If something goes wrong, you can access the build and deployment history through the logs to immediately determine the failing step in the process. This is what we mean by a single real-time source of truth, it is having instant access to the complete deployment history.

- **API rollout history**: As we have just seen, the Kubernetes API provides you with a way to surface real-time issues about a deployment's status. This provides the means for any developer on the team with access to the cluster to explore and discover what's happening with the delivery. They will be able to view all the end status of the commands that were run, thereby identifying the problem and perhaps even resolving the issue. All this is done through the audit log, which is the one-stop place for viewing changes between deployments and gives a chance to roll back to any precious last-known-working versions of the app.

Simple health check capability

Keeping track of the system's health is a critical process in your application's lifecycle. This is especially true during the deployment phase where things can go unexpectedly wrong. In the past, when applications were deployed into production, they very often did not have an automatic kill or restart process that would kick in if the application crashed or hung. Kubernetes resolves this issue as it has automatic health checks deployed by default, and if an application fails to respond to health checks, Kubernetes will automatically restart it.

Kubernetes doesn't just monitor your application to see if it is alive, it also checks whether it is responsive and in a condition that is ready to accept workloads. Kubernetes makes it simple to configure several types of health checks for your application, but generally, you check the application's health in one of the following two ways:

- **The Liveness probe**: This health check is applied to an application to determine its current health as well as to track if it fails, i.e., goes from a healthy state to an unhealthy state. If the application fails to respond or indicates a failed response, Kubernetes will restart your application.

- **The Readiness probe**: This is an interesting probe as it checks to see if an application is actually in a state where it is ready to accept traffic. An application may be alive and running but still not fully initiated, so sending it a workload would be pointless. Kubernetes determines whether the application is indeed ready to accept a workload before it sends it any traffic. This is to ensure that a new pod is given sufficient time to allow new containers to be spun up, running, and healthy before it sends them a workload.

Both liveness and readiness probes are useful tools, and Kubernetes makes them easy to use.

Rolling updates and native rollback

Another key deployment feature of Kubernetes is its ability to do rolling updates with native rollback. The problem this solves is that traditionally, if you wanted to deploy an application into production, the process required the server to upload the latest version code and then restart your application. If something went wrong, you would need to upload the last-working-version of the code and restart the application, causing downtime. Instead, Kubernetes does a deployment rollback that has no downtime.

Kubernetes 1.2 and all subsequent versions use a declarative manifest, which is a document containing everything that will be delivered in the deployment. The manifest file details the version of the software image to be used as well as the number of replicas. The manifest-based configuration enables better CD workflows and evolving best practices with Kubernetes and CI/CD in the organization.

Resilience

Granting Kubernetes, the autonomy to shut down and restart nodes in a cluster may be seen as risky. However, even though Kubernetes has the capability to shut down and spin up nodes in a cluster as it deems fit, it does so in a manner likely to reduce any downtime. Kubernetes performs a shut down and restart process by starting to spin up new replacements before it shuts down any existing application containers. Furthermore, you can configure Kubernetes to store the last few changes so that you can revert to previous deployments with a single Kubernetes command.

Simplified monitoring

Monitoring is the cornerstone of security, so it is a critical process; this is especially true when we consider Kubernetes clusters. Due to the perceived complexity of a cluster infrastructure, it might seem counter-intuitive to suggest that Kubernetes makes monitoring your applications easier. This is because Kubernetes will ensure that all your applications are running in a healthy state in consistent pods and correct deployments. This enforces consistency of deployment and of operation, which then makes it easier for monitoring tools to track and detect any abnormal behavior.

With regard to monitoring, GKE is natively integrated with Google Cloud Operations suite (formerly Stack Driver), which provides it with logging and monitoring services for GKE observability. GKE, however, also works alongside Prometheus, which is an open-source monitoring tool that has gained popularity among the cloud-native community. Prometheus provides the advanced monitoring and alerting capabilities for the GCP, and it is tightly integrated with Kubernetes.

For example, when Prometheus monitors a Kubernetes cluster, its focus is on a few key components, such as the Kubernetes nodes (these are the underlying servers), the Kubernetes system deployments, and the application itself.

Aligns with business objectives

When undertaking any major project or initiative in the organization, it is essential to ensure that it aligns with the organizations business goals. This is true with DevOps and CI/CD initiatives as aligning with the organizations goals and culture is the best path to success. Hence, you should adopt a CI/CD pipeline strategy that is aligned to the priorities and practices of the organization. That will determine what processes to improve, develop, and automate and what platform stacks to use.

The best way to get the low-hanging-fruit results is to focus on the existing business priorities and align your plans and objectives for DevOps and CI/CD with them. It can be an ideal time to focus on the CI/CD pipeline when new applications are being developed. This is when you might want to consider if there is a need for ongoing feature development.

Let the system engineers implement CD

Implementing a CI/CD pipeline is always going to be tricky, even in a cloud environment, as continuous deployment or delivery takes a lot of scripting, which, in turn, requires a good knowledge of the computing (cloud) architecture and solid pre-requisite knowledge of the application's specifications and requirements. Thus, this is a job for the engineers.

It might seem educational and even democratic to allow your team's developers, particularly in a DevOps environment, to run their own CI/CD tools. Unfortunately, developers always find the most convenient path around a rule.

Kubernetes and CI/CD a divine combo

Kubernetes has many features that make it ideal for CI/CD:

- With Kubernetes, builds become a lot faster. Setting up a CI/CD pipeline on top of a Kubernetes cluster will speed up your release lifecycle, enabling you to release multiple times a day, and let your team iterate quickly. Instead of spinning up entirely new servers, your build process is quick, lightweight, and straightforward.

- A good CI/CD workflow should include a strong test suite. While not unique to Kubernetes, a containerized approach can make tests more straightforward to run as Kubernetes simplifies CI/CD.

- Kubernetes' zero-downtime deployment capability relieves a lot of the administration stress, making scheduled downtime a lot easier.

- As part of a rolling update, Kubernetes spins up a set of new pods concurrently with the running pods. When the new pods are healthy and up and running, Kubernetes deletes the old ones. The tests and health checks can prevent bad code from reaching production.

Complementary tools

CI/CD tools and practices are still evolving with the advent of cloud-native deployments on Kubernetes. As a result, we have seen several useful DevOps tools emerge. It's worth highlighting a few DevOps tools that were built for the purpose of cloud-native applications:

- **Draft**: This targets developer workflows with an easy-to-use UI. For example, a few CLI commands is all it takes for Draft to containerize and deploy an application to Kubernetes.

- **Helm**: This is a package manager that simplifies deploying applications to Kubernetes. Deployment configurations for projects are available in *charts*.

- **Skaffold**: This is a standard CI/CD workflow with an option to build and deploy code to a Kubernetes development environment each time the code changes locally.

- **Spinnaker**: This is a cloud-native pipeline management tool that supports integrations with all the major cloud providers: AWS, Azure, Google Cloud Platform, and OpenStack.

Today, Kubernetes is chosen instead of other orchestration tools as it is the best container deployment and management solution available.

The Promise of GitOps

Software file systems are complex, and when developers collaborate in projects to develop code, then coordinating updates is a problem as changes from different developers can be hard to track and even incompatible.

The practice of CI was created to address these problems. CI follows the principle that repeatable action through automation can remove many pain points by creating rapid feedback loops that ensure developers can effectively work in small batches. As a result, CI enables teams to produce high-quality software to reduce the cost and increase the productivity of development teams.

How to implement CI in GitOps?

When your organization practices CI, your developers integrate all their work into the main version of the code base (known as trunk or main) on a regular basis. A set of automated tests is run both before and after the merge in order to validate that the changes don't introduce any regression bugs. If these automated tests fail, the team stops what they are doing to fix the problem.

CI ensures that the software is always in a working state and that developer branches don't diverge significantly from trunk. The benefits of CI are significant as it leads to higher deployment frequency, more stable systems, and higher quality software.

The key elements in successfully implementing continuous integration are:

- Each commit should trigger a build of the software

- Each commit should trigger a series of automated tests that provide feedback in a few minutes

To implement these elements, you need the following:

- **An automated build process**: The first step in CI is to have an automated script that creates packages that can be deployed to any environment. The packages created by the CI build should be authoritative and used by all downstream processes. These builds should be numbered and repeatable. You should run your build process successfully at least once a day.

- **A suite of automated tests**: If you don't have any tests, then you need to start by writing a handful of unit and acceptance tests that cover the high-value functionality of your system. Make sure that the tests are reliable, inspire confidence, and can run quickly. Your tests should run successfully, and the developers should get feedback from them daily.

- **A CI system that runs the build and automated tests on every check-in**: The system should also make the test status visible to the team. For example, you can use klaxons or traffic lights to indicate when the build is broken.

- **Continuous integration** also includes two other practices, which are also predictive of higher software delivery performance:

  o The practice of trunk-based development in which developers work off trunk/mainline in small batches. They merge their work into a shared trunk/mainline at least daily, rather than working on long-lived feature branches.

  o An agreement that when the build breaks, fixing it should take priority over any other work.

Creating maintainable automated unit tests is complex. A good way to solve this problem is to practice **test-driven development (TDD)**, which ensures developers write code that's modular and easy to test.

Objections to CI

As described earlier, CI can require that your developers break up large features into smaller incremental steps that can be integrated frequently into a trunk. When teams switch to using small steps, it can take longer to get the large features completed. However, in general, you want to be able to get changes reviewed, integrated, tested, and deployed as quickly as possible. The CI process results in software development and delivery that is faster and more stable when the changes are small and self-contained.

Despite these objections, helping software development teams implement continuous integration should be the number one priority for any organization wanting to start the journey to continuous delivery.

Common pitfalls

The following are some common pitfalls that prevent wide adoption of CI:

- Not putting everything into the code repository. Everything that's needed to build and configure the application and the system should be in your repository.

- Not fully automating the build process.

- Not triggering quick tests on every change.

- Not fixing broken builds right away.

- A key goal of CI is having a stable build from which everyone can develop. If the build can't be fixed in a few minutes, the change that caused the build to break should be identified and reverted.

- Having tests that take too long to run. The tests should not take more than a few minutes to run, with an upper limit of about 10 minutes max.

- Not merging into the trunk often enough. Many organizations have automated tests and builds but don't enforce a daily merge into trunk. This leads to long-lived branches that are much harder to integrate, and to long feedback loops for the developers.

Measuring CI

Gathering some key metrics allows you to optimize your processes. This leads to better CI practices and shorter feedback loops for your developers. The trick is knowing what to measure.

GitOps-style continuous delivery with Cloud Build

The goal of automating the deployment process is to develop a process that can deploy your software into production with just the push of a button. Traditionally, this final step has been done manually, whereas deployment into staging and testing has been automatic. However, automation of the deployment process is considered to be critical in reducing the risk of production deployments. Providing an autonomous automated process is also deemed crucial for receiving feedback on your application; it is also essential as it allows quality teams to do comprehensive testing after changes come about and before the application reaches production.

An automated deployment process will typically have these inputs:

- Packages created by the continuous integration (CI) process (these packages should be deployable to any environment, including production).

- Scripts to configure the environment, deploy the packages, and perform tests.

- Environment-specific configuration information.

In a GitOps-style continuous deployment model, the storing of the scripts and configuration information in version control should be considered mandatory. Your deployment process should download the packages only from a trusted source code repository (for example, Artifact Registry or your CI tool's built-in repository).

The scripts usually perform the following tasks:

- Prepare the target environment, perhaps by installing and configuring any necessary software or by starting up a virtual host from a pre-prepared image in a cloud provider such as Google Cloud.

- Deploy the designated packages.

- Perform any deployment-related tasks such as running database migration scripts.

- Perform any required configuration tasks.

- Perform the deployment test to check whether all required external services are reachable, and that the system is working as intended.

Implementing an automated deployment process

When you design your automated deployment process, you may well want to follow these best practices:

- Use the same tried and tested deployment process for each environment, including deploying into production. Adherence to the rule will ensure that you have tested the deployment process several times across the different stages of development, staging, testing, etc. before you use it to deploy to production.

- You should allow anyone to deploy code to any environment on-demand in a fully automated fashion. If it isn't just a click of a mouse or a press of a button, then don't have a fully automated deployment process.

- Use the same packages for each environment. This rule determines that you should not include environment-specific configurations within the package. That way, you know that the packages you are due to be deploying to production are exactly the same as the ones that you have worked on and tested.

- Make sure that you can recreate the environment state from information stored in version control. This rule helps ensure that deployments are repeatable and can be restored in a deterministic way.

Ideally, you will want to have a tool that you can use autonomously to make deployments. It will be capable of recording which builds are currently in each environment, and it will record the output of each of the deployment process runs for audit purposes. There are many CI tools available as open-source or proprietary software that have these commonly required features.

Common pitfalls in deployment automation

When you automate your deployment process, you will face the following pitfalls:

- The inherent complexity within the existing process

- The number of dependencies between services

- Critical components that are not designed for automation

- Poor collaboration between developer or operations teams

Complexity

Automating a complex, fragile manual process is unlikely to work as it typically results in a complex, fragile automated process. You will first need to re-architect your existing process for deployability. This means making the deployment script as simple as possible and pushing the complexity into the application code and infrastructure platform. Cloud-native applications running on a platform-as-a-service, such as App Engine or Cloud Run, can typically be deployed by running a single command, with no deployment scripting required at all: this is the ideal process.

There are two important properties of a reliable deployment process. First, the individual steps are repeatable so that they can be rerun in the case of a failure, and second, they should be order independent with no tight coupling between dependencies.

Dependencies

Often, you will need to deploy multiple services together in a particular order. Although many enterprise deployment workflow tools exist to help with this situation, these tools are band-aids over an architectural problem: tight coupling between the various components and services. Over time, you must address this tight coupling. The goal is that services should be independently deployable with no orchestration required. It's important to ensure that services can continue to operate (perhaps with some functionality unavailable) even if they are unable to connect to other services that they depend on.

Not designed for automation

A third common pitfall is components that are not designed for automation. Today, most platforms (including Google Cloud) offer an API that your deployment script can use.

Poor collaboration between teams

The last pitfall occurs when developers and IT operations teams aren't in sync. This can happen if the environments are configured differently, you substantially increase the risk of the deployment process being manually performed by IT operations, which introduces inconsistencies and errors. The deployment automation process must be created by developers and IT operations working together. This approach ensures that both teams can understand, maintain, and evolve deployment automation.

Ways to improve deployment automation

The first step is to document the existing deployment process in a common tool that developers and operations have access to, such as Google Docs or a wiki. Then, work to incrementally simplify and automate the deployment process. This approach typically includes tasks such as packaging code in ways suitable for deployment and creating pre-configured virtual machine images or containers. The goal is to work to remove any toil, that is, manual steps, and implement idempotent (repeatable) and order independence wherever possible. Additionally, try to leverage the capabilities of your infrastructure platform wherever possible. Remember that deployment automation should be as simple as possible.

Ways to measure deployment automation

Measuring deployment automation is, fortunately, pretty much straightforward. Continuous delivery is measured by the ability of the process to release changes of all kinds on demand quickly, safely, and sustainably.

When your team practices continuous delivery, you can answer *yes* to the following questions:

- Is our software in a deployable state throughout its lifecycle?

- Do we prioritize keeping the software deployable over working on new features?

- Is fast feedback on the quality and deployability of the system we are working on available to everyone on the team?

- When we get feedback that the system is not deployable (such as failing builds or tests), do we make fixing these issues our highest priority?

- Can we deploy our system to production or to end users at any time, on demand?

Continuous Delivery vs Continuous Deployment

Continuous delivery is commonly conflated with continuous deployment, but they are separate practices. Continuous deployment is when teams try to deploy every code change to production as soon as possible. Continuous deployment works well for web services but can't be applied to software such as firmware or mobile apps. Continuous delivery is applied to all kinds of software, including firmware and mainframe systems, in highly regulated environments. You can and should start with continuous delivery, even if you never intend to start using continuous deployment.

Continuous delivery and continuous deployment are mistakenly viewed as risky and unsuited to regulated or safety critical domains. In fact, the goal of continuous delivery is to reduce software risk, and research has shown consistently that high performers achieve higher levels of reliability and availability. The technical practices that drive continuous delivery—continuous testing, shifting left on security, and comprehensive testing and observability—are even more important in highly regulated and safety-critical domains. Continuous delivery has been successfully applied many times in highly regulated domains like financial services and the government.

Implementing continuous delivery

The following technical capabilities drive the ability to successfully achieve continuous delivery. Transformational leadership within the organization drives the implementation of many of these technical capabilities.

To help your team get higher throughput and lower risk releases, implement the following continuous delivery practices:

- **Test automation**: The use of comprehensive automated test suites that find real failures and only pass releasable code.

- **Deployment automation**: All deployments are fully automated and do not require manual intervention.

- **Trunk-based development**: Characterized by fewer than three active branches in a code repository, branches and forks having very short lifetimes (for example, less than a day) before being merged into mainline, and application teams rarely or never having code lock periods.

- **Shift left on security**: Including security in the design and testing phases of the software development process. Using pre-approved security libraries and packages and testing security features as a part of the automated test suite.

- **A loosely coupled architecture**: Having a loosely coupled architecture allows your teams to work independently, which, in turn, enables them to work quickly.

- **Empowering teams to choose tools**: Teams that can choose which tools to use do better at continuous delivery as they know what they need to be effective.

- **Continuous integration (CI)**: A development practice where code is regularly checked in and each check-in triggers a set of quick tests to discover regressions, which developers fix immediately. The CI process creates canonical builds and packages that are ultimately deployed and released.

- **Version control**: The use of a version control system, such as Git or Subversion, for all production artifacts, including application code, application configurations, system configurations, and scripts for automating build and configuration of environments.

- **Test data management**: Effective practices include having adequate data to run your test suite, the ability to acquire necessary data on demand, and the data not limiting the number of tests you can run.

- **Comprehensive monitoring and observability**: Allow teams to understand the health of their systems.

- **Proactive notifications**: Monitoring system health so that teams can preemptively detect and mitigate problems.

- **Code maintainability**: Systems and tools that make it easy for developers to change code maintained by others, find examples in the codebase, reuse other people's code, and add, upgrade, and migrate to new versions of dependencies without breaking their code.

While continuous delivery is often combined with continuous integration and shortened to CI/CD, research shows that continuous integration is only one element of implementing continuous delivery. To achieve reliable, low-risk releases, you need close collaboration between everyone involved in the software delivery process, not just software developers, and your team needs to adopt new ways of working and learn new skills.

Common pitfalls of implementing continuous delivery

Many descriptions of continuous delivery focus on the pipeline and patterns. However, using modern tools without implementing the necessary technical practices and process change described in this document won't produce the expected benefits.

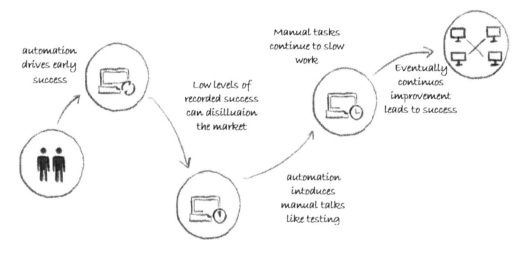

Figure 10.1: J-curve in Transformation

In the diagram, the following stages are labeled:

- At the beginning of the curve, teams begin transformation and identify quick wins.

- In an initial improvement, automation helps low performers progress to medium performers.

- In a decrease to efficiency—the bottom of the J curve—automation increases test requirements, which are dealt with manually. A large amount of technical debt blocks progress.

- As teams begin to come out of the curve, technical debt and increased complexity cause additional manual controls and layers of process around changes, slowing work.

- At the top of the curve, relentless improvement work leads to excellence and high performance. High and elite performers leverage expertise and learn from their environments to see increase in productivity.

Measuring continuous delivery

Ultimately, the goal of continuous delivery is to ensure that releases are performed in a low-risk manner. How well you are doing at continuous delivery is reflected in the outcomes that you achieve. You can take the following DevOps quick check to see how you're doing with the key continuous delivery metrics:

- Short lead times for both regular and emergency changes, with a goal of using your regular process for emergency changes.

- Low change fail rates.

- Short time to restore service in the event of outages or service degradations.

- Release frequencies that ensure that high-priority features and bug fixes are released in a timely manner.

As discussed at the start of this chapter, implementing continuous delivery should also lead to lower levels of rework, reduced deployment pain, and less time spent doing rework and unplanned work:

- Examine the existing process and count the number of manual steps in your deployment process. The objective is to replace those manual steps with automated steps. Manual steps will increase the deployment time as well as the opportunity for error.

- Measure the level (or percentage) of automation in your deployment pipeline. The objective should be to increase that level as a continuous improvement process.

- Determine the time lost to delays within the deployment pipeline. The objective is to try to eliminate these costly delays and understand why they came about.

Interactive tutorial 10.1: GitOps-style continuous delivery with Cloud Build

Overview

This tutorial uses two Git repositories:

- **app repository**: Contains the source code of the application itself.

- **env repository**: Contains the manifests for the Kubernetes Deployment.

When you push a change to the **app** repository, the Cloud Build pipeline runs tests, builds a container image, and pushes it to Container Registry. After pushing the image, Cloud Build updates the Deployment manifest and pushes it to the **env** repository. This triggers another Cloud Build pipeline that applies the manifest to the GKE cluster and, if successful, stores the manifest in another branch of the **env** repository.

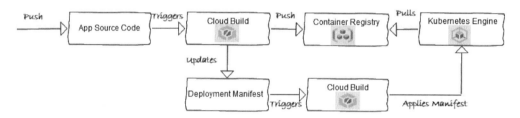

Figure 10.2: *Automated Deployment Process*

We keep the **app** and **env** repositories separate because they have different lifecycles and uses. The main users of the **app** repository are humans, and this repository is dedicated to a specific application. The main users of the env repository are automated systems (such as Cloud Build), and this repository might be shared by several applications. The **env** repository can have several branches, each of which maps to a specific environment (you only use production in this tutorial) and references a specific container image, whereas the app repository does not.

When you finish this tutorial, you have a system where you can easily:

- Distinguish between failed and successful deployments by looking at the Cloud Build history.

- Access the manifest currently used by looking at the production branch of the env repository.

- Roll back to any previous version by re-executing the corresponding Cloud Build build.

This tutorial uses Cloud Source Repositories to host Git repositories, but you can achieve the same results with other third-party products such as GitHub, Bitbucket, or GitLab. This pipeline does not implement a validation mechanism before the deployment. If you use GitHub, Bitbucket, or GitLab, you can modify the pipeline to use a Pull Request for this purpose.

While we recommend Spinnaker to the teams who want to implement advanced deployment patterns (blue/green, canary analysis, multi-cloud, etc.), its feature set might not be needed for a successful CI/CD strategy for smaller organizations and projects. In this tutorial, you will learn how to create a CI/CD pipeline fit for applications hosted on GKE with tooling. For simplicity, this tutorial uses a single environment —production— in the env repository, but you can extend it to deploy to multiple environments if needed.

Objectives

- Create Git repositories in Cloud Source Repositories.

- Create a container image with Cloud Build and store it in the Container Registry.

- Create a CI pipeline.

- Create a CD pipeline.

- Test the CI/CD pipeline.

Prepare

Set your **Project_ID** in Cloud Shell:

gcloud config set project [PROJECT_ID]

1. In Cloud Shell, enable the required APIs.

   **gcloud services enable container.googleapis.com **

   **cloudbuild.googleapis.com **

   **sourcerepo.googleapis.com **

   containeranalysis.googleapis.com

```
alasdair_gilchrist@cloudshell:~ (supple-design-329501)$ gcloud services enable container.googleapis.com \
>     cloudbuild.googleapis.com \
>     sourcerepo.googleapis.com \
>     containeranalysis.googleapis.com
Operation "operations/acf.p2-6891695393-615469d9-7d53-46c6-b43d-ea848c16b905" finished successfully.
```

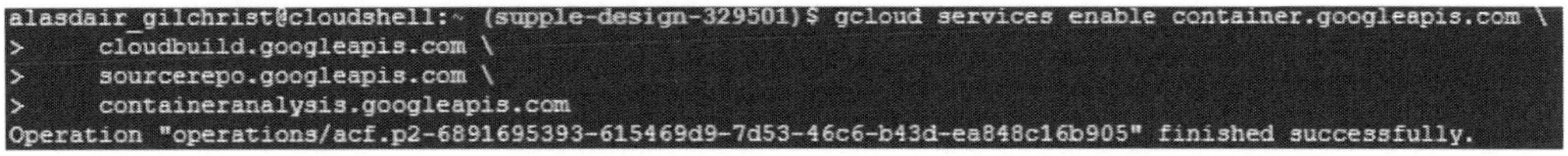

Figure 10.3: APIs enabled

2. In Cloud Shell, create a GKE cluster that you will use to deploy the sample application of this tutorial.

3. Create a cluster named **hello-cloudbuild**:

```
gcloud container clusters
create  hello-cloudbuild \
  --region us-central1
```

4. If you have never used Git in Cloud Shell, configure it with your name and email address. Git will use those to identify you as the author of the commits you will create in Cloud Shell:

```
git config --global user.email "[YOUR_EMAIL_ADDRESS]"
git config --global user.name "[YOUR_NAME]"
```

5. Run the gcloud credential helper. This will connect your Google Cloud user account to Cloud Source Repositories.

```
git config --global credential.helper gcloud.sh
```

Creating the Git repositories in Cloud Source Repositories

In this section, you create the two Git repositories (**app** and **env**) used in this tutorial and initialize the **app** one with some sample code:

1. In Cloud Shell, create the two Git repositories:

```
gcloud source repos create hello-cloudbuild-app
gcloud source repos create hello-cloudbuild-env
```

Figure 10.4: Source Repositories created

2. Clone the sample code from GitHub:

```
cd ~

git clone https://github.com/GoogleCloudPlatform/gke-gitops-
tutorial-cloudbuild \

Hello-cloudbuild-app
```

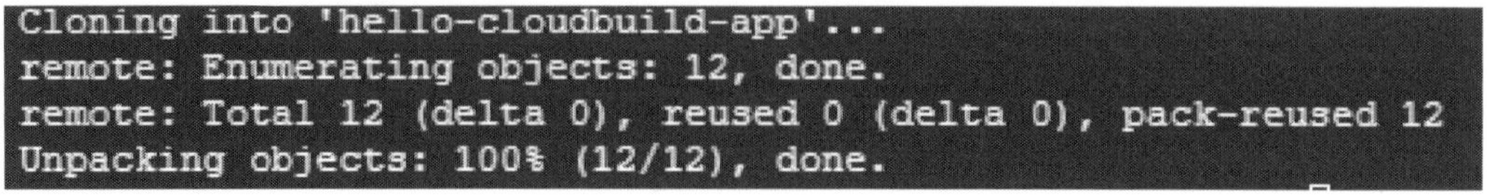

Figure 10.5: Cloning the App

3. Configure Cloud Source Repositories as a remote:

```
cd ~/hello-cloudbuild-app
PROJECT_ID=$(gcloud config get-value project)
git remote add google \
    "https://source.developers.google.com/p/${PROJECT_ID}/r/
hello-cloudbuild-app"
```

The code you cloned contains a **Hello World** application:

```
app.py
from flask import Flask
app = Flask('hello-cloudbuild')


@app.route('/')
def hello():
  return "Hello World!\n"


if __name__ == '__main__':
  app.run(host = '0.0.0.0', port = 8080)
```

Creating a container image with Cloud Build. The code you cloned contains the following Dockerfile:

Dockerfile

```
FROM python:3.7-slim
RUN pip install flask
WORKDIR /app
COPY app.py /app/app.py
ENTRYPOINT ["python"]
CMD ["/app/app.py"]
```

With this Dockerfile, you can create a container image with Cloud Build and store it in the Container Registry.

4. In Cloud Shell, create a Cloud Build build based on the latest commit with the following command:

```
cd ~/hello-cloudbuild-app
COMMIT_ID="$(git rev-parse --short=7 HEAD)"
```

```
gcloud builds submit --tag="gcr.io/${PROJECT_ID}/hello-
cloudbuild:${COMMIT_ID}" .
```

```
ID: b0674458-548d-4ac1-87a9-f9a4b58813ba
CREATE_TIME: 2021-10-29T21:22:51+00:00
DURATION: 21S
SOURCE: gs://supple-design-329501_cloudbuild/source/1635542569.257964-d7937c6769934e1fa696e78b9be35a49.tgz
IMAGES: gcr.io/supple-design-329501/hello-cloudbuild:5b55cac
STATUS: SUCCESS
```

Figure 10.6: *Cloud Build Success*

Cloud Build streams the logs generated by the creation of the container image to your terminal when you execute this command.

5. After the build finishes, verify that your new container image is available in the Container Registry.

    Go to Container Registry:

	Name	Tags	Virtual size ❓	Created	Uploaded ↓	Vulnerabilities	
☐	🐳 99cf981c70a0	5b55cac	47.3 MB	in 3 minutes	in 3 minutes	⚠ 37	⋮

Figure 10.7: *Container Registry contents*

Creating the continuous integration pipeline

In this section, you will configure Cloud Build to automatically run a small unit test, build the container image, and then push it to the Container Registry. Pushing a new commit to Cloud Source Repositories automatically triggers this pipeline. The **cloudbuild.yaml** file included in the code is the pipeline's configuration.

```
Cloudbuild.yaml

# This step runs the unit tests on the app
- name: 'python:3.7-slim'
  id: Test
  entrypoint: /bin/sh
  args:
  - -c
  - 'pip install flask && python test_app.py -v'


# This step builds the container image.
- name: 'gcr.io/cloud-builders/docker'
  id: Build
  args:
```

```
    - 'build'
    - '-t'
    - 'gcr.io/$PROJECT_ID/hello-cloudbuild:$SHORT_SHA'
    - '.'


# This step pushes the image to Container Registry
# The PROJECT_ID and SHORT_SHA variables are automatically
# replaced by Cloud Build.
- name: 'gcr.io/cloud-builders/docker'
  id: Push
  args:
  - 'push'
  - 'gcr.io/$PROJECT_ID/hello-cloudbuild:$SHORT_SHA'
```

1. Open the Cloud Build Triggers page. Go to Triggers.

2. Click on **Create trigger**.

3. Fill out the following options:

     i.   In the **Name** field, type **hello-cloudbuild**.

     ii.   Under **Event**, select **Push to a branch**.

     iii.   Under **Source**, select **hello-cloudbuild-app** as your **Repository** and **^master$** as your **Branch**.

     iv.   Under **Build configuration**, select the **Cloud Build** configuration file.

     v.   In the Cloud Build configuration file location field, type **cloudbuild. yaml** after the **/**.

4. Click on Create to save your build trigger.

   In Cloud Shell, push the application code to Cloud Source Repositories to trigger the CI pipeline in Cloud Build:

   cd ~/hello-cloudbuild-app

   git push google master

5. Open the Cloud Build console. Your recently run and finished builds appear. You can click on a build to follow its execution and examine its logs.

Creating the continuous delivery pipeline

Cloud Build is also used for the continuous delivery pipeline. The pipeline runs each time a commit is pushed to the candidate branch of the **hello-cloudbuild-env** repository. The pipeline applies the new version of the manifest to the Kubernetes cluster and, if successful, copies the manifest over to the production branch. This process has the following properties:

- The **candidate** branch is a history of the deployment attempts.

- The **production** branch is a history of the successful deployments.

- You have a view of successful and failed deployments in Cloud Build.

- You can roll back to any previous deployment by re-executing the corresponding build in Cloud Build. A rollback also updates the production branch to truthfully reflect the history of deployments.

You will modify the continuous integration pipeline to update the candidate branch of the **hello-cloudbuild-env** repository, triggering the continuous delivery pipeline.

Note: You can extend the system described in this tutorial to manage several environments. The easiest way to achieve this is to have a pair of branches for each environment env: a candidate-env branch and an env branch.

Granting Cloud Build access to GKE

To deploy the application in your Kubernetes cluster, Cloud Build needs the Kubernetes Engine Developer Identity and Access Management Role.

In Cloud Shell, execute the following command:

```
PROJECT_NUMBER="$(gcloud projects describe ${PROJECT_ID}
--format='get(projectNumber)')"

gcloud projects add-iam-policy-binding ${PROJECT_NUMBER} \

    --member=serviceAccount:${PROJECT_NUMBER}@cloudbuild.
gserviceaccount.com \

    --role=roles/container.developer
```

Initializing the hello-cloudbuild-env repository

You need to initialize the **hello-cloudbuild-env** repository with two branches (**production** and **candidate**) and a Cloud Build configuration file describing the deployment process.

1. In Cloud Shell, clone the **hello-cloudbuild-env** repository and create the production branch:

```
cd ~
gcloud source repos clone hello-cloudbuild-env
cd ~/hello-cloudbuild-env
git checkout -b production
```

2. Copy the **cloudbuild-delivery.yaml** file available in the **hello-cloudbuild-app** repository and commit the change:

```
cd ~/hello-cloudbuild-env

cp ~/hello-cloudbuild-app/cloudbuild-delivery.yaml ~/hello-cloudbuild-env/cloudbuild.yaml

git add .

git commit -m "Create cloudbuild.yaml for deployment"
```

3. The **cloudbuild-delivery.yaml** file describes the deployment process to be run in Cloud Build. It has two steps:

   - Cloud Build applies the manifest on the GKE cluster.

   - If successful, Cloud Build copies the manifest on the production branch.

4. Create a candidate branch and push both branches for them to be available in Cloud Source Repositories:

```
git checkout -b candidate
git push origin production
git push origin candidate
```

5. Grant the Source Repository Writer IAM role to the Cloud Build service account for the **hello-cloudbuild-env** repository:

```
PROJECT_NUMBER="$(gcloud projects describe ${PROJECT_ID} \
  --format='get(projectNumber)')"
cat >/tmp/hello-cloudbuild-env-policy.yaml <<EOF
bindings:
- members:
  - serviceAccount:${PROJECT_NUMBER}@cloudbuild.gserviceaccount.com
  role: roles/source.writer
EOF
```

```
gcloud source repos set-iam-policy \ hello-cloudbuild-env /tmp/
hello-cloudbuild-env-policy.yaml
```

Creating the trigger for the continuous delivery pipeline

In this section, you configure Cloud Build to be triggered by a push to the **candidate** branch of the **hello-cloudbuild-env** repository.

1. Open the Triggers page of Cloud Build. Click on **Create trigger**.

2. Fill out the following options:

   i.   In the **Name** field, type **hello-cloudbuild**-deploy.

   ii. Under **Event**, select **Push to a branch**.

   iii. Under **Source,** select **hello-cloudbuild-env** as your **Repository** and **^candidate$** as your **Branch**.

   iv. Under **Configuration**, select **Cloud Build** configuration file (yaml or json).

   v.   In the Cloud Build configuration file location field, type **cloudbuild.yaml** after the /.

3. Click on **Create**.

Modifying the continuous integration pipeline to trigger the continuous delivery pipeline

In this section, you will add some steps to the continuous integration pipeline that generates a new version of the Kubernetes manifest and push it to the **hello-cloudbuild-env** repository to trigger the continuous delivery pipeline.

1. Replace the **cloudbuild.yaml** file with the extended example in the **cloudbuild-trigger-cd.yaml** file:

   ```
   cd ~/hello-cloudbuild-app
   ```

   ```
   cp cloudbuild-trigger-cd.yaml cloudbuild.yaml
   ```

   ```
   cd ~/hello-cloudbuild-app
   cp cloudbuild-trigger-cd.yaml cloudbuild.yaml
   ```

2. The **cloudbuild-trigger-cd.yaml** is an extended version of the **cloudbuild.yaml** file. It adds steps to generate the new Kubernetes manifest and trigger the continuous delivery pipeline.

> **This pipeline uses a sed to render the manifest template. In reality, you might benefit from using a dedicated tool such as kustomize or skaffold. These tools give you more control over the rendering of the manifest templates.**

```
Cloudbuild-trigger-cd.yaml
# This step clones the hello-cloudbuild-env repository
- name: 'gcr.io/cloud-builders/gcloud'
  id: Clone env repository
  entrypoint: /bin/sh
  args:
  - '-c'
  - |
    gcloud source repos clone hello-cloudbuild-env && \
    cd hello-cloudbuild-env && \
    git checkout candidate && \
    git config user.email $(gcloud auth list --filter=status:ACTIVE
--format='value(account)')


# This step generates the new manifest
- name: 'gcr.io/cloud-builders/gcloud'
  id: Generate manifest
  entrypoint: /bin/sh
  args:
  - '-c'
  - |
      sed "s/GOOGLE_CLOUD_PROJECT/${PROJECT_ID}/g" kubernetes.
yaml.tpl | \
      sed "s/COMMIT_SHA/${SHORT_SHA}/g" > hello-cloudbuild-env/
kubernetes.yaml


# This step pushes the manifest back to hello-cloudbuild-env
- name: 'gcr.io/cloud-builders/gcloud'
  id: Push manifest
```

```
entrypoint: /bin/sh
args:
- '-c'
- |
  set -x && \
  cd hello-cloudbuild-env && \
  git add kubernetes.yaml && \
  git commit -m "Deploying image gcr.io/${PROJECT_ID}/hello-
cloudbuild:${SHORT_SHA}
  Built from commit ${COMMIT_SHA} of repository hello-
cloudbuild-app
  Author: $(git log --format='%an <%ae>' -n 1 HEAD)" && \
  git push origin candidate
```

3. Commit the modifications and push them to Cloud Source Repositories:

   cd ~/hello-cloudbuild-app

   git add cloudbuild.yaml

   git commit -m "Trigger CD pipeline"

   git push google master

4. This triggers the continuous integration pipeline in Cloud Build.

5. Examine the continuous integration build.

6. Go to Cloud Build. Your recently run and finished builds for the **hello-cloudbuild-app** repository appear. You can click on a build to follow its execution and examine its logs. The last step of this pipeline pushes the new manifest to the **hello-cloudbuild-env** repository, which triggers the continuous delivery pipeline.

7. Examine the continuous delivery build. Go to Cloud Build.

8. Your recently run and finished builds for the **hello-cloudbuild-env** repository appear. You can click on a build to follow its execution and examine its logs.

Testing the complete pipeline

The complete CI/CD pipeline is now configured. In this section, you will test it from end to end.

1. Go to the GKE Services page.

2. The list contains a single service called **hello-cloudbuild** created by the recently completed continuous delivery build.

3. Click on the endpoint for the **hello-cloudbuild** service. **Hello World!** appears. If there is no endpoint, or if you see a load balancer error, you might have to wait a few minutes for the load balancer to be completely initialized. Click on **Refresh** to update the page if needed.

4. In Cloud Shell, replace **Hello World** with **Hello Cloud Build**, both in the application and in the unit test:

   ```
   cd ~/hello-cloudbuild-app

   sed -i 's/Hello World/Hello Cloud Build/g' app.py

   sed -i 's/Hello World/Hello Cloud Build/g' test_app.py
   ```

5. Commit and push the change to Cloud Source Repositories:

   ```
   git add app.py test_app.py

   git commit -m "Hello Cloud Build"

   git push google master
   ```

6. This triggers the full CI/CD pipeline.

7. After a few minutes, reload the application in your browser. **Hello Cloud Build!** appears.

Testing the rollback

In this section, you will roll back to the version of the application that said **Hello World!**.

1. Open the Cloud Build console for the **hello-cloudbuild-env** repository.

2. Click on the second most recent build available.

3. Click on **Rebuild**.

4. When the build is finished, reload the application in your browser. **Hello World!** appears again.

Congratulations! You have just built a GitOps-style continuous delivery pipeline using Cloud Build.

Clean up!

Deleting the resources

If you want to keep the Google Cloud project you used in this tutorial, delete the individual resources:

- Delete the local Git repositories:

```
cd ~
rm -rf ~/hello-cloudbuild-app
rm -rf ~/hello-cloudbuild-env
```

- Delete the Git repositories in Cloud Source Repositories:

```
gcloud source repos delete hello-cloudbuild-app --quiet
gcloud source repos delete hello-cloudbuild-env --quiet
```

- Delete the Cloud Build Triggers.

  - Open the Triggers page of Cloud Build.

  - For each trigger, click on **More** and then **Delete**.

- Delete the images in Container Registry:

```
gcloud beta container images list-tags \
    gcr.io/${PROJECT_ID}/hello-cloudbuild \
    --format="value(tags)" | \
    xargs -I {} gcloud beta container images delete \
    --force-delete-tags --quiet \
    gcr.io/${PROJECT_ID}/hello-cloudbuild:{}
```

- Remove the permission granted to Cloud Build to connect to GKE:

```
PROJECT_NUMBER="$(gcloud projects describe ${PROJECT_ID} \
    --format='get(projectNumber)')"
gcloud projects remove-iam-policy-binding ${PROJECT_NUMBER} \
    --member=serviceAccount:${PROJECT_NUMBER}@cloudbuild.
gserviceaccount.com \
    --role=roles/container.developer
```

- Delete the GKE cluster:

```
gcloud container clusters delete hello-cloudbuild \
   --region us-central1
```

Conclusion

This chapter was heavy on process as that is what CI/CD is, a strict automated process consisting of preconfigured steps with corresponding unit tests at every stage. You learned why we do this in Continuous Integrate and in Continuous Delivery. You learned how to identify potential pitfalls and effectively measure your processes. You also learned the fundamentals of creating a GitOps-style Continuous delivery pipeline that incorporated much of the lessons that you have learned in this chapter.

In the next chapter, we will build on what you have learned here by building a modern CI/CD pipeline using Anthos.

CHAPTER 11
Build a Software Delivery Platform with Anthos

In the previous chapter, you learned how to create a GitOps-style continuous delivery pipeline using Cloud Build. This introduced you to several of the components and skills you will build upon in this chapter as we continue our journey by building a modern software delivery platform using Anthos.

Although that seems like a major sidestep as you are being introduced to a new technology late in the book, but it isn't really. Anthos is an umbrella technology that combines many of the GCP services we have become familiar with, such as kubernetes, Cloud Build and Artifact Repository, among many others. So, we will be taking the next logical step in the learning process and building upon your existing knowledge and skills.

Structure

We will cover the following topics in this chapter:

- An introduction to Anthos
- Anthos technical drill-down
- Designing modern CI/CD with Anthos
- Interactive tutorial: Building a CI/CD in Anthos

Objectives

After completing this chapter, you will be able to define the purpose and features of Anthos and how it operates in a hybrid or multi-cloud environment. You will also be familiar with Anthos features and architecture and understand how it is deployed in real-world scenarios. In addition, you will know how to design, configure, and deploy a CI/CD solution with Anthos.

Defining Anthos

A simple way of describing Anthos' purpose or functionality is to suggest that it is an orchestrator for managing hybrid Cloud and on-prem environments. So, you could say that Anthos is just like Kubernetes, which we have covered extensively in this book. However, Anthos does a lot more than Kubernetes does for containers. Nonetheless, it is a good-enough example to get us started with understanding Anthos as one of its main features is that it is a platform for managing your hybrid Kubernetes clusters for you.

Anthos has three key areas of functionality:

- Anthos is capable of provisioning infrastructure in cloud, on-premise, and in hybrid environments.

- Anthos has capabilities in infrastructure management, domain security as well as in policies and compliance solutions.

- Anthos is used in application development, network service discovery and telemetry, and workload migration from cloud to cloud or from on-premises to cloud.

Another key characteristic of Anthos that it shares with Kubernetes is that they are both best used in a declarative manner. Indeed, with Anthos, you will tell it what you want your Kubernetes clusters to look like, and Anthos will then make sure your desired states are met. Initially, you might not find that particularly impressive, but if you are managing hybrid and on-prem environments with a mixture of flavors of Kubernetes, it is important that those different clusters are not limited to only GKE clusters.

The way Anthos works

The underlying concept of Anthos infrastructure management is based on a declarative GitOps approach, whereby you start out with a Git repo as this is where you manage your configuration (YAML) files. These config files contain the details for the desired states for your environment. Anthos ensures that they are kept under strict version management as they are in the context of the infrastructure, the blueprint or essentially the single source of truth. Anthos does this by adopting the now familiar GitOps way of working.

Anthos agent

Again, simplistically, Anthos installs an Anthos GKE Connect Agent on your Kubernetes clusters. This allows the cluster to be located anywhere as long as it has a network to connect to Anthos. The Anthos agent on each Kubernetes cluster will retrieve and load the appropriate config (YAML) files from the Git repository when there is a change in the desired state or to maintain a present state.

Anthos hub

Anthos is responsible for communicating with Anthos Hub, which is the managed service running on Google Cloud. Anthos communicates with the Hub to check the desired state and then figure out how to make changes where needed. Importantly, GitHub or GKE Hub do not have any access to your clusters as this would be a security vulnerability. Instead, Anthos utilizes the local intelligence of the Anthos Agent residing in each cluster to interrogate the cluster when integrating with the Hub. This means that Google Cloud does not need to have or store credentials to your cluster. Instead, the Agent performs the interactions with the GKE Hub in Google Cloud to request the desired state and act accordingly.

Anthos Service Mesh

In modern microservice architecture, managing the spider's web of interrelated and loosely coupled services can be a nightmare. However, Anthos helps by streamlining and automating the service discovery process and application development/ management via the Anthos (Istio) Service Mesh. A core module in Anthos, the **Cloud Service Mesh** (**CSM**) allows all workloads in all clusters to have the potential to talk to each other, if you so wish. The way this works is that if workloads wish to communicate within a single cluster, the regular DNS can be used to resolve the `.local` domain.

However, for inter-cluster communications where you want to reach workloads running in another cluster, you leverage `ServiceEntries`. This is a separate DNS managed on each cluster that handles the forwarding of any permitted traffic that is external to the cluster, referred to with a `.global` domain. To resolve these global DNS queries, the Anthos Agent leverages Stub Domains.

Anthos operations suite

Anthos performs much of the heavy lifting when handling and managing clusters and microservices architectures on your behalf. This makes it easier for you as an administrator and/or developer. This is simply because when you have several clusters controlled autonomously by Anthos, it frees you from all the operational burden. However, to prevent you from getting mentally disconnected from the workloads running in those managed clusters, CSM provides a Topology View.

The Topology view lets you easily visualize the workloads running within your clusters. CSM is based on Istio and Stackdriver, the former being a service-mesh providing connectivity, and the latter being a suite of operational tools. Combined, they form CSM, which provides unique insights into your clusters and their workloads.

Stackdriver, or Operations Suite as it is now renamed in GCP, is what allows CSM to provide you with out-of-the-box SLIs like errors and latency metrics, which, in turn, allows you to create operations dashboards or even set SLOs based on them. CSM will help you track these SLOs and maintain your error budget, which are core SRE principles. Anthos also provides an out-of-the-box structured view of the entire system, including services, clusters, and more. This simplifies the view and management so that you can improve security, use resources more efficiently, and demonstrate measurable success.

Anthos's business utility

An enterprise today will often have its infrastructure architecture spread across hybrid cloud and on-prem data centers. Hence, it is common to have an architecture where existing networking, storage, and compute services are established on multiple clouds as well as in your own data centers. Of course, you will need to provision and administrate applications and the underlying services on each of these platforms, and this can lead to huge levels of complexity. However, Anthos provides platform administrators a single place to monitor and manage their landscape from, including policy control and marketplace access across hybrid, multi-cloud, and on-prem environments and platforms.

Today's hybrid and multi-cloud ecosystems

In a typical use case, you may use containers in the cloud and develop apps using services on Google Cloud, Azure and AWS cloud platforms in addition to on-prem. Regardless of platform, you will need consistent policy development and enforcement across all your IT footprint. However, to possibly manage policy across diverse platforms, you will need flexible monitoring and logging systems. Additionally, you will need to integrate your data from across all your platforms into meaningful categories, such as business data, analytical data, operational data, and house-keeping data like logging and alerts. Further, when you come to use this data, you might find that you need to stream operational data and alerts to inform optimizations and automations and to set policies or SLOs, again, from across all platforms. However, you might probably also need to use business intelligence data to feed into SLOs or use operational data to deploy third-party apps. That's just the beginning of the complexity as you need to act on different specific parts of the different platforms to consume the data in the manner you have planned. That will mean interrogating each platform for policy enforcement, securing services, orchestrating containers, and managing infrastructure management. All this work is in addition to what it takes to develop, deploy, and manage your own apps. With all this complexity comes resistance to change, so it's hard to stay current, understand business implications, and ensure compliance. Anthos helps overcome these challenges.

With Anthos, you get a consistent way to manage with similar infrastructure management, container management, service management, and policy enforcement across all your platforms. As a result, you gain observability across your platforms in one single place, including business information, alerts, and operational information. With this information, you might decide to optimize, automate, and set policies or SLOs, or you might rely on our machine learning models to make automated suggestions. You take those recommendations or make your own decisions and apply them to the different management layers and let Anthos manage it for you. Unfortunately, it is not that easy.

This is because enterprises typically have a global reach, so you may have different geographical regions that need different policies, or you may be a single regional business but perhaps have different development, staging, or production environments that need different operational policies and permissions. Also, there will likely be parts of your work that may need confidentiality and hence, security. That's where Anthos and environs come in.

Anthos fleets

Environs are the way to create logical sets of underlying Kubernetes clusters, regardless of which platform these clusters live on. This enables you to group and manage sets of clusters as logical environments named *Fleets*, regardless of where or on what platform they are located. You can then think about and work with your applications in the right way and at the required level of detail for the task at hand.

By using Fleets, organizations are able to manage multi-clusters more easily as fleets provides a method for logically grouping clusters to make administration easier. For example, in a multi-cluster environment, there may well be reuse of namespace terms across clusters. This is commonly found in DevOps environments where there may well be reuse of Dev, Test, and Prod as namespaces dedicated to specific stages in the CI/CD process. With Fleets, all the Devs could be grouped together as they have similar sameness, and as could Test and Prod. By doing so, you logically group them together, making it easier to apply consisted policy and configuration across the multi-cluster environment.

In short, fleets help you enforce policies and processes as it abstracts the complexities of the underlying infrastructure, cluster, and container management from the namespace view or workspace. Anthos simplifies and provides a consistent view across your company's clusters, which has benefits in improved security and the efficient use of resources, and it helps teams innovate faster when working in multi-cluster environments.

By using Fleets, Google Anthos Cloud provides the user with the flexibility to run and deploy their applications from anywhere, either as a cloud service or from their own data center. This might not seem too important, but it prevents cloud vendor lock-in where an enterprise shifts its workloads to a specific cloud provider and so, becomes locked into that provider's services. Importantly, Anthos' unified dashboard can show views of Fleets, whereby it combines all the data from each cluster and displays it on a single pane in the dashboard view. This makes deploying an app across several clusters easily achievable and manageable.

Anthos technical drill-down

Anthos is a modern application management platform that provides a consistent development and operations experience for cloud and on-premises environments. As such, we will get a technical overview of each layer of the Anthos infrastructure and see how you can leverage its features to develop a cloud native approach to CI/CD.

The following diagram shows Anthos components and features and how they provide Anthos's functionality across your environments, from infrastructure management to facilitating application development:

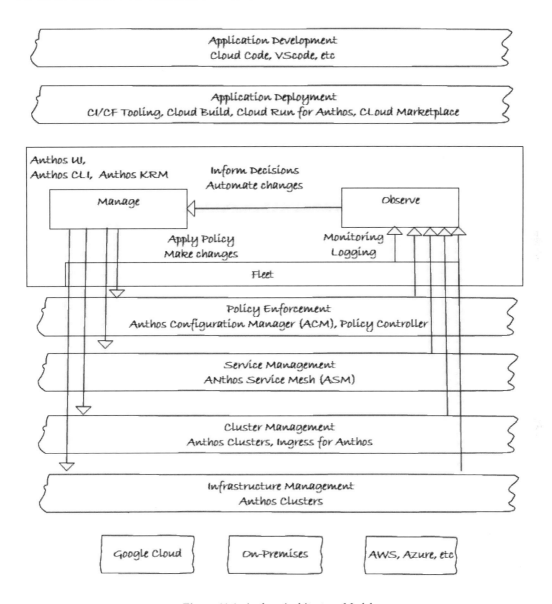

Figure 11.1: Anthos Architecture Model

Computing environment

Anthos' primary computing environment is Anthos clusters, which extends the GKE for use on Google Cloud, on-premises, or multi clouds. With Anthos, you get management capabilities for creating, scaling, and upgrading conformant Kubernetes clusters. With Kubernetes, you have access to a common orchestration layer that manages application deployment, configuration, upgrade, and scaling.

Kubernetes has two main parts: the control plane and the node components. How the environments host the control plane and node components for GKE is described below:

- **Anthos on Google Cloud**: With Anthos on Google Cloud, only access to the Kubernetes API server is given to customers. GKE manages the node components in the customer's project using Compute instances.

- **Anthos on-prem**: With Anthos clusters on VMware, all components are hosted in the customer's on-prem virtualization environment.

- **Anthos on AWS**: With Anthos clusters on AWS, all components are hosted in the customer's AWS environment.

Multi-cluster management

Anthos clusters are registered as part of a Google Cloud fleet using Cloud Connect; this allows for multiple clusters to be viewed and managed together in the Anthos dashboard.

Connecting across environments

You can connect your on-premises, multi cloud, attached clusters, and Google Cloud environments in various ways. The easiest way to get started is by implementing a site-to-site VPN between the environments using Cloud VPN.

Connecting to Google services

Your Anthos environments outside Google Cloud must be able to reach Google's API endpoints for connect at a minimum.

Microservice architecture support

In Kubernetes, services are composed of many Pods, which execute containers. In a microservices architecture, a single application may consist of numerous services, and each service-to-service communication occurs over the network.

Networks can be unreliable and insecure, so services must be able to identify and deal with network idiosyncrasies. To solve these problems, you can install Anthos Service Mesh on GKE or attached clusters in your chosen environment. Anthos Service Mesh is based on Istio, which is an open-source implementation of the service mesh infrastructure layer.

Managed service mesh

For workloads running on Anthos on Google Cloud, Anthos Service Mesh manages your service mesh environment and provides you with many features, along with all of Istio's functionality:

- Service metrics and logs for all traffic within your mesh's GKE cluster are automatically ingested into Google Cloud.

- Automatically generated dashboards display in-depth telemetry in the Anthos Service Mesh dashboard, letting you dig deep into your metrics and logs, filtering and slicing your data on a wide variety of attributes.

- Service-to-service relationships at a glance; you can understand who connects to each service and the services it depends on.

- Secure your inter-service traffic; Anthos Service Mesh certificate authority (Mesh CA) automatically generates and rotates certificates so that you can enable mutual TLS authentication (mTLS) easily with Istio policies.

- Quickly see the communication security posture not only of your service but also its relationships with other services.

- Dig deeper into your service metrics and combine them with other Google Cloud metrics using Cloud Monitoring.

- Gain clear and simple insight into the health of your service with **service level objectives** (**SLOs**) that allow you to easily define and alert on your own standards of service health.

Centralized config management

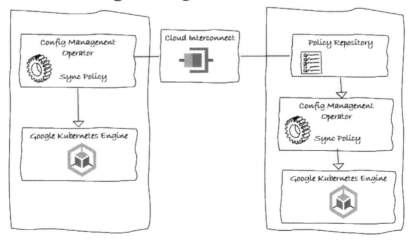

Figure 11.2: *Centralized Config management*

Anthos provides a unified declarative model for computing, networking, and even service management across clouds and data centers.

Spanning multiple environments adds complexity in terms of resource management and consistency. Configuration as data is one common approach to managing this complexity, allowing you to store the desired state of your hybrid environment under version control and apply it directly with repeatable results. Anthos makes this possible with Anthos Config Management, which integrates with Anthos clusters on-premises or in the cloud. It lets you deploy and monitor configuration changes stored in a central Git repository.

The Git approach leverages some of the core Kubernetes concepts, such as Namespaces, labels, and annotations, to help in configuration management. Namespaces and labels determine how and where Anthos is to apply the config changes across your Kubernetes clusters. The repository maintains a controlled, versioned, secured, single source of truth for all your Kubernetes configurations.

Anthos Config Management provided the following benefits for your multi-cluster environments:

- Single source of truth
    - Provides a definitive controlled version for configurations
    - Enables code reviews, validation, and rollbacks
    - Defeats shadow ops, where Kubernetes clusters can drift out of policy adherence due to manual changes.
    - Drives the use of CI/CD pipelines for automated testing and rollout
- One-step deployment across all clusters
    - Anthos Config Management autonomously converts a single Git commit into multiple kubectl commands delivered across all the relevant clusters.
    - Rollback can be performed automatically by reverting the change in the Git repository. The code reversion is then automatically deployed as per the CI/CD process.
- Rich inheritance model for applying changes
    - Using Fleets or Namespaces, you have the granularity to create configurations for all similar clusters, just some clusters, or even for a custom group of resources.
    - Using Fleets or Namespace inheritance, you can create a layered Namespace model so that you can effectively configure inheritance to be applied across and down through the repository folder's structure.

- Advanced policy enforcement and auditing with Policy Controller

  o Use the included policy guardrails to enforce security best practices across your entire environment

  o Continuously audit your environment for configuration that violates business policies

  o Define and deploy your own custom rules using an expressive custom policy language to encode your unique business logic

Cloud Run for Anthos

Cloud Run for Anthos provides a serverless platform for creating modern applications. Cloud Run abstracts away the complexities of the underlying platform, making it easier to design and generate your containerized applications.

Developers deliver more in less time because Cloud Run provides a layer of abstraction when defining and deploying services, freeing up the developer to concentrate on the code. Cloud Run autonomously manages how the service is run. It can do this either in the cloud or on-premise. It controls not just how the service runs but also how it adjusts to fluctuating demand. As a result, Cloud Run for Anthos will optimize resource utilization, horizontal scaling, and integration with networking and Anthos Service Mesh during runtime if required. Cloud Run can even scale apps to and from zero instances based on demand.

Cloud Run for Anthos is generally available for Anthos on Google Cloud and Anthos on-prem deployment options and is on the roadmap for multi-cloud and attached clusters.

Secure software supply chain

How do you trust what is running on the production infrastructure? After all, the software is deployed as a final stage in the CI/CD pipeline typically after undergoing stringent testing. However, what is to prevent working and non-conformant containers from slipping through. This is where Binary Authorization comes into play.

Binary Authorization was designed as a solution for exactly that issue as it is a container security feature integrated into Anthos clusters. Binary Authorization sits close to the endpoint of a CI/CF pipeline and provides a policy enforcement chokepoint to ensure that only signed and authorized images are deployed in the production environment.

Consolidated logging and monitoring

Logging and monitoring are the foundation of diligent security. Hence, access to logs for applications and infrastructure components is critical for running and maintaining production infrastructure.

Cloud Logging provides a place to store and analyze logs. For Anthos, workloads running inside your clusters will have logs automatically enriched with relevant labels like the pod labels, pod name, and the cluster's name that generated them. Labels make logs easier to explore through advanced queries.

In Anthos, the Cloud Audit Logs capture and analyze the interactions between your application's control components and your users. This is essential when you need to know who did what and when they did it.

On the other hand, Kubernetes Engine Monitoring provides an integration that stores your application's critical metrics for use in debugging, alerting, and post-incident analysis. For Anthos on Google Cloud, Kubernetes Engine Monitoring is enabled by default.

Unified user interface

As the purpose of Anthos is to manage across hybrid environments, it must have a dashboard in the Google Cloud Console that provides you with a secure, unified user interface to view and manage your applications across all your Anthos resources. The Anthos default dashboard's landing page provides you with an at-a-glance runtime status summary for all your services and clusters. The Dashboard's default out-of-the-box has three views:

- **Cluster management**: The Anthos cluster management view provides a secure console to view the state of all your registered clusters and create new clusters for your project. You add clusters to this view by registering them with Connect to your Google Cloud project fleet.

- **Service Mesh dashboard**: Anthos Service Mesh, by default, will upload metrics and logs to Cloud Monitoring and Cloud Logging for all the traffic it sees within your cluster. This amount of detailed telemetry data will enable operators to act upon their observations and highlight and mitigate any anomalous behavior.

- **Configuration management**: The Anthos dashboard's Configuration Management view provides a unified overview of the status of all your clusters. With Anthos Config Management enabled, you can readily highlight and then track multi-cluster configuration changes. You can also drill-down to see which specific branch and commit tag was applied to each cluster during the change.

Anthos for development

Developers use the Anthos platform to quickly and easily build and deploy existing container-based applications and microservices-based architectures across multi-cluster environments.

Key benefits for developers are:

- Anthos provides a Git-compliant repository with Git style process management driving CI/CD workflows for configuration as well as code

- Delivery of telemetry and data using Anthos Service Mesh and Cloud Monitoring and Cloud Logging

- Security of services using mTLS and throttling

- Inbuilt support for Google Cloud Marketplace to install off-the-shelve-software into clusters

Anthos for operations

For Operations, Anthos provides a method for centralized and efficient deployment and management of clusters. This allows the operations team to quickly provide and manage infrastructure that is compliant with corporate standards using templates and code.

Key benefits include:

- Centralized configuration management, which drives compliance with policy, configuration-as-code, and infrastructure-as-code.

- Simplified CI/CD deployments and rollbacks with Git style check-ins.

- A unified dashboard with a single pane of glass view across all the clusters.

Anthos for security

For Security, Anthos enforces policy and security standards on clusters, deployed applications, and even configuration management workflow by using a configuration-as-code approach supported by centralized management.

Key benefits include:

- Centralized and securable workflow using a centralized, Git-compliant configuration repository.

- Policy and Compliance enforced on cluster configurations using Namespaces and inherited config.

- Security, by default, ensures that microservices use the Anthos Service Mesh, which gives them in-cluster mTLS with certificate-level protection.

- Built-in services protection using Anthos Service Mesh authorization and routing.

Designing modern CI/CD with Anthos

To improve software delivery performance, you need to implement CI/CD components and other technical best practices needed to support the software delivery lifecycle and understand how to consistently manage that infrastructure with Anthos.

Software delivery platforms

A software delivery platform unifies the tools and streamlines the processes needed to build, deliver, deploy, and operate applications.

It has the responsibility to maintain an application's configuration, stability, uptime, and scale varies between operators, security, and developer teams, but all the components and teams need to work together to speed up releases. Although this document describes methods to improve source control management and application observability, it focuses mainly on **continuous integration (CI)**, **continuous delivery (CD)**, and configuration management.

Software delivery workflow

A core component of the software delivery platform is the CI/CD system. When platform builders begin to define the CI/CD process, they need to ensure that each component produces or consumes artifacts that adhere to a standardized interface. Using a standardized interface simplifies the replacement of components when a better implementation comes to the market.

When you create a platform for containerized applications, you can use the three standardized interfaces between components: Git repositories, Docker images, and Kubernetes manifests. These interfaces let you create a reusable and flexible CI/CD pipeline with a development, build, and release workflow, as shown in the following diagram:

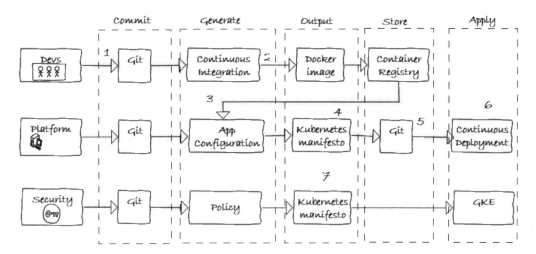

Figure 11.3: CI/CD Workflow

This workflow works as follows:

- Developers commit their application code to the code repositories.

- The CI system tests the code, creates a Docker image artifact, and stores the artifact in a registry.

- After the artifact is ready for deployment, a reference to it is added to the application configuration.

- That application configuration is rendered into a Kubernetes-readable format and stored in a code repository. Updates to this repository trigger deployments to a pre-production environment.

- After the configuration is stored in the code repository, operators review the changes and merge them into the mainline branch. At that point, the configuration is deployed to the production environment.

- When operators make changes to the base configurations, those changes are applied across the organization. As operators commit changes to their repositories, application configuration updates (and subsequent deployments) can be triggered automatically. Alternatively, operators' changes can be picked up the next time developers deploy their changes.

- In parallel, security engineers can implement and tweak policies that define what can be deployed, and then commit those policies to their policy repository.

Using a GitOps methodology, you can require a declarative approach for any changes to applications and clusters. With this approach, all changes are subject to audit and review before they can be enforced. In this declarative model, you store your configuration files in a Git repository that lets you maintain a log of changes, easily roll back failed deployments, and see the potential impact of the changes being proposed.

Code repositories

Source code repositories are at the heart of the CI/CD system. Operators, developers, and security engineers should probably each have their own repositories, but this is not always the case as it enables them to autonomously propagate their changes into the platform. Using a Git repository as the basis for all changes in the system provides several benefits:

- **Built-in auditability**: Commits contain information about when, what, and who changed the system.

- **A simplified rollback process**: Git's revert functionality lets you roll back to a previous state of the system.

- **Versioning**: You can tag Git commits to denote a version of the system's state.

- **Transactions**: You must explicitly resolve state conflicts and review them before you can integrate the changes into the state.

Application landing zones

A landing zone is a locked-down logic entity that lets developers deploy and iterate on their applications autonomously. Namespaces within clusters is a good way to manage this as you create a Kubernetes namespace in each cluster for each environment (for example, for production, QA, or staging).

Operating model

It is important to take time to plan your operating model as consistency is critical when you operate a software delivery platform with modern CI/CD. It's important to keep the environments, infrastructure, and processes naming and terminology consistent and up to date.

Governance

The pursuit of consistency in the prior step leads to the main goal of all software delivery platforms and modern CI/CD systems, which is to improve the efficiency of the overall software delivery process. When managing the platform, you will typically have two primary considerations: application onboarding, which generally falls under the category of governance, and any ongoing development and maintenance of the platform, which is when you are treating the platform like a product.

Platform as a product

The CI/CD workflow is a software product, except that the users of the product are development, operations, and security teams. With that in mind, the platform requires the same software development roles and processes, such as user feedback loops and feature development cycles.

Deploying CI/CD with Anthos

As you begin to deploy modern CI/CD with Anthos to the organization, choosing the best pilot applications is critical. Development, operations, and security teams also need to consider other factors as they work, which this section discusses.

Selecting a pilot application

This refers to choosing the first few good candidates as pilots are services that process data or handle requests but don't store data, for example, caching layers, web front ends, or event-based processing applications. Typically, these applications are more resistant to small amounts of downtime and deployment errors.

Developer considerations

When you work in a modern CI/CD development process, features, changes, and deployments can occur both with increased frequency and more asynchronously. It's a good practice to invest in better versioning practices both for applications and the data contracts by which the different services communicate. Along with improving communication methods and versioning, implementing features in small pieces and utilizing feature branches and flags can improve how you test and release features.

Operator considerations

With a software delivery platform, operations teams need to function more like development teams. Instead of building externally facing features, they're building internal tools and processes that help facilitate the development, deployment, and operation of external-facing applications. Platform tools are used by their own team as well as the development and security teams. Operators should build tools to aid in rolling out new versions of applications and rolling them back in case of application errors or deployment failures. Operators should also emphasize more on building monitoring and alerting systems to proactively detect failures and throw alerts accordingly.

Security team considerations

Security teams should work to make security more of a shared responsibility between themselves and the operations and development teams. This pattern is commonly called *shifting left* on security, in which information security (InfoSec) is involved early in the development process, developers work with pre-approved tools, and security testing is automated. In addition to these techniques, you can programmatically define and enforce security policy with Anthos Config Management. The combination of techniques and tools puts security enforcement in a more proactive posture.

CI/CD workflow

To build out a modern CI/CD system, you first need to choose tools and services that perform the main functions of the system. This reference architecture focuses on implementing the core functions of a CI/CD system, which are shown in the following diagram:

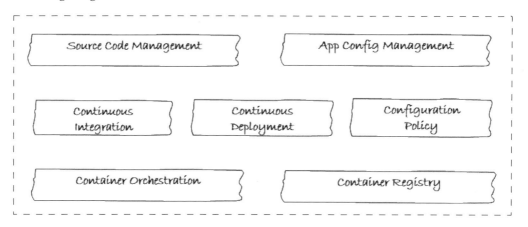

Figure 11.4: CI/CD Reference Architecture

This reference implementation uses the following tools for each component:

- For source code management: GitLab
    - o   Stores application and configuration code
    - o   Let's you review changes

- For application configuration management: kustomize
  - o Defines the desired configuration of an application
  - o Let's you reuse and extend configuration primitives or blueprints
- For continuous integration: GitLab
  - o Tests and validates source code
  - o Builds artifacts that the deployment environment consumes
- For continuous delivery: GitLab
  - o Defines the rollout process of code across environments
  - o Provides easy rollback for failed changes
- For the infrastructure configuration and policy engine: Anthos Config Management
  - o Provides a mechanism that you can use to define what is allowed to run in a given environment based on the organization's policies.
- For container orchestration: Anthos clusters
  - o Runs the artifacts that are built during CI
  - o Provides scaling, health checking, and rollout methodologies for workloads
- For container registry: Artifact Registry
  - o Stores the artifacts (container images) that are built during CI

Architecture

This section describes the CI/CD components that you implement by using this reference architecture: infrastructure, code repositories, and application landing zones.

Platform infrastructure

The infrastructure for this reference architecture consists of Kubernetes clusters to support development, shared tools, and application environments. The following diagram shows the logical layout of the clusters:

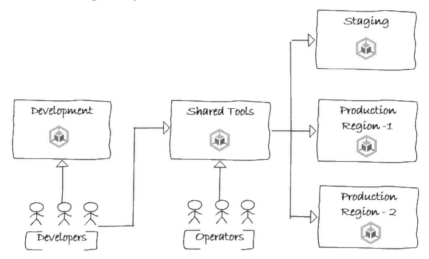

Figure 11.5: *Infrastructure Architecture*

Code repositories

Using this reference architecture, you set up individual repositories for operators, developers, and security engineers.

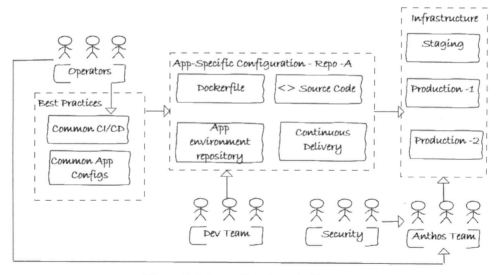

Figure 11.6: *Source Repository Architecture*

In this workflow, your operators will directly manage their own repository for storing their best practices for CI/CD and any application configuration in the operator repository. When the developers onboard any new applications in their own development repository, they will automatically get access to the operators' repository of best practices and any specialized configuration necessary for their application to operate properly. Meanwhile, the operations and security teams can manage their own repositories for consistency and security of the platform in the configuration and policy repositories, respectively.

Application landing zones

You will have landing zones, which are pre-configured environments for running workloads in specific namespaces, such as Dev, Test, and Prod.

Each namespace includes a service account that the CI/CD system uses to deploy Kubernetes resources such as Pods and Services. To follow the principle of least privilege, we recommend that you give the service account access to only its own namespace. You can define service account access in Anthos Config Management and implement it by using Kubernetes role-based access control (RBAC) roles and role bindings. With this model in place, teams can deploy any resources directly into the namespaces they manage but are prevented from overwriting or deleting resources from other namespaces.

Technical walkthrough 11.1: Building a CI/CD in Anthos

Overview

In this tutorial, we will be learning how to build a Continuous Integration Continuous Deployment pipeline in Anthos. We will also be examining the resultant architecture and explore some of the required code repositories.

Objectives

- Deploy the reference architecture infrastructure
- Explore the infrastructure
- Explore the code repositories and pipelines
- Explore an example application landing zone

Before you begin

- Select or create a Google Cloud project.

> **If you don't plan to keep the resources that you create in this procedure, create a project instead of selecting an existing project. After you finish these steps, you can delete the project, removing all resources associated with the project.**

- Make sure billing is enabled for your Cloud project. Learn how to confirm that billing is enabled for your project.

Part 1

Step 1: Deploying the reference architecture

1. In the Cloud Console, activate Cloud Shell.

2. In Cloud Shell, clone the Git repository:

   ```
   git clone https://github.com/GoogleCloudPlatform/solutions-modern-cicd-anthos.git
   ```

   ```
   cd solutions-modern-cicd-anthos
   ```

3. Set the environment variables for this project:

   > **In the following command replace PROJECT_ID with your Cloud project ID.**

   ```
   export PROJECT_ID=PROJECT_ID
   ```

   ```
   export PROJECT_NUMBER=$(gcloud projects describe ${PROJECT_ID} --format 'value(projectNumber)')
   ```

   ```
   export REGION="us-central1"
   ```


   ```
   gcloud config set compute/region ${REGION}
   ```

   ```
   gcloud config set core/project ${PROJECT_ID}
   ```

4. Enable the Cloud Build, Anthos, Service Usage, Cloud Key Management Service (Cloud KMS), Binary Authorization, Secret Manager, and Container Analysis APIs:

   ```
   gcloud services enable cloudbuild.googleapis.com
   ```

   ```
   gcloud services enable anthos.googleapis.com
   ```

   ```
   gcloud services enable serviceusage.googleapis.com
   ```

```
gcloud services enable cloudkms.googleapis.com

gcloud services enable binaryauthorization.googleapis.com

gcloud services enable secretmanager.googleapis.com

gcloud services enable containeranalysis.googleapis.com
```

5. Update **Identity and Access Management (IAM)** roles and permissions for the Cloud Build service account:

```
gcloud projects add-iam-policy-binding ${PROJECT_ID} \

    --member serviceAccount:${PROJECT_NUMBER}@cloudbuild.
gserviceaccount.com \

    --role roles/owner

gcloud projects add-iam-policy-binding ${PROJECT_ID} \

    --member serviceAccount:${PROJECT_NUMBER}@cloudbuild.
gserviceaccount.com \

    --role roles/containeranalysis.admin
```

6. Run Cloud Build to deploy the clusters:

```
gcloud builds submit --substitutions=_PROJECT_ID=${PROJECT_ID}
```

This process takes about 30 minutes. When it finishes, you can explore the infrastructure.

Step 2: Exploring the infrastructure

In this section, you will explore the main components of the CI/CD system, including the infrastructure, code repositories, and a sample landing zone:

- In the Google Cloud Console, go to the Kubernetes clusters page. This page lists the clusters that are used for the development (**dev-us-west1**), shared tools (gitlab), and application environments (**staging-us-west2**, **prod-us-central1**, **prod-us-east1**):

Figure 11.7: Kubernetes Cluster View

Development cluster

The development cluster (**dev-us-west1**) gives your developers access to a namespace that they can use to iterate on their applications. We recommend that teams use tools like Skaffold that provide an iterative workflow by actively monitoring the code under development and reapplying it to the development environments as changes are made. This iteration loop is similar to hot reloading, but instead of being programming language-specific, the loop works with any application that you can build with a Docker image. You can run the loop inside a Kubernetes cluster.

Shared tools cluster

Any software delivery system uses a mixture of tools to support the software development lifecycle. Following the principle of least privilege, the reference implementation provides a dedicated cluster for storing tools (GitLab). We recommend that you deploy each tool to its own namespace.

In this reference implementation, you use GitLab for source code management and continuous integration. You install GitLab in the tools cluster by using the GitLab on GKE Terraform module.

Application environment clusters

Also included in the reference architecture are clusters (**staging-us-west2**, **prod-us-central1**, **prod-us-east1**) to run your applications for both pre-production (staging) and production deployments. You should deploy your applications to at least one cluster in each environment. For geo-redundancy or high-availability (HA) systems, we recommend that you add multiple clusters to each environment. For all clusters where applications are deployed, it's ideal to use regional clusters. This approach insulates your applications from zone-level failures and any interruptions caused by cluster or node pool upgrades.

We recommend that you use Anthos Config Management to sync the configuration of cluster resources such as namespaces, quotas, and RBAC. For more details on how to manage those resources, see Configuration and policy repositories later in this chapter.

Exploring the code repositories

In this section, you will explore the code repositories.

Log in to the GitLab instance

1. In Cloud Shell, get the GitLab URL:

    ```
    echo "https://gitlab.endpoints.${PROJECT_ID}.cloud.goog"
    ```

2. Copy the URL because you need it for a later step.

3. Retrieve the GitLab User and Password, which are stored in Secrets Manager:

```
export GITLAB_USER=$(gcloud secrets versions access latest
--secret="gitlab-user")

export GITLAB_PASSWORD=$(gcloud secrets versions access latest
--secret="gitlab-password")


echo "User: ${GITLAB_USER}"
echo "Password: ${GITLAB_PASSWORD}"
```

4. Copy these credentials because you need them for a later step.

5. In a web browser, go to the GitLab URL that you copied earlier.

6. Using the User and Password credentials that you copied, log in to your GitLab instance.

The Projects page for your GitLab instance is displayed.

Explore the operator repositories

The operator, starter, and configuration repositories are where operators and platform administrators define the common best practices for building on and operating the platform. These repositories are all located in the platform-admins group:

1. In the GitLab instance, click on **Groups**, and then select **Your Groups**.

2. Click on **platform-admins**.

A list of repositories is displayed:

Step 3: Applying the reference architecture

Now that you've explored the reference architecture, you can explore a developer workflow that is based on this implementation:

1. If you've never used Git in Cloud Shell, configure Git with your name and email address. Git uses this information to identify you as the author of the commits that you create in Cloud Shell.

Replace the values in the following command:

- **GIT_EMAIL_ADDRESS**: The email address associated with your Git account.

- **GIT_USERNAME**: The username associated with your Git account:

```
git config --global user.email "GIT_EMAIL_ADDRESS"
git config --global user.name "GIT_USERNAME"
```

Part 2: Applying the developer workflow

Overview

When you use a CI/CD pipeline, the idea is that when you develop a new feature, you need to quickly deploy your changes into a development sandbox in order to test and iterate on them. In this tutorial, you will use Skaffold to actively monitor your changes and deploy them to a development sandbox.

Objectives

- Onboard a new application.

- Use Skaffold to develop a new feature and then test it live.

- Deploy the new feature to a pre-production environment.

- Use GitOps to deploy the new feature to multiple production clusters.

Step 1: Onboarding a new application

The reference architecture contains a command-line interface (CLI), anthos-platform-cli, that streamlines application management processes, such as creating and deleting applications. anthos-platform-cli uses starter repositories to initialize the new application and pull in best practices that the operation and platform administration teams manage. The CLI also establishes the landing zone for your new application by defining the namespace and base policies in the anthos-config-management repository.

1. In Cloud Shell, download the anthos-platform-cli CLI:

   ```
   cd $HOME

   wget -O anthos-platform-cli https://storage.googleapis.com/
   solutions-public-assets/anthos-platform-cli/latest/anthos-
   platform-cli-vlatest-linux-amd64
   ```

2. Make the CLI executable:

   ```
   chmod +x anthos-platform-cli
   ```

3. Create an application:

   ```
   ./anthos-platform-cli add app \
       --name hello-world-golang \
   ```

```
  --gitlab-hostname $GITLAB_HOSTNAME \
  --gitlab-token $GITLAB_PASSWORD \
  --template-name golang-template
mv hello-world-golang hello-world-golang.bak
```

Step 2: Adding a new feature to the application

When you develop a new feature, you need to quickly deploy your changes into a development sandbox in order to test and iterate on them. In this tutorial, you will use Skaffold to actively monitor your changes and deploy them to a development sandbox.

Skaffold generates a configuration file named **skaffold.yaml**. This file defines the Docker images and Kubernetes manifests that you use to deploy the application. When you run skaffold dev, the continuous development loop begins. As you make changes to the application, Skaffold automatically rebuilds the necessary Docker images and deploys the latest version of your development code to the development cluster.

In their work, developers build many images and need a place in a container registry to store them. We recommend that you give each developer access to a subpath in the container registry where they store their development images. For example, your project might give them access to the **gcr.io/my-project/alice** repository in Container Registry. After you give them administrative access to push and pull images from that repository, they can set the default-repo Skaffold configuration to use that repository for their development images.

1. Connect to the development cluster. In Cloud Shell, get credentials to the development cluster:

   ```
   gcloud container clusters --region us-west1 get-credentials dev-
   us-west1
   ```

2. 2.2 Rename your context:

   ```
   kubectx development=gke_${PROJECT_ID}_us-west1_dev-us-west1
   ```

3. Switch to your development cluster context:

   ```
   kubectx development
   ```

Step 3: Set up your development environment

1. In Cloud Shell, clone your application repository:

   ```
   git clone git@$GITLAB_HOSTNAME:hello-world-golang/hello-world-
   golang.git
   cd hello-world-golang
   ```

2. Create an Artifact Registry repository for your user:

```
gcloud beta artifacts repositories create $USER --repository-
format=Docker \
    --location=us-central1
gcloud beta artifacts repositories add-iam-policy-binding \
    --member serviceAccount:tf-sa-dev-us-west1@${PROJECT_ID}.iam.
gserviceaccount.com \
    --role roles/artifactregistry.reader \
    --location us-central1 $USER
```

3. Set up Docker authentication to your Artifact Registry repository:

```
gcloud beta auth configure-docker us-central1-docker.pkg.dev
```

4. Create your own namespace on the development cluster to serve as your development sandbox:

```
kubectl create namespace $USER
kubens $USER
```

5. Create a service account for your application:

```
kubectl create serviceaccount hello-world-golang-ksa
```

6. Configure Skaffold to use your Artifact Registry repository:

```
skaffold config set default-repo us-central1-docker.pkg.
dev/$PROJECT_ID/$USER
```

7. Start the Skaffold development loop:

```
skaffold dev --port-forward
```

On the Cloud Shell toolbar, click on **Web Preview**, and then click on **Preview** on port **8080**:

The output is the following:

```
Hello World!
```

Keep this Cloud Shell session open.

Step 4: Update the application

1. On the Cloud Shell toolbar, click on add **Open a new tab** to activate a new session. Create a feature branch for your work:

```
cd hello-world-golang
git checkout -b my-feature
```

2. Update the application to output a different message:

```
sed -i "s/Hello World/My new feature/g" main.go
```

Skaffold monitors your working directory for changes and is automatically rebuilding and deploying your application to the development cluster.

3. To see your changes, refresh the web preview.

4. In your original Cloud Shell session, press *Ctrl + C* to exit Skaffold.

5. Commit and push your changes into the feature branch:

```
git add .
git commit -m "Changed the message"
git push -u origin my-feature
```

6. Close the other Cloud Shell session.

Step 5: Deploying your change to the staging cluster

After you successfully push your changes into the feature branch of the application code repository, you can deploy them to the staging cluster. To deploy to the staging cluster, merge your changes into the main branch of the application repository. This action triggers a CI process to test the code, render the Kubernetes manifests, and push the rendered manifests into the staging branch of the application's configuration repository. When the CI process pushes the manifests into the application's configuration repository, a CD job starts, which deploys the manifests to the staging cluster.

To deploy your changes to the staging cluster, do the following:

1. In a web browser, go to GitLab and log in using the URL and username and password from the reference architecture.

2. Click on **Groups**, and then select **Your Groups**.

3. Click on **hello-world-golang**.

4. Click on **hello-world-golang** to go to the application code repository. To see your changes in the repository, select your feature branch from the Branches list:

Figure 11.8: GitLab Branch and Tags View

5. In the adjacent pane, click on **Merge Requests**, and then click on **Create merge request** to create a merge request.

6. Select the **Delete source branch** when merge request is accepted option, and then click on **Submit merge request**.

    Click on **Merge**. In the menu, click on **CI/CD** to view the execution of the CI pipeline.

7. Click on **Running** to get more details.

    > **When the pipeline is completed, the updated manifests have been pushed into the hello-world-golang-env repository. That push triggered a CD job to deploy your code changes to the staging cluster.**

8. Click on **Groups**, and then select **Your Groups**.

9. Click on **hello-world-golang**.

10. Click on **hello-world-golang-env** to view the application configuration repository.

    In the menu, click on CI/CD to view the execution of the CD pipeline.

> **When the pipeline is completed, the code changes have been deployed to the staging cluster.**

View the changes on the staging cluster

1. In Cloud Shell, get credentials to the staging cluster:

    ```
    gcloud container clusters --region us-west2 get-credentials
    staging-us-west2
    ```

2. Rename your context:

```
kubectx staging=gke_${PROJECT_ID}_us-west2_staging-us-west2
```

3. Switch to your staging cluster context:

```
kubectx staging
```

4. Create a port forward:

```
kubectl port-forward svc/hello-world-golang-app -n hello-world-golang 8080:8080
```

5. On the Cloud Shell toolbar, click on preview **Web Preview**, and then click on **Preview** on port **8080**.

   The output is the following:

   ```
   My new feature!
   ```

6. In Cloud Shell, press *Ctrl + C* to end the port forward.

Step 7: Promoting to the production clusters

After you verify your changes in the staging cluster, you are ready to promote the changes to the production clusters. The **hello-world-golang-env** repository contains a branch for each application environment. Updates to the application configuration automatically trigger the CD pipelines, which deploy the application to the environments associated with the branch; for example, updates to the staging branch trigger a deployment to the staging environment. Storing the application configuration in Git and automating the deployment of the applications form the foundation of the GitOps process. Storing the manifests in Git improves the auditability of configuration changes and deployments.

To trigger the deployment to production, you merge the application configuration from the staging branch into the main branch of the **hello-world-golang-env** repository.

1. In GitLab, click on **Groups**, and then select **Your Groups**.

2. Click on **hello-world-golang**.

3. Click on **hello-world-golang-env**.

4. In the adjacent pane, click on **Merge Requests**, and then click on **Create merge request** to create a merge request.

5. Unselect **Delete** source branch when merge request is accepted.

6. Click on **Submit** merge request.

7. Click on **Merge**.

8. In the menu, click on **CI/CD** to view the pipeline execution.

9. After the deployment to the prod-us-central1 cluster completes, click on **play_arrow** play to approve the rollout to the prod-us-east1 cluster.

Step 8: View the changes on a production cluster

1. In Cloud Shell, get credentials to the **prod-us-central1** cluster:

   ```
   gcloud container clusters get-credentials prod-us-central1
   ```

2. Rename your context:

   ```
   kubectx prod-central=gke_${PROJECT_ID}_us-central1_prod-us-central1
   ```

3. Switch to your **prod-central** cluster context:

   ```
   kubectx prod-central
   ```

4. Create a port forward:

   ```
   kubectl port-forward svc/hello-world-golang-app -n hello-world-golang 8080:8080
   ```

5. On the Cloud Shell toolbar, click on preview **Web Preview**, and then click on **Preview** on port **8080**.

   The output is the following:

   ```
   My new feature!
   ```

6. In Cloud Shell, press *Ctrl + C* to end the port forward.

Congratulations! You just built a CI/CD Pipeline on Anthos.

Clean up!

To avoid incurring charges to your Google Cloud account for the resources used in this tutorial, delete the project.

Conclusion

In this chapter, you learned about Anthos from a deeper technical inspection of its architecture and features. You also learned how Anthos can be used for CI/CD and how we can set up isolated repositories and workspaces using namespaces and labels. Additionally, you learned the best practices for planning software and security workflows as well as best practices in infrastructure management. Finally, you put everything, and a little bit more, into building a modern CI/CD pipeline on Anthos.

In the next chapter, we will build on what you learnt in this chapter to learn more about deploying, managing, and exploring Anthos in a real-world scenario.

CHAPTER 12

Application Management with Anthos

In the previous chapter, we learned about Anthos and what we needed to know in order to build a modern software CI/CD pipeline. You learned a lot, and it was a technical accomplishment to successfully build your software pipeline. Nonetheless, Anthos is still most likely a mystery to you as we have only investigated a single, albeit a very popular use case, reason for deploying Anthos. In this chapter, we will dive deeper into Anthos, its architecture, and how it works. Up to now, we have just accepted that Anthos is a solution for managing our applications that are deployed on hybrid and/or multi cloud Kubernetes clusters without questioning how it manages to do this. Taken at face value, it is a fantastic solution to many of our issues with deploying cloud native apps across on-prem and other cloud environments. However, it is essential that we get a grounding as to what is going on under the hood so that we can be confident that our apps are optimized, cost-effective, and secure. In this chapter, we will take a deeper dive into Anthos to see how it works its magic under the hood.

The goal of this chapter will be to introduce Anthos to any developer or user familiar with Kubernetes. You will learn about Anthos architecture and the control plane, and we will then deploy a full sample Anthos cluster to see some of these things in action.

Structure

In this chapter, we will cover the following topics:

- Kubernetes technical architecture
- Kubernetes as a hybrid, multi-cloud orchestrator
- Cloud logging, monitoring, and observability
- Interactive tutorial: Deploying Anthos on Google Cloud
- Exploring Anthos cluster security
- Exploring Anthos cluster's policy configuration

Objectives

When you finish going through this chapter, you will have a good understanding of the Kubernetes technical architecture and how Kubernetes can spam multi-cloud and hybrid environments. You will be familiar with Anthos as a multi-cloud, multi-cluster orchestrator and, through hands-on tutorials, be able to connect to and explore an Anthos environment.

The rise of Kubernetes

At the beginning of the last decade, the very technology that had revolutionized the on-prem data center was now a problem. VMs were propagating wildly throughout the enterprise, and IT faced a challenge with what they called the **virtual machine (VM)** sprawl. The harsh reality was that VMs were so cheap and easy to provision that any user, developer, or administrator with access to the VMware environment launched a new virtual machine as the answer to any issue. But it didn't take long before enterprise IT realized that there were literally hundreds of zombie VMs running across multiple departments that were active, unmonitored, and not visible to IT administrative software or managed by IT.

Virtual machine sprawl inevitably led to the loss of control and fragmentation of resources. A change in fashion and a shift in trend from VMs to containers put paid to VM sprawl rather effectively, but at a price. Fast forward to 2020, and now we find that enterprise IT is experiencing Kubernetes cluster sprawl. Once again, users at a departmental level are spinning up clusters in on-premises, private cloud, and public cloud environments. Each department runs multiple clusters or managed CaaS offerings such as Google Kubernetes Engine and Azure Kubernetes Service.

Enterprise IT is facing the same challenges with cluster sprawl that it once saw with VM sprawl. Kubernetes clusters have become the new deployment boundaries for applications. Though namespaces provide the required isolation and boundaries, customers find it much easier to isolate their applications completely by running them on different clusters, often on different clouds.

Today, it is not uncommon to find departments with multiple shadow clusters running across different environments—on-premises, private cloud, self-provisioned clusters in the public cloud and managed clusters in the public cloud. Moreover, trying to enumerate these clusters, let alone manage them, poses a huge challenge to the IT and DevOps teams.

Thankfully, one technology has come to the forefront for orchestrating clusters: Kubernetes. Normally, having one dominant technology is not a good thing, but such is the scale of the problem with shadow clouds and offshore clusters that this time it's a blessing. You see, bringing all the clusters under an umbrella of centralized management requires centralized control. For example, multiple Kubernetes clusters can happily coexist on-prem or in the cloud so long as a single set of kubectl commands is simultaneously run on each cluster to ensure that they have a consistent configuration. Automation is a necessity as to apply configurations, policies, quotas, RBAC roles to each cluster is not just time-sensitive but also laborious and error-prone. That is why we need Anthos.

The meta control planes

A Kubernetes cluster is under the direct control of the control plane, which, as its name suggests, controls the master nodes within a cluster. Having mastery over the Kubernetes control plane effectively gives you full jurisdiction of the cluster. This is effectively what Google does with its fully managed GKE service as it locks out the customer from unrestricted access to the control plane. Of course, if you have several clusters under your domain, then you need to find a way to orchestrate and synchronize your control over the group of clusters. The term meta control plane has been used because this virtual entity has dominance over the control plane of each Kubernetes cluster: the master nodes. Hence, a command sent to the meta control plane is automatically applied to the control plane of each cluster. And this is what Anthos does, it acts as a virtual multi-cluster control plane or what is popularly termed a Meta Control Plane.

An effective meta control plane is just what enterprise IT needs to take back control of the cluster sprawl. It needs this meta control plane to act as an overarching single source of mastery that monitors and orchestrates all Kubernetes clusters launched within or even outside an organization's boundaries. Even with the best will in the world, running multiple autonomous clusters will eventually become an issue due to configuration drift. The meta control plane can enforce strict rules that can detect a drift in the cluster configuration and bring them back to the desired state of the organization's configuration.

Monitoring

Since the meta control plane has visibility and omniscience into the workings of each cluster, it can collect and aggregate relevant metrics related to the infrastructure and your application's health. The meta control plane becomes the single pane of glass for both configuration and observability. Indeed, observability is the foundation of Site Reliability Engineering, a close cousin of modern DevOps. With SRE, Service Level Objectives are king as these go a long way to designing creative and effective Service Level Agreements, which are legally enforceable contracts with the customers. Without an all-seeing and all-knowing entity concurrently monitoring all the Service Level Indicators within every cluster in the domain, effective SLAs would be almost impossible.

Just like the Kubernetes controller maintains the desired state of deployments, statefulsets, jobs, and the daemonsets, the meta control plane ensures that the entire cluster maintains the desired state of the configuration. For example, if a participating cluster is expected to run a role and a rolebinding, the meta control plane can detect when the role gets deleted and automatically reapplies the configuration. This is just like the Kubernetes controller maintains the desired count of replicas of a deployment.

As the number of clusters grows within an organization and beyond, customers will need a meta control plane to take charge of the cluster management; that's where Anthos rides to the rescue as it ensures that the participating clusters are normalized and consistent with their configuration. In short, we can say that the meta control plane is to Kubernetes cluster what the controller is to a deployment.

Anthos Cloud

What is Anthos Cloud? Simply put, the popular definition going around is that it is the meta control plane of Kubernetes from Google. Though this definition may be technically correct, it doesn't do justice to the platform. Apart from being a meta control plane, Anthos plays other nuanced orchestration roles that are subtle yet critical to managing infrastructure and workloads in hybrid and multi-cloud environments.

The core components of Anthos, in most cases, are invisible to users. Just like Google hides the master nodes of a GKE cluster, Anthos hides the workings of the underlying control plane. This is because the only interaction customers require with the control plane is via exposed APIs. Anthos exposes the API for managing the lifecycle of Kubernetes clusters and registering external clusters with Anthos.

Anthos — Hybrid and multi cloud dexterity

Though Anthos' control plane runs in the context of GCP, it can launch managed Kubernetes clusters in a variety of environments, including on-premises data centers, AWS, and Azure clouds. The managed Kubernetes clusters launched via Anthos have the same reliability and stability of a typical GKE cluster running in GCP.

For Anthos to launch a managed Kubernetes cluster on-premises, it relies on vSphere 6.5, vCenter, vSphere storage, and F5 BIG-IP or a bundled software load balancer based on a Google open-source project called Seesaw. Anthos first provisions an admin cluster in vSphere that can spawn multiple user clusters. Think of the admin cluster as the local Anthos control plane that handles the lifecycle of managed clusters running in vSphere.

Anthos for Amazon Web Services, which become generally available in May 2020, can run managed Kubernetes clusters in the context of AWS. By taking advantage of Amazon EC2, Amazon EBS, AWS VPC, and Amazon ELB, Anthos can launch highly available Kubernetes clusters that span multiple availability zones. Just like the admin cluster in vSphere, Anthos first launches a management cluster in AWS VPC, which is responsible for launching additional user clusters.

When Anthos for Azure becomes available, it will leverage Azure VMs, Azure Premium Storage, Azure Virtual Networks, and Azure Load Balancer for running HA Kubernetes clusters. Technically speaking, Anthos can launch a managed cluster in any programmable infrastructure that supports running Kubernetes in high availability mode.

Apart from managing clusters launched through Anthos, the platform supports connecting external, unmanaged clusters to the control plane. The key difference between the two—managed and unmanaged—is the lifecycle management. While Anthos can own everything from the creation and termination of managed clusters, it can partially control the external, unmanaged clusters.

Key components of Anthos

Apart from being a hybrid, multicloud control plane for Kubernetes clusters, Anthos can manage the network policies, routing, security, configuration management of workloads deployed across clusters.

Let's take a look at the key components of Anthos:

- **Anthos Control Plane**: This component is the meta control plane of Anthos. It's responsible for managing the lifecycle of managed clusters and the registration and un-registration of external, unmanaged clusters. Anthos exposes the API for this through the Hub and Connect services.

- **Anthos Service Mesh**: This component is a commercially available implementation of Istio service mesh that's optimized for Anthos. It delivers three capabilities:

  o Secure communication among microservices

  o Network and routing policies

  o Observability

- **Anthos Config Management**: This component is based on GitOps and enables a centralized mechanism to push deployments, configuration, and policies to all the participating clusters, both managed and unmanaged. A centrally accessible Git repository acts as a single source of truth for all the clusters. An Anthos Config Management agent running in each cluster will monitor the change of state in a cluster. When deviated from what's defined in the Git, the agent automatically applies the configuration that will bring the cluster back to the desired state.

- **Cloud Run for Anthos**: Cloud Run is a serverless and clusterless environment to run containers in GCP. It's a layer above Knative that delivers an optimal developer experience to deploy and run containers without the need to launch a GKE cluster or define a pod specification. Cloud Run for Anthos brings the same developer experience to the managed clusters.

- **Ingress for Anthos**: This component routes the traffic to the microservices in conjunction with the Envoy proxy configured through Anthos Service Mesh. Ingress for Anthos becomes the entry point to access workloads running in Anthos clusters. It currently works only for workloads running in GKE clusters launched by Anthos.

- **Kubernetes Apps on GCP Marketplace**: This acts as the catalog for a variety of stateless and stateful workloads targeting Kubernetes. Customers can push a button to deploy applications from the marketplace in Anthos managed clusters, irrespective of where they are provisioned.

Cloud logging, monitoring, and observability

Logging and monitoring are the cornerstones of application and network security as they enable application analysis, network forensics, access patterns, and performance profiling, among other things. Indeed, without monitoring, it is very difficult to know exactly what is happening. Additionally, when incidents occur, monitoring and logging are also needed to help identify security or operational risks to your organization.

The GCP Cloud Operations service formerly known as but still commonly referred to as Stackdriver enables debugging, monitoring, and diagnostics for applications and provides a centralized place to manage and analyze operational resources. The Cloud Operations suite, which is a pertinent example of why it is still called **'Stackdriver'**, helps you increase application reliability when running in the cloud. The Cloud Operations suite module that handles logging is aptly named Cloud Logging; this tool lets you capture, store, search for, and analyze configurable system events. With the complementary service, Cloud Monitor, you can also track and trigger alerts on log data and events from the Google Cloud platform. In addition, Cloud Logging is a fully managed service that performs at scale and can ingest application and system locked data from thousands of data sources. Plus, you can analyze all that log data in real-time.

Combined with powerful visualization tools such as DataView, Cloud Operations Suite helps you identify trends and be more proactive in preventing issues. The Cloud Operations Suite provides tools for error reporting, tracing, and debugging applications so that you can quickly locate and fix problems in production systems. However, security nowadays is about more than vulnerability scanning of code; there is the need to ensure regulatory compliance, which extends well beyond traditional security borders of firewalls as you also need data protection and compliance with a variety of regulatory standards.

In addition, Anthos provides access to a service operations dashboard that greatly simplifies what it takes for you to keep your applications up and running at peak efficiency across heterogeneous platforms. The key to making this happen are Cloud monitoring, cloud logging, Service Mesh, and a focus on what we call the golden signals.

If you can only measure four metrics of your user-facing systems, focus on:

- Latency, which is the average time (RTT) it takes to service a request. It's important to distinguish between the latency of successful requests and the latency of failed requests. Latency can be fixed as in high delay caused by packets traveling over long distances, and there is not a lot you can do about that. However, latency can also be variable due to network and environmental factors, and this variation in latency is termed as jitter.

- Traffic or load, which is the measure of how much demand is being placed on your system measured in high-level, system-specific metrics. Traffic or load placed upon the system can again be stable or highly volatile; benchmarking typical traffic peaks over time is critical for understanding the operating environment of your application.

- Errors, which are the percentage of requests that fail, either explicitly--for example, HTTP 500s; implicitly--for example, **HTTP 200** success responses but coupled with the wrong content; or by policy--for example, if you committed to one-second response times, any request over one second is an error.

- Saturation, which is the point of service overload; this is a measure of your system capacity emphasizing the resources that are most constrained.

These golden signals are the cornerstone of establishing and embracing SRE best practices at your organization. With Anthos, you can adopt SRE best practices and improve your observability using those four golden signals.

Anthos application security

Despite the best efforts of Google and its Cloud Operations Suite security on the GCP remains a shared responsibility between Google and the customer. The division of responsibilities vary depending on the services being used. For example, if you build an application with On-Premises infrastructure, you are fully aware of your responsibility for the physical security of the hardware, software, and the premises in which it is housed. This drills down to a responsibility for the encryption of the data on disk, the integrity of your network, and the security of any personal information or confidential content stored in your application. However, when you move an application to Google Cloud Platform, the responsibility for security becomes opaque as Google handles many of the lower layers of the security stack on your behalf. This is not a problem as Google can deliver a higher level of security at these layers than most customers could afford to do on their own. However, the upper layers of access and authority management in the security stack should always remain the customer's responsibility.

One aspect of security that is almost always impractical to outsource is the responsibility of data access or who has access to your data. This is one of the core responsibilities of system administrators establishing and maintaining a workable identity, authentication, and Authorization system. The same constraints apply when you move to GCP, but you have tools and mechanisms to help you design and implement these access controls, including Cloud Identity and Access Management, Access Control lists, and Firewall rules. However, in order to protect your data, these must be properly configured, and that is down to you.

Nonetheless, Google provides tools to make life easier even in those upper security layers, such as Cloud Identity Access Management and Cloud IAM, which helps customers implement the policies they define. One aspect of security that is almost always the responsibility of the customer is Data access. This simply means that you are the one who controls who has access to your data. GCP provides mechanisms to help implement these access controls.

Service accounts

Automation is at the core of Cloud Native applications, so there has to be a way to initiate commands and services without a user with sufficient authority and privileges being logged in. For example, when calling a Google API to retrieve data, the API requests are done via a REST service call, but from where and on whose authority?

The answer is, via a service account. If you are building an automated pipeline of tasks, then you will want to have it initiated and run by a dedicated service account with just the right number of permissions and no more to fulfill the tasks.

Cloud Identity and Access Management

Google Cloud Identity is an Identity as a Service solution for managing who has appropriate access to your organization's resources and services. It is currently used by hundreds of thousands of business customers to manage millions of users on devices. Cloud Identity provides a single Admin console, so users, groups, and domain-wide security settings can be managed for your entire organization from a central location. Cloud Identity can work with any domain name that is able to receive email, so you can use your existing web and email addresses.

When you migrate to Cloud Identity, you must verify that you own the domain name; then, you can create an account for each of your users. You will manage all users from the Google Admin console as it provides a central management location or a single pane of glass for managing your security policies and roles as well as setting users' identity and access permissions across your entire domain.

Managing users manually can also add significant operational overhead, and most organizations already have something similar to a Microsoft Active directory or LDAP database containing user and group information. The Google Cloud Directory Sync tool can synchronize IAM accounts to match the data in an existing active directory so that your Google users' groups and shared context are synchronized to match the information in your Windows or LDAP server.

Zero Trust

The concept of the Zero Trust approach is that there should not be implicit trust in any single entity or service as this can create a security risk. Instead, there is enforcement of mutual trust between communicating or interacting components within the network, and this should be established via mutual authentication and be continuously verified. End-user access is one domain to which this model can be applied, but it also applies to end-to-end processes and cloud-native applications and even workloads running on cloud infrastructure.

Anthos allows you to define and enforce these zero-trust perimeters via network and workload segmentation so that you can readily separate trust and access to clusters and workloads. This Zero Trust approach is enforced across the production environment, ensuring that software interacts with other software in a secure and authenticated manner with no inherent mutual trust between any components or services. To assist with this security approach for users and software, Google has its own in-built security method called **BeyondProd** that applies even to microservices.

For your convenience, you should have at least two organizational admins. This provides redundancy in case one of them is not available for any reason or if an account is lost. But be careful of adding too many admins to your organization. A general principle is to add no more than three.

When the organization is first created, all users in your domain are automatically granted project creator and billing account creator IAM roles at the organization level. This enables users in your domain to continue creating projects without disruption. However, organizational admins should remove these organization-level permissions and start.

A security best practice is to enforce two-step verification (2SV) on all accounts. At the minimum, 2SV should be enforced for all super admin accounts and elevated privilege accounts.

Technical walkthrough 12.1: Launching Anthos using the sample deployment

Before we go ahead and deploy the Google Cloud Platform Anthos sample (preview and not for production) it is probably advisable to create a new project for Anthos. When you have a new project ready, then to launch a fully functional demo of Anthos, you can go to this link at Google.

You will land at this page; click on **LAUNCH** to continue:

Anthos Sample Deployment on Google Cloud (Preview)

Google Click to Deploy

Experience Anthos on Google Cloud with a sample deployment

LAUNCH   VIEW PAST DEPLOYMENTS

Figure 12.1: GCP Marketplace Anthos Sample Deployment

The next page in the deployment process asks you to enable the required APIs, which are Compute Engine, Cloud Deployment Manager, and Cloud Runtime Configuration API.

Click on enable and wait for them to get the green icon next to them:

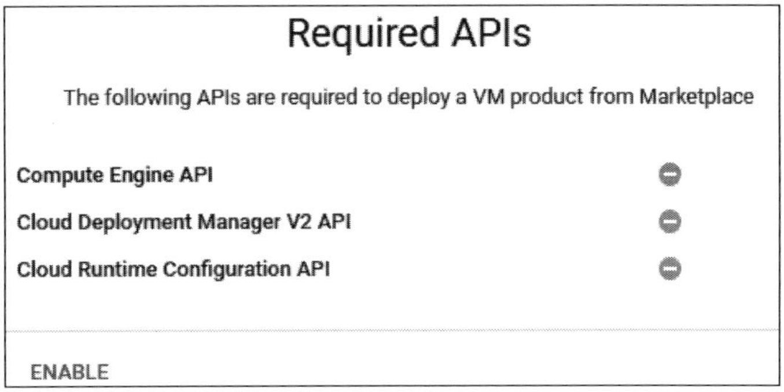

Required APIs

The following APIs are required to deploy a VM product from Marketplace

Compute Engine API   ⊖

Cloud Deployment Manager V2 API   ⊖

Cloud Runtime Configuration API   ⊖

ENABLE

Figure 12.2: Check that APIs are enabled

Once the APIs are enabled, you will be directed to the **Deployment** page. Here, you will confirm that all prerequisites have been met and create a service account (unless you already have one that has the required permissions):

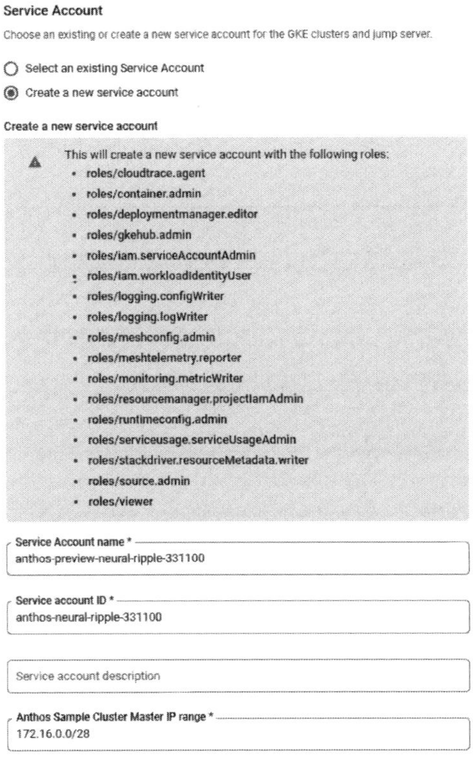

Service Account

Choose an existing or create a new service account for the GKE clusters and jump server.

◯ Select an existing Service Account

◉ Create a new service account

Create a new service account

⚠ This will create a new service account with the following roles:
- roles/cloudtrace.agent
- roles/container.admin
- roles/deploymentmanager.editor
- roles/gkehub.admin
- roles/iam.serviceAccountAdmin
- roles/iam.workloadidentityUser
- roles/logging.configWriter
- roles/logging.logWriter
- roles/meshconfig.admin
- roles/meshtelemetry.reporter
- roles/monitoring.metricWriter
- roles/resourcemanager.projectIamAdmin
- roles/runtimeconfig.admin
- roles/serviceusage.serviceUsageAdmin
- roles/stackdriver.resourceMetadata.writer
- roles/source.admin
- roles/viewer

Service Account name *
anthos-preview-neural-ripple-331100

Service account ID *
anthos-neural-ripple-331100

Service account description

Anthos Sample Cluster Master IP range *
172.16.0.0/28

Figure 12.3: Create a Service Account

Now, deploy sample Anthos:

Figure 12.4: Deploy the Sample Anthos Deployment

The deployment will take a while, so be patient. You will be rewarded for your patience with the following:

Figure 12.5: Success! Anthos is deployed

Anthos is now deployed on your GCP Project and ready for us to play with!

The first thing to do is to go to the console menu and select **Anthos** and **Dashboard**. On the dashboard, you can see the health of our sample Anthos Clusters at a glance.

You should see that there is Anthos Cluster ready and healthy and that it is Synced, so let's click on view clusters and then on the sample-cluster (it's the only one). The following details will appear:

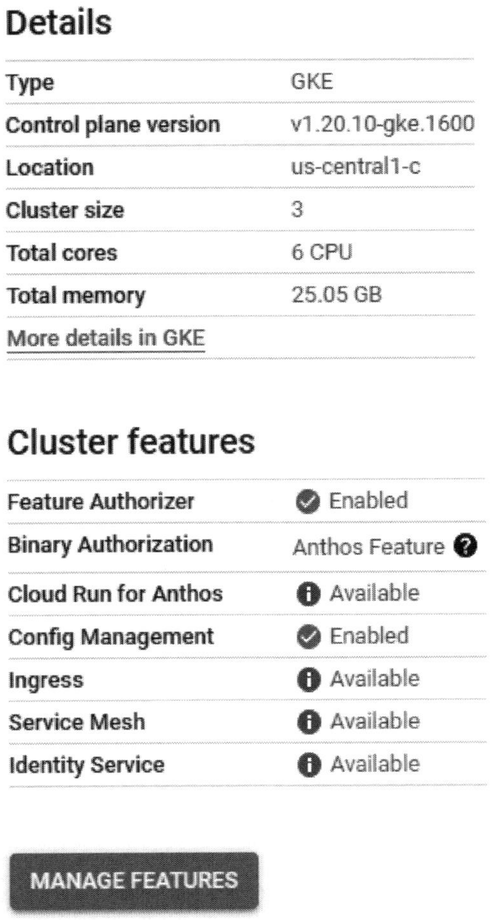

Details

Type	GKE
Control plane version	v1.20.10-gke.1600
Location	us-central1-c
Cluster size	3
Total cores	6 CPU
Total memory	25.05 GB

More details in GKE

Cluster features

Feature Authorizer	✓ Enabled
Binary Authorization	Anthos Feature ❓
Cloud Run for Anthos	ⓘ Available
Config Management	✓ Enabled
Ingress	ⓘ Available
Service Mesh	ⓘ Available
Identity Service	ⓘ Available

MANAGE FEATURES

Figure 12.6: Anthos Manage Deployment Features

Note not all the features are enabled. The notable ones available but not switched on are Service Mesh, Binary Authorization, Cloud Run for Anthos, Identity Service, and Ingress. However, as this is a local deployment, we don't need any of those quite yet; so, leave them disabled for now.

Click on **Security** in the left-hand menu and note the following:

Binary Authorisation

ⓘ

Enable Binary Authorisation API to ensure that only trusted container images are deployed

Kubernetes network policy

ⓘ

Enable network policy for this cluster to specify which pods are allowed to communicate
Learn more

Figure 12.7: Anthos Binary Authorization and Network Policy are not yet enabled

Service access control

No workloads adhere to authorisation policies
Learn more

mTLS status

mTLS is permissive for all workloads
Learn more

Figure 12.8: Service Access Control and mTLS status are enabled but not configured securely

TLS is enabled, but all workloads are presently in the permissive state, which means they can use plain-text and http.

It looks like we have a bare bones Anthos deployment, so let's go ahead and see how to configure it to do something useful.

The Anthos Sample Deployment on Google Cloud (Preview) is a Google Cloud Marketplace solution that you can preview now. It deploys a real Anthos hands-on environment with a GKE cluster, service mesh, and an application with multiple microservices. This tutorial introduces you to these features, letting you learn about Anthos deployed on Google Cloud with a fictional bank. You can then explore Anthos features that interest you by following the bank's Anthos story further in our follow-up tutorials.

Your journey

You are the platform lead at the Bank of Anthos. Bank of Anthos started as a small business for payment processing on two servers almost 10 years ago. Since then, it has grown into a successful commercial bank with thousands of employees and a growing engineering organization. Bank of Anthos now wants to expand its business further.

Throughout this period, you and your team have found yourself spending more time and money on maintaining infrastructure than on creating new business value. You have decades of cumulative experience invested in your existing stack, but you know it's not the right technology to meet the scale of global deployment that the bank needs as it expands.

You've adopted Anthos to modernize your application and migrate successfully to the cloud to achieve your expansion goals.

Objectives

In this tutorial, you'll be introduced to some of the key features of Anthos through the following tasks:

- Deploy your Anthos environment with clusters, applications, and Anthos components: Anthos Service Mesh and Anthos Config Management.

- Use the Google Cloud Console to explore the Anthos clusters resources used by your application.

- Use Anthos Service Mesh to observe application services.

Costs

We recommend cleaning up after finishing the tutorial or exploring the deployment to avoid incurring further charges. The Anthos Sample Deployment is not intended for production use, and its components cannot be upgraded.

Before you begin

The Anthos Sample Deployment on Google Cloud requires that you use a new project with no existing resources. The following additional project requirements apply:

- You must have enough quota in the target deployment project and zone for at least 7 vCPUs, 24.6 GB of memory, 310GB of disk space, one VPC, two firewall rules, and one Cloud NAT.

- Your organization does not have a policy that explicitly restricts the use of click-to-deploy images.

Before you start the tutorial:

- In the Google Cloud Console, on the project selector page, select or create a Google Cloud project. Go to **Project selector**.

- Make sure that billing is enabled for your Cloud project. Learn how to confirm that billing is enabled for your project.

- Enable the Compute Engine and Service Management APIs. **Enable the APIs**.

Then, do the following to ensure that your project meets the requirements for running the Anthos Sample Deployment:

1. In your new project, launch Cloud Shell by clicking on Activate Cloud Shell in the top toolbar. Cloud Shell is an interactive shell environment for Google Cloud that lets you manage your projects and resources from your web browser.

2. Configure Cloud Shell with the target deployment zone, replacing ZONE in the following command:

```
gcloud config set compute/zone ZONE
```

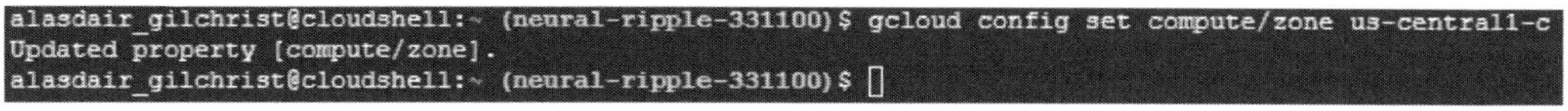

```
alasdair_gilchrist@cloudshell:~ (neural-ripple-331100)$ gcloud config set compute/zone us-central1-c
Updated property [compute/zone].
alasdair_gilchrist@cloudshell:~ (neural-ripple-331100)$ []
```

Figure 12.9: *Compute Zone Set*

3. Enter the following command to run a script that checks whether your project meets the necessary requirements:

```
curl -sL https://github.com/GoogleCloudPlatform/anthos-sample-
deployment/releases/latest/download/asd-prereq-checker.sh | sh -
```

Expected output (example):

```
Your active configuration is: [cloudshell-4100
```

```
Checking project my-project-id, region us-central1, zone us-central1-c
```

```
PASS: User has permission to create a service account with the required
IAM policies.
```

```
PASS: Org Policy will allow this deployment.
```

```
PASS: Service Management API is enabled.
```

```
PASS: Anthos Sample Deployment does not already exist.
```

```
PASS: Project ID is valid, does not contain colon.
```

```
PASS: Project has sufficient quota to support this deployment.
```

Caution

If anything doesn't PASS, you will need to investigate and fix it; if you don't fix these errors, you might be unable to deploy the sample.

What's deployed?

The Anthos Sample Deployment on Google Cloud provisions your project with the following:

- One GKE cluster running on Google Cloud: **anthos-sample-cluster1**.

- Anthos Service Mesh installed on the cluster. You will use Anthos Service Mesh to manage the service mesh on **anthos-sample-cluster1**.

- You can find out how to use Anthos Config Management to manage configuration and security policies on **anthos-sample-cluster1** in our follow-up tutorial, Secure Anthos.

- Bank of Anthos application running on the cluster. This is a web-based banking app that uses a number of microservices written in various programming languages, including Java, Python, and JavaScript.

- A single Compute Engine instance (virtual machine) that performs several automated tasks to jump-start the tutorial environment after the cluster is created: **asd-jump-server**.

- A VPC with a subnetwork within the target deployment region for the GKE cluster and Compute Engine instance, a Cloud NAT gateway on a Cloud Router, and firewall rules for connectivity to and between the deployment's components.

Launch the Anthos sample deployment on Google Cloud

Launch the Anthos Sample Deployment on Google Cloud through the Cloud Marketplace:

1. Open the Anthos Sample Deployment on Google Cloud. Select and confirm the Google Cloud project to use. This should be the project that you created in the *Before you begin* section.

2. Click on **LAUNCH**. It can take several minutes to progress to the deployment configuration screen while the solution enables a few APIs.

3. Select the confirm that all prerequisites have been met checkbox to confirm that you have successfully run the prerequisites script.

4. (Optional) In the deployment configuration screen, specify your chosen deployment name, zone, and Service Account. However, for your first deployment, we recommend that you accept all the provided default values, including creating a new Service Account.

5. Click on **Deploy**. Deploying the trial can take up to 15 minutes, so don't be concerned if you have to wait for a while.

While the deployment is progressing, the Cloud Console transitions to the **Deployment Manager view**. After the sample is deployed, you can review the full deployment. You should see a list of all enabled resources, including one GKE cluster (**anthos-sample-cluster1**) and one Compute Engine instance (**asd-jump-server**).

Using the Anthos Dashboard

Anthos provides an out-of-the-box structured view of all your applications' resources, including clusters, services, and workloads, giving you an at-a-glance view of your resources at a high level while letting you drill down when necessary to find the low-level information that you need. To see your deployment's top-level dashboard, go to your project's Anthos Dashboard in the Google Cloud Console.

You should see:

1. A **Service mesh** section that tells you that you have 9 services (but that they need action to see their health). You'll find out more about what this means later in the tutorial.

2. A **Cluster status** section that tells you that you have one healthy GKE cluster:

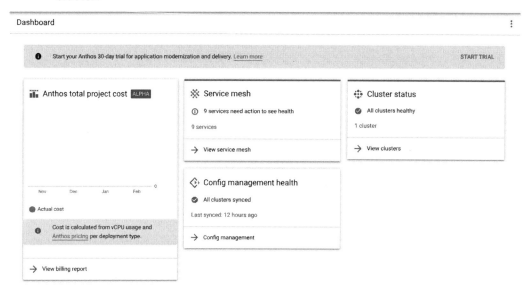

Figure 12.10: *Anthos Dashboard*

Explore Anthos clusters resources

The Anthos Clusters page shows you all the clusters in your project registered to Anthos, including clusters outside Google Cloud. You can also use the Google Kubernetes Engine Clusters page to see all the clusters in your project. In fact, the Anthos Clusters page lets you drill down to the GKE pages if you need to see more cluster and node details.

In this section, you'll take a closer look at Bank of Anthos' GKE resources.

Cluster management

1. In the Google Cloud Console, go to the **Anthos Clusters** page.

Click on the anthos-sample-cluster1 cluster to view its basic details in the right pane, including its **Type**, **Master version**, and **Location**. You can also see which Anthos features are enabled in this cluster in the **Cluster features** section.

2. For more detailed information about this cluster, click on **More details** in GKE. This brings you to the cluster's page in the Google Kubernetes Engine console, with all the current settings for the cluster.

3. In the Google Kubernetes Engine console, click on the **Nodes** tab to view all the worker machines in your cluster. From here, you can drill down even further to see the workload Pods running on each node as well as a resource summary of the node (CPU, memory, and storage).

Cluster workloads

The Google Kubernetes Engine console has a Workloads view that shows an aggregated view of the workloads (Pods) running on all your GKE clusters:

*   In the Google Kubernetes Engine console, go to the GKE Workloads page.

    Workloads from the GKE cluster and namespaces are shown. For example, workloads in the **boa** namespace are running in **anthos-sample-cluster1**:

Name ↑	Status	Type	Pods	Namespace	Cluster
accounts-db	✅ OK	Stateful Set	1/1	boa	anthos-sample-cluster1
balancereader	✅ OK	Deployment	1/1	boa	anthos-sample-cluster1
canonical-service-controller-manager	✅ OK	Deployment	1/1	asm-system	anthos-sample-cluster1
contacts	✅ OK	Deployment	1/1	boa	anthos-sample-cluster1
frontend	✅ OK	Deployment	1/1	boa	anthos-sample-cluster1
gatekeeper-audit	✅ OK	Deployment	1/1	gatekeeper-system	anthos-sample-cluster1
gatekeeper-controller-manager	✅ OK	Deployment	1/1	gatekeeper-system	anthos-sample-cluster1
git-importer	✅ OK	Deployment	1/1	config-management-system	anthos-sample-cluster1
gke-connect-agent-20211028-04-00	✅ OK	Deployment	1/1	gke-connect	anthos-sample-cluster1
istio-ingressgateway	✅ OK	Deployment	2/2	istio-system	anthos-sample-cluster1

Figure 12.11: Anthos Cluster Workloads Status

Services and Ingress

The **Services and Ingress** view shows the project's Service and Ingress resources. A Service exposes a set of pods as a network service with an endpoint, while an Ingress manages external access to the services in a cluster. However, rather than a regular Kubernetes Ingress, Bank of Anthos uses an Istio ingress gateway service for traffic to the bank, which Anthos Service Mesh meshes can use to add more complex traffic routing to their inbound traffic. You can see this in action when you use the service mesh observability features later in this tutorial.

1. In the Google Kubernetes Engine console, go to the **Services & Ingress** page. To find the **Bank of Anthos** ingress gateway, scroll down the list of available services to find the service with the name **istio-ingressgateway**.

2. Click on the down arrow at the end of the row for **istio-ingressgateway** to see more information about the service, including all its external endpoints. An ingress gateway manages inbound traffic for your application service mesh, so in this case, we can use its details to visit the bank's web frontend.

3. Click on the **istio-ingressgateway** external endpoint using port **80**. You should be able to explore the Bank of Anthos web interface:

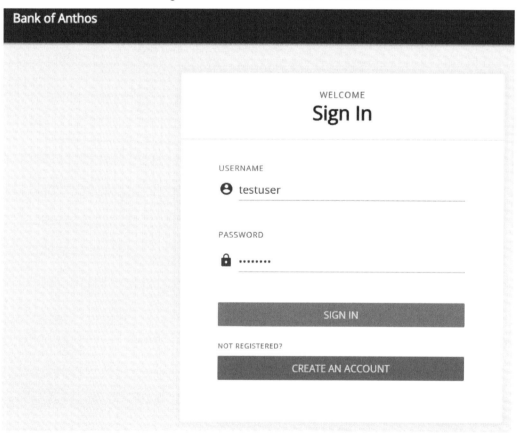

Figure 12.12: *Bank of Anthos Login Page*

Observing services

Anthos's service management and observability is provided by Anthos Service Mesh, a suite of tools powered by Istio that helps you monitor and manage a reliable service mesh. To find out more about Anthos Service Mesh and how it helps you manage microservices, see the Anthos Service Mesh documentation. If you're not familiar with using microservices with containers and what they can do for you, see Preparing an application for Anthos Service Mesh. In our example, the cluster in the sample deployment has the microservice-based Bank of Anthos sample application running on it. The application also includes a loadgenerator utility that simulates a small amount of load to the cluster so that you can see metrics and traffic in the dashboard.

In this section, you'll use the Anthos Service Mesh page to look at this application's services and traffic.

Observe the services table view

1. Go to the Anthos Service Mesh page.

2. The page displays the table view by default, which shows a list of all your project's microservices, including system services. To filter only the Bank of Anthos services, select **boa** from the Namespace dropdown at the top left of the page.

Each row in the table is one of the services that makes up the Bank of Anthos application; for example, the frontend service renders the application's web user interface, and the **userservice** service manages user accounts and authentication.

Each service listing shows up-to-date metrics, such as error rate and key latencies, for that service. These metrics are collected out-of-the-box for services deployed on Anthos. You do not need to write any application code to see these statistics.

You can drill down from this view to see further details about each service. For example, to learn more about the **transactionhistory** service:

1. Click on **transactionhistory** in the services list. The service details page shows all the telemetry available for this service.

2. On the **transactionhistory** page, on the **Navigation** menu, select **Connected Services**. Here, you can see both the Inbound and Outbound connections for the service. An unlocked lock icon indicates that some traffic has been observed on this port that is not encrypted using mutual TLS

(mTLS). You can find out more about how this works in the Secure Anthos tutorial.

Figure 12.13: Requests per Frontend services

Observe the services topology view

The table view isn't the only way to observe your services in Anthos. The topology view lets you focus on how the services interact:

- If you haven't done so already, return to the table view from the service details view by clicking on the back arrow at the top of the page.

- At the top-right of the page, click on **Topology** to switch from the table view to the workload/service graph visualization. As you can see from the legend, the graph shows both the application's Anthos Service Mesh services and the GKE workloads that implement them.

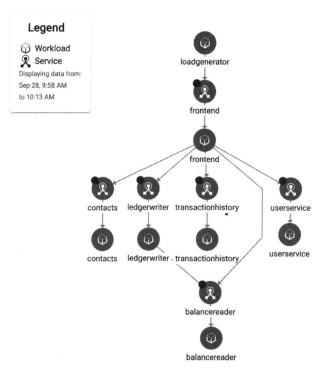

Figure 12.14: Anthos Topology Diagram

Now, you can explore the topology graph. Anthos Service Mesh automatically observes which services are communicating with each other to show service-to-service connections details:

- Hold your mouse pointer over an item to see additional details, including outbound QPS from each service.

- Drag nodes with your mouse to improve your view of particular parts of the graph.

- Click on service nodes for more service information.

- Click on **Expand** when you hold the pointer over a workload node to drill down for further details, including the number of instances of this workload that are currently running.

It may take some time for the topology view to render completely. If you see a partial diagram or even no data, you can move along to the next section and check back later.

Exploring Anthos further

While this tutorial has shown you many Anthos features, there's lots more to see and do in Anthos with our deployment. Visit one of our follow-up tutorials to try some hands-on tasks with Anthos, or continue to explore the Anthos Sample Deployment on Google Cloud yourself before following the cleanup instructions in the next section.

Setting up your Cloud Shell environment

In this tutorial, you will use the Cloud Shell command line and editor to make changes to cluster configuration. To initialize the shell environment for the tutorial, the Anthos Sample Deployment provides a script that does the following:

1. Installs any missing command-line tools for interactively working with and verifying changes to the deployment:

   - **kubectl**
   - **kubectx**
   - **istioctl**
   - **nomos**

2. Sets the Kubernetes context for **anthos-sample-cluster1**.

3. Clones the repository that Anthos Config Management uses for synchronizing your configuration changes to your cluster. Changes that you commit and

push to the upstream repository are synchronized to your infrastructure by Anthos Config Management. This is the recommended best practice for applying changes to your infrastructure.

To set up your environment:

1. Ensure that you have an active Cloud Shell session. You can launch Cloud Shell by clicking on Activate Cloud Shell from the Cloud Console in your tutorial project.

2. Create a directory to work in:

   mkdir tutorial

   cd tutorial

3. Download the initialization script:

   curl -sLO https://github.com/GoogleCloudPlatform/anthos-sample-deployment/releases/latest/download/init-anthos-sample-deployment.env

4. Source the initialization script into your Cloud Shell environment:

   gcloud container clusters get-credentials anthos-sample-cluster1

   Then,

   source init-anthos-sample-deployment.env

   /google/google-cloud-sdk/bin/gcloud

   /google/google-cloud-sdk/bin/kubectl

   Expected output:

   Your active configuration is: [cloudshell-13605]

   export PROJECT as anthos-launch-demo-1

   export KUBECONFIG as ~/.kube/anthos-launch-demo-1.anthos-trial-gcp.config

   Fetching cluster endpoint and auth data.

   kubeconfig entry generated for anthos-sample-cluster1.

   Copying gs://config-management-release/released/latest/linux_amd64/nomos...

   \ [1 files][40.9 MiB/ 40.9 MiB]

   Operation completed over 1 objects/40.9 MiB.

   Installed nomos into ~/bin.

   Cloned ACM config repo: ./anthos-sample-deployment-config-repo

5. Change the directory to the configuration repository and use it as the working directory for the remainder of this tutorial:

```
cd anthos-sample-deployment-config-repo
```

Enforcing mTLS in your service mesh

In anticipation of global expansion, your CIO has mandated that all user data must be encrypted in transit to safeguard sensitive information to be in compliance with regional data privacy and encryption laws.

So, is all your traffic currently secure?

1. Go to the Anthos Service Mesh page in your project where you have the Anthos Sample Deployment deployed.

2. Click on **transactionhistory** in the services list. As you saw in Explore Anthos, the service details page shows all the telemetry available for this service.

3. On the **transactionhistory** page, on the **Navigation** menu, select **Connected Services**. Here, you can see both the **Inbound and Outbound** connections for the service. An unlocked lock icon indicates that some traffic has been observed on this port that is not using mutual TLS (mTLS).

mTLS is a security protocol that ensures that traffic is secure and trusted in both directions between two services. Each service accepts only encrypted traffic from authenticated services. As you can see, Anthos Service Mesh clearly shows that you have unencrypted traffic in your mesh. Different colors are used in Anthos Service Mesh to indicate whether the unencrypted traffic has a mix of plaintext and mTLS (*orange*) or only plaintext (*red*).

With Anthos, you're only a few steps away from being compliant. Rather than making changes at the source code level and rebuilding and redeploying your application to address this situation, you can apply the new encryption policy declaratively through configuration by using Anthos Config Management to automatically deploy your new configuration from a central Git repository.

In this section, you'll do the following:

1. Adjust the policy configuration in your Git repository to enforce those services; use encrypted communications through mTLS.

2. Rely on Anthos Config Management to automatically pick up the policy change from the repository and adjust the Anthos Service Mesh policy.

3. Verify that the policy change occurred on your cluster that is configured to sync with the repository.

Confirm Anthos Config Management setup

1. The nomos command is a command-line tool that lets you interact with the Config Management Operator and perform other useful Anthos Config Management tasks from your local machine or Cloud Shell. To verify that Anthos Config Management is properly installed and configured on your cluster, run nomos status:

   nomos status

   Expected output:

   ```
   Connecting to clusters...

   Current    Context                    Sync Status  Last Synced Token
   Sync Branch    Resource Status

   -------    -------                    -----------  -----------------
   -----------    ---------------

   *          anthos-sample-cluster1     SYNCED       abef0b01
   master         Healthy
   ```

2. The output confirms that Anthos Config Management is configured to sync your cluster to the master branch of your configuration repository. The asterisk in the first column indicates that the current context is set to **anthos-sample-cluster1**. If you don't see this, switch the current context to **anthos-sample-cluster1**:

   kubectl config use-context anthos-sample-cluster1

   Expected output:

   Switched to context "anthos-sample-cluster1".

3. Ensure that you're on the master branch:

   git checkout master

   Expected output:

   Already on 'master'
   Your branch is up to date with 'origin/master'.

4. Verify your upstream configuration repository:

   git remote -v

   Expected output:

   origin https://source.developers.google.com/.../anthos-sample-deployment-config-repo (fetch)

```
origin  https://source.developers.google.com/.../anthos-sample-
deployment-config-repo (push)
```

5. Ensure that you're still in the **anthos-sample-deployment-config-repo** directory and run the following command to check your git setup. This helper function is sourced into your environment by the initialization script and runs git config commands to check your git config's existing **user. email** and user.name values. If these values are not configured, the function sets defaults at the repo level based on the currently active Google Cloud account:

```
init_git
```

Expected output (example):

```
Configured local git user.email to user@example.com
```

```
Configured local git user.name to user
```

You are now ready to commit policy changes to your repository. When you push these commits to your upstream repository (origin), Anthos Config Management ensures that these changes are applied to the cluster that you have configured it to manage.

Update a policy to encrypt all service traffic

Configuration for Anthos Service Mesh is specified declaratively by using YAML files. To encrypt all service traffic, you need to modify both the YAML that specifies the types of traffic that services can *accept*, and the YAML that specifies the type of traffic that services send to particular destinations.

1. The first YAML file that you need to look at is: **namespaces/istio-system/ peer-authentication.yaml**. This is a mesh-level authentication policy that specifies the types of traffic that all services in your mesh accept by default:

```
cat namespaces/istio-system/peer-authentication.yaml
```

Expected output:

```
apiVersion: "security.istio.io/v1beta1"
kind: "PeerAuthentication"
metadata:
  name: "default"
  namespace: "istio-system"
spec:
  mtls:
    mode: PERMISSIVE
```

2. As you can see, the **PeerAuthentication mTLS** mode is **PERMISSIVE**, which means that services accept both plaintext HTTP and mTLS traffic.

3. Modify **namespaces/istio-system/peer-authentication.yaml** to allow only encrypted communication between services by setting the mTLS mode to STRICT:

```
cat <<EOF> namespaces/istio-system/peer-authentication.yaml

apiVersion: "security.istio.io/v1beta1"

kind: "PeerAuthentication"

metadata:

  name: "default"

  namespace: "istio-system"

spec:

  mtls:

    mode: STRICT

EOF
```

4. Next, look at the **Destination Rule** in **namespaces/istio-system/destination-rule.yaml**. This specifies rules for sending traffic to the specified destinations, including whether the traffic is encrypted. Notice that TLSmode is **DISABLE**, meaning that traffic is sent in plaintext to all matching hosts:

cat namespaces/istio-system/destination-rule.yaml

Expected output:

```
apiVersion: networking.istio.io/v1alpha3

kind: DestinationRule

metadata:

      annotations:

       meshsecurityinsights.googleapis.com/generated:
    "1561996419000000000"

    name: default

    namespace: istio-system

  spec:

    host: '*.local'

    trafficPolicy:

     tls:

        mode: DISABLE
```

5. Modify **namespaces/istio-system/destination-rule.yaml** to have Istio set a traffic policy that enables TLS for all matching hosts in the cluster by using TLSmode **ISTIO_MUTUAL**:

```
cat <<EOF> namespaces/istio-system/destination-rule.yaml
apiVersion: networking.istio.io/v1alpha3
kind: DestinationRule
metadata:
  annotations:
    meshsecurityinsights.googleapis.com/generated:
"1561996419000000000"
  name: default
  namespace: istio-system
spec:
  host: '*.local'
  trafficPolicy:
    tls:
      mode: ISTIO_MUTUAL
EOF
```

Push your changes to the repository

You are almost ready to push your configuration changes; however, we recommend a few checks before you finally commit your updates:

1. Run nomos vet to ensure that your configuration is valid:

   nomos vet

2. No output indicates that there were no validation errors.

3. As soon as you push your changes, Anthos Config Management picks them up and applies them to your system. To avoid unexpected results, we recommend checking that the current live state of your configuration hasn't changed since you made your edits. Use kubectl to check that the **destinationrule** reflects that mTLS is disabled for the cluster:

   kubectl get destinationrule default -n istio-system -o yaml

   Expected output:

   ```
   apiVersion: networking.istio.io/v1alpha3
   kind: DestinationRule
   ...
   spec:
   ```

```
host: '*.local'
trafficPolicy:
  tls:
    mode: DISABLE
```

4. Now, commit and push these changes to the upstream repository. The following command uses a helper function called **watchmtls** that was sourced into your environment by the **init** script. This helper function runs a combination of nomos status and the kubectl command that you tried earlier. It watches the cluster for changes until you press *Ctrl + C* to quit. Monitor the display until you see that the changes are applied and synchronized on the cluster.

```
git commit -am "enable mtls"

git push origin master && watchmtls
```

5. You can also see the changes reflected on the Anthos Service Mesh pages in Anthos.

6. You should see that the red unlocked lock icon has changed. The lock icon appears orange (mixed traffic) rather than green (entirely encrypted traffic) because we're looking, by default, at the last hour with a mix of mTLS and plaintext. If you check back after an hour, you should see a green lock that shows that you have successfully encrypted all the service traffic.

mTLS status

mTLS is strict for all workloads

Figure 12.15: mTLS is successfully updated

Using Policy Controller to set up guardrails

Your security team is concerned about potential root attacks that might occur when running pods with privileged containers (containers with root access). While the current configuration does not deploy any privileged containers, you want to guard against as many threat vectors as possible that could compromise performance or, even worse, customer data.

Despite the team's diligence, there is a risk that you could find yourself vulnerable to root attacks unintentionally from future configuration updates through your continuous delivery process. You decide to set up a security guardrail to protect against this danger.

Apply guardrails

Guardrails are automated administrative controls intended to enforce policies that protect your environment. Anthos Config Management includes support for defining and enforcing custom rules not covered by native Kubernetes objects. The Anthos Config Management Policy Controller checks, audits, and enforces guardrails that you apply that correspond to your organization's unique security, regulatory compliance, and governance requirements.

Use Policy Controller

Anthos Config Management Policy Controller is built on an open-source policy engine called Gatekeeper that is used to enforce policies each time a resource in the cluster is created, updated, or deleted. These policies are defined by using constraints from the Policy Controller template library or from other Gatekeeper constraint templates.

The Anthos Sample Deployment on Google Cloud already has Policy Controller installed and the Policy Controller template library enabled. You can take advantage of this when implementing your guardrail by using an existing constraint for privileged containers from the library.

Apply a policy constraint for privileged containers

To address your security team's concerns, you apply the K8sPSPPrivilegedContainer constraint. This constraint denies pods from running with privileged containers.

1. Using the Cloud Shell terminal, create a new **constraint.yaml** file with the text from the library constraint, as follows:

```
cat <<EOF> ~/tutorial/anthos-sample-deployment-config-repo/
cluster/constraint.yaml
apiVersion: constraints.gatekeeper.sh/v1beta1
kind: K8sPSPPrivilegedContainer
metadata:
  name: psp-privileged-container
spec:
  match:
    kinds:
      - apiGroups: [""]
        kinds: ["Pod"]
    excludedNamespaces: ["kube-system"]
EOF
```

2. Use nomos vet to verify that the updated configuration is valid before you apply it:

nomos vet

3. The command returns silently as long as there are no errors.

4. Commit and push the changes to apply the policy. You can use nomos status with the watch command to confirm that the changes are applied to your cluster. Press *Ctrl* + *C* to exit the watch command when finished:

git add .

git commit -m "add policy constraint for privileged containers"

git push && watch nomos status

Expected output:

```
Connecting to clusters...

Current    Context                      Sync Status  Last Synced Token
Sync Branch    Resource Status

-------    -------                      ----------   -----------------
----------     ---------------

*          anthos-sample-cluster1       SYNCED       f2898e92
master         Healthy
```

Test your policy

After you've applied the policy, you can test it by attempting to run a pod with a privileged container:

1. In the Cloud Shell terminal, use the following command to create a new file in the tutorial directory, **nginx-privileged.yaml**, with the contents from this example spec:

```
cat <<EOF> ~/tutorial/nginx-privileged.yaml

apiVersion: v1

kind: Pod

metadata:

  name: nginx-privileged-disallowed

  labels:

    app: nginx-privileged

spec:

  containers:

  - name: nginx
```

```
    image: nginx

    securityContext:

        privileged: true

EOF
```

2. Attempt to launch the pod with **kubectl apply**:

kubectl apply -f ~/tutorial/nginx-privileged.yaml

Expected output:

```
Error from server ([denied by psp-privileged-container]
Privileged container is not allowed: nginx, securityContext:
{"privileged": true}): error when creating "~/nginx-privileged.
yaml": admission webhook "validation.gatekeeper.sh" denied
the request: [denied by psp-privileged-container] Privileged
container is not allowed: nginx, security
```

Context: {"privileged": true}

```
alasdair_gilchrist@cloudshell:~/tutorial (golden-ego-331620)$ kubectl apply -f nginx-priviliged.yaml
Error from server ([denied by psp-privileged-container] Privileged container is not allowed: nginx,
equest: [denied by psp-privileged-container] Privileged container is not allowed: nginx, securityCon
alasdair_gilchrist@cloudshell:~/tutorial (golden-ego-331620)$ []
```

Figure 12.16: Access denied as Privileged containers not allowed

3. The error shows that the Gatekeeper admission controller monitoring your Kubernetes environment enforced your new policy. It prevented the pod's execution due to the presence of a privileged container in the pod's specification.

The concept of version-controlled policies that you can apply to set up guardrails with Anthos Config Management is a powerful one because it standardizes, unifies, and centralizes the governance of your clusters, enforcing your policies through active monitoring of your environment post-deployment. You can find many other types of policies to use as guardrails for your environment in the Gatekeeper repository.

Conclusion

In this chapter, you learned why we need Anthos in a hybrid or multi cloud environment. You also learned how Anthos manages heterogeneous clusters and how you can benefit from deploying Anthos. Furthermore, you learned, through an interactive tutorial, how to deploy Anthos using a sample app, and explored Anthos features such as service mesh and monitoring and logging. You also explored policy configuration and security policies.

In the next chapter, we will look at hosting, optimizing, and securing your own applications on Anthos in the most cost-optimized manner.

CHAPTER 13

Securing Cloud Native Apps in Anthos

In the last chapter, you built and deployed an Anthos cluster with the Bank of Anthos application. You explored some of Anthos's features and even set some security properties. In this chapter, we will dive deeper into security, identity management, and policy enforcement.

It can be challenging to maintain identities across different environments and hybrid and multi-cloud deployments. It is not often that you can leverage your existing **identity and access management (IAM)** systems. However, if you are running hybrid or multi-cloud environments on GCP, you can use Anthos to simplify your Identity management for users and workloads.

In this chapter, you will learn all about security in the Kubernetes cluster, how IAM roles work, and what makes Anthos a modern approach to security. You will see how Anthos differs from the traditional approach to security and how it is structured into a four-layer model. We will examine each layer, i.e., infrastructure, guardrails and policy, app security, and monitoring, and we will see how Anthos addresses security at each level. Then, we will examine the Anthos Configuration Manager and its tools and techniques for securing hybrid and multi-cloud environments such as the Config Controller, Config Synch, and Policy Controller.

Structure

We will cover the following topics in this chapter:

- Anthos core functional modules for security (AIS and IAM)

- GKE IAM Role Based Access Control

- Technical Walkthrough on IAM Least Privilege in Anthos

- Anthos 4-layer modern security model

- Anthos Config Controller and Config Sync

- Anthos Policy Controller

- Interactive Tutorial

Objectives

After going through this chapter, you will be knowledgeable in administering identity and access management at the GKE level and understand the principles of least privilege and how to enforce the policy on a real cluster. You will also be familiar with some Anthos specific security modules such as the Config Controller, Config Sync, and, through some hands-on work, the Policy Controller.

Anthos Identity Service (AIS)

With Anthos, there is a seamless approach for you to modernize and manage your workloads in an environment that you prefer, whether it is on-prem, Google Cloud, Edge, or on a different cloud altogether. This is because Anthos can span across multiple environments, even if each is built on a different identity store, for example, Active Directory for on-prem, Cloud Identity for Google Cloud, and AWS IAM for AWS.

What makes Anthos special from an identity management perspective is that today, in addition to managing employee identity, you almost always need to manage partner, project, workload, or customer identity, increasing the complexity of integrating with these diverse data stores.

Traditionally, the way that hybrid and multi-cloud environments were handled was for one party, that is, for Google Cloud to offer a synchronization-based identity model, while the other parties were required to synchronize their identities with them. Although it did work for certain scenarios, and while this was indeed the de-facto method for many years, it did have some shortcomings. Specifically, the issues that the synchronization identity model had were concerns around consistency and latency. This was particularly true when deployed for a hybrid or multi-cloud environment.

Google's Anthos has taken a new approach to multi-platform identity management with **Anthos Identity Service (AIS)** adopting a federation-style model. This modern approach enables Anthos to support customers who wish to use third-party identity providers and existing authentication protocols. Anthos Identity Service spans the existing capabilities, so it can be deployed quickly into your Anthos GKE cluster, enabling standard protocols such as OpenID Connect. This means that you no longer need to synchronize identities to Google Cloud or worry about consistency across heterogeneous environments. It also saves time and reduces friction during the onboarding process as Anthos on-prem offers OIDC support, which enables authentication via G Cloud or through the Cloud Console.

To demonstrate how this works in practice, let's take a look at a typical use case. In this scenario, a platform administrator is managing a small project team of developers, and the team has requested access to the Kubernetes API server to debug issues or perform cluster management tasks using Kubectl. The admin creates a user cluster for GKE on-prem by running a `-gkectl-` command to generate a login configuration file. The admin will then need to populate this file with values specific to the identity provider, such as issuer URL, redirect URL, and client ID. However, the admin can, if they wish to, enable one or multiple identity providers to support the needs of different user groups. Once completed, the identity configuration file can be securely distributed to the team of developers using an accessible URL. However, the admin will still need to restrict access based on privileges granted to authenticated users. To do this, the admin can use Kubernetes **role-based access control (RBAC)** to create cluster roles that grant specific privileges to individual users and groups.

As a developer, you can install the G Cloud SDK with the Anthos authentication components to enable third-party OIDC authentication. To do this, simply run the `-gcloud anthos auth login-` command to view the list of available clusters and then specify a cluster flag to log in. Based on your Kubernetes RBAC privileges, you can now run Kubectl commands to complete your required tasks.

Anthos Identity Service is designed to work seamlessly with other Anthos components as well as your existing identity systems and identity stores and sources. Hence, Google is working to enable support for additional standard protocols, such as LDAP, to support authentication needs for multiple environments, including Google Cloud, on-prem, and other clouds. Google is also extending the existing OIDC capabilities to other clouds to create a consistent multi-cloud experience.

Beyond user identity

Anthos Identity Service reaches beyond user authentication as you can also enable authentication for workloads running in GKE to consume services provided by

Google APIs. To do this, you simply configure a Kubernetes service account to automatically authenticate when accessing Google Cloud APIs. Using this method means there is no need to worry about safeguarding private keys for PKI and client certificates or managing bearer and bootstrap tokens.

As you can see, AIS offers a seamless solution for managing authentication to multiple Anthos GKE environments. AIS allows you to leverage the existing identity investments as it is a fully integrated, enterprise-ready solution for authentication that is built with security in mind.

Kubernetes Engine (GKE) IAM roles

Authenticating a user identity is one thing, but you still need to provide the correct level of access to resources, and this is done via Cloud IAM. However, when a Google Cloud Administrator is planning their IAM strategy for how to best use the built-in GKE IAM Roles, there are a few details that might be confusing and/or surprising, and these could have unforeseen consequences. Therefore, we need to clarify some of the possible ambiguities that exist.

An interesting thing about Identity in GCP is that instead of binding roles to a member to define what access they have, users attach IAM Policies to resources. IAM Policies define who has what type of access to the resource they are attached to by binding members to a role on the resource (where roles are a defined set of individual permissions). For example, if you want to grant User A permission to list objects in a Kubernetes cluster, say cluster B, but restrict their access to list objects in any other cluster, you would create an IAM Policy that binds User A to the Kubernetes Engine Cluster Viewer role and attach it to cluster B. This way, you grant list access to the specific cluster, in this case cluster B, and deny User A list permissions to any other cluster.

These IAM Policies can be set at any level in the GCP resource hierarchy (organization level, folder level, project level, resource level), and are transitively inherited by descendant resources. This decentralization makes it difficult to enumerate all possible permissions granted to a member. Additionally, there are numerous ways for members to assume other members' identities (for example, service account impersonation), and permissions can be easily assigned across projects, provided that the appropriate organization policy is disabled. For an organization with many projects, the number of all possible IAM permissions increases significantly.

Clarifying the GKE predefined IAM roles

	Type	Title	Used in	Status	
☐	◉	Kubernetes Engine Admin	Kubernetes Engine	Enabled	⋮
☐	◉	Kubernetes Engine Cluster Admin	Kubernetes Engine	Enabled	⋮
☐	◉	Kubernetes Engine Cluster Viewer	Kubernetes Engine	Enabled	⋮
☐	◉	Kubernetes Engine Developer	Kubernetes Engine	Enabled	⋮
☐	◉	Kubernetes Engine Host Service Agent User	Kubernetes Engine	Enabled	⋮
☐	◉	Kubernetes Engine Service Agent	Service Agent Roles	Enabled	⋮
☐	◉	Kubernetes Engine Viewer	Kubernetes Engine	Enabled	⋮

Figure 13.1: GKE IAM roles

Here's a listing of the predefined IAM Roles for Kubernetes Engine purposes, along with their official Google IAM documentation descriptions. We have added some notes to help clarify some points of potential confusion:

- **Kubernetes Engine Admin**

  o **Description**: "Full administrative control of the Kubernetes Clusters and all the Kubernetes API objects."

  o **Intended use**: Generally, this role is assigned to users or service accounts that are required to manage all aspects of the GKE clusters in a project. They can create/manage/delete clusters as well as node pools, and this role can create/manage/delete all the workloads deployed to them.

This role is often confused with the role of Kubernetes Engine Cluster Admin.

- **Kubernetes Engine Cluster Admin**

  o **Description**: "Full Administrative control of Kubernetes Clusters."

  o **Intended use**: Generally, this role would be assigned to designated users or automation service accounts that are just responsible for creating/managing/deleting any GKE clusters, but they would not need access to the workloads running on them.

- **Kubernetes Engine Cluster Viewer**

    o **Description**: "Get and list access to GKE Clusters."

    o **Intended use**: Generally, this role is assigned to designated users or automation service accounts that need only sufficient IAM access to query the GCP APIs to search, discover, and connect to a given GKE cluster, but they have no access permissions to Kubernetes API resources.

- **Kubernetes Engine Developer**

    o **Description**: "Full access to Kubernetes API objects inside Kubernetes Clusters."

    o **Intended use**: Generally, this role is assigned to designated users who need permissions to administer most of the Kubernetes API resources; there are some exceptions for some privileged permissions.

- **Kubernetes Engine Host Service Agent User**

    o **Description**: "Allows the Kubernetes Engine service account in the host project to configure shared network resources for cluster management."

    o **Intended use**: Generally, this role is assigned for granting the GKE service project's "robot" account the necessary access to a host project in a Shared VPC scenario as well as for granting access to view firewalls and network resources.

- **Kubernetes Engine Service Agent**

    o **Description**: "Gives Kubernetes Engine account access to manage cluster resources and includes access to service accounts."

    o **Intended use**: This role is purely intended to be assigned to only the project's GKE "**robot**" account. It is not really ideal for tenant/customer use as it contains ~1000 permissions and `iam.serviceAccounts.actAs`, which is not ideal from a security perspective. It also has lots of compute, container, and network services resources, which defeats the principle of least privilege.

- **Kubernetes Engine Viewer**

    o **Description**: "Read-only access to Kubernetes Engine resources."

    o **Intended use**: Typically, this role will be assigned to designated users or automation service accounts that require only the ability to discover GKE clusters and have "read-only" access to all non-sensitive Kubernetes API resources.

It is commonly confused with Kubernetes Engine Cluster Viewer during assignment, but because it contains all those permissions, nothing seems out of place; however, it does not follow the least privilege principle.

Potential risks and privilege elevation paths

A potential abuse of the user privileges can come about perhaps unintentionally by assigning users to an incorrect RBAC group. For example, some groups appear to be pretty toothless by their title until you dig deeper and check the permissions. For example, check these two RBAC roles:

- **Kubernetes Engine Viewer**
  - o Having **container.pods.list** (and cronjobs, deployments, jobs, and statefulsets list) and **container.configMaps.list** can potentially leak sensitive credentials and/or details from pod environment variables or what is stored in **configMaps**. Note that viewing secrets is not allowed by this role.

- **Kubernetes Engine Developer**
  - o Having **container.secrets.list** allows reading secret contents in all namespaces in the GKE cluster, including kube-system. Kubernetes secrets are also where Kubernetes service account tokens are stored, so a **Developer** is actually the union of all permissions granted to all service accounts in the cluster.

Defining exactly what permissions developers require to do their job with minimal interruption when working with complex access control systems such as GCP's Cloud IAM is no trivial task. This task becomes even harder to design correctly and consistently in an existing environment, where standard template 'least privilege' permissions can disrupt developer workflows. Ideally, engineers would, in theory, be granted only a minimal set of permissions required to complete their everyday tasks. Any operation that requires elevated privileges would be handled via a unique, separate, and well-defined process. However, in practice, many organizations do not have formal policies for this escalation process, and the process often devolves into undocumented, persistent elevated privileges.

The strategy of least privileges demands that you only give the minimum access rights that a user needs to fulfil their job. However, for GKE, this can be a little bit tricky as there is Google Cloud Platform IAM, and then you have Kubernetes Roles.

GCP IAM defines what actions you are allowed to take on GCP (for example create a Compute VM or a Cloud Storage Bucket). However, Kubernetes Roles are much more specific as they define the permissions you have within a single cluster. However, some GCP IAM roles propagate down from the project to their own GKE clusters. For example, the project level GCP IAM role Kubernetes Engine Developer will give edit access to every cluster in the project, and that's probably not what you want.

One problem is that Kubernetes does not have the concept of users, so GKE relies upon GCP IAM to Authenticate users. However, that's used for authentication (who are you?), and you need to set authorization (what are you allowed to do?) for the second part of access control. You should rely on specific Kubernetes Roles as much as possible for this job. Therefore, to appease least-privilege, we will grant minimal roles on the GCP IAM side that can be used to identify yourself to a cluster (authenticate). Then, the GKE cluster itself will decide whatever you are allowed to do (authorization) based on a specific Kubernetes Role.

Google Cloud Platform IAM

The minimal set of permissions you need on the GCP IAM side are the following:

- `container.apiServices.get`
- `container.apiServices.list`
- `container.clusters.get`
- `container.clusters.getCredentials`

So, let's create a custom role for these permissions in the Cloud Shell terminal:

```
gcloud iam roles create $ROLE_NAME -- file iam.yaml -- project $PROJECT
```

Group membership over individual access

Another best practice for enforcing the principle of least privilege is to rely on granting group membership for access rather than granting individual users' specific access. This is almost always the case, except for very high-level security roles in high-security use-cases.

The reason for grouping users into groups is that working at the user level is simply unsustainable. This is why we use RBAC and Groups to make the process feasible. Let's give all members from the development team our custom role, by granting it to the group. To do this, run the following command:

```
gcloud projects add-iam-policy-binding $PROJECT -- member group:$DEV_
GROUP -- role projects/$PROJECT/roles/$ROLE_NAME
```

There is a problem however: Google Kubernetes Engine does not respect group membership. In order to force Kubernetes to recognize the development group, you will have to define that group as a member of a dedicated GKE group, which is called **gke-security-groups@[your-domain]**.

Once we do so, we can create our cluster with this specific security-group as a root group that will contain all groups.

To do this, type in:

```
gcloud beta container clusters create $CLUSTER_NAME -- project $PROJECT
-- zone $ZONE -- security-group=$GKE_DOMAIN_GROUP
```

We have the developer team now a member of team 1, which, in turn, is a member of the Google Group **team_1@xxxx.io**, and any member of this group is allowed to authenticate itself against our Kubernetes cluster on GKE.

Alas, remember that access control is set at two levels: authentication and authorization. Authentication merely proves that you are who you claim you are, whereas Authorization determines what you are permitted to do. Kubernetes will authenticate you as it now knows who you are, but it will not allow you to perform any meaningful operation as we still need to get through the second obstacle: Authorization. For that, we need to revisit RBAC and configure and apply some roles.

Role-based Access Control

Now, we'll tell this specific cluster that it should create a namespace **team-1** for the first group and allow members of the dedicated Google Group **team_1@xxxx. io** pod level access in this namespace. All developers of the team are members of this Google Group. We do this by creating a Role and then applying this as a **RoleBinding**. Note the **Subjects** element that refers to which subject to bind to the specified Role.

As a cluster admin, we first get our credentials:

```
gcloud container clusters get-credentials $CLUSTER_NAME --project
$PROJECT --zone $ZONE
```

Then, we create the namespace, role, and rolebinding:

```
kubectl apply -f rbac.yaml
```

And there you have it! Now, any member of the Google Group **team_1@xxx.io** will be able to manage Deployments in the **team_1** namespace of this cluster, leaving other namespaces and other clusters in the same GCP projects out of their reach.

All they need to do is configure their kubectl using:

```
gcloud container clusters get-credentials $CLUSTER_NAME --project
$PROJECT --zone $ZONE
```

The final task for the administrator will be to make a test deployment in both the default as well as the team-1 namespaces. You will then see that these **team_1** namespace users will not be able to get access to deployments that are in the default namespace:

```
$kubectl get deployments
```

Expected output:

```
 Error from server (Forbidden): deployments.extensions is forbidden:
User "X.Y@xxxx.io"  cannot list resource "deployments" in API group
"extensions" in the namespace "default"
```

However, they will be able to access the deployments in the team-1 namespace:

```
$kubectl get deployments -n team-1
```

Expected output:

```
NAME                  DESIRED CURRENT UP-TO-DATE    AVAILABLE AGE
first-deployment      1 1 1            0 4s
```

Anthos: Modernize your security posture

Anthos is a modern application management platform from Google Cloud that delivers a consistent development, operations, and security experience across hybrid and multi cloud environments. Anthos is designed for enterprise organizations that want to modernize their security and accelerate the development and deployment of dynamic apps with granular security controls.

With Anthos, you can modernize your approach to app security without any detrimental impact on rapid development and deployment initiatives. Anthos aims to provide granular security controls by default, which can help you automate the following security operations:

- Enforcing consistent policy across environments

- Isolating workloads with different risk profiles

- Deploy only trusted workloads

A modern approach to security in cloud architectures is essential as the security challenges of modern apps are more complex and differ considerably from traditional apps, particularly in three key areas:

- In Microservices architecture

- Declarative configurations

- Where there is a high degree of automation

However, with Anthos, the problems are amplified as there may not be a way to enforce consistency and manage workloads that span environments. If that is the case, then your organization can face security challenges when modernizing their apps.

The following are three key security challenges that emerge with modern apps:

- Applying consistent organization-level policies across heterogeneous environments

- Securing the software supply chain

- Securing multi-tenant environments across a shared platform

Consistent policies

Microservices are dynamic and ephemeral and as such, you can distribute them across many hosts, clusters, or even clouds. As your services are deployed, shutdown, and redeployed, it's difficult to maintain security policies that are consistent; this problem is known as **cluster sprawl**.

The adoption of an infrastructure as code approach, along with automation and the use of declarative policies that you deploy through configuration management tooling, helps you ensure consistency across heterogeneous environments. However, it isn't all cutting-edge technologies as old established techniques have found a place in Anthos. The use of namespaces and labels long established in Unix and Linux today provide for workspace isolations through logical group abstractions across services. Isolation lets you establish coherent policies in setting up guardrails for tenant-specific environments. You can also use traditional techniques like inheritance to delegate organization-level policies to tenants.

In this new model, the key functions of access control and policy enforcement must be declarative and automated to conform to controls that meet your organization's security and risk appetite as well as for strict adherence to governance and compliance requirements.

Software supply chain security

Today, the DevOps and Agile development methodologies drive Continuous Integration and Continuous deployment (CI/CD) practices for modern development of cloud native apps. These automated processes drive your development teams to ship code faster, better, and scale more easily. You may well be building production-ready containers from scratch inside CI/CD systems at record speeds. However, the ease and flexibility with which you can build these application containers and the resulting workflow where containers are replaced frequently to add new functionality or patch vulnerabilities does bring along its own unique set of security challenges.

Each container build starts with a base **operating system (OS)**. A frequent challenge is the proliferation of base OSs, often with varying patch levels. You might have provenance of code issues because your developers can download new components and libraries and incorporate them into builds with increasing ease and often without due diligence or challenge.

While a developer-centric build and deploy model enables rapid deployment, security practices such as vulnerability scanning and patching, which were once hard to enforce are now a fundamental step in the build process, leading to standardization and adherence to policy and ultimately, strong governance. Indeed, today's modern CI/VD pipelines are the means for automating the process of deploying only trusted workloads.

Security of multi-tenant environments across a shared platform

In a container architecture, multiple containers run on the same host and share the same set of machine resources. This architecture delivers portability and resource efficiency benefits but introduces a different threat model—workloads running in the cluster can have different risk profiles and need to be treated accordingly, while sharing the same host. For example, you can't apply traditional IP-based authorization in this new architecture. The mechanisms that separate containers such as control groups (cgroups) and namespaces, and security modules such as **AppArmor** can be adequate for some workloads but inadequate for the risk profile of others.

This new model requires new security controls that address network policies, workload isolation, and service authentication Anthos improves security across a hybrid production environment via a portfolio of products and features. Therefore, it is quite challenging to visualize all the features that are available and on which environment or which platform it's available. To help you get to grips with this, you will learn about the four-step workflow to configure Anthos security across multiple different platforms to modernize your security posture.

So, why does Anthos modernize security? What is so different from the tried and tested traditional models? Well, to begin with, traditional security models were based on homogeneous production environments. Today, however, platforms and environments are now a heterogeneous mixed lot of hybrids, multi-cloud, and on-prem platforms, so there are often several production security environments to harden simultaneously.

In addition, the advent of Kubernetes and containers has really changed a lot of our security assumptions about production infrastructure. Where previously we might have had an application running on a virtual machine that acted as a server with a static IP, this mirrored the traditional data center model on which security practices were developed such as access-lists, firewall rules, and other IP centric rules. However, today we find with Kubernetes and containers that we have applications being dynamically scaled, scheduled across different virtual machines, and with dynamically allocated IPs that change every time a container spins up or down.

That changes the approach to security as we no longer have a static anchor, the IP address, for identification, which is quite a difference in security properties. We also have big changes in how applications are built today; gone are the big monoliths as these have been broken down into microservices. And all those microservices now need authentication and authorization to be able to talk to each other. This needs to happen across the network rather than inside the application.

Consequently, security demands have radically changed over the last decade, and this is where Anthos really starts to help us cope. For example, if we look at a typical hybrid infrastructure where we have clusters running on Google Cloud, other clouds, and on-prem, we are going to need some help as the threat surface area is now vast. This is where Anthos comes into play.

There are four key areas where Anthos can bring its influence to bear: at the infrastructure level, at a separate policy layer, with services and application security, and with monitoring and detection. So, if we look at those four key areas as security concepts, then we can turn them into four manageable steps. Breaking down the problem into four key concepts allow us to manage the seemingly unmanageable problem.

Stage 1: The infrastructure

The first of the four steps is about infrastructure hardening such as patching, compliance, and hardening configuration across all environments in a uniformed fashion. The second step has you contemplating about the guardrails -- segmentation, isolation, and the application of a common policy across lots of clusters on diverse platforms. The third step focuses on securing workloads and applications and locking down security and compliance. The goal is to only run what you trust and have fine-grained authorization through policy adherence. Lastly, there comes monitoring and detection, which entails surfacing misconfigurations and detecting vulnerabilities and hidden threats to your clusters.

Moreover, the real challenge is that you need to perform these four tasks uniformly and simultaneously across all of your different environments. After all, it is pointless having strict policy driven processes in GKE if on-prem is a lawless domain with no policy enforcement.

However, it is not all doom and gloom as a lot of this heavy lifting has been done for you when Google was developing Anthos. Let's take a look at step 1: hardening the infrastructure. This task involves security patching and hardening. However, if we look at Kubernetes clusters, everything from the hardware right up to application containers, each one of these layers will need security patching, and it will need initial hardening.

When we're running on our own infrastructure with GKE, Google basically takes the responsibility for most of that technology stack. However, for your environments that aren't GKE, for example, clusters on-prem and AWS, Google is running on the customer's infrastructure. Anthos can, if permitted, directly manage the VMs running on-prem, but control of the virtual machines running in AWS or other clouds will be limited, and this can be problematic.

Nonetheless, where Anthos does control that infrastructure is on GKE, and then they can deliver advanced security functionality that's on by default or is enabled with simplified configuration. Some of the things Google is doing in GKE is that they are introducing Shielded VMs and nodes. These features provide verifiable integrity from Google's own Titan hardware security chip and the verifiable integrity of the underlying firmware and up through the kernel.

There is also the virtual TPM that provides a secure bootstrap and a way to join the node to the cluster securely in GKE. In addition, there are options for Customer managed encryption keys for disk encryption. So, every VM is encrypted automatically by default in Google Cloud with a key that is managed by Google internally. However, if you want to re-encrypt the disk, you can do that using managed encryption keys that you store in Cloud KMS. There is a similar feature for Kubernetes secrets. You can encrypt Kubernetes secrets using a Cloud KMS managed key as well.

On GKE, the control plane and the node–the cluster infrastructure itself–automatically upgrade themselves by default. This means that if you create a cluster and forget about it, it will not become a security hazard as it will keep upgrading itself and keep itself in a good, security configuration.

GKE also offers some control over how those upgrades happen as there are different release channels–rapid, regular, and stable–that you can choose to really dial up or down how quickly those updates are happening on your clusters. Also, there's additional features like maintenance windows and exclusions.

Over the last decade or so, compliance in its many forms has risen to match security in importance, and if we consider compliance, then GKE starts with the Kubernetes CIS benchmark. The Center for Internet Security has created a Kubernetes benchmark that tells you how to run Kubernetes in a hardened configuration. Nonetheless, there are a lot of settings in this benchmark, but GKE has done the hard work to configure all those settings and published the full results for GKE and for on-prem. Google also developed a GKE-specific CIS benchmark that basically just takes their own hardening guide in a checklist form.

To wrap up stage 1, the infrastructure hardening layer, if you follow Google's guidelines for multi-tenancy on GKE, then Anthos does most of the work for you here across all the platforms.

Stage 2: Guardrails and policy

So, once you've made some clusters and have some infrastructure to use, the next step is to establish some guardrails around that infrastructure to ensure that it's not being abused and is used appropriately.

The key feature here is Anthos Config Management:

- **Anthos Config Management**: ACM provides the ability to manage cross-cluster and cross-cloud environments having a lot of different policies. The strategy is to use a GitOps model where infrastructure as code is checked into source control. Using source control to manage infrastructure in a declarative manner has advantages like automatic review. Additionally, you have a history, and you have a way to templatize and create new pieces of infrastructure easily and quickly. Anthos uses Terraform to make the base layer of infrastructure as code, automating the building of things like projects, VPCs, and Kubernetes clusters.

- **ACM Config Sync**: The next level of infrastructure as code is setting guardrails, and this is where ACM comes in. This is where the ACM Config Sync module, which is generally available across all three Anthos platforms, gives you the ability to create namespaces, configure RBAC and security controls, and create identities through service accounts. ACM Config Sync is what manages any Kubernetes object at scale across many clusters and across all the hybrid environments.

- **Policy controller**: Policy controller is another ACM feature that also works across all three environments, and it allows you to really control what the pods are doing inside that cluster. If you want to ensure that containers aren't doing things like running as root or doing other dangerous things like fetching and running binaries, then you need to use the Policy Controller within the ACM.

  The Policy Controller provides you with a comprehensive policy library that you can apply to your clusters. When you're running Policy Controller on GKE itself, there are some other things you can do, such as set org policies. An org policy sits above all your clusters, even above all your projects at the organization level, and it allows you to have macro policy control across many objects.

So, for example, you can set org policy to restrict regions from accessing resources or set different policies per region to meet legal and regulatory requirements. Similarly, the Policy controller can also set the standard that a container must achieve before being permitted into production. For example, it must pass a vulnerability scan. Another thing you can do for your Kubernetes clusters is to restrict how services are exposed to the internet. Many organizations want to avoid someone accidentally putting an untested or a kind of poorly configured application on the internet.

So, summing up this section, we want to use ACM to do the vast majority of our policy configuration enforcement across our hybrid infrastructure.

Then, on GKE cloud, we have some extra controls that we can use to establish some extra guardrails.

Stage 3: Securing the workloads

So far, you have learned how to configure a secure infrastructure and set up guardrails. Now, it's time to see how we can secure workloads with Anthos. The good news is that Anthos provides tools to implement a defense in-depth architecture or a zero-trust architecture. There are four basic steps that you can use to secure workloads on Anthos:

- The first step is securing your build and deployment pipelines, ensuring that your entire supply chain for your code from source to production is secure.

- The second is to ensure that all workloads deployed to production are appropriately isolated from the internet and from each other within your production.

- You should isolate your pods on the node if multiple applications are deployed on a single cluster.

- Lastly, you want to ensure that services that are exposed to the internet are done so with appropriate protection against internet facing attacks.

So, let's consider the first step, which is to secure workloads.

The objective of securing workloads is to ensure that only trusted code can be deployed to production. To ensure that, Anthos recommends that you lock down your CI/CD pipelines, always use a secure base image, and scan that base build image for vulnerabilities. Google Cloud's Container Registry provides incremental and continuous monitoring against a known vulnerability database as a stage in the build process. The output of the scans is available as metadata with your pod. The fact that you have gone through all the above steps can be asserted using binary authorization.

Binary authorization allows you to define a policy that checks for attestation from each step of your CI/CD Pipeline. When using Binary authorization, you can either leverage the tools provided by GCP for building and deploying your containers, or you can bring your own build and deployment tools. It doesn't matter so long as your tools are trusted by binary authorization.

With binary authorization enabled, only workloads that have the right attestations can be deployed to production, and all deployment and denials are audited. By using Binary authorization, you can trust the code running in production with a privileged identity.

The next step is to isolate the deployed code from the internet, and you can do this by ensuring that all clusters are private and any service that is exposed to the internet is done so using an internet facing load balancer. This is because the Google Cloud's load balancer provides DDoS protection, but you can also configure web application firewall policies via Cloud Armor. Additionally, you have the option to configure zero trust access by your employees using Identity via proxy.

Nonetheless, it's not sufficient to just isolate the applications from the internet; it is also necessary to isolate workloads from each other to prevent lateral movement of traffic or what's known as east-west traffic flows. To prevent lateral movements over the network and between pods on the same node, Anthos provides two technologies: Anthos service mesh and Kubernetes network policy to isolate workloads on the network.

Depending on your security profile and the nature of your application, you might want a second layer of isolation between your container workloads on a shared host, and Anthos also provides two technologies for this: GKE Sandbox and AppArmor. These are tools that you can deploy to isolate applications on the cluster nodes. GKE Sandbox provides an extra layer of security to prevent untrusted code from affecting the host kernel on your cluster nodes. AppArmor is a Linux security module that supplements the standard Linux user and group-based permissions to confine programs to a limited set of resources.

A common approach with Anthos is to create clusters that are shared across multiple teams. Each team gets one or more name spaces into which to deploy their application workloads. Thus, namespaces form a natural boundary for isolation. Kubernetes network policy allows you to isolate applications on a single cluster based on namespaces. You can then define ingress and egress rules based on IP CIDRs or Kubernetes objects, such as namespaces and labels. This approach can be called micro-segmentation. It's a good approach if you don't have too many exceptions to manage.

However, a lot of east-west communications between apps is common, and when we implement shared services, such as a common database, we effectively break isolation. Thus, Anthos recommends using coarse-grained segments for mandatory controls and defining fine-grained policies at the application level.

Then, you can set custom application-level policies and a broad end-to-end zero trust access solution using Anthos service mesh and identity via proxy.

Anthos Service Mesh

With Anthos service mesh, all communications are encrypted in transit. Further, all workload-to-workload communications can be strongly authenticated, authorized, and logged. Workloads are authenticated using certificates instead of bare tokens.

Using mutual TLS for authentication helps mitigate the risk of impersonation and privilege escalation through replay or man-in-the-middle attacks. ASM also provides you with the context of policies that allows you to define access controls based on peer request and application contexts.

For example, you can state that only the credit card front end can access the credit card back end. You do this in terms of identities. Thus, a credit card front end can be deployed anywhere, and access policy remains the same irrespective of the network context of the credit card front end.

On GCP, they provide identity via proxy for authenticating and authorizing user access based on BeyondCorp principles. You can also use your own user authentication solution with Anthos service mesh. And you can do all of this without changing your application code.

Now, let us look at a summary of this section. So, we provide a defense in depth approach to secure your workloads, from securing your build and deployment pipelines to isolating your applications on the network. We can do that with a different in-depth approach using segmentation and zero trust approach with Anthos service mesh and isolating your pods on a shared node.

Finally, we provide you with the ability to protect your internet exposed services using Google Cloud load balancer and CloudArmor. Now, let us look at the fourth step to secure your applications with Anthos. The fourth step is to enable monitoring and detection for any incidents. Now, you have done your best to configure everything securely, but how do you know you did it right?

Stage 4: Monitoring and detecting flaws

In order to know that you have correctly configured everything securely, Anthos provides you with the three-layered stack. Starting at the lowest layer of the stack, Anthos provides you with Security Health Analytics, which helps prevent threats by telling you about problems before they get exploited by an attacker.

Moving up the stack, there is the Security Scanner that analyzes your configuration to prevent threats due to a misconfiguration. The third layer is a set of threat detection capabilities known as container threat detection, which helps you detect potential attacks in real-time by monitoring for suspicious behavior inside containers. In addition to container threat detection, Anthos provides event threat detection for suspicious events and logs, such as traffic to known bad domains and IPs.

To summarize this section on GCP, we provide a number of tools to help you analyze your posture and detect incidents. This information is available in Cloud Security Command Center or a tool of your choice. You can view all your alerts in the Cloud Security Command Center.

To recap what we just covered, there are four steps to securing your modern applications using Anthos:

- You harden your infrastructure.

- You then establish guardrails.

- Once you have a secured landing zone, you can secure your workloads by securing your deployment pipelines and isolating your workloads in your production environment.

- And finally, you enable monitoring and detection to ensure that you have the right posture and that you are alerted to incidents.

You can enable this four-step workflow across all your environments, whether it's GCP or on-premises on AWS and perhaps others in the future.

Anthos: Modernizing security for hybrid and multi-cloud

By using Anthos, you can enforce consistent policy across environments, deploy only what you trust, and isolate workloads with different risk profiles.

Enforcing consistent policies across environments

Anthos helps your organization enforce consistent policy across clusters through Anthos Config Management, a centralized, declarative configuration manager that works consistently across on-premises and multi-cloud deployments. You can use Anthos Config Management to create a common configuration for all your admin policies and apply it to all your clusters, wherever they're deployed.

A GitOps approach

A central Git repository hosts a common configuration that can cover access-control policies, resource quotas, and namespaces. Anthos Config Management evaluates each commit to the repository and then rolls out configuration changes to all clusters so that the state you want is quickly reflected. A built-in validator checks for misconfigurations submitted to the repository to prevent the pushing of bad configurations. ACM prevents configuration drift with continuous monitoring of each cluster's state by using the declarative model to apply policies that enforce compliance.

By automating and scaling policy creation, rollout, audit, and enforcement continuously across all Anthos environments, your developers can execute as fast as the business requires while staying within the guardrails put in place by security.

Deploying only trusted workloads

Regardless of environment, you need to know that the container images you deploy are trusted. Arbitrary public container images can include unpatched vulnerabilities, or even embedded, malicious code that can expose your enterprise to preventable attacks.

The following diagram illustrates how your enterprise organization can modernize your app security approach. You build container images by taking a minimal OS base image and adding the packages, libraries, and binaries that you need for your app. You can reduce the surface of attack of these container images by doing the following:

- Use images purpose-built for containers

- Make sure that images are up-to-date with the latest available patches

- Use deploy-time checks for supply chain integrity

Anthos helps guard against vulnerable container images with a defense-in-depth approach. GCP provides managed base images that you can use to build container images. Managed base images are built reproducibly and are patched automatically when patches are available upstream. GCP also provides distroless images, a more minimal alternative to managed base images. When you build container images with distroless images as their base image, it contains only your app and its runtime dependencies, greatly reducing the potential attack surface.

When you use Anthos, you benefit from the native vulnerability scanning capabilities of Container Registry. Container Registry vulnerability scanning looks for known vulnerabilities (based on the **Common Vulnerability and Exposures (CVE)** database). Having knowledge of image vulnerabilities prior to deployment enables your developers and operators to prevent patchable and potentially high-risk images from being deployed into production. The scanning results show the severity (based on the **Common Vulnerability Scoring System (CVSS)** score), availability of a fix, and the name of the package that contains the vulnerability.

By using Anthos, you can also benefit from Binary Authorization, a deploy-time control that lets your organization define the requirements for a container image that you want to deploy and stop deployment if an image doesn't meet your requirements. While each organization has different definitions of what constitutes a trusted image, common requirements are vulnerability scanning, verification of a legitimate build, and review by the **quality assurance (QA)** team. Binary Authorization integrates into many popular CI/CD tools and uses cryptographic attestations to verify that requirements are met prior to deploying an image.

With tools such as managed base images, Container Registry vulnerability scanning, and Binary Authorization, you can *shift security left* by building defined security checks into the development process and making security a part of the app lifecycle.

Isolating workloads with different risk profiles

To gain resource efficiency, containers with different risk profiles can share the same host kernel or cluster of machine nodes. You need to isolate and segment your apps with different risk profiles running on this shared infrastructure so that only authorized services can communicate with each other and access the intended resources.

The following diagram illustrates how Anthos delivers a full suite of security capabilities to isolate apps at multiple levels, including host, cluster, network, and service:

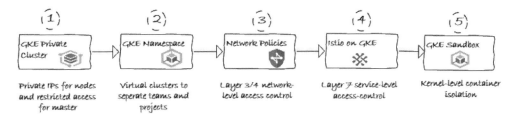

Figure 13.2: Isolate apps at multiple levels

- At the cluster level, you can deploy GKE private clusters, node clusters that aren't exposed to the internet because they don't have public IP addresses. Access to the master is also restricted. You can authorize external networks to access the master.

- Within the cluster, you can separate teams and projects using namespaces that have different Kubernetes identities provisioned, and you can assign quotas for memory and CPU usage.

- At the network level, you can control access to the workloads and pods by using GKE network policies at layers 3 and 4. From a multi-tenancy perspective, this helps you ensure that pods from different apps or different tenants aren't able to communicate.

- At the app level, you can use Anthos Service Mesh for service-to-service and end-user-to-service authorization at different levels of granularity, including namespace level, service level, and method level. (For additional reading on zero trust security and user access controls, see BeyondCorp.)

- At the host level, GKE Sandbox provides an extra layer of isolation between the host kernel and containers for sensitive or untrusted workloads. GKE Sandbox limits the host kernel surface area accessible to the app while still giving the app the ability to perform the system operations it needs. Anthos facilitates this modernization, enabling enterprises to evolve to a platform where automated security operations that deploy only trusted workloads, isolate workloads with different risk profiles, and enforce consistent policies across heterogeneous environments.

Anthos under the hood

So far, we have taken a high-level administrative approach to Anthos, but now we are going to look under the hood and see just how Anthos Config Management works.

Anthos Config Controller

Config Controller is a hosted service that is responsible for provisioning and orchestrating Anthos and Google Cloud resources. The service offers, among other things, an API endpoint that can provision, actuate, and orchestrate Google Cloud resources as part of Anthos Config Management.

Config Controller leverages another ACM service called Config Connector, which maps resources using the **Kubernetes Resource Model** (**KRM**). This enables Kubernetes resources to be declaratively mapped to their Google Cloud counterparts by making the necessary Google Cloud API calls. ACM also includes Config Sync that connects to a Git repository, making configuration changes as easy as git push. Finally, it comes with the Policy Controller, which lets you roll your own custom policies that you will utilize to enforce the security and compliance of your resource configurations.

Config Controller lets you define the desired state and operate with a simple, declarative configuration in Kubernetes KRM style. This declarative configuration as code approach provides several benefits:

- **Simplified management**: Leverage the tools and workflows for Kubernetes to manage Anthos and Google Cloud resources.

- **Declare desired state**: Focus on what your resources look like rather than the specifics of how they are created.

- **Automatically detect and repair drift**: Continuously monitor your infrastructure for drift from the desired state and enable automatic repairs.

- **Consistency with GitOps**: Collaborate with your colleagues on potential changes and preview modifications before they are made.

- **Enforce policy guardrails**: Enforce policies earlier in the development cycle and detect violations before they are deployed.

- **Audit continuously**: Maintain an audit trail of all changes that can be used to understand the provenance of infrastructure.

- **Codifying best practices**: Codify common patterns as blueprints that can be rolled out across your organization.

- **Increase velocity**: Improve the safety and velocity of your cloud adoption journey by reusing the existing best practices.

Managing Anthos and Google Cloud with your Kubernetes tools

Config Controller, which is part of the Anthos Config Management ACM program, exposes an API endpoint that works with the existing Kubernetes tools to manage Anthos and Google Cloud resources. Hence, if you are already familiar with running workloads in Kubernetes, you can leverage your tooling, pipelines, and knowledge to manage Anthos and Google Cloud resources. You can even use the Config Controller to create Google Kubernetes Engine (GKE) clusters using kubectl.

Focus on what you want, Config Controller takes care of the rest

Config Controller is powered by a Kubernetes API server that takes your declarative configurations that are written in KRM to construct your desired state. Using this favored DevOps approach, this declarative model allows you to forget about the underlying infrastructure. Instead, you can concentrate entirely on what you want your resources to look like rather than the specifics of how they will be created. Config Controller takes your intent and creates resources to reconcile your desired state. Furthermore, after the resources are deployed and running, the Config Controller tracks them and continuously monitors them for drift detection and automatic repairs. As Config Controller is managed by Google, you get these benefits out of the box in the fully managed GKE service.

Consistency with GitOps

Anthos ACM is steeped in DevOps culture, and now it is adopting the emerging GitOps culture. In this emerging paradigm, the Config Controller uses one of its component services called Config Sync to connect and, as the name suggests, sync to a Git repository. As a result, the Config Sync service continuously reconciles the state of the Config Controller with files stored in one or more Git repositories. This GitOps code versioning strategy lets you manage and deploy common configurations with a process that is auditable, transactional, reviewable, and version controlled. It also enables collaboration with your colleagues on potential changes and lets you preview modifications before they are made.

Policy guardrails and auditing

Config Controller comes with another interesting service called Policy Controller, which lets you create custom policies to enforce the security and compliance of your resource configurations. You can use these policies to actively block non-compliant API requests or simply to audit the configuration of your resources and report violations. Working in tandem with Config Sync, the Policy Controller can ensure that the same process of auditable, transactional, reviewable, and version-controlled code applies to documented policies as well. This docs-as-code approach means policies are now tethered to code revisions and their life cycles are intertwined as they are stored together, in the same Git versioning repository.

Config Sync lets cluster operators and platform administrators deploy consistent configurations and policies. You can deploy these configurations and policies to individual Kubernetes clusters, multiple clusters that can span hybrid and multi-cloud environments, and multiple namespaces within clusters. This process simplifies and automates configuration and policy management at scale. Config Sync also lets development teams independently manage their namespaces within clusters while still being subject to policy guardrails set by administrators.

Using the same principles as Kubernetes itself, Config Sync continuously reconciles the state of registered clusters with a central set of Kubernetes declarative configuration files called configs. Configs are stored in one or more Git repositories, and Config Sync keeps them consistent with the configured Kubernetes objects. This GitOps approach (sometimes also referred to as configuration as code) lets you manage and deploy common configurations with a process that is auditable, transactional, reviewable, and version controlled.

> **Config Sync is available for Anthos and GKE customers. Anthos customers have the added benefit of utilizing Config Sync on other cloud providers and on-premises.**

Config sync benefits

The following points highlight some of the benefits that Config Sync provides you with:

- **Reduce the risk of "shadow ops"**: If unvetted changes are pushed to live clusters, it can be difficult to understand the differences between documented configuration and your live environment. You can require that all cluster configuration changes are applied using Config Sync, lock down direct access to the Kubernetes API, and trace changes back to their sources of truth in Git.

- **Use GitOps best practices**: Before any changes are pushed to your live environment, you can require code reviews using any repository management tools that you prefer. Use Config Sync to audit exactly which commit caused a configuration change.

- **Reduce downtime due to configuration-related outages**: Config Sync lets you use a *"revert then investigate"* strategy to roll back breaking changes and get your live clusters back into a good working state before fixing the problematic change and applying it as a new commit.

- **Use Continuous Integration / Continuous Deployment (CI/CD) pipelines**: You can use a CI/CD workflow to render configuration using any tools and formats you prefer, test, and validate your changes, and commit them automatically when tests pass. Config Sync then applies the changes and then monitors and remediates configuration drift.

Configuring clusters

Config Sync lets you create a common set of configuration and cluster-level policies, such as Policy Controller constraints, and consistently apply them across registered and connected clusters from a single source of truth in Git. Before you can configure a cluster, you need to create a config and a repository.

Configs

A config is a Kubernetes configuration declaration written in YAML or JSON. Config Sync reads and applies the config to one or more clusters to create or configure a Kubernetes object or resource in those clusters, or to provide information needed by Config Sync itself. A config can contain any configuration detail you could apply to a Kubernetes cluster using `kubectl edit` or `kubectl apply`. You can also declare multiple configs in a single file. Config Sync reads three types of files: `.yaml`, `.yml` and `.json`. Files with other suffixes are ignored.

Repositories

The repo is the Git repository where configs are stored. When you initially configure Config Sync, you configure three things: the repository, the branch, and the subdirectory that Config Sync monitors for changes.

Config Sync lets you sync configurations from multiple repositories to the same set of clusters, enabling the ability to sync from multiple repositories gives you access to additional functionality (for example, drift prevention and ignoring object mutations). You can enable this functionality even if you only want to use a root repository and don't want to use namespace repositories.

You can create a root repository and namespace repositories:

- **Root repository**: This repository lets you sync cluster-scoped and namespace-scoped configs. Each cluster can only have one root repository, and a central administrator typically governs this repository.

  You can use two different structures for your root repository:

  o **Unstructured**: The unstructured source format lets you organize the configs in your repository in whatever way is most convenient.

  o **Hierarchical**: The hierarchical, or structured, source format separates configs into distinct categories for system configuration, cluster metadata, cluster-level configuration, and namespace configuration to help you organize the configs. Hierarchical is the default repository format for Config Sync.

- **Namespace repositories**: Namespace repositories are optional and can contain namespace-scoped configs synced to a particular namespace across clusters. Namespace repositories must use the unstructured repo format.

Policy Controller overview

Anthos Config Management's Policy Controller enables the enforcement of policies for your clusters. These policies act as *guardrails* and prevent any changes to the configuration of the Kubernetes API from violating security and operational or compliance controls.

You can set policies to actively block non-compliant API requests or simply to audit the configuration of your clusters and report violations. Policy Controller is based on the open-source Open Policy Agent Gatekeeper project and comes with a full library of pre-built policies for common security and compliance controls.

In addition to actively controlling your Kubernetes environment, you can optionally use Policy Controller to analyze configuration for compliance prior to deployment.

This helps provide valuable feedback during the process of configuration changes and ensures that any non-compliant changes are caught early before they might be rejected during application.

Constraints

Policy Controller enforces your clusters' compliance using objects called constraints. For example, you can use the following constraints:

- Require each namespace to have at least one label. This constraint can be used to ensure accurate tracking of resource consumption when using GKE Usage Metering, for example.

- Enforce many of the same requirements as **PodSecurityPolicies**, but with the added ability to audit your configuration before enforcing it, ensuring that any policy changes aren't disruptive to running workloads.

- Restrict the repositories a given container image can be pulled from. This constraint ensures that any attempt to pull containers from unknown sources is denied, protecting your clusters from running potentially malicious software.

These are just a few of the constraints provided as part of the constraint library that is included with the Policy Controller installation. This library contains numerous policies that help enforce best practices and limit risk.

Constraints can be applied directly to your clusters using the Kubernetes API or distributed to a set of clusters from a central Git repository by using Config Sync.

Constraint templates

Policy Controller also lets you add your own custom policies by creating constraint templates. Constraint templates define policy parameters, error messages, and custom logic.

Once created, these templates let anyone invoke the policy using a constraint, which sets the parameters and defines the scope of resources and namespaces to which the policy applies. This separation lets subject matter experts write policies once and then enables others to use them in various contexts without the need to write or manage policy code.

Interactive tutorial 13.1: Validating apps against policy

Overview

This tutorial demonstrates how to validate your apps against the company policies in a CI pipeline.

If your organization uses Anthos Config Management and Policy Controller to manage policies across its Anthos clusters, then you can validate an app's deployment configuration in its **continuous integration** (**CI**) pipeline. Validating your app is useful if you are a developer building a CI pipeline for an app or a platform engineer building a CI pipeline template for multiple app teams.

Policies are an important part of the security and compliance of an organization. Policy Controller, which is part of Anthos Config Management, allows your organization to manage those policies centrally and declaratively for all your clusters. As a developer, you can take advantage of the centralized and declarative nature of those policies. You can use those characteristics to validate your app against those policies as early as possible in your development workflow. Learning about policy violations in your CI pipeline instead of during the deployment has two main advantages: it lets you shift left on security, and it tightens the feedback loop, reducing the time and cost necessary to fix those violations.

If you are in charge of Anthos Config Management and Policy Controller and want to build a CI pipeline for them (and not for a specific app), see using *Policy Controller* in a CI pipeline. This tutorial uses Cloud Build as a CI tool and a sample GitHub repository containing policies for demonstrations.

Resources

This tutorial uses several Kubernetes tools. This section explains what those tools are, how they interact with each other, and whether you can replace them with something else. The tools that you will use in this tutorial include the following:

- **Policy Controller**: Policy Controller is a Google Cloud product that is part of Anthos Config Management. It's based on the open-source project Open Policy Agent - Gatekeeper. Policy Controller enforces policies about the objects that are created in a Kubernetes cluster (for example, preventing the usage of a specific option or enforcing the usage of a specific label). Those policies are called constraints. Constraints are defined as Kubernetes Custom Resources. Config Sync lets you declare those constraints in a Git repository and apply traditional development workflows to your policy management process. Config Sync is available both as a standalone product and as a part of Anthos Config Management. You can use Open Policy Agent - Gatekeeper instead of Policy Controller for your implementation.

- **GitHub**: In this tutorial, we will use GitHub to host the Git repositories: one for a sample app, and one for Anthos Config Management (which contains the constraints for Policy Controller). For simplicity, the two repositories are two different folders in a single Git repository. In reality, they would be different repositories. You can use any Git solution.

- **Cloud Build**: Cloud Build is Google Cloud's CI solution. In this tutorial, we will use it to run the validation tests. While the details of the implementation can vary from one CI system to another, the concepts outlined in this tutorial can be used with any container-based CI system.

- **Kustomize**: Kustomize is a customization tool for Kubernetes configurations. It works by taking "*base*" configurations and applying customizations to them. It lets you have a **Don't Repeat Yourself (DRY)** approach to Kubernetes configurations. With Kustomize, you keep elements that are common to all your environments in the base configurations and create customizations per environment. In this tutorial, we will keep the Kustomize configurations in the app repository, and we will "*build*" (for example, apply the customizations) the configurations in the CI pipeline. You can use the concepts outlined in this tutorial with any tool that produces Kubernetes configurations that are ready to be applied to a cluster (for example, the helm template command).

- **Kpt**: Kpt is a tool to build workflows for Kubernetes configurations. Kpt lets you fetch, display, customize, update, validate, and apply Kubernetes configurations. As it works with Git and YAML files, it is compatible with most of the existing tools of the Kubernetes ecosystem. In this tutorial, we will use kpt in the CI pipeline to fetch the constraints from the Anthos Config Management repository and validate the Kubernetes configurations against those constraints.

Pipeline

The CI pipeline we will use in this tutorial is shown in the following diagram:

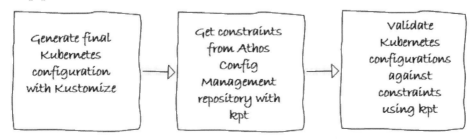

Figure 13.3: Validating Apps against policy pipeline

CI pipeline for Policy Controller

The pipeline runs in Cloud Build, and the commands are run in a directory containing a copy of the sample app repository. The pipeline starts by generating the final Kubernetes configurations with Kustomize. Next, it fetches the constraints that we want to validate against from the Anthos Config Management repository using kpt. Finally, it uses kpt to validate the Kubernetes configurations against those constraints. To achieve this last step, we use a specific config function called gatekeeper-validate that performs this validation. In this tutorial, you will trigger the CI pipeline manually, but in reality, you would configure it to run after a git push to your Git repository.

Objectives

- Run a CI pipeline for a sample app with Cloud Build.

- Observe that the pipeline fails because of a policy violation.

- Modify the sample app repository to comply with the policies.

- Run the CI pipeline again successfully.

> **You don't need an Anthos entitlement to run this tutorial. However, you do need one to run Anthos Config Management in a cluster.**

Before you begin

- Select or create a Google Cloud project.

  To execute the commands listed in this tutorial, open Cloud Shell. In Cloud Shell, run the below command:

  ```
  gcloud config get-value project
  ```

  If the command does not return the ID of the project that you just selected, configure Cloud Shell to use your project: Replace **PROJECT_ID** with your project ID.

  ```
  gcloud config set project PROJECT_ID
  ```

- In Cloud Shell, enable the required Cloud Build API:

  ```
  gcloud services enable cloudbuild.googleapis.com
  ```

Step 1: Validating the sample app configurations

In this section, you will run a CI pipeline with Cloud Build for a sample app repository that we provide. This pipeline validates the Kubernetes configuration available in that sample app repository against constraints available in a sample Anthos Config Management repository.

1. To validate the app configurations, in Cloud Shell, clone the sample app repository:

   git clone https://github.com/GoogleCloudPlatform/anthos-config-management-samples.git

Step 2: Run the CI pipeline with Cloud Build

1. Run the pipeline; the logs of the build are displayed directly in Cloud Shell:

   cd anthos-config-management-samples/ci-app/app-repo

   gcloud builds submit .

   The pipeline that you run is defined in the following file:

   ci-app/app-repo/cloudbuild.yaml

```
01.  steps:
02.  - id: 'Prepare config'
03.    # This step builds the final manifests for the app
04.    # using kustomize and the configuration files
05.    # available in the repository.
06.    name: 'gcr.io/google.com/cloudsdktool/cloud-sdk'
07.    entrypoint: '/bin/sh'
08.    args: ['-c', 'mkdir hydrated-manifests && kubectl kustomize config/prod > hydrated-manifests/prod.yaml']
09.  - id: 'Download policies'
10.    # This step fetches the policies from the Anthos Config Management repository
11.    # and consolidates every resource in a single file.
12.    name: 'gcr.io/kpt-dev/kpt'
13.    entrypoint: '/bin/sh'
14.    args: ['-c', 'kpt pkg get https://github.com/GoogleCloudPlatform/anthos-config-management-samples.git
15.  /ci-app/acm-repo/cluster@1.0.0 constraints
16.                 && kpt fn source constraints/ hydrated-manifests/ > hydrated-manifests/kpt-manifests.yaml']
17.  - id: 'Validate against policies'
18.    # This step validates that all resources comply with all policies.
19.    name: 'gcr.io/config-management-release/policy-controller-validate'
20.
```

Figure 13.4: cloudbuild.yaml code

2. Analyze the code.

   While the pipeline is running, take the time to review the YAML file. In the **cloudbuild.yaml** file the 2nd step:

```
01.  - id: 'Download policies'
02.    # This step fetches the policies from the Anthos Config Management repository
03.    # and consolidates every resource in a single file.
04.    name: 'gcr.io/kpt-dev/kpt'
05.    entrypoint: '/bin/sh'
06.    args: ['-c', 'kpt pkg get
07.
```

Figure 13.5: cloudbuild.yaml – step 2

We see that the **kpt pkg get** command is needed and used to download both constraint templates and constraints before they are used in step 3:

```
01.
02.   - id: 'Validate against policies'
03.       # This step validates that all resources comply with all policies.
04.
```

Figure 13.6: cloudbuild.yaml -step3

After a few minutes, observe that the pipeline fails with the following error:

[...]

Step #2 - "Validate against policies": [RUNNING] "gcr.io/kpt-fn/gatekeeper:v0"

Step #2 - "Validate against policies": [FAIL] "gcr.io/kpt-fn/gatekeeper:v0"

Step #2 - "Validate against policies":   Results:

Step #2 - "Validate against policies":   [ERROR] Deployment objects should have an 'owner' label indicating who created them. violatedConstraint: deployment-must-have-owner in object "apps/v1/Deployment/nginx-deployment" in file "prod.yaml"

Step #2 - "Validate against policies":   Stderr:

Step #2 - "Validate against policies":   "[error] apps/v1/Deployment/nginx-deployment : Deployment objects should have an 'owner' label indicating who created them."

Step #2 - "Validate against policies":   "violatedConstraint: deployment-must-have-owner"

Step #2 - "Validate against policies":   ""

Step #2 - "Validate against policies":   Exit code: 1

[...]

Step 3: View the Logs in the console

1. Note that the constraint that the configuration is violating is defined in the following file. It's a Kubernetes custom resource called **K8sRequiredLabels**:

   ci-app/acm-repo/cluster/deployment-must-have-owner.yaml

```
01.   apiVersion: constraints.gatekeeper.sh/v1beta1
02.   kind: K8sRequiredLabels
03.   metadata:
04.     name: deployment-must-have-owner
05.   spec:
06.     match:
07.       kinds:
08.         - apiGroups: ["apps"]
09.           kinds: ["Deployment"]
10.     parameters:
11.       labels:
12.         - key: "owner"
13.       message: "Deployment objects should have an 'owner' label indicating who created them."
```

Figure 13.7: *deployment-must-gace-owner*

For the constraint template corresponding to this constraint, see **requiredlabels.yaml** on GitHub.

2. 3.2 Build the full Kubernetes configuration yourself and observe that the owner label is indeed missing.

    To build the configuration:

    kubectl kustomize config/prod

3. Fix the app to comply with company policies. In this section, you will fix the policy violation using Kustomize. In Cloud Shell, add a **commonLabels** section to the base Kustomization file:

    cat <<EOF >> config/base/kustomization.yaml

    commonLabels:

    ** owner: myself**

    EOF

4. Build the full Kubernetes configuration, and observe that the owner label is now present:

    kubectl kustomize config/prod

5. Rerun the CI pipeline with Cloud Build:

    gcloud builds submit .

The pipeline now succeeds with the following output:

```
[...]
Step #2 - "Validate against policies": [RUNNING] "gcr.io/kpt-fn/
gatekeeper:v0"
Step #2 - "Validate against policies": [PASS] "gcr.io/kpt-fn/
gatekeeper:v0"
[...]
```

> **You can run and debug Cloud Build pipelines locally without having to trigger an actual build or pushing to your Git repository using `cloud- build-local`.**

Congratulations! You have just completed the last tutorial in the book!

Cleaning up!

1. As this is the last interactive tutorial in the book, you can safely delete the project.

2. In the project list, select the project that you want to delete, and then click on **Delete**.

3. In the dialog, type the project ID, and then click on **Shut down** to delete the project.

Conclusion

In this chapter, you were introduced to some of the security features shared by KGE and Anthos. You learned how to deploy a Sample Anthos deployment and how to use Config Sync and the Policy Controller to enforce organizational policy across the CI/CD pipeline.

You learnt a lot about GKE and Anthos as ideal cloud-native platforms for deploying your cloud native applications.

Index

Printed in Great Britain
by Amazon

83885969R00240